OXFORD WORLD'S

SELECTED LE

MARCUS TULLIUS CICERO (106–43 BC) was the son of a Roman
equestrian from Arpinum, some 70 miles south-east of Rome. He
rose to prominence through his skill in speaking and his exceptional
success in the criminal courts, where he usually spoke for the
defence. Although from a family that had never produced a Roman
senator, he secured election to all the major political offices at the
earliest age permitted by law. His consulship fell in a year (63) in
which a dangerous insurrection occurred, the Catilinarian conspiracy; by his persuasive oratory and his controversial execution of five
confessed conspirators, he prevented the conspiracy from breaking
out at Rome and was hailed as the father of his country. Exiled for
the executions by his enemy Clodius in 58 but recalled the following year, he lost his political independence as a result of the domination of politics by the military dynasts Pompey and Caesar. His
governorship of Cilicia (51–50) was exemplary in its honesty and
fairness. Always a firm republican, he reluctantly supported
Pompey in the Civil War, but was pardoned by Caesar. He was not
let into the plot against Caesar. After Caesar's assassination (44), he
supported the young Octavian (the future emperor Augustus) and
led the Senate in its operations against Mark Antony. When
Octavian and Antony formed the 'second triumvirate' with Lepidus
in 43, Cicero was their most prominent victim; he met his end with
great courage.

Cicero's letters, together with his speeches and his political and
philosophical works, form the chief source for the history of the late
republic. His philosophical treatises, written in periods when he was
deprived of his political freedom, are the main vehicle by which
Hellenistic philosophy was transmitted to the west. His prose style
raised the Latin language to an elegance and beauty that was never
surpassed.

P. G. WALSH is Emeritus Professor of Humanity in the University
of Glasgow. This is the seventh of his translations of Latin authors
in Oxford World's Classics, following Apuleius, *The Golden Ass*,
Petronius, *Satyricon*, Cicero, *The Nature of the Gods* and *On
Obligations*, Boethius, *The Consolation of Philosophy*, and Pliny's
Complete Letters. He has also published extensively on Livy, on the
Roman novel, and on patristic and medieval Latin.

OXFORD WORLD'S CLASSICS

For over 100 years Oxford World's Classics have brought readers closer to the world's great literature. Now with over 700 titles—from the 4,000-year-old myths of Mesopotamia to the twentieth century's greatest novels—the series makes available lesser-known as well as celebrated writing.

The pocket-sized hardbacks of the early years contained introductions by Virginia Woolf, T. S. Eliot, Graham Greene, and other literary figures which enriched the experience of reading. Today the series is recognized for its fine scholarship and reliability in texts that span world literature, drama and poetry, religion, philosophy, and politics. Each edition includes perceptive commentary and essential background information to meet the changing needs of readers.

OXFORD WORLD'S CLASSICS

===

CICERO

Selected Letters

===

Translated with an Introduction and Notes by
P. G. WALSH

OXFORD
UNIVERSITY PRESS

OXFORD
UNIVERSITY PRESS

Great Clarendon Street, Oxford ox2 6DP

Oxford University Press is a department of the University of Oxford.
It furthers the University's objective of excellence in research, scholarship,
and education by publishing worldwide in

Oxford New York

Auckland Cape Town Dar es Salaam Hong Kong Karachi
Kuala Lumpur Madrid Melbourne Mexico City Nairobi
New Delhi Shanghai Taipei Toronto

With offices in

Argentina Austria Brazil Chile Czech Republic France Greece
Guatemala Hungary Italy Japan Poland Portugal Singapore
South Korea Switzerland Thailand Turkey Ukraine Vietnam

Oxford is a registered trade mark of Oxford University Press
in the UK and in certain other countries

Published in the United States
by Oxford University Press Inc., New York

British Library Cataloguing in Publication Data

Data available

Library of Congress Cataloging-in-Publication Data

Data available

Typeset by Cepha Imaging Private Ltd., Bangalore, India
Printed in Great Britain
on acid-free paper by
Clays Ltd., St Ives plc

ISBN 978-0-19-921420-4

1

PREFACE

THE aim of this selection from the 914 letters of Cicero's correspondence is to present, month by month as far as is possible, the history of the collapse of the Roman republic between 68 and 43 BC as witnessed and interpreted by Cicero. The obvious difficulty for an editor lies in the choice of those most apposite for this purpose. In order to concentrate upon Cicero's own views, I have excluded letters written by others, even where such letters appear cheek by jowl with the replies to them by Cicero. Since there are few letters which do not provide some information relevant to the history of the period, some readers will inevitably regret the absence of particular letters in this selection.

The editions and translations of Shackleton Bailey, especially his Cambridge commentaries and his eight volumes in the Loeb series (1999–2002), have been my chief resource. For the wider historical background I have relied particularly on the chapters of Peter Wiseman and Elizabeth Rawson in the second edition of the *Cambridge Ancient History*. My gratitude as always is owed to Judith Luna at Oxford University Press for her patience, expertise, and genial interest, and to Elizabeth Stratford for her careful scrutiny and correction of the typescript.

CONTENTS

INTRODUCTION

IT is a commonplace to observe that our knowledge of the last years of the Roman republic is greater than that of any other period of ancient history, and that this is attributable chiefly to the writings of Cicero. The 58 extant speeches, the rhetorical and philosophical treatises, and above all the corpus of 914 letters provide a detailed account from the inside of this momentous period. Two important limitations are, however, to be borne in mind when assessing the importance of the letters. The first is chronological: no letters survive from the years before 68 BC (indeed, even those written between 68 and 62 are of slight interest from the historical perspective), and the last surviving correspondence was written in July 43; moreover there are significant gaps in the twenty-five-year period between 68 and 43, not least in the years 64–63. The second limitation lies in Cicero's political standpoint; as a traditionalist, he is the spokesman for the selfish senatorial government. Though frequently critical of the opportunism and blindness of individual optimates, he harks back to his consulship as a golden age, and is insufficiently critical of the narrow and selfish concerns of the nobility. It is vital to lay the writings of Sallust as a corrective alongside Cicero's idealized picture, to illuminate the social and economic problems besetting Rome; as Sallust put it, 'All things divine and human lay in the hands of the few' (*Jugurtha* 31.20).

The momentous change in Roman politics from senatorial government to the rule of one man owed its beginnings to the tribunates of the Gracchi in the 130s and 120s BC. Their successive land-bills aimed not merely to improve the economic status of impoverished citizens, but also to adjust the balance of power between Assembly and Senate. This prompted the emergence of a series of 'people-pleasers' (*populares*), who followed the example of Gaius Marius in exploiting their successes as military commanders to confront the Senate with the backing of their armies and their discharged veterans. The letters of 61 to 43 reveal how Pompey, Caesar, Mark Antony, and Octavian successfully imposed their personal ambitions on a Senate which initially resisted them fiercely, but ultimately was forced to comply. This occurred when the three dynasts Pompey, Caesar, and Crassus made an informal alliance in 60 and renewed it at Luca in 56, and again when Antony, Octavian, and Lepidus established a formal triumvirate in 43. The selected letters, divided in this edition into eight sections, allow us to trace these significant political developments in detail.

1. Cicero's career

Cicero was born to a non-senatorial family in 106 BC in Arpinum, a small Volscian hill-town lying some seventy miles south-east of Rome, close to the modern Montecassino. His father was a well-heeled, well-read equestrian who owned a second house on the Esquiline hill in Rome, so that the young Marcus and his younger brother Quintus were able to attend the seminars of eminent rhetoricians and philosophers; indeed, the famous Stoic Diodotus resided in their Roman house. Though Cicero served in Sulla's army in the later days of the Social (also called the Italian) War of 91–87, which the Senate could bring to a close only by reluctantly conceding citizenship to the Italians, he took no part in the ensuing civil conflict (83–82) between the optimates, jealously preserving the privileges of the nobility, and the *populares*, who included idealists seeking political reform, but also more prominently ruthless individuals aspiring to personal power. At this stage the optimates triumphed, and Sulla as dictator was able to carry through reforms which assured senatorial control of the state. Meanwhile Cicero sought to launch his career as an advocate in the courts, first in a civil action on behalf of Quinctius, and then in 80 BC in a criminal case in defence of Sextus Roscius of Ameria. Roscius was the innocent victim of a 'frame-up' engineered by Sulla's agent Chrysogonus after the Civil War. Sulla deemed it politic not to interfere, especially as Cicero in his speech for the defence demonstrated his political leaning towards the optimates. He duly won the case.

After a two-year period spent chiefly in Greece and in Rhodes to improve his health and to promote his rhetorical and philosophical studies, Cicero returned to Rome to resume his activities in the courts and to seek political advancement. In 75 he was elected quaestor, which gained him membership of the Senate, and in 69 he obtained the plebeian aedileship, a post useful for seeking prominence by mounting public games. In the meantime he had won popularity with the Sicilians, and fame at Rome, by undertaking in 70 the prosecution of Verres, the rapacious governor of Sicily. In conducting this case he outshone the defending counsel Hortensius, the pre-eminent forensic orator of the day. It was no surprise when in 67 Cicero was not merely elected praetor, but also emerged at the top of the poll. He was now a leading candidate for the consulship of 63. His prospects and his rivals are well documented in the *Handbook for Candidates Seeking Office* (see p. xvi). Having to reinforce his candidature, he voiced his support for the proposal advanced by the tribune Manilius that Pompey should replace Lucullus as commander in the war against Mithradates, an astute move because Pompey was a popular figure, having safeguarded the Roman corn-supply by the suppression of piracy throughout the Mediterranean. In this same year, 66, his defence of a prominent equestrian, Cluentius, who was indicted for murder, signalled his long-term ambition to promote the *concordia ordinum*, the alliance of senators and equestrians to control the policies of state. With support from both orders (partly motivated by apprehensions of the intentions of his unscrupulous rival the *popularis* Catiline), he was elected consul for 63, the first such ennoblement of a *novus homo*—a 'new man'—for thirty years. His period in office was marked by closer adhesion to the optimates in his denunciation of proposals for agrarian reform, and by the detection and suppression of the Catilinarian conspiracy, which culminated in the execution without trial of the ringleaders who had remained in Rome.

The subsequent history of Cicero's career, visualized against the background of the momentous political developments, can be followed by scrutiny of his letters, which survive up to July 43. The return of Pompey to Rome in 62, flushed with military success, and the subsequent alliance with Caesar and Crassus in 60, overshadowed Cicero's eminence as *Pater patriae* (father of his country), the title awarded for his suppression of the Catilinarians. He was increasingly hounded by Clodius, a former ally of Catiline and an inveterate foe of Cicero owing to the Bona Dea scandal. Under the threat of indictment by Clodius for the execution of Roman citizens without trial, he was persuaded to retire into exile, and spent an unhappy period, first at Thessalonica and then at Brundisium, lamenting his inglorious fall. Though the proposal for his restoration was supported by both Pompey and Caesar, Cicero was obliged to accept a humbler political role while forging good relations with the dynasts. For the next few years he devoted himself to work in the courts and to rhetorical writing. In 51–50 he was obliged to accept the governorship of Cilicia, on the southern coast of modern Turkey, a role which he discharged with some distinction and without corruption.

He returned to Rome in January 49, to find the capital in severe crisis. Caesar responded to the threat of indictment by marching on Rome, Pompey, now the bastion of the Senate, took his forces south to Luceria. Cicero's hope was for a settlement brokered between the two dynasts; this was dashed when Pompey evaded a meeting with Caesar by quitting Italy for Macedonia, to organize republican resistance there. Cicero's quandary—his support for the republican cause was qualified by his dismay at Pompey's leadership and his distaste for the bellicosity of his optimate supporters—held him paralysed until June, when he finally set out to join Pompey. He was coldly received there by Cato and his supporters, and his low morale, accentuated by ill-health, caused him to reject participation in military activity at Dyrrhachium and later at Pharsalus. He made his way back to Brundisium, where he was detained by Antony in durance vile for a year until Caesar on his return to Italy signalled approval of his move back to Rome.

Cicero was there, lamenting his political isolation, when the republicans succumbed to the Caesarian forces at Thapsus in Africa in February 46. The senatorial rump acknowledged Caesar's sovereignty by bestowing a ten-year dictatorship upon him. Caesar's clemency towards prominent Pompeians initially encouraged Cicero to hold some hope for modified republican institutions, but increasing disillusionment drove him to abandon political life in favour of philosophical study. For twenty months from late 46 onwards he worked at a ferocious rate, producing the equivalent of a history of philosophy, with separate treatises on the theory of knowledge, the highest good, the means to happiness, and the nature of the gods.

Cicero took no part in the assassination of Caesar on the Ides of March 44, and though he expressed his delight to the conspirators, he also upbraided them for allowing Antony to escape a similar fate. He knew that the surviving consul had ambitions to establish himself in Caesar's place. The arrival of Caesar's heir, the youthful Octavian, a month after the assassination introduced a new factor into the power-struggle. Once Cicero had decided to abandon his plan to retire to Athens, and had returned to confront Antony in the series of speeches which he called the *Philippics*, he cultivated the young man and initially succeeded in grooming him to oppose Antony on behalf of the Senate.

Meanwhile Antony was claiming his province of Cisalpine Gaul, currently administered by the senatorial nominee Decimus Brutus, whom he enclosed and besieged in Mutina. The senatorial forces, led by the consuls Pansa and Hirtius and supported by Octavian, worsted Antony's troops, but Decimus Brutus allowed the depleted army to escape. At the point when the extant letters come to an end in July 43, Cicero is vainly beseeching Marcus Brutus to return to Italy from Macedonia to undertake the leadership of the senatorial forces.

The final months of Cicero's life can be briefly recounted. In November 43 Antony, Octavian, and Lepidus met near Bononia and established a formal triumvirate. By the *lex Titia* they awarded themselves five-year appointments, with authority to promulgate laws and to appoint city-magistrates and provincial governors. Following the precedent set by Sulla and Marius, they issued a decree proscribing 300 senators and 2,000 equestrians; Cicero headed the list. The poignant details of his final moments are preserved in a long fragment from Livy:

Marcus Cicero had withdrawn from Rome before the imminent arrival of the triumvirs. He regarded as inevitable what actually ensued, that he would no more be delivered from the clutches of Antony than Brutus and Cassius could escape from Caesar. Initially he fled to his Tusculan estate. From there he journeyed cross-country to his residence at Formiae, intending to take ship from Caieta. From there he put out to sea several times, but at one moment he was carried back by adverse winds, and at the next he was unable to endure the ship's tossing induced by the groundswell. Eventually he tired of both flight and life, and he retired to his house further inland, a little more than a mile from the sea. 'I shall die', he said 'in the fatherland which I have often delivered.' It is well established that his slaves were ready to fight bravely and faithfully, but Cicero himself bade them lay down the litter, and to endure without a struggle the necessity imposed by an unjust fate. As he leaned from his litter, and offered his neck without resistance, his head was hacked off. This was not enough for the soldiers' heartless cruelty; they also hacked off his hands, reproaching them for having penned words injurious to Antony. His head was accordingly borne back to Antony, and on his instructions it was set between his hands on the rostra, where as consul, and on numerous occasions as a consular, and in that very year in opposing Antony, he had been greeted with adulation for his eloquence greater than had ever been accorded to any human voice. Men could scarcely raise their eyes, blinded with tears, to gaze on his slaughtered bodily parts. (Livy, Book 120)

2. *The letters and Cicero's correspondents*

The 914 extant letters are separated into four groups:

(*a*) *The Letters to Atticus* (*Att.*), 426 in number, are arranged chronologically into sixteen books. All the letters in them were written by Cicero, and we may accordingly assume that they were stored and published by Atticus. In addition, Cicero enclosed with his own correspondence some 26 letters sent to or from others, which he forwarded for Atticus' perusal. The most important of these were sent to or from Pompey (*Att.* VIII 11A–D), Caesar (*Att.* IX 6A, IX 11A, X 8B), and Antony (X 8A, XIV 13 A–B).

T. Pomponius Atticus (110–32 BC) was the subject of an extant biography by his contemporary Cornelius Nepos. From it we learn that Pomponius was a companion of Cicero's from childhood, and the two remained intimate friends throughout Cicero's life. Pomponius left Italy in 85, during the disturbances, to reside in Athens, where he became a popular figure, acquiring the surname Atticus ('the Athenian') from his close familiarity with Greek language and literature, and more generally through his friendship with and philanthropy towards the Athenians. According to Nepos (4.5), he returned to Rome in 65, and thereafter divided his time between the capital and Epirus, where he had acquired an estate near Buthrotum.

Cicero's letters to him span the years from November 68 to the last months of 44, though with notable gaps when the two were in close personal contact, from July 65 to January 61, from November 54 to May 51, and from May 49 to January 48. At other times they corresponded with each other virtually every day when couriers were available. These letters are the most precious of the body of correspondence for the insights they provide into political events at Rome. Atticus was on friendly terms not only with optimates like Marcus Cato and Hortensius, but also with Cicero's adversaries, so that he served as a mine of information which is reflected in Cicero's responses.

Cicero did not intend these letters for publication, and he writes with uninhibited candour about the leading personalities and their activities. Again, since the two men were related (Cicero's brother Quintus was married to Atticus' sister Pomponia), and since Cicero relied on his friend's business acumen to restore to order his frequently chaotic finances, the letters provide a mine of information about his domestic affairs.

A fitting tribute to the political importance of these letters is provided by Cornelius Nepos in his Life of Atticus. Nepos possessed a copy of the sixteen books to Atticus:

The person who reads them does not have much need of a connected history of these times, for all the details of the rivalries of the dominant figures, the faults of the leaders, and the changes in the political scene have been penned in such a way that there is nothing which is not clearly set out in them. (*Atticus* 16.3 f.)

(*b*) *The Letters to Friends (Fam.).* These letters, assembled like those to Atticus in sixteen books, were written in the period between January 62 and July 43. They differ from the Atticus collection in two ways. First, they include upwards of seventy letters written by correspondents other than Cicero. Secondly, the letters are not arranged chronologically, but are for the most part grouped round individual correspondents. Thus *Fam.* I 1–9 are addressed to Lentulus Spinther; the letters of Book III are all to Appius Claudius; VII 6–22 are addressed to Cicero's young protégé Trebatius; Letters 17–28 of Book XIII embody correspondence with Servius Sulpicius Rufus; Book XIV is devoted to his wife Terentia and the family; Book XV is confined to correspondence with his secretary and confidant Tiro, who assembled and published the whole collection during the Augustan era.

The 'friends' to whom the letters refer (in fact, the heading *Ad Familiares* is a coinage as late as the Renaissance), some ninety in number, include individuals like Crassus (Letter 44), for whom Cicero has to struggle to show friendly feelings. The most significant of these correspondents include Pompey (Letter 5), Caesar (VII 5, XIII 15–16; see Letters 45 and 115), Cato (XV 3–6; see Letter 63). Cassius Longinus (XII 1–12, XV 14–19; see Letters 139, 146, 147, 154, 156, 163, and 100), and Marcus Brutus (XI 17), with letters also from both to the triumvir Lepidus (X 27, 34–34a; see Letter 158).

(*c*) *The Letters to Quintus his Brother* (*Q. fr.*). The 27 letters in this collection all date from the years 60–54, when for the most part Quintus was serving in Asia, Sardinia, and Gaul. They are all written by Marcus. (There is one surviving letter from Quintus to Marcus in *Ad fam.* (XVI 16), together with three from Quintus to Tiro (XVI 8, 26–7).

Quintus Cicero (102–43 BC), four years younger than his brother, studied with him in Rome and Athens. He reached the praetorship in 62, and thereafter became governor of Asia (61–58). Having returned to Rome to facilitate Marcus' restoration from exile, he was next appointed legate in Sardinia by Pompey to secure the corn-supply (57–6), and then served with Caesar in Gaul (54–51) and Britain (54). He subsequently served as his brother's legate in Cilicia (51–50). He fought with the Pompeians in the Civil War, and was allowed to return to Rome by Caesar in 47. He was later proscribed by the triumvirs, and was murdered with his son in December 43.

The Handbook for Candidates Seeking Office (*Commentariolum Petitionis*), which is ascribed to Quintus as advice to his brother when he was a candidate for the consulship in 64, is now regarded by most scholars as spurious. But it is knowledgeable about both procedures and candidates, and is probably dated as early as the Augustan era.

(*d*) *The Letters to Marcus Brutus* (*Brut.*). These letters are all dated between March/April and July 43. They were early divided by editors into two books. The first five letters of Book II consist of four from Cicero and one (II 3) from Brutus. These letters have survived only in the printed edition of 1528, since the manuscript from which it was copied has not survived. The remaining letters are allotted to Book I; of them, 16–17 are spurious, crude forgeries composed by an early hand; 1, 4, 7, and 11 are by Brutus, and the rest by Cicero. Probably all 24 surviving letters in this Brutus collection originally rounded off a large body of correspondence between the two intimate friends.

Marcus Junius Brutus (*c.*85–42) was brought up by his uncle Marcus Cato, and was highly educated in rhetoric and philosophy. The letters of Cicero record his dubious financial dealings in the eastern provinces, notably in Cyprus. After early differences with Pompey, he attached himself to the republican cause, and after Pharsalus was pardoned by Caesar, who in 43 favoured him by appointing him governor of Cisalpine Gaul. After Caesar crushed the republican remnants in Africa and then in Spain, Brutus enjoyed close relations with him, while maintaining a cordial friendship with Cicero. But when Caesar assumed a perpetual dictatorship, Brutus headed the conspiracy to assassinate him. The ensuing unpopularity compelled him to quit Rome, and later Italy. In 43–42 he gathered forces and finances in Asia and Syria. In 42, after the defeat at Philippi, he followed the example of his colleague Cassius, and committed suicide.

3. *The letters: content and texture*

In a note addressed to his friend Scribonius Curio (*Fam.* II 4), Cicero remarks that letters fall into several categories. The most important is the informative, the purpose for which letter-writing was invented; the other two are 'the friendly and jocular' on the one hand, and 'the earnest and serious' on the other. But at this tragic crisis for Romans (the date is 53) neither is appropriate; the only suitable theme which remains for him is the exhortation, 'to seek the pursuit of the highest fame'.

In this passage, however, Cicero is alluding to letters exchanged between intimate friends, and there are types in the correspondence which fall outside the three categories. The most obvious of these is the letter of recommendation; Book XIII of *Letters to Friends* contains 79 such missives, for Cicero as senior statesman was often requested to use his influence on behalf of youthful acquaintances to further their careers. A typical example is Letter 45, in which Cicero solicits Caesar on behalf of Trebatius. A familiar pattern emerges; initially he exploits his friendship with the dynast. He then praises the merits of his protégé ('no man alive . . . is more honourable, virtuous, or decent'), and he exhorts Caesar, 'Take him to your heart with all your courtesy.' Clearly, however, the pattern must vary with the identity of the person addressed and the nature of the request. When in Letter 7 Cicero recommends Atticus to his cordially disliked former colleague Antonius, the tone is less ingratiating. Requests advanced on behalf of Pompeians, as in Letter 117 to Dolabella and Letter 102 to Plancus, have to be pressed more delicately. In some cases, as in Letter 125, a plea on behalf of Precilius, Cicero exploits the genre to apologize to Caesar for his political stance.

Another type which falls outside Cicero's three categories is the consolatory theme, examples of which are assembled in Book IV of the *Letters to Friends*. They include the famous letter from Servius Sulpicius on the death of Tullia (*Fam.* IV 5), which elicits Letter 121, Cicero's mordant reply. Again, the informal note struck in the letters to Terentia and the family, gathered in Book XIV, together with the letters to Tiro in Book XVI, lie outside the three categories distinguished by Cicero.

Many formal letters to political associates, however, can be subsumed under the heading of 'earnest and serious'. Cicero exercises expertise and artistry in framing these addresses on the political scene, so that in word order, rhythmical effects, and periodic structure they become the written equivalent of the speeches for which he was so celebrated. He intended that these letters, as distinct from his indiscreet observations to Atticus, would reach a wider readership. The letters which he penned from exile, and again those composed under pressure of duties in his province of Cilicia, do not betray the same care and polish, but those addressed, for example, to Lentulus Spinther, which Tiro when editing the *Letters to Friends* placed at the forefront to advertise their stylistic merit, are impressive productions.

Standing out as the most impressive of these letters from the literary standpoint is the address to Lucceius (Letter 40) which requests him to compose an account of Cicero's varied career. With its wealth of literary, historical, and philosophical allusions, it induced Cicero himself to praise it as 'a handsome effort' (Letter 41.3).

But the great majority of the letters, especially those to Atticus, are centred on Cicero's own activities, ambitions, reflections on contemporary events, and reminiscences of past glories. When we examine the texture of these descriptions, we are made aware that Cicero stands at the centre of a highly educated community of scholars. In addressing men like Paetus, Marius, his brother Quintus, friends like Brutus, and above all Atticus, he constantly underscores his views by apposite parallels from the past. He is able to assume that his correspondents recognize and appreciate the literary allusions he draws from his rich store of learning. He enriches his and their vision of contemporary events by evocation of the Greek (and occasionally Latin) masterpieces.

Of these authors, Homer is most frequently exploited, and in particular, his *Iliad*, from which are regularly deployed citations illustrative of Cicero's own situation. So, for example, his patriotism is summarized in Homer's 'The best, the only omen is defence | Of one's own native land' (Letter 18.4; *Iliad* 12.268). Elsewhere (Letter 19.1) he argues that he must not quit Rome for fear of the reproaches of his fellow-citizens, and in particular of Cato; here he assumes the persona of Hector, who refuses to flee from Achilles because he fears 'the Trojans and their wives with trailing gowns . . . Polydamas will be the first' (*Iliad* 22.105 and 100). In recounting his policy of non-aggression in his tussles with Clodius, he claims that it is his practice merely to respond to provocation and not to initiate it, 'to strike back when a man shows violence first' (Letter 20.3; *Iliad* 24.369). In describing his reaction to the news that Pompey has quitted Italy, he recites: 'My heart does not stand firm, but I am tortured' (Letter 75.4; *Iliad* 10.93 f.). A little later in the same letter he expresses regret that Atticus cannot join him so that they can plan a joint strategy, for 'Two heads together grasp advantages which one would miss' (*Iliad* 10.234). When he explains how Clodius secured his acquittal in the Bona Dea outrage, he begins: 'Ye Muses, tell me now how first the fire descended', a passage in which Homer describes how the Achaean ships were set on fire. He likens that disaster to the destructive effect of Clodius' release on the collapsing republic (Letter 12.5; *Iliad* 16.112). Such evocations as these are ubiquitous in the letters.

Cicero elsewhere similarly exploits the *Odyssey*, but more sparingly. In Letter 66 (in which there are further quotations from the *Iliad*), he confesses that he has not followed his friend's advice, as Odysseus rejected the promptings of Circe and Calypso: 'But never did you stir the heart within my breast' (*Odyssey* 9.33). Elsewhere he quotes from the Greek tragedians, above all Euripides, to achieve similar effects; other quotations come from Hesiod, Aristophanes, and various lesser lights. There are also apposite citations from Latin authors, though these are less in evidence. Ennius' *Annals* are exploited for a sardonic comparison of Bibulus with Fabius Maximus Cunctator (Letter 23.2), and a citation from Terence in a letter to Cornificius (157.5) hails the happier prospects for the body politic, if only traditional republicans pull together: 'The day now brings fresh life, demands fresh ways.'

Perhaps the most notable example of such citations deployed for the serious purpose of underlining Cicero's attitudes is found in Letter 125, which is addressed to Caesar. It purports to be a letter of recommendation of a young friend, but it emerges as an apologia for Cicero's political stance. Caesar had done him the honour of inviting him to join the Caesarians, but Cicero had resisted. 'Never did he win the heart within my breast' (*Odyssey* 9.33, cited above) and 7.258, where Odysseus resists the blandishments of Callipso). Instead, Cicero had hearkened to republican leaders who were urging him 'Be brave, to win the praises of posterity' (*Odyssey* 1.302). Caesar's reaction to this rejection is that of Laertes at *Odyssey* 24.315: 'At these words grief's black cloud encompassed him.' Even at this late stage Cicero was being exhorted to aspire to immortal fame: 'May I not die ignobly and ingloriously, | But do some mighty deed, which men to come may learn' (*Iliad* 22.306 f.). But he resists this siren-song and listens instead to Euripides: 'I hate the wisdom-teacher who himself's not wise.' But he will listen to the words of Glaucus' father in the *Iliad* (6.208): 'Strive to be best, and rise superior to the rest.' Cicero deluges Caesar with this array of quotations as the surest way of maintaining his benevolence, engaging him as scholar to scholar.

So much for the serious aspects of the literary texture. But Cicero was celebrated (in his speeches as in his letters) for his sardonic wit. One obvious example of this is his denigration of leading figures by derisive nicknames. Crassus becomes 'old Baldhead' (Letter 12.5) because earlier members of the family bore the name Calvus ('Bald'). Clodius' surname was Pulcher ('Beautiful'), so he becomes 'our little Beauty' (Letters 17.4, 22.3). His sister Claudia, celebrated for her bright gaze, becomes 'Lady Ox-eyes', a learned reminiscence of Homer's description of the goddess Hera (Letter 20.1; *Iliad* 1.551, etc.). Pompey's eastern conquest is recalled by the nickname Sampsiceramus, the name of a minor Syrian prince (Letters 21.2, 25.2); elsewhere he is referred to as 'Epicrates' ('the Powerful One'; Letter 18.1). Antony's nominee for the province of Africa, Calvisius Sabinus, and his legate Statilius Taurus, are designated as 'the Minotaur' (half-man, half-beast; see Letter 157). Antony is labelled 'Stratyllax', the name of a braggart soldier in an unidentified play (Letter 151.3). Leading optimates, including Hortensius, are derisively called 'Tritons of the fish-ponds' (Letter 20.1), because they are more concerned for their private property than for the welfare of the republic. Caesar (whom earlier Cicero treats respectfully) in his role as benevolent dictator is designated as a second Pisistratus (Letter 74.2).

Elsewhere many of these joking references are less barbed, and indeed more genial. When Atticus prepares to go to Sicyon to reclaim a loan, Cicero depicts him as a campaigning general, first offering sacrifice before launching his attack (Letter 9.1). At Letter 16.7, he refers to 'the Cincian Law' because his bequest has won the approval of Atticus' agent Cincius. In similar vein he refers to '*The Education of Cyrus*', indicating not Xenophon's biography, but the instruction of the architect Vettius Cyrus (Letter 18.2).

Cicero's most telling taunts are directed against his two bitter enemies, Clodius and Antony. Letter 17.5 records his witticism about Clodius' defence of alibi in the Bona Dea episode: 'Sicily to Rome in a week, but Rome to Interamna in three hours?' This letter continues with an innuendo about Clodius' sexual relations with his sister (Cicero admits that Atticus will regard the comment as unworthy of a former consul). Antony is the target when Cicero repeatedly expresses his regret at not having accompanied the conspirators when they assassinated Caesar: 'I only wish you had invited me to the dinner on the Ides of March; there would have been nothing left over!' (Letter 154.1 to Cassius Longinus); 'How I wish that you had invited me to that most attractive feast on the Ides of March! We would have had no left-overs' (Letter 155, to Trebonius).

Cicero draws effortlessly on his knowledge of history and philosophy to add a spice of learning to his joking. So during his campaigning in Cilicia, when he encamps with his army at Issus he recalls that Alexander the Great ('a considerably better commander than you or I') had done likewise (Letter 59.3), Another letter (Letter 61.26), also sent from his province, is dated 'The 765th day after the battle of Leuctra', which commemorates not the famous victory of Thebes over Sparta in 371, but the street-battle between the hoodlums of Milo and those of Clodius, when Clodius met his end. Elsewhere we read the anecdote, a favourite of Cicero's, which recounts how when the tyrant Dionysius was expelled from Syracuse, he became a schoolmaster at Corinth because he could not forgo the right to rule (Letter 76.1 and n.; Letter 106.1).

Atticus claimed allegiance to the doctrines of Epicurus, and Cicero misses no opportunity of joking at the expense of the school. Thus at Letter 66.1 he castigates the slow progress of Saufeius, another Epicurean, as courier, as symptomatic of philosophers. At Letter 143.4, Cicero remonstrates with Atticus for condemning his plan to retire to Athens. That would be a forgivable option, Atticus had suggested, if Cicero were an Epicurean. What a pity that you did not make this objection, retorts Cicero, for then you could have played your usual role as a Cato! (Atticus as an Epicurean is acidly associated with the Stoics.)

In short, the literary texture of the letters regularly incorporates, as befits a man of learning, reminiscences of literature, history, and philosophy.

4. Cicero and domestic life

After the happy childhood at Arpinum and Rome, and his two years of study abroad, Cicero returned to Rome to lay the foundations of his married life. If his daughter Tullia was born in 79 (some scholars would place the birth two years later) he must have married before his departure or immediately on his return. His wife Terentia was of good family (her half-sister Fabia was a Vestal virgin) and had considerable private means. A son, Marcus, was born in 65, many years after Tullia. Though the marriage lasted until the winter of 47/46, when the break-up occurred for reasons probably financial (Cicero shows discretion in discussing it, but Terentia's freedman may have been implicated with her), the relationship was never a close one. Terentia is alleged to have remarried after the divorce, her second husband being the historian Sallust, and to have survived to the age of 103; Cicero almost immediately married a slip of a girl called Publilia, probably, as Tiro explained, to relieve his debts. This marriage, however, lasted only a few months, and when friends offered him a third possible bride, Cicero is said to have remarked: 'It is difficult to attend to philosophy and a wife at the same time.' As Boissier remarks in his classic book *Cicero and his Friends*, it was a wise answer, but Cicero should have thought of it sooner.[1]

The letters frequently advert to Tullia, on whom Cicero lavished much more affection than on Terentia. (Publilia's cold indifference to her sad death in February 45 may have precipitated Cicero's second divorce.) Tullia was married three times. Her first husband, Calpurnius Piso, whom she married in 62 and whom Cicero regarded highly, died in 57. In 55 she married Furius Crassipes, but he divorced

---

[1] G. Boissier, *Cicero and his Friends* (London, 1899; French edn. 1865), 99.

her a few years later. In 50 she married a third time; Cicero was absent
in his province when the negotiations took place. Her new husband,
Cornelius Dolabella, joined Caesar, and after the dictator's murder he
was advanced into the vacant consulship. Cicero sought to detach him
from his colleague Antony, and in spite of his divorcing Tullia when
she was pregnant with his child in 46, the two men initially remained
on friendly terms. Cicero, however, broke decisively with his former
son-in-law when Dolabella threw in his lot with Antony; he vainly
sought to recover Tullia's dowry until finally Dolabella committed suicide when besieged by Cassius at Laodicea.

Cicero's son, Marcus, born in 65, gave early signs of becoming a
better soldier than a scholar. He had already served with some distinction at Pharsalus, and had been pardoned by Caesar when his
father arranged for his further education at Athens in April 45. But
he abandoned his studies, and in April 43 won praise from Brutus for
his part in the military operations. After Cicero senior was
butchered, his son fought with Sextus Pompeius. He was again pardoned in 39, and became a favourite of Octavian, sharing the consulship with him in 30, and thereafter became governor of Syria and
then of Asia.

Cicero's brother Quintus had married Pomponia, sister of his
friend Atticus, in 70/69. The marriage, punctuated by constant
bickering, ended in divorce in 45. There was one son, Quintus, born
in 66. His boyhood was spent in close proximity to his cousin
Marcus, supervised by his uncles Cicero and Atticus during his
father's lengthy absences on duties abroad. Young Quintus fought in
support of Pompey at Pharsalus. He was a temperamental youth, and
became bitterly hostile to Cicero. While serving with Caesar, he
sought to blacken Cicero's reputation, and to cause a rift between the
supremo and Cicero. He was proscribed in 43, and perished with his
father.

Cicero's confidential secretary, Tiro, became virtually one of the
family when he was manumitted at the age of 50 in the year 53. The
27 letters of Book XVI of *Letters to Friends*, written between 56 and
44, reveal the strong feelings of family affection shown to Tiro not
only by the immediate family, but also by Cicero's brother Quintus.
In general, Cicero showed himself a model master towards his slaves,
as the loyalty of those attending him at his death demonstrated.
His many houses demanded a large retinue; Letter 51.4 expresses

gratitude to Quintus for his promise to provide new recruits from Gaul or Britain.

The considerable number of slaves was necessary for the upkeep of his many villas. We hear of no contemporary who possessed as many residences. Besides his splendid town house on the Palatine hill at Rome, he owned inland villas close to the capital at Tusculum and Arpinum. He owned houses on the coast of Latium, similarly close to Rome, at Formiae, Astura, and Antium, though he sold this last when purchasing that at Cumae. In Campania, in addition to his acquisition at Cumae, he owned villas at Puteoli and Pompeii. Thus in his later years he had eight houses to be staffed by slaves.

The correspondence of Cicero has won the attention of minds and hearts of civilized readers throughout the centuries in the West. There are several reasons for this. First, the sheer body of the 914 letters which have survived, most of them covering the events of a mere twenty years, has ensured that the wide-ranging content, together with Cicero's reflections upon it, provides astonishing detail. In particular, Cicero's letters to Atticus, incorporating reflections sent virtually every day with no thought of publication to the world at large, are fascinating documents. In general, the letters range widely over both public policies and private concerns; as the Younger Pliny commented when contrasting his own correspondence with them, 'My situation is different from that of Marcus Cicero . . . He had not only the most abundant talent, but he also matched it with the supply of varied and important topics' (9.2.2). But the chief attraction of the letters is the light they cast on the day-to-day politics in a world which witnessed the collapse of the republic, and its replacement by a tyranny, however benevolent. Cicero's sense of political decency in condemning the blatant self-interest of Pompey's later supporters, his passive resistance on principle to Caesar's monarchy, and his outspoken opposition to Mark Antony, Caesar's self-appointed successor, have won for these letters the continuing study of them over two millennia later.

NOTE ON THE TEXT AND TRANSLATION

THIS translation is based on the texts of the letters edited by W. S. Watt and D. R. Shackleton Bailey. For the *Letters to Atticus*, see *Epistulae ad Atticum I–VIII* (ed. Watt, Oxford Classical Texts, 1965; *IX–XVI* (ed. Shackleton Bailey, OCT, 1961). A revised edition of *I–XVI* by Shackleton Bailey was published by Teubner (Stuttgart, 1987–8).

For the *Letters to Friends*, see *Epistulae ad Familiares* (ed. Watt, Oxford Classical Texts, 1982); ed, Shackleton Bailey (Teubner, Stuttgart, 1988).

For the *Letters to Quintus and Brutus*, see *M. Tulli Ciceronis Epistulae*, vol. iii (ed. Watt, Oxford Classical Texts, 1958); ed. Shackleton Bailey (Teubner, Stuttgart, 1988).

The recent Loeb editions of *Letters to Atticus*, 4 vols. (1999), *Letters to Friends*, 3 vols. (2001), *Letters to Quintus and Brutus* (2002), edited and translated by Shackleton Bailey, embody the Stuttgart texts.

Readers interested in the complex and disparate textual traditions can consult the summaries by R. H. Rouse in *Texts and Transmissions* (ed. L. D. Reynolds, Oxford, 1983), 135–42.

The following standard abbreviations are used throughout for the sources of the letters in this volume:

Att.   Letters to Atticus
Fam.   Letters to Friends
Brut.   Letters to Marcus Brutus
Q. fr. Letters to Quintus

In translating the Letters, I have benefited from the Loeb renderings of Shackleton Bailey. Following the practice of earlier editors, I have resorted to French to convey an effect similar to Cicero's extensive use of Greek, but, as in my translation of Pliny, where the Greek citations are more extensive I have rendered them in English.

NOTE ON ROMAN NAMES

IN the late republic a male Roman citizen generally had three names: a *personal name*, (*praenmen*), a *clan name* (*nomen*), and a *surname* (*cognomen*)—for example Marcus Tullius Cicero. The *clan name* ('Tullius') would be borne not only by his extended family, but also by various people, such as freed slaves, who gained citizenship through him: thus Cicero's secretary Tiro on being freed took the name Marcus Tullius Tiro. Hence sharing a clan name often did not involve a blood relationship. To these names a further one (*agnomen*) was sometimes added as an honorific title (Africanus) or by adoption (Aemilianus).

The *surname* ('Cicero') was usually inherited within families though it might be a nickname personal to an individual; thus brothers, for example, might sometimes have different surnames.

Few *personal names* were available to choose from: the main ones were Appius, Aulus, Decimus, Gaius, Gnaeus, Lucius, Manius (M'.), Marcus, Publius, Quintus, Servius, Sextus, Spurius, Tiberius, and Titus. These might be used alone by close family and intimate friends, but outside those circles a Roman would typically be addressed by surname alone, or by a combination of personal name and *either* clan name *or* surname—'Marcus Tullius' or 'Marcus Cicero'.

Female names under the republic had normally been simply a feminine version of the father's clan name—thus Cicero's daughter was called 'Tullia'. Once again under the empire this often became more complex, and women would sometimes have names derived from, for example, their maternal family background, or from surnames; now too women would sometimes have more than one name.

This translation employs the names that Cicero himself uses; in the index, however, the full names (where these are known) are given, to assist cross-referencing with other works where different versions of the person's name might be used.

SELECT BIBLIOGRAPHY

Asterisks indicate fuller bibliographies

Editions of and Commentaries on the Letters

Works additional to those listed in the Note on the Text and Translation:

Abbott, F. E., *Select Letters* (Norman, Okla., 1964).

Constans, L.-A., Bayet, J., and Beaujeu, J, *Cicéron: Correspondance*, 11 vols. (Paris, 1934–96).

How, W. W., *Cicero: Select Letters*, 2 vols. (Oxford, 1925–6).

Shackleton Bailey, D. R., *Cicero's Letters to Atticus*, 7 vols. (Cambridge, 1965–70).

—— *Ad Familiares*, 2 vols. (Cambridge, 1977).

—— (tr.), *Cicero's Letters to his Friends*, 2 vols. (Harmondsworth, 1978; repr. Atlanta, Ga., 1988).

—— *Cicero: Select Letters* (Cambridge Greek and Latin Classics, Cambridge, 1980).

Tyrrell, R. Y., and Purser, L. C., *The Correspondence of Cicero*, 7 vols. (Dublin, 1904–33).

Wilkinson, L. P., *Letters of Cicero* (London, 1966).

*Willcock, M. M., *Cicero: The Letters of January to April 43 BC* (Warminster, 1995).

Ancillary Texts, Translations, and Commentaries

Appian, *Civil Wars*, tr. J. Carter (Harmondsworth, 1996).

[Asconius,] *A Historical Commentary on Asconius* by B. A. Marshall (Columbia, Mo., 1985).

Caesar, *The Gallic War*, tr. C. Hammond (Oxford World's Classics, 1995).

—— *The Civil War*, tr. J. Carter (Oxford World's Classics, 1997). This volume usefully incorporates translations of the Alexandrian, African, and Spanish wars, composed by authors other than Caesar.

[Cicero,] *The Speeches of Cicero*, ed. P. Mackendrick (London, 1995).

—— *The Philosophical Works of Cicero* ed. P. Mackendrick (London, 1989).

—— *Caesarian Speeches*, ed. H. C. Gotoff (Chapel Hill, NC, 1995).

—— *Defence Speeches*, tr. D. H. Berry (Oxford World's Classics, 2001).

—— *Philippics*, ed. and tr. D. R. Shackleton Bailey (Chapel Hill, NC, 1986).

—— *Political Speeches*, tr. D. H. Berry (Oxford World's Classics, 2006).

Cornelius Nepos, *Atticus*, in N. Horsfall (ed. and tr.), *Cornelius Nepos: A Selection* (Oxford, 1989).

Plutarch, *Roman Lives*, tr. R. Waterfield, ed. P. A. Stadter (Oxford World's Classics, 1999).

Sallust, *Catiline*, tr. S. A. Hansford (Harmondsworth, 1963).

Suetonius, *Lives of the Caesars*, tr. C. Edwards (Oxford World's Classics, 2000).

General

Mini-biographies by E. Badian of the major players in the *Oxford Classical Dictionary*, 3rd edn. (Oxford, 1996), should be consulted.

Badian, E., 'M. Porcius Cato and the Annexation and Early Administration of Cyprus', *Journal of Roman Studies*, 55 (1965), 110–21.

Balsdon, J. P. V. D., *Life and Leisure in Ancient Rome* (London, 1960).

—— 'Fabula Clodiana', *Historia*, 15 (1966), 65–73.

—— 'Cicero the Man' in Dorey, ch. 7.

Boissier, G., *Cicero and his Friends* (London, 1899; orig French edn. 1865).

Broughton, T. R. S., *The Magistrates of the Roman Republic*, 3 vols. (repr. Atlanta, 1984–6).

Cambridge Ancient History, IX² (Cambridge, 1994), chs. 9–10 (T. P. Wiseman); chs. 11–12 (E. Rawson).

Dorey, T. A. (ed.), *Cicero* (London, 1964).

Douglas, A. E., 'Cicero the Philosopher', in Dorey, ch. 6.

—— Cicero, *Brutus* (Oxford, 1966).

Dyck, A. R., *A Commentary on Cicero, De legibus* (Ann Arbor, 2004).

*Edwards, Catherine, 'Epistolography', in S. Harrison (ed.), *A Companion to Classical Literature* (Oxford, 2004).

Fox, M., *Cicero's Philosophy of History* (Oxford, 2007).

Griffin, M., 'Cicero and Rome', in J. Boardman, J. Griffin, and O. Murray (eds.), *The Oxford History of the Classical World* (Oxford, 1986), ch. 4.

*Gruen, E. S., *The Last Generation of the Roman Republic* (Berkeley, 1994).

*Hutchinson, G. O., *Cicero's Correspondence: A Literary History* (Oxford, 1995).

Lintott, A. W., *Violence in Republican Rome* (Oxford, 1988).

—— 'Electoral Bribery in the Roman Republic', *Journal of Roman Studies*, 80 (1990), 1–16.

—— 'Cicero and Milo', *Journal of Roman Studies*, 64 (1974), 62–78.

Malherbe, A. J., *Ancient Epistolary Theorists* (Atlanta, 1988).

*Mitchell, T. N., *Cicero, the Ascending Years* (New Haven, 1979).

—— *Cicero, the Senior Statesman* (New Haven, 1991).

Nisbet, R. G. M., 'The Speeches', in Dorey, ch. 3.

Powell, J. G. F. (ed.), *Cicero the Philosopher* (Oxford, 1995).

Ramsey, J. T., *Cicero and Sallust on the Conspiracy of Catiline* (White Plains, NY, 1988).

Scullard, H. H., 'The Political Career of a Novus Homo', in Dorey, ch. 1.

Shackleton Bailey, D. R., *Cicero* (London, 1971).

Steel, C. E. W., *Cicero: Rhetoric and Empire* (Oxford, 2001).

Stockton, D., *Cicero: A Political Biography* (Oxford, 1971).

Syme, R., *The Roman Revolution* (Oxford, 1939).

Weigel, E. D., *Lepidus. The Tarnished Triumvir* (London, 1992).

Wilkinson, L. P., 'Cicero . . . Letters', in *The Cambridge History of Classical Literature II* (Cambridge, 1982), 247 ff., 834 ff.

A CHRONOLOGY OF CICERO

Dates are BC

106   Cicero born (3 January).

91–87   Social War; Cicero serves under Gnaeus Pompeius Strabo (89) and Sulla (88); Italians win Roman citizenship (90, 89).

88   Sulla occupies Rome.

88–85   First Mithradatic War.

87   Marius and Cinna occupy Rome; domination of Cinna (87–84).

86   Marius dies.

83–81   Second Mithradatic War.

82   Sulla occupies Rome and is made dictator (82–81); proscriptions (82 to 1 June 81).

81   Sulla's reforms, including establishment of seven permanent criminal courts with senatorial juries; *Pro Quinctio*.

80   *Pro Roscio Amerino*; and the defence of the freedom of a woman from Arretium (80 or 79) wins Cicero popularity with Italians.

79(?77)   Birth of Tullia.

79–77   Travels in Athens and Rhodes.

78   Sulla dies.

75   Cicero quaestor in western Sicily; henceforward a senator.

73–71   Spartacus' slave revolt; Verres governor of Sicily.

73–63   Third Mithradatic War.

70   Pompey and Crassus consuls; *In Verrem*; *lex Aurelia* makes juries two-thirds equestrian.

69   Cicero plebeian aedile.

67   Lucullus relieved of Mithradatic command; *lex Gabinia* gives Pompey command against pirates.

66   Cicero praetor in charge of extortion court; *De imperio Cn. Pompei*; *lex Manilia* gives Pompey Mithradatic command; *Pro Cluentio*.

65   Birth of Marcus.

63   Cicero consul; *De lege agraria*; *Pro Rabirio perduellionis reo*; Catilinarian conspiracy; *Pro Murena*; execution of the conspirators (5 December).

62   Catiline defeated and killed; Bona Dea scandal; Pompey returns to Italy.

61 Clodius acquitted of sacrilege.

60 Publication of *In Catilinam*; formation of first 'triumvirate'.

59 Caesar consul; Clodius adopted into a plebeian family; *Pro Flacco*.

58. Clodius tribune; Cicero exiled in Thessalonica and Dyrrhachium; Caesar conquers Gaul (58–50).

57 Cicero recalled; returns to Rome (4 September); *Post reditum in senatu*; *Post reditum ad quirites*; *De domo sua*.

56–52 Activity in courts; 'first triumvirate' reaffirmed; *Pro Balbo*.

55 Pompey and Crassus consuls; *In Pisonem*; Cicero begins philosophical and rhetorical works (*De oratore*, *De republica*).

54 Defends Vatinius; Delegibus? defends Gabinius (54 or 53).

53 Crassus killed at Carrhae; Cicero is made augur (53 or 52); *Pro Rabirio Postumo* (53–52); *Pro Sestio*; writing *The Laws* (53–51).

52 Clodius killed by Milo (18 January), Pompey appointed sole consul; Cicero defends Milo (7 April); publication of *Pro Milone* (52–51).

55–51 Writes *De oratore*, *De republica*.

51–50 Cicero governor of Cilicia.

50 Hortensius dies.

49 Cicero back in Rome (Jan.). Caesar dictator; Civil War begins; Pompey crosses to Greece (17 March); Caesar visits Cicero (28 March); Cicero crosses to Greece (7 June).

48 Pompey defeated at Pharsalus (9 August) and murdered in Egypt (28 September); Cicero returns to Brundisium.

47 Cicero pardoned and allowed to move on to Rome.

47/6 Divorce from Terentia.

46 Marriage to Publilia. Pompeians defeated in Africa at Thapsus; Cato commits suicide; Cicero resumes philosophical and rhetorical works; *Pro Ligario*; *Stoic Paradoxes*.

45 Death of Tullia. Pompeians defeated in Spain at Munda (17 March); *Pro rege Deiotaro*; *Academica*; *On Ends*; *Tusculans*; *Nature of the Gods*.

44 Caesar and Antony consuls; Caesar *dictator perpetuo*; Caesar assassinated (15 March); Octavian named as his heir; Cicero attacks Antony (September); *Philippics* 1–4; *On Divination*; *On Fate*; *On Old Age*; *On Friendship*; *De officiis*; *On Obligations*.

43 Civil War; *Philippics* 5–14; Antony declared public enemy (April); Octavian occupies Rome and is elected consul (August); formation of 'second triumvirate'; proscriptions; Cicero murdered (7 December).

MAP 1 Italy and Africa marking Cicero's residences (see p. xxiv)

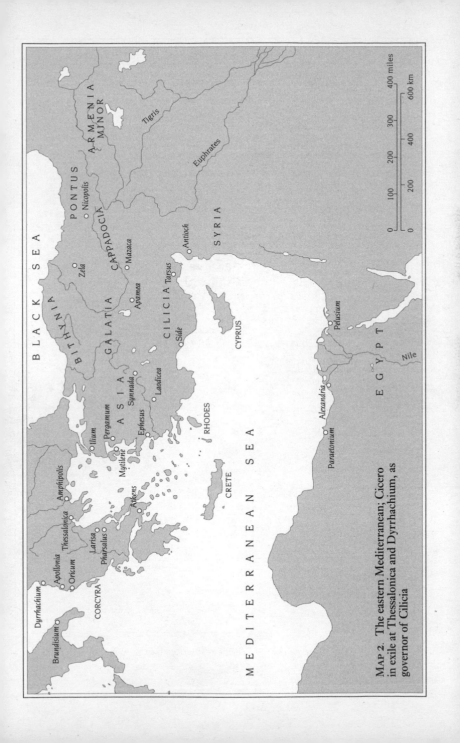

MAP 2. The eastern Mediterranean; Cicero in exile at Thessalonica and Dyrrhachium, as governor of Cilicia

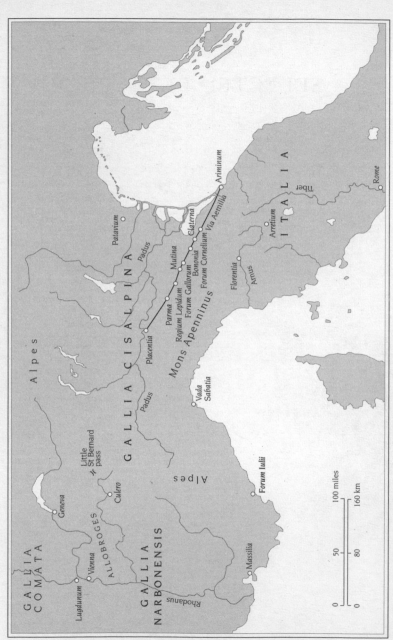

MAP 3 Civil War in Cisalpine Gaul; senatorial forces versus Mark Antony

SELECTED LETTERS

1

THE YEARS BEFORE THE CONSULSHIP (68–65 BC)

THE first surviving letters of Cicero which we possess (*Att.* I 1–11) document the period November 68–July 65. Thus no letters survive which recount his early life and family background at Arpinum, his precocious advocacy as a youth in the courts, his studies in oratory and philosophy which took him to Athens and Rhodes, or his election as quaestor in 75, a position which took him to Sicily and provided him with the material evidence for his crushing condemnation of Verres in 70.

These early letters are predominantly concerned with private rather than public issues. The first letter in this selection is actually the earliest; it provides information on family issues. The second makes passing reference to Cicero's campaign for the praetorship, which he held in 66. The third discusses in some detail his rivals for election to the consulship.

No letters survive from the years 64–63. We lament the absence not only of letters written during Cicero's consulship of 63, but also of the canvassing immediately preceding it. This lends particular relevance to *The Handbook for Candidates Seeking Office*. The question of the authenticity of this document, which purports to be an extended letter of advice from Quintus Cicero, has divided scholars. Though the prevailing modern view is against authenticity, the comment of Elizabeth Rawson (*Cicero, a Portrait* (London, 1975), 57) is relevant: 'More plausibly to be regarded as a rhetorical exercise of imperial date. But it is probably well informed on Roman elections in general, and Cicero's in particular.'

Letter 1 (*Att.* I 5)

Rome, November 68

CICERO TO ATTICUS

The close bond between us can enable you to gauge both my deep   1 feelings of sorrow and the great blessings, public and private, of which I have been deprived by the death of my cousin Lucius.*

I received from him all the pleasures which can be gained from the kindness and character of another. So I have no doubt that you share my unhappiness, since you are moved by my distress, and since you have lost a family connection and friend who was highly endowed with every good quality and sense of obligation, and who regarded you with affection both of his own accord and from my mentioning him to you.

2 In your letter to me you raise the topic of your sister. She herself will witness to you my deep concern that the attitude of my brother* Quintus towards her should be as it ought to be. I thought that he was being rather offensive, so I sent a letter to him to placate him as a brother, to counsel him as one younger than myself, and to rebuke him for his errant ways. From several letters which he has since written to me, I am sure that all is as it should be, and as we would both wish it.

3 Your reproach about my dispatch of letters is groundless, for our Pomponia never informed me that there was anyone to whom I could entrust a letter. However, I myself do not chance to have anyone going to Epirus,* and I have as yet no word of your being at Athens.

4 As for the business concerning Aemilius,* I dealt with it as you had instructed me, as soon as I reached Rome after our parting. As it happened, however, there was no pressing need, and since I decided that you had a sufficient strategy mapped out, I thought it better that Peducaeus should send you a letter of advice rather than I myself. Indeed, since I had bent my ear to Aemilius over several days (I imagine that you are well aware of his mode of discourse), I do not consider it an imposition to write to you about his complaints, when I have made light of the rather tiresome task of listening to them. But let me tell you that despite your accusation, I have received just one epistle from you, though you have more leisure to write, and greater facilities for the dispatch of letters.

5 As for your claim that even if a certain person* feels rather resentful towards you, I ought to make him more amenable, I take on board what you say and have not fallen down on the task, but he is surprisingly irked. I have missed no chance of saying all the right things about you, but I think I ought to decide what line of argument I should adopt in deference to your wishes. If you enclose them in a letter, you will find that on the one hand I have not sought to be more conscientious than yourself, and on the other that I will not be more slipshod than you wish.

On the issue affecting Tadius, he himself mentioned to me that 6
you had written that he has no grounds for concern, since the inheritance is his by uninterrupted possession.* (I am surprised that you
do not know that nothing can be taken by such uninterrupted
possession from the legal protection which the girl enjoys.)

I am delighted that your purchase in Epirus is to your satisfaction. 7
As suggested in your letter, I should like you to superintend what I
have entrusted to you, and whatever you consider appropriate for my
house at Tusculum, so long as you can do this without inconvenience
to yourself. That house is the one place where I can relax from all my
troubles and toils.

We expect my brother Quintus every day. Terentia* suffers badly
from arthritis. She is extremely fond of you, your sister, and your
mother. She sends her warmest greetings, as does my darling Tullia.
Look after yourself, and keep me in your affections. Impress upon
yourself that I love you like a brother.

Letter 2 (*Att.* I 11)

Rome, August 67

CICERO TO ATTICUS

I was already of my own accord working on your behalf, but then 1
when your two letters insistently made the same point, I was stirred
to make greater efforts. Further pressure came from the attentive
urging of Sallustius,* inciting me to work on Lucceius* as energetically as possible to restore your long-standing regard for each other.
But in spite of all my efforts, not only was I unable to establish afresh
the goodwill which he had earlier felt for you, but I could not even
coax out of him the reason for the change in his attitude. Though he
makes much of that arbitration* affecting him, and though I knew of
those other issues which alienated him when you were here, there is
undoubtedly some further deep-seated resentment preying on his
mind. Neither your letters nor my representations can expunge it as
readily as your presence here will remove it, not merely by your
words but also by those genial looks of yours—that is, as long as you
think it worth the effort, as you certainly will if you listen to me and
wish to make your courtesy manifest. Do not be surprised that in
spite of previous intimations in my earlier letters of my hopes of

bringing him round, I now appear to lose heart, for I find it astonishing how much more unrelenting and how much more obdurate in his anger his attitude is. But either your arrival will heal these wounds, or whichever of you is guilty will feel the pain.

2　　　As for the comment in your letter that you regard my election as already sewn up,* you are to realize that at present in Rome there is no harassment to match all the unfair barbs which the candidates endure, and it is not known when the elections will take place. But Philadelphus will inform you on these matters.

Do please send with all speed the items you have bought for my Academy.* I take remarkable pleasure not only in using it, but even in contemplating it. Be sure not to pass on your books; keep them for me, as you write that you will. My boundless enthusiasm for them is commensurate with the loathing I feel for all else. It is beyond belief how much worse you will find things.

Letter 3 (*Att.* I 1)
Rome, July 65

CICERO TO ATTICUS

1　　So far as one can forecast at present, the situation with regard to my candidature (I know that you are deeply concerned about it) is something like this. Publius Galba is the only person canvassing, and he is meeting the plain and unambiguous refusals typical of former days. The general view is that his premature canvassing is doing my prospects no harm, because people are commonly saying no to him, with the claim that they owe an obligation to me. So I hope that some advantage accrues to me when the news gets round that friends of mine are in evidence in great numbers. My plan has been to begin my canvassing at the very time that Cincius tells me that your slave is leaving with this letter, that is, on 17 July,* when the tribunes are elected on the Campus. Galba, Antonius, and Quintus Cornificius* appear to be definite rivals—I think I hear your laughter or groaning! Some people believe—this will make you beat your forehead—that Caesonius* too will be a candidate. As for Aquilius,* I doubt that he will stand, for he has said that he will not, pleading illness and the excuse of his kingship of the courts. Catiline* is certain to be a fellow-candidate, if the courts decree that it is still dark at midday.

I hardly think that you are waiting for me to write anything about Aufidius and Palicanus.

Of the candidates standing for immediate election, Caesar* is considered a certainty, while Thermus and Silanus are thought to be in competition. Both are so impoverished in friends and in reputation that it does not seem to me *impossible* to have Turius* block their prospects, though no one thinks so except myself. From my perspective, it seems best for Thermus to be elected with Caesar, for none of the present contenders seems to be a stronger candidate if he were relegated to my year. This is because he is Curator of the Flaminian Way, which will quite easily be completed by then. I should gladly see him lumped in with consul Caesar here and now.

Such is my thinking in outline about the candidates up to now. For myself, I shall exercise the utmost care in performing the whole gamut of my functions as a candidate, and since Gaul seems to exercise a powerful effect on the voting, once the courts are in abeyance at Rome and public life is at a standstill, I shall perhaps take a trip in September to join Piso* as a member of his staff, intending to return in January. Once I have investigated the intentions of the nobles, I shall write to you. I hope that my other plans are running smoothly, at any rate so far as these city rivals are concerned. Since you are quite near at hand, you must make yourself responsible for the band of supporters of our friend Pompey. Assure him that I will not be angry if he does not appear for my election.

So that is the situation. But there is a matter about which I should like to seek your indulgence. Your uncle Caecilius was cheated of a large sum of money by Publius Varius. He has taken an action against Caninius Satyrus,* Varius' brother, about some articles which he stated had been fraudulently obtained by him from his brother. The other creditors are joining him in the action, among them Lucullus, Publius Scipio, and Lucius Pontius,* who they believe will be the official receiver if the goods are sold, though this business of the official receiver is a nonsense. But hark to the point at issue. Caecilius has asked me to be prosecutor against Satyrus. Scarcely a day passes on which this Satyrus does not appear at my door. He pays court most of all to Lucius Domitius,* and after him to me. He has been a great help both to me and to my brother Quintus in our canvassing.

I am indeed much exercised because of my friendship with both Satyrus himself and Domitius, on whom alone my prospects chiefly rest. I pointed this out to Caecilius, at the same time indicating that if the dispute had been between him alone and Satyrus alone I should have complied with his request. But as things stood, since the case involved all the creditors, especially as they were most distinguished men who could readily conduct their common case without anyone whom Caecilius might introduce on his own account, it was right that he should show consideration for both my obligation and the circumstances. He seemed to me to be more offended by this than I would have wished or than genial men usually are, and thereafter he has totally withdrawn from the friendly connection which he had established with me only a few days before.

I beg you to pardon me for this, and to believe that it was kindness which prevented me from acting against a friend of the highest repute at a time of utter wretchedness for him, after he had lent me all his support and services due. If you permit yourself to take a harsher view of me, you will regard my candidature as having been the stumbling-block. I believe that even if this were the case, pardon is my due, 'for the prize is no sacrificial beast or oxhide.'* You know the race I am running, and my conviction that I am not merely to maintain old favours but also to gain new ones. I hope that I have justified my case to you, for I am certainly anxious to do so.

5   Your Hermathena* is a source of great delight to me. It is so admirably placed that the entire hall seems to be an *offrande votive* to her. I am most grateful.

THE RETURN OF POMPEY, AND THE ENMITY OF CLODIUS (62–60 BC)

IN 70, as consul with Crassus, Pompey restored their powers to the tribunes, and became the people's champion. In 67 he was rewarded with an unprecedented command to suppress the pirates, with pro-consular authority throughout the Mediterranean. Having achieved prodigious success, in 66 he was given command of the Mithradatic War in place of Lucullus. Having routed the Mithradatic forces, he annexed Syria, settled Judaea, and organized the eastern provinces. During these years in the East he continued to dominate the political scene at Rome through his supporters, and obtained unprecedented honours. Thus, when he returned to Rome in late 62 he was a popular hero, overshadowing Cicero's fame. To the surprise of many, he disbanded his army and sought an accommodation with the optimate leaders in the Senate. His increasingly warm relations with Cicero are a persistent theme in the letters of these years.

In December 62 a major scandal erupted during the ceremony of the Bona Dea held at the house of the Pontifex Maximus Julius Caesar. A quaestor, Publius Clodius, was discovered in transvestite garb, apparently pursuing an adulterous relationship with Caesar's wife Pompeia. He was indicted for sacrilege. Cicero played a major role in denouncing him. But Clodius was acquitted, thanks to blatant bribery of the jurors organized by Crassus. Thereafter Clodius sought revenge by gaining election to the tribunate and pursuing Cicero relentlessly. Though Cicero was dismayed by the acquittal, regarding it as a significant blow against the senatorial government, he fatally underestimated the danger to his own person.

Letter 4 (*Fam.* V 2)

Rome, mid-January 62

CICERO TO METELLUS CELER

If you and the army are in good shape, that is welcome.   1

You write that our friendly spirit towards each other, and the restoration of our good relations, had led you to believe that you would never be made a laughing stock by me. I cannot grasp the purport of this, but I suspect that report has reached you of my comments in the Senate: that when I maintained that there were very many who were resentful* that I had saved the state, I remarked that relatives of yours, to whom you could not say no, had induced you to suppress what you had decided ought to be said in praise of me in the Senate. When making that statement I added that we had divided between us the duty of preserving the republic. I was to protect the city from ambush within and from internal villainy, and you were to defend Italy from both armed enemies and a hidden conspiracy. That alliance of ours in performing this great and exemplary duty, I said, had been undermined by your relatives. They feared, when I honoured you in most ungrudging and munificent terms, that you would contribute your share of our mutual goodwill by honouring me.

2   When in the course of my remarks I recounted my eager anticipation of your speech and the extent of my delusion, my words seemed to be without malice, and were greeted with gentle laughter, directed not against you but rather against my misconception and admission, made openly and naively, that I had been eager to seek your praise. My remark that I had sought to have an attestation from your lips when my achievements had won such great fame and distinction can be interpreted only as paying tribute to you.

3   As for your phrase 'our friendly spirit towards each other', I do not know what your view of reciprocal friendship is. My own conception is that it lies in well-wishing both welcomed and returned. If I were to claim that I had not taken up a province for your sake, you would regard me as less than sincere, for my own calculations prompted that decision, and this strategy of mine brings me greater profit and pleasure every day. What I do claim is that as soon as I renounced the province in the Assembly, I at once began to ponder how I could consign it to you. I say nothing about the drawing of lots* among you; I would merely like you to suspect that my colleague took no steps in that matter without my knowledge. Bear in mind what followed, the speed with which I convened the Senate that day once the lottery had been held, and the lengthy speech which I made about you. Why, you yourself told me that not only did my speech do you honour, but it also cast aspersions on your fellow-praetors.

Moreover, the preamble to the senatorial decree* passed that day 4
attests that as long as that document survives, my obligation to you
cannot be hidden. Please remember too the motions which I proposed about you in the Senate once you had departed to your
province, the speeches which I made in public assemblies, and the
letters I dispatched to you. Once you have assembled all these, you
must judge for yourself whether you regard your recent visit to
Rome to have sufficiently reciprocated all these tributes of mine.

As for your comment about the restoration of good relations, 5
I do not understand why you speak of 'restoration', for they never
deteriorated.

You write that your brother Metellus* ought not to have been 6
attacked by me because of the statement he made. With regard to
this, I should like to assure you first of all that I strongly approve this
attitude of yours, which reflects brotherly feeling so full of kindness
and devotion. Secondly, if I have opposed your brother on any
matter in the interests of the state, I beg you to pardon me, for I am
as much devoted to the republic as any man. But if I have defended
my reputation against the most cruel attack which he launched
against me, you should be content that I do not raise with you
any complaint about your brother's injustice towards me. When
I ascertained that he was preparing and planning the entire thrust
of the tribunate to bring me down, I discussed the matter with
your wife Claudia and your sister Mucia;* I had observed that
because of my friendship with Gnaeus Pompey, Mucia supported
me on many issues. I urged them to make him desist from that injurious attitude toward me. Yet—and I am sure that you have heard 7
of this—on 31 December he inflicted on me as consul an insult such
as was not sustained by the most worthless citizen in any
magistracy, and this after I had been the salvation of the state. As I
was quitting office, he deprived me of the opportunity of convening
a public assembly. That injustice, however, won for me the greatest
esteem. When he allowed me to take the oath* and no more, at the
top of my voice I swore the most truthful and noble oath, and the
citizens likewise at the tops of their voices swore that I had sworn
truthfully.

Even after sustaining this notable insult, on that very day I sent to 8
Metellus friends whom we shared to induce him to abandon his
attitude. His answer to them was that this was not open to him, for

shortly before at a public assembly he had declared that a person who had punished others unheard* ought not to have the opportunity to speak. What a specimen of high dignity, what a noteworthy citizen he is! To pronounce the man who had saved the Senate from massacre, the city from arson, and Italy from war as deserving of the same punishment as, with the unanimity of all honourable men, the Senate had imposed on those who had sought to set fire to the city, to slaughter the magistrates and senators, and to unleash the most dreadful war!

So I took my stand against your brother Metellus face to face, for in the Senate on 1 January I disputed with him about the political situation so vehemently that he realized that he would do battle against a brave and unshakeable man. When he launched into a speech on 3 January, every third word in it mentioned and threatened me. He had nothing more firmly in mind than to bring me low by every possible means, not through argumentation in court, but by violent assaults. Had I not stood fast with courage and spirit against his rash behaviour, who would have believed that my brave bearing as consul was deliberate rather than accidental?

9   If you were unaware that Metellus was forming these designs against me, you should realize that your brother has kept you ignorant of affairs of the greatest moment. But if he disclosed to you some element of his plans, you must regard me as a gentle and affable soul for not broaching these matters indignantly with you. Once you realize that I was roused not, as you write, by that statement of Metellus but by his designs and most hostile attitude towards me, you must now acknowledge my indulgent attitude, if 'indulgent' is an appropriate epithet for a relaxed and easygoing response in the face of the bitterest insult. I have never passed any judgement in the Senate against your brother. Whenever such proposals against him were made, I remained seated, associating myself with those who seemed to me to advocate the most lenient course. Let me further say that while it was not expected that I should be concerned to secure his acquittal, I was not averse to it, and I furthered that outcome as best I could because he was your brother, so that he should be lent a helping hand by a senatorial decree.

10   So I did not assail your brother, but defended myself against him. I was not, as you write, fickle in your regard, but I remained constant in my cordial feelings towards you, even when I lost your

kindly support. Even now, though you have written a letter virtually threatening me, I say this in reply: not merely do I pardon your resentment, but I praise it in the loftiest terms, for I am guided by my own experience of the depth of a brother's affection. I beg you likewise to adjudge my wounded feelings equally fairly, and since I have been assailed so bitterly and so cruelly without due cause, to concede that not only was I not to give way, but that I ought to have enjoyed the assistance of you and your army in a matter of this kind.

I have always desired your friendship, and have worked hard to enable you to understand that I am very well disposed towards you. I remain supportive, and will continue to be for as long as you wish it. I would sooner abandon my ill-feeling towards your brother out of affection for you than let ill-feeling for him cause any diminution in our regard for each other.

Letter 5 (*Fam.* V 7)

Rome, April 62

CICERO TO POMPEY*

If you and the army are in good shape, that is welcome; I too am well.   1
The letter which you addressed to the state at large gave me and all citizens pleasure beyond belief, for the expectation of untroubled peace which you hold out is such as I have ever promised to all citizens, in our reliance upon you alone. But you must realize that your former enemies, now your recent friends,* were considerably shaken by your letter, and now that their high hopes have not materialized their morale is low.

Though the letter which you addressed to me contained only the   2
merest suggestion* of your regard for myself, you can none the less rest assured that I was delighted by it, for nothing habitually gives me greater joy than my awareness of the services I have bestowed on others. If ever they fail to be equally reciprocated, I am quite readily content to have shown the greater observance. I have no doubt that if my total support for you has failed sufficiently to win your allegiance to me, the concerns of the state will reconcile us in harmony with each other.

I do not wish to leave you unaware of what I found lacking in your   3
letter, so I shall state it explicitly, as both my character and our

friendship demand. My achievements* have been such as to lead me
to expect a note of congratulation in your letter by virtue of both our
friendship and the interests of the state. I imagine that you have
refrained from expressing this because you were afraid of alienating
some individual.* But you must realize that my actions on behalf of
the safety of the state have won approval in the judgement and
testimony of the world. On your arrival here you will come to know
that these achievements of mine have been performed with such
forethought and such high-mindedness that you will readily
acknowledge that I have not fallen far behind Laelius in both public
policy and private friendship in my association with you, who are so
much greater than Africanus* ever was.

Letter 6 (*Fam.* V 6)

Rome, December 62

CICERO TO SESTIUS

1 When your secretary Decius approached me, and in discussion urged
me to ensure that no successor to you should be appointed at present, despite my belief that he was honest and well disposed to you,
I recalled the tenor of your earlier letters to me, and so I did not put
great trust in that circumspect man's assurance that your outlook had
changed so dramatically. But after your wife Cornelia met up with
Terentia, and I had discussed it with Quintus Cornelius,* I took care
to attend every meeting of the Senate, and I went to a great deal of
trouble there to compel the plebeian tribune Quintus Fufius, and the
others to whom you had written, to trust me rather than your letters.
The whole issue has been deferred until January, but we are getting
our way without difficulty.

2 Ages ago you wrote to me wishing me success in my purchase of
Crassus' house.* I was roused to action by your good wishes, and a
little later after receiving them I bought the house for 3,500,000 sesterces. So kindly realize, now that I am plunged so deeply into debt, that
I am keen to join a conspiracy,* should anyone admit me! But some
are barring the door on me because they loathe me, and openly show
that loathing for me as one who came down hard on a conspiracy.
Others do not trust me, being fearful that I am laying an ambush

for them. They do not believe that one who rescued usurers when they were under siege can be short of money! It is certainly the case that there is a great deal of cash available on loan at 6 per cent monthly, and I can thank my achievements for the status of being thought a reliable debtor. I have had a good look at your house and 3 all the building-works, and I thoroughly approve of them.

Though all the world regards Antonius' obligations towards me as lacking, I have with the utmost dignity and scrupulousness defended him in the Senate. Senators were profoundly stirred by my words and their compelling force.

Do write to me more frequently.

Letter 7 *(Fam.* V 5)
Rome, December 62

CICERO TO ANTONIUS

I had decided to send no letters to you other than recommendations 1 (as for these, it was not that I thought that they carried enough weight with you, but I did not wish to reveal to those who asked for them that our relationship had at all deteriorated). But now that Titus Pomponius,* who is especially aware of all my gestures of support and obligation towards you, and who moreover is a keen supporter of yours and a most devoted friend of mine, is setting out to join you, I thought that I should write a note to you, especially as I cannot accommodate Pomponius himself in any other way.

No one should be surprised at my expecting the greatest services 2 from you, for I have accorded you everything which advanced your interest, honour, and distinction. You yourself are the best witness that I have received no favour from you in return; indeed, I have heard from many that you have adopted the opposite attitude. I do not presume to say that I have 'ascertained'* this, to avoid using the very word which people say you often attribute to me, quite unjustly. I want you, however, to learn of the reports which have reached me, not from any letter of mine but from Pomponius, who found them equally infuriating, The Senate and people of Rome both attest that my attitude towards you has been one of unparalleled observance.

You yourself can measure how grateful you have been to me; others must measure the extent of your debt to me.

3　My earlier undertakings on your behalf were induced by my goodwill and later in the interests of consistency. But believe me, the demands that remain* require a much greater application of my support, and greater earnestness and hard work. I shall apply these with all my strength so long as I do not appear to be vainly expending and wasting my efforts. But if I feel that they are not appreciated, I shall not so act that you take me for a madman. You will be able to elicit from Pomponius the issues and their nature.

As for Pomponius himself, I commend him to you. Though I am sure that you will do everything for his sake, I beg of you that if you retain any vestige of affection for me, please direct it entirely to Pomponius' concerns.* There is nothing you can do which I appreciate more.

Letter 8 (*Att.* I 12)

Rome, January 61

CICERO TO ATTICUS

1　That Teucris is a slow operator indeed, and Cornelius* has never subsequently returned to see Terentia. I think that I shall have to have recourse to Considius or Axius or Selicius. As for Caecilius,* his own relatives can't get a penny out of him at less than 12 per cent. But to return to my first point, I have never encountered shamelessness, craftiness, or procrastination worse than hers. 'I am sending a freedman,' or 'I have sent instructions to Titus,' she says. *Ce ne sont que prétextes et ajournements*, but perhaps *le hazard décide mieux que nous.* For the advance party of Pompey* tells me openly that he is to propose to have Antonius replaced, and at the same time a praetor will put the proposal to the popular Assembly. The situation is such that in all honesty I cannot defend the man, in view of the attitude of the loyalists and of the citizens at large. Nor should I care to do so, and that is the most important thing.

2　There is in fact an additional consideration, and I am charging you to investigate its nature. I have a freedman, an absolute scoundrel. I'm talking about Hilarus, that accountant and protégé of yours. The interpreter Valerius sends me reports of him, and Thyillus writes that he has heard he is closeted with Antonius, and further that Antonius when extorting money* keeps saying that a part of it is being exacted on my behalf, and that I have dispatched a freedman to safeguard the profits which we share. I am quite exercised about this, though I do not believe the story. But at any rate it has caused some gossip. You must look into the whole matter, elicit the facts, subject them to scrutiny, and get that scoundrel away from your region by every possible means. Valerius has cited Gnaeus Plancius as the source of this gossip. I commit the whole business to you to see what the story is.

It is clear that Pompey is extremely well disposed to me. There is 3 strong approval of his divorce of Mucia.* I believe that you have heard that Publius Clodius, son of Appius, was caught red-handed wearing women's clothing during the state ritual at Gaius Caesar's house,* that a wee servant-girl saved his skin and got him out, and that the incident has caused a mighty scandal. I am sure that you disapprove.

I have nothing else to write about to you, and indeed I write this 4 in some distress. My *lecteur* Sositheus has died. He was a genial youth, and his death has affected me more than a slave's death seemingly should. Do, please, write to me often. If you have no news of substance to report, write anything that comes to mind.

1 January, in the consulship of Marcus Messalla and Marcus Piso

Letter 9 (*Att.* I 13)

Rome, January 61

CICERO TO ATTICUS

I have now received three letters from you, the first delivered by 1 Marcus Cornelius which I believe you gave him at Tres Tabernae, the second which your host at Canusium passed to me, and the third, as your letter states, dispatched from the small boat once you had quitted the shore. All of them, as young students of rhetoricians put it, were both sprinkled with the salt of gentility and notable for their marks of affection. In those letters you especially urge me to reply, but I am slower in doing so because I have no reliable courier at hand (how few there are who can carry a rather weighty letter without lightening it by reading it!). Then too I imagine that though they all set out for Epirus, they do not reach you, for I think that, having slain some victims in the shrine of your Amalthea,* you set off at once to launch your attack on Sicyon, but I am not certain when you are to journey to Antonius, or how much time you are spending in Epirus. So I do not presume to entrust a somewhat indiscreet letter to either Achaeans or Epirotes!

2   Since you left me, events have occurred which merit a letter from me, but they are not to be exposed to the hazard of being lost or opened or intercepted. The first thing you should know is that I was not asked to initiate the debates,* but the man who pacified the Allobrogians was given precedence over me, a proceeding which caused whispered comments in the Senate, but which I did not resent, for I am both absolved of showing respect to that awkward individual, and free to maintain my political prestige by opposing his wishes. Moreover, being second in line to speak has almost equal authority to being first, and my views are not over-inhibited by my being the recipient of the consul's favour. Third in line was Catulus, and fourth, if you are still keen to hear, was Hortensius. The consul himself has a childish mind, but one which is also perverse. He is a quibbler of the peevish type who raises a laugh though bereft of wit, for his features cause more amusement than his wisecracks. He plays no part in political debate, and distances himself from the optimate party. You would anticipate no benefit to the state from him because of his indifference, and you would fear no harm from him because he is so timid. His fellow-consul,* however, is most respectful to me personally, as well as being a zealous champion of the optimate party.

3   At present the disagreement between them is minor, though I fear that the contagion may spread. I believe that you have heard that when a state ritual* was being conducted at Caesar's house, a man was present dressed in women's clothes; that after the sacrifice had been repeated by the Vestals, the issue was raised in the Senate by Quintus Cornificius* (he was the first to raise it, in case you happen to think that it was one of our number); that subsequently by senatorial decree the matter was referred to the Vestals and the pontiffs, and that they formally pronounced it a sacrilege; that then the consuls in accordance with a senatorial decree published a bill; that then Caesar gave his wife an intimation of divorce. In this process Piso has been induced by his friendship with Publius Clodius to ensure that

the bill which he himself is proposing (proposing, mind you, in accordance with a senatorial decree, and on a matter of religion) should be rejected. Up to now Messalla has been outspoken in his stern attitude to the case. The optimates are being induced by pleas of Clodius to distance themselves from it. Gangs of thugs are being assembled. I myself, a veritable Lycurgus,* am cooling towards it every day. Our Cato, however, is insistently on the attack. Enough said. My fear is that the indifference to the case shown by the optimates, and the defence of it by the unscrupulous, may cause great damage to the state.

That friend of yours* (you surely know the one I mean; you wrote 4 that he began to praise me once he had not the effrontery to criticize me) on the surface now shows fondness for me, welcomes me, is openly friendly, praises me, but the jealousy he seeks to hide is all too obvious. There is no graciousness, no candour, no generosity. But I will write to you about this with greater precision another day; as yet I am not sufficiently aware of the whole situation, and I dare not entrust a letter on such a momentous matter to this nobody of a courier.

The praetors* have not yet drawn lots for the provinces; the posi- 5 tion is just as it was when you left. I shall insert in my speech,* as you demand, *la peinture idéale* of Misenum and Puteoli. I had noticed that the date 1 December was in error. Believe me, I was extremely pleased myself with the passages from my speeches which you praise but I did not presume to say so earlier. But now that you have approved of them, they seem to me to contain *bien plus d'atticisme*. I have made some additions to my speech against Metellus; the text will be dispatched to you, for your affection for me has made you *un amateur d'éloquence*.

What news have I to pass on to you? Yes, there is some. The 6 consul Messalla has bought Autronius' house for 13,400,000 sesterces. You will ask, 'How does that concern me?' Merely that the purchase indicates that I have done well with mine. People have begun to realize that it is possible to exploit the wealth of friends in house-purchase to attain greater respectability. That Teucris* is a slow operator in business, but I still pin my hopes on her. You must deal with affairs at your end. Await a less guarded letter from me.

25 January, in the consulships of Marcus Messalla and Marcus Piso

Letter 10 (*Att.* I 14)

Rome, February 61

CICERO TO ATTICUS

1 It is tiresome, I fear, to recount to you how busy I am, but I have been so distracted that even for this short letter I have barely spared the time and I have had to filch it from most important concerns.

I wrote to you previously* to describe Pompey's first speech in public. The impoverished elements did not find it a delight, the scoundrels thought it pointless, the well-to-do did not welcome it, and the honourable men found it lightweight. So it was a flop. Then the consul Piso prompted that utterly shallow plebeian tribune Fufius* to present Pompey to the Assembly. The meeting took place in the Circus Flaminius, the very place where that day *les grandes assises* of the market were gathered. Fufius asked Pompey whether he approved the selection of the jurymen* by the praetor, when that same praetor would be enrolling them as his panel (this was the procedure that the Senate had laid down for the hearing of Clodius' sacrilege).

2 Pompey then gave answer* *comme grand seigneur*, and at great length. He said that he always considered the authority of the Senate as supreme on all issues. Thereafter the consul Messalla asked Pompey in the Senate for his view on the issue of sacrilege and the published bill. Pompey stated in the Senate that he praised all decrees of the order *en bloc*, and when he sat down by me, he told me that he thought that he had now given a sufficient reply 'on these issues of yours'.

3 Once Crassus* realized that Pompey had gained approval because people suspected that he thought well of my consulship, he rose and spoke in the most honorific terms about it, going so far as to say that he owed his existence as senator and as citizen, his liberty and his life, to me. He added that whenever he gazed on his wife, his home, his native land, he gazed on gifts which I had conferred on him. Enough said. With supreme gravity he interwove the whole rigmarole which I habitually deploy in different ways in my speeches (which you, Aristarchus that you are,* criticize), dilating on fire and sword—you know those lurid colours! I was sitting next to Pompey. I realized that he was irritated, whether because Crassus was garnering the

popularity which he himself had failed to grasp, or because, to the pleasure of the Senate, my great achievements were being lauded by none other than the man who had less obligation to applaud me, since he had been savaged in all that I had written in praise of Pompey.

That day allied me closely to Crassus, yet I welcomed with pleas- 4 ure any tributes from Pompey, whether open or covert. As for my own part, dear heaven, *comme je me vantais* in front of Pompey, who had never heard me before! Then, if ever, I had periods, transitions, syllogisms, and argumentation at my fingertips. I need not elaborate on the cries of approval. My theme was the dignity of the Senate, harmony with the equestrians, the one mind throughout Italy, the dying dregs of the conspiracy, the corn dirt-cheap, and our lives untroubled. You know by now how I turn up the volume on these topics. I waxed so loud that I need not elaborate, for I imagine that you heard it even from over there!

The situation in Rome is like this. The Senate is a veritable 5 Areopagus,* as steadfast and serious and brave as can be. When the day dawned for the proposal to be put to the Assembly in accordance with the Senate's decree, the young bloods with their goatees, Catiline's entire flock, made a concerted rush headed by that dear little girlie* of Curio's, and begged the people to reject the measure. The consul Piso, sponsor of the bill, actually spoke against it. Clodius' hoodlums had laid siege to the gangways; voting-papers were being issued, none of them in support of the motion. Just then, however, Cato, mark you, flew up to the rostrum and gave Piso a remarkable dressing-down, if that is the right expression for a speech thoroughly dignified, authoritative, and salutary. Our friend Hortensius rallied to him in this, as did many other loyalists as well. The support lent by Favonius was especially notable. Thanks to this united charge of the optimates, the Assembly was dissolved, and the Senate was convoked. There was a crowded attendance, and a decree was passed that the consuls should urge the people to ratify the bill, in spite of Piso's opposition and Clodius' going down on his knees before each of us individually. About fifteen senators supported Curio's proposal that there should be no senatorial decree, while there were easily four hundred opposing him. That ended the debate.

The tribune Fufius then vetoed the decree. Clodius is making wretched speeches in which he abusively attacks Lucullus, Hortensius, Gaius Piso, and the consul Messalla. The only charge he levels against me is that I 'ascertained' all the facts.* The Senate has decreed that no action is to be taken on the allocation of provinces to praetors, or about embassies or other business, until this bill has been put to the Assembly.

6   This is the news for you of events at Rome. But cock your ears at this additional item, which I did not anticipate. Messalla is outstanding, brave, steady, and energetic. He lavishes praise and affection on me, and follows my example. That other consul* has a single vice which makes him less objectionable. He is lazy, somnolent, unpractised, *très paresseux*. But his disposition is so *malveillant* that he has begun to loathe Pompey, following that speech of Pompey's in which he started to praise the Senate. Hence Piso has become unpopular, quite remarkably so, with all the optimates. It is as much his propensity for criminal practices and criminal factions as his friendship with Clodius that led him to behave as he did. But there is no one similarly inclined among the magistrates except Fufius. We have reliable plebeian tribunes at our disposal; Cornutus in particular is a Cato in disguise. No need to say more.

7   To return to private matters, Teucris has kept her promises. Do carry out all the instructions you got. My brother Quintus, who has purchased the other three-quarters of the house in the Argiletum for 725,000 sesterces, is trying to sell his house at Tusculum in order to buy the residence of Pacilius, should that be possible. I am back on good terms with Lucceius;* I see that he has caught a bad dose of candidate-ambition. I shall do my best for him. Do keep me carefully informed of your activities and whereabouts, and the state of your affairs.

13 February

Letter 11 (*Att.* I 15)

Rome, March 61

CICERO TO ATTICUS

1   You have heard that my brother Quintus, of whom I am very fond, has obtained Asia* as his province, for I have no doubt that rumour has brought you wind of this more speedily than a letter from any of us,

So now, since we have always been most eager for glory, and since we both are more philhellenic than the rest and are regarded as such, and since in our devotion to the state we have incurred the hatred and enmity of many, 'summon all the courage you can',* and ensure that we win the praise and affection of all.

I shall write further on these matters in the letter to you which I 2 shall entrust to Quintus. Please let me know what you have done about my instructions and about your own affairs too, for no letters from you have been delivered to me since you set out from Brundisium. I am extremely eager to know how you are doing.

15 March

Letter 12 (*Att.* I 16)

Rome, *July 61*

CICERO TO ATTICUS

You ask me about the outcome of the trial,* that it turned out so con- 1 trary to the general expectation, and at the same time you are keen to know how it was that I entered the lists less than usual. I will answer you as Homer does,* putting the cart before the horse.

For so long as it was necessary for me to defend the authority of the Senate, I entered the lists so keenly and enthusiastically that people crowded round and praised me, shouting for all they were worth. If ever you thought me a stalwart figure in public life, I would certainly have won your esteem on that occasion, for when Clodius had recourse to haranguing the citizens and in his speeches was citing my name to rouse odium against me, ye immortal gods, what battles I fought, what slaughter I inflicted, what assaults I made on Piso, on Curio, and on that entire crew! How I inveighed against the fickleness of the old guard, and the wantonness of the youth! Often, so help me God, I longed to have you not just to counsel my strategy, but also to witness my wondrous battles.

But then Hortensius devised the plan that Fufius the plebeian 2 tribune should propose a law on religion. It differed in no way from the consular bill except on the composition of the jury*—mind you, everything hung on that! He fought hard to have it passed, for he had persuaded both himself and others that Clodius could not escape conviction by any conceivable jury. But I noted the bankruptcy of the jurors, and I drew in my sails, and offered in evidence only what was so well known and attested that I could not omit it.

So, to revert to the *première question*, you ask why he was acquitted; the answer lies in the poverty of the jurymen and their lack of principle. The outcome resulted from the strategy of Hortensius, who in his fear that Fufius would veto the law which was proposed in accordance with the senatorial decree, did not realize that it would have been better to leave Clodius sunk in notoriety and disgrace rather than subjected to an unreliable tribunal. But his loathing for Clodius led him to make haste to bring the case to court, saying that even a sword of lead would be enough to cut his throat.

3   However, if you are enquiring how the trial went, the outcome was so astonishing that others are blaming Hortensius' tactics now that it is all over, whereas I did so from the very outset. The disqualification of jurymen took place amidst the greatest uproar. The prosecutor, like a worthy censor, rejected the most dissolute individuals, while the defendant, like a kindly gladiator-trainer,* excluded all the decent men. As soon as the jury was empanelled, honest men began to have grave misgivings, for a more grisly crew never assembled at a low dancing-show. There were disreputable senators, bankrupt equestrians, and tribunes not so much moneyed as on the make, as their title implies.* There were a few honest souls among them, whom Clodius had been unable to reject by disqualifying them. These few sat dejected and depressed among characters wholly different from themselves, profoundly unhappy at being polluted by such degradation.

4   During the preliminaries, as each question was referred to the jury, their serious demeanour was amazing; there were no differences in the views expressed. The defendant obtained no concessions, and the prosecutor was awarded more than he demanded. As you might expect, Hortensius waxed triumphant at his great foresight, and no one envisaged Clodius as merely on trial rather than condemned a thousand times over. You have heard, I imagine, how when I was brought in to give evidence, and Clodius' supporters began howling, the jury rose to their feet, stood round me, and exposed their bared throats to Publius Clodius in defence of my person. This seemed to me a much greater compliment than that when your fellow-citizens prevented Xenocrates from taking the oath as he gave evidence, or that when Roman jurymen refused to examine the accounts of

Metellus Numidicus* when they were circulated in the usual way. Indeed, I claim that what happened in my case was much more impressive.

So when I was protected in this way by the jurymen as the salva- 5 tion of our native land, the defendant and all his advocates with him had the wind taken from their sails. The next day a crowd gathered at my house, as large as that which escorted me home when I laid down my consulship. Our distinguished Areopagites* cried that they could not attend unless they were given a bodyguard. The issue was referred to the tribunal, where there was just one vote claiming that bodyguards were unnecessary. The question was referred to the Senate. A most solemn and elaborate decree was passed. The jurors were praised; the business was entrusted to the magistrates. No one believed that Clodius would answer the charge.

'Ye Muses, tell me now how first the fire descended.'* You know old Baldhead of the Nanneian household,* that panegyrist of mine whose complimentary address to me I mentioned in my letter. Within two days, employing a single slave—and him from the school of gladiators—he brought the whole affair to a conclusion. He summoned the jurors to his house, made promises to them, stood surety for them, or gave them cash. In addition—good God, how low can men sink?—nightly favours with certain ladies, and introductions to youths from noble families were offered to several jurors to top up the payments. Even so, while the decent men totally withdrew, and the Forum was awash with slaves, twenty-five jurors showed such courage that in the face of supreme danger they preferred even to forfeit their lives rather than to lose all self-respect. On the other hand there were thirty-one for whom hunger counted for more than good repute. When Catulus* later caught sight of one of them, he asked him: 'Why did you ask us to provide you with a bodyguard? Was it your fear that you would be mugged for your pennies?'

I have given you as briefly as I can an account of the trial, and the 6 reason for the acquittal. You next enquire about the present political situation and my own position. You should be aware that the condition of the state, which you believe was stabilized by my policy, and I myself believe was by heaven's design, and which appeared so firmly established by the alliance of all honourable men and by the authority of my consulship, has—unless some god takes pity on us— slipped from our grasp through this one trial. That is, if 'trial' is the right word when thirty of the most fickle and most depraved members of the Roman people pocket their wretched cash and extinguish all law, human and divine, and Talna and Plautus and Spongia,* and the other riff-raff of that ilk, announce that no crime was ever committed, when not only humans but also beasts of the field knew that there had been.

7 However, the political scene offers you some consolation. Wickedness does not eagerly exult in its victory as much as evil men hoped, after the republic sustained so grievous a wound. They obviously imagined that when religion, moral values, the integrity of the courts, and the authority of the Senate had collapsed, wickedness and lustful practices would openly parade their victory, and would exact punishment for the suffering with which the severity of my consulship had branded the most depraved among them.

8 But again it was I myself—I do not think that I am vaingloriously boasting in referring to myself in discussion with you, especially in a letter which I do not wish others to read—yes, it was I who restored the depressed spirits of honourable men by strengthening and rousing them one by one. Moreover, by assailing and harassing the venal jurors, I deprived all those who enthusiastically hailed that victory, of their *franc-parler*. I gave the consul Piso no respite at any point, and I deprived him of the province of Syria* which had already been promised him. I recalled the Senate to its stern practice of old, and roused it from its despondency, I crushed Clodius face to face in the Senate, not only in a full-length speech of the most measured seriousness, but also in verbal exchanges, which I detail. You can capture the flavour from these few excerpts; the rest cannot retain the impact or wit when detached from the liveliness of the argument, which you Greeks term a *combat*.

9 When we assembled in the Senate on 15 May, and I was asked for my view, I spoke at length on the supreme issues of state, and my heaven-inspired theme was that the conscript fathers should not be demoralized or disheartened by this single blow. The wound, I said, was one which I considered should cause neither disregard nor panic, so that on the one hand we should not be accounted utter fools by ignoring it, nor, on the other, sheer cowards through fear of it. Lentulus, I added, had been acquitted twice, and so had Catiline.* In Clodius, jurors had now launched a third foe against the state. 'You are misled, Clodius. The jury has not preserved you to walk free in

Rome, but to be imprisoned. They did not want to keep you in the community, but to deprive you of the prospect of exile.* This is why, conscript fathers, you must raise your spirits, and maintain your dignity. That harmony between honourable men in the state still obtains. Good men have experienced resentment, but their valour has not diminished. No additional damage has been done; we have merely unearthed what already existed. In this trial of one depraved man, more like him have come to light.'

But what am I up to? I have almost enclosed my speech in this 10 letter. I now revert to the verbal exchanges. Our fancy little fellow* gets up and accuses me of having been at Baiae. This was untrue, but no matter. I commented: 'So what? Is this the same as your saying that I was lurking under cover?'* 'What was a native of Arpinum,' he asked, 'doing at the hot springs?' 'Mention that to your defence counsel,'* I replied, 'for he was keen to sample the waters of a man from Arpinum' (you know that the waters were the preserve of Marius). 'For how long', he asked, 'will we have to endure this king?' 'Do you call me a king,' I replied, 'when Rex* made no mention of you?' (He had hoped to inherit Rex's money in order to squander it.) 'You have bought a house,' he said. 'One would think', I countered, 'that you were claiming that I have bought a jury.' 'They didn't give credit to your words though you swore an oath,' he said. 'In fact,' I replied, 'twenty-five jurors did credit my words, whereas thirty-one gave you no credit, for they had already got their money.' The shouts of approval discomfited him, and he relapsed into silence.

My personal situation is this. I have the same standing with decent 11 men as when you left them, and I am in even better standing with the dregs and dross of the city than at your departure. The fact that my evidence seems not to have carried the day has not prejudiced my position. The blood-letting of my unpopularity has been discharged without pain, all the more so as all the supporters of that outrageous trial admit that our clear case was bought off from the jury. Moreover, the unhappy, starving rabble, blood-suckers of the Treasury, who attend the Assembly, believe that I have the unchallenged affection of our friend Pompey the Great,* and indeed he and I are closely joined in a deep and rewarding relationship, to the point that those young men of ours, sporting their goatee beards, who revelled in the conspiracy, are in their chatter calling him Gnaeus Cicero! Accordingly

I came away from the shows and gladiatorial contests greeted with remarkable *cris d'acclamation*, with no rustic whistling.

12   We now await the elections, for which our Magnus is urging the claims of Aulus' son* to universal disapproval. He promotes his candidature not with his authority and influence, but with those engines with which Philip used to say* that all fortresses could be stormed, so long as a donkey laden with gold could mount up to them! It is said that the consul, who like an actor plays a *rôle secondaire*, has undertaken the business, and that he has agents of bribery in his house. I do not believe this, but already two objectionable senatorial decrees have been passed which are thought to be levelled at the consul.* Cato and Domitius have proposed them, the first that it should be permitted to search the house of any magistrate, and the second that anyone keeping agents of bribery in his house is acting against the interests of the state.

13   Lurco, the plebeian tribune (who embarked on that magistracy in the company of the Aelian law), has been freed from the provisions of both Aelian and Fufian laws* to allow him to propose a law on bribery; being a cripple he has published it with a fair augury of success. So the elections have been postponed until 27 July. What is new in the law is that any member of a tribe who proclaims a promise of money should not be punished as long as he does not pay out, but if he does pay it, he must contribute 3,000 sesterces to every tribe for as long as he lives. I stated that Publius Clodius had already observed that law, for he regularly promised money, but never delivered it. But see now, do you realize that this noble consulship of ours, which Curio earlier described as *une apothéose*, will be worth no more than the proverbial bean if this fellow Afranius is elected? So in my view I must repair to *philosophie*, as you do, and cease to care a jot for those consulships of theirs.

14   You write to tell me that you have decided not to go to Asia. I should indeed have wanted you to go, and I fear that the outcome may be less pleasant* if you don't. However, I can hardly censure your decision, especially as I myself have not quitted Rome for a province.

15   I shall rest content with those epigrams of yours* which you have laid in your shrine of Amalthea, especially as Thyillus has abandoned me, and Archias* has composed nothing about me. I fear that now that he has written his Greek poem for the Luculli he may be contemplating a Caecilian drama.

I have thanked Antonius in your name, and have entrusted the 16
letter to Mallius. My reason for having written less often to you in
the past has been that I had no suitable courier to whom I could
entrust letters, and I was not altogether sure of an address to which
to send one. I was lavish in my praise of you.

If Cincius lands any of your business in my lap, I shall undertake
it, but at the moment he is more taken up with his own, and I am
giving him a hand with it. If you are to be settled in one place, you
must anticipate an avalanche of letters from me, but you must
likewise send me more.

Please write a description to me of your shrine of Amalthea, the
decoration and *l'aménagement* of it. Send me any poems or historical
accounts of her which you possess. I should like to set one up in
my house at Arpinum. I shall be sending you one or other of my
compositions, but none of them have had the final touches.

Letter 13 (*Att.* I 17)

Rome, December 61

CICERO TO ATTICUS

I have detected a great change of feeling and an inconsistency of 1
attitude and judgement on the part of my brother Quintus in the
copies of his letters enclosed with yours which you have sent to me.
This has caused me considerable distress which my boundless
affection for you both must inevitably provoke, and also surprise, for
I wonder what has happened to cause my brother Quintus such deep
offence and so marked a change of attitude. I had already realized
earlier (and I saw that you too suspected it when you were leaving)
that he was nurturing some tiresome notion below the surface, that
he was wounded at heart, and that some unkind suspicions had taken
root there. I was eager to assuage those feelings, both on several occasions earlier and also more earnestly after he had been allotted his
province, but I was not aware of the depth of alienation as was
revealed in your letter. My attempts did not have the success which
I desired.

However, I consoled myself with the thought that he would 2
undoubtedly meet you at Dyrrhachium or at some other place over
there. I was confident and had persuaded myself that, once the

meeting took place, all would be reconciled between you, not merely through discussion and conversation, but even by setting eyes on each other and getting together. There is no need for me to recount to you how genial and pleasant my brother Quintus is, and his sensitivity in both taking offence and dismissing it, for you are well aware of this. But it was unfortunate that you did not set eyes on him anywhere, for he was affected more by remarks made to him by several designing persons* than by a sense of duty or friendship or the long-standing affection between you, which ought to have carried the greatest weight.

3   As for where the blame for this unfortunate situation lies, it is easier for me to imagine than to write, for I fear that defence of my relatives may lead me not to spare yours. I realize that even though the wound was not inflicted by members of his household, they could at least have healed it once it was in evidence. But I shall more conveniently explain to you face to face the canker lying below all this, for it has wider implications than at first appears.

4   So far as concerns the letter which he sent you from Thessalonica, and the remarks which you believe he passed both at Rome in the company of your friends and on his outward journey, I have no idea what trivial reason occasioned them. But my entire hope of relieving this oppressive unpleasantness lies in your kindly disposition. If you conclude that the best of men are often both easily provoked and also easily mollified, that this vacillation, so to speak, and natural sensitivity are usually the marks of a good heart, and most important of all, that the embarrassments or faults of injuries which we inflict upon each other must be readily borne, these present difficulties will, I hope, be easily resolved. I beg you to adopt this attitude, for, as one whose affection for you is unmatched, I make it my greatest concern that none of my circle should fail to show you affection, or to experience it from you.

5   The part of your letter was wholly unnecessary in which you recount the opportunities for advancement* you have forgone both at other times and during my consulship, not only in the provinces but also at Rome. I am eminently aware of both your decency and your magnanimity. I have never thought that there was any difference between us other than our choice of career; while some sort of ambition led me to seek high positions, your different decision, deserving of no blame whatsoever, directed you to an honourable life of leisure. In what is truly praiseworthy—integrity, honesty, industry,

and piety—I regard neither myself nor any other as superior to you, and as for affection towards me, my brother and family connections apart, I award you the palm.

I have noted, yes, noted and closely observed both your worries 6 and your joys at my varying fortunes. Your felicitations at the time of my fair fame were a frequent pleasure, and your consolation in times of fear was welcome. Indeed, now that you are away, I miss not only your outstanding advice but also the conversations between us which I regularly find most engaging. Am I to say that I miss these most in the political sphere, the type of activity in which I cannot be remiss, or in the labour of the courts (which earlier I practised out of ambition, and nowadays continue so as to be able to preserve my standing through my influence), or in my family concerns, in which both previously and especially after my brother's departure I have felt the loss of your presence and of our discussions? In short, both in my labours and my relaxation, in my activities and my leisure, in the Forum and at home, in matters both public and private, I cannot for too long dispense with your most engaging and affectionate advice and conversation.

Truth to tell, our native reticence has hindered both of us from 7 mention of these facts. But it has now become necessary, because of that section of your letter in which you sought to vindicate and justify yourself and your behaviour to me. However, in this embarrassment of Quintus' estranged and offended outlook, there is the positive point that both your other friends and I knew that you had made it clear somewhat earlier that you intended not to visit the province. So the fact that you are not together does not seem to be the result of disagreement and rupture between you, but the outcome of your intention and decision. So on the one hand the breach between you will be healed, and on the other our relationship, which has been most devotedly preserved, will maintain its sanctity.

Here in Rome the republic in which we dwell is enfeebled, 8 wretched, and unstable. I think you have heard that our equestrian friends have virtually parted from the Senate. Initially they took it very badly that a senatorial decree was issued declaring that those who had received money for jury-service* should be investigated. I happened to be absent when this decree was passed. I realized that the equestrian order was incensed by it without criticizing it openly. So I berated the Senate with what I considered all the weight I could muster; though the cause was not a seemly one, I spoke quite earnestly and fluently.

9   Then, lo and behold, the equestrians advanced another precious plea. It was virtually intolerable, though I not merely tolerated it but also enhanced it. The tax-farmers, who had made a contract with the censors for the tax-collection in Asia, complained in the Senate that their greed had misled them into paying too high a price for the contract. They demanded the annulment of the lease. I was the first to lend them support, or rather the second, for Crassus urged them to make that shameless request. What an odious business, what a disgraceful demand, what an admission of rash behaviour! But the supreme danger loomed that if they obtained no concession, there would be a total rupture from the Senate. In this matter I have lent them the greatest support. I ensured that they had the benefit of a very well-attended and very indulgent Senate. On 1 December, and again on the next day, I spoke at length on the great worth of the orders and the harmony between them. The issue is not yet decided, but the good-will of the Senate is clear. The sole opposition came from the consul-designate Metellus; our famed champion Cato* was about to speak, but the curtailment of daylight prevented his turn being reached.

10   In this way, by preserving my policy and practice, I am defending as best I can the harmony which I myself welded. But since the situation is so unstable, I am building another path* which I hope is secure, in order to maintain my influence. I cannot explain this adequately to you by letter, but I shall briefly allude to it: I am on most intimate terms with Pompey. I know what you are saying, and I shall take the necessary precautions. I shall write further at another time about my plans for political engagement.

11   Let me tell you that Lucceius* is thinking of standing for the consulship at once. Only two are being talked of as likely candidates. The first is Caesar; Lucceius is thinking of linking up with him through Arrius. The other is Bibulus; Lucceius believes that cooperation with him is possible through Gaius Piso. Do I hear you laughing? Believe me, it is beyond a joke.

What other news am I to pass on to you? Is there anything? Yes, quite a lot, but that is for another time. Be sure to let me know when I can expect you. I am delicately begging for what I most urgently desire, that you come with all speed.

5 December

Letter 14 (*Att.* I 18)

Rome, January 60

CICERO TO ATTICUS

Believe me, there is nothing I need at the present moment so much 1
as the one man with whom I can share all the problems which cause
me some concern, that affectionate and wise friend with whom I can
converse without hypocrisy, pretence, or reserve. My brother, who
is wholly *sans artifice* and most affectionate, is away, while Metellus[?]*
is no human being but merely 'seashore and air', 'sheer emptiness'.
But where are you? You have so often with your conversation and
advice relieved my anxiety and mental anguish, you are my ally in
public life, my confidant in domestic affairs, regularly involved with
me in all my discussions and my plans. I am so deserted by all that
the only relaxation I have is spent with my wife, my dear daughter,
and my darling son Cicero, for those self-seeking, bogus friendships
of mine exist in the bright light, so to say, of public life, but they lack
the rewards bestowed by my household. So my house is well and
truly crowded in the early morning; I walk down to the Forum
escorted by flocks of friends; but among that huge mêlée I can find
not one with whom to share an unguarded joke or intimate sigh of
regret. This is why I anticipate and long for your coming, and why
I am even summoning you back, for I have many worries and
anxieties which I think I can banish by claiming your ear in the
conversation of a single stroll.

So far as family worries are concerned, I shall say nothing about 2
the pricks and aches. I refuse to entrust them to this letter, or to a
courier I do not know. They are not thoroughly troublesome (I would
not have you worried) but they preoccupy and oppress me, and I
have no one's friendly advice or reassurance to lay them to rest. As
for the political situation, though the spirit is willing, the healing
process itself repeatedly reopens the wound. To sum up briefly, all
that has occurred since your departure makes one cry out that the
Roman state can no longer survive.

It was, I think, after your departure that the first scene of the
Clodian drama was enacted. I thought it gave me a chance to cut
back licentious behaviour, and to restrain our young men, so I
trumpeted the message loudly, and I exerted the full force of my
heart and talent. I was motivated not by hatred of any individual,

but by the hope, not of putting the community to rights, but of healing its wounds.

3 Through that trial, which was besmirched by bribery and debauchery, the republic is in the throes. Now observe the sequel. A consul* has been imposed on us, the likes of whom no one but philosophers like us could observe without a sigh. What a heavy blow this is! The Senate passed a decree on bribery and the courts,* but no law has been enacted. The Senate has been affronted, and the Roman equestrians estranged, owing to the clause 'Any man who for judging a lawsuit . . .'. Thus the one year has brought down the two bastions of the state which were established by myself alone, for it has both deprived the Senate of its authority, and has disrupted the harmony between the orders. Now this noteworthy new year looms over us. Its beginning was marked by the omission of the ritual of the goddess Juventas, for Memmius* has initiated the wife of Marcus Lucullus into rites of his own. Menelaus resented this and divorced his wife, yet the celebrated shepherd of Mount Ida cuckolded only Menelaus, whereas this Paris of ours has treated Agamemnon as well as Menelaus as a contemptible slave.

4 There is a certain Gaius Herennius,* a plebeian tribune, whom you perhaps do not even know, though you may have had knowledge of him as he is a member of your tribe, and his father Sextus used to dole out the electoral gratuities. He is seeking to transfer Publius Clodius* into the ranks of the plebeians, and is proposing that the whole citizen–body should vote on this issue concerning Clodius, in the Campus Martius. I greeted Herennius in the Senate in my usual way, but he is the greatest sluggard alive.

5 Metellus is an outstanding consul, who is amiable to me, but his authority is diminished because for appearance's sake he has issued the same proposal* about Clodius. As for Aulus' son, ye immortal gods, what a cowardly trooper, lacking all spirit! He is fit for nothing but to lend his ears to Palicanus' denunciations day after day, which is precisely what he does.

6 Flavius has published a proposal for an agrarian law,* a quite light-weight proposal, virtually identical with the Plotian. In the meantime, *pas l'ombre d'un homme politique* is to be found. Pompey, that intimate of mine (for that is what he is, I would have you know), guards that fond embroidered toga of his with a wall of silence, Crassus does not utter a word to prejudice his popularity. The rest

of them you already know. They are such fools that they seem to anticipate that their fish-ponds will be safe, though the republic is lost.

The one man who shows concern is Cato, but in my view more with 7
resolve and integrity than with any strategy and intelligence. For more
than two months now he has been harassing the wretched tax-farmers,
who were most devoted to him, and he refuses to allow the Senate to
give them an answer. Because of this we are forced to refrain from
passing decrees* on other measures until the tax-farmers obtain a
reply. So I believe that even the embassies will be postponed.

You now realize the heavy seas which are tossing us about, and if 8
what I have written gives you an insight into the great issues I have
not mentioned, you must get back to us after all this time. Though
the scene to which I am summoning you is one to be avoided, you
must regard my affection for you sufficiently highly as to be willing
to experience it in person, troublesome though things are. As for the
census, I shall ensure that in your absence your name is registered
and posted everywhere. It is a real businessman's trick to be entered
on the census list at the close of the period! Ensure that I set eyes on
you with all speed.

20 January, in the consulships of Quintus Metellus and Lucius Afranius

Letter 15 (*Att.* I 19)

Rome, March 60

CICERO TO ATTICUS

If only I had as much leisure as you, and indeed if only I were dis- 1
posed to send you letters as short as those which you usually send to
me! I should easily have the upper hand in writing much more
frequently than you do! But in addition to my wholly taxing and
incredibly busy activities, I am also keen that no letter of mine should
reach you without some important topic, and my view on it. So first
I shall explain the present political situation to you as to a citizen as
patriotic as you are, and secondly, since I am so close in affection to
you, I shall also inform you about personal details which I think you
are not averse to knowing.

In the political sphere the chief concern at present is fear of war in 2
Gaul,* for our brothers the Aedui have of late been worsted in battle,
and the Helvetii have undoubtedly taken up arms and are making

forays into the Province. The Senate has decreed that the consuls should draw lots for the two Gauls, should conduct a levy permitting no exemptions, and in addition that Quintus Metellus Creticus, Lucius Flaccus, and (*comme parfum aux lentilles*) Lentulus* son of Claudianus should be sent as plenipotentiary ambassadors to the communities in Gaul to ensure that they do not unite with the
3 Helvetii. I cannot forbear to leave unmentioned while on this subject that when my name was drawn out first among the consulars, a crowded Senate unanimously decreed that I should be detained in Rome. The same thing happened to Pompey after me, so it seemed that the two of us were being kept here as pledges for the safe-keeping of the state. (Why should I wait for accolades from others, when they are sprouting in my own soil?)

4   The situation at Rome is this. The agrarian law* is being aggres-sively promoted by the plebeian tribune Flavius; Pompey is behind it. There is nothing 'people-pleasing' about it except its sponsor. With the approval of a public Assembly, I proposed the deletion of all the clauses in the bill prejudicial to private citizens. I favoured freeing the land which was the property of the state in the consul-ships of Publius Mucius and Lucius Calpurnius.* I supported confirmation of holdings allotted to Sulla's veterans. I proposed that the citizens of Volaterrae and Arretium,* whose lands Sulla had nationalized but not allocated, should continue to possess them. There was one proposal which I did not reject, that land should be purchased from the windfall* accruing from new taxes levied abroad over a five-year period. The Senate is opposed to the entire agrarian scheme, suspecting that new powers are being sought for Pompey from it. Pompey has in fact buckled down to his aim of getting the bill passed, whereas I have been winning the utmost gratitude of landowners by securing the holdings of all private individuals, for as you know, these wealthy people form the backbone of my army.* But I also seek to satisfy the common folk and Pompey (this too I am keen to achieve) by land-purchase, for my thinking is that if this is care-fully carried through, the dregs of the city can be drained off, and deserted areas of Italy can be inhabited. But this entire process has been interrupted by war, and has ground to a halt.

Metellus is an admirable consul, and quite an intimate of mine. As for that other consul,* he is such a cipher that clearly he has no notion of the position he has bought.

That is all that is happening in the public domain, unless you 5 think it politically important that one Herennius,* a plebeian tribune who is a member of your tribe and a wholly despicable bankrupt, has now started making repeated attempts to have Publius Clodius transferred to the ranks of the plebeians. This proposal is being vetoed by many. That is the sum, I think, of the affairs of state.

As for my own role, ever since that historic Fifth of December* 6 when I gained outstanding and immortal fame conjoined with the jealousy and enmity of many, in the same greatness of spirit I have not ceased to be active in politics, and to safeguard the high standing which I had established and assumed. But once I observed, first of all the inconstancy and instability of the courts through the acquittal of Clodius, and secondly that my allies the tax-farmers were being detached without difficulty from the Senate (though not breaking off relations with me), and in addition that those affluent individuals (I refer to those friends of yours, the fish-pond owners*) were not cloaking their jealousy of me, I thought that I had better hunt out some greater resources and some more unflinching support.

So to start with I induced Pompey, who for too long had made no 7 reference to my achievements, to become so well disposed as to attribute to me in the Senate the salvation of the empire and the world, not once, but repeatedly at great length. This was in the interest not so much of myself (after all, those events are not so little known as to need a witness, nor so dubious as to require commendation) as of the state, because there were certain blackguards who believed that some dispute would develop between Pompey and myself because of diversity of views about these events. But I have attached myself to him in such friendship that through this alliance each of us in his own situation can gain greater protection and greater stability in affairs of state.

The feelings of hatred entertained by wanton and degenerate 8 youths and stirred up against me have been so softened by a show of affability on my part that they now cultivate me like no other. In short, not one harsh word do I now direct at anyone, though nothing I say is 'people-pleasing' or unprincipled. My entire strategy is ordered in such a way that I show resolution in affairs of the state, but in my personal capacity, owing to the weakness of honourable men, the wickedness of the ill-disposed, and the hatred directed at me by the reprobates, I adopt a degree of caution and circumspection.

Yet I am tied to these new friendships only to the extent that the Sicilian rascal Epicharmus* often whispers that familiar refrain of his in my ear: 'Keep sober, and remember to be sceptical; these are the joints on which the senses turn.' I think that you can now visualize a certain shape in my strategy and conduct of life.

9   You keep writing to me about that business of yours,* but at present I can offer no remedy, for that senatorial decree was passed with the most enthusiastic support of the silent majority, but without the authority of any of our senior circle. You notice that I appended my name to the resolution, but you can infer from the senatorial decree itself that it was directed at another issue, and that the clause on free communities was an irrelevant appendage. That indeed was how it was incorporated by the younger Publius Servilius, one of the final speakers, but it cannot be amended at present. So the meetings which were initially crowded have for some time now ceased to assemble. Please inform me if by your coaxing you have extracted a few sesterces from the people of Sicyon.

10   I have sent you the record of my consulship, composed in Greek. If there is anything in it which an Atticist* finds un-Greek and unlearned, I shall not repeat what I believe Lucullus said* to you at Panhormus about his histories, that in order to demonstrate more readily that they were the work of a Roman, he had interspersed them with barbarisms and solecisms. If any blemishes of that kind appear in my work, they will be unforeseen and unintended. If I complete a Latin version, I shall send it to you. As a third contribution you are to await a poem, so that I shall leave no genre untouched in recounting my own praises! Be sure not to say at this point, 'Who will praise his father?',* for if anything on earth is worthier of praise, I am to be censured for not lauding those other achievements—though these writings of mine belong to *l'histoire* rather than to panegyric.

11   My brother Quintus has written to me, clearing himself and maintaining that he has said nothing untoward to anyone about you. But we must deal with this very circumspectly and carefully when we meet. Just come back to me at long last. Cossinius here, to whom I am entrusting this letter, seems to me to be an excellent man, serious and devoted to you, and very much the kind of person your letter to me made him out to be.

15 March

Letter 16 (*Att.* I 20)

Rome, May 60

CICERO TO ATTICUS

On my returning to Rome from my house at Pompeii on 12 May, 1
our friend Cincius delivered to me the letter which you sent on
5 February. This present letter will be my reply to it.

First of all, I am delighted that you know perfectly well my high
opinion of you. Secondly, I am overjoyed at your most temperate
reaction to what seemed to you rather prickly behaviour on my part,
or rather, the somewhat unkind attitude of ray kin, a reaction which
I consider to be a mark of no slight affection, as well as of outstanding
intelligence and wisdom. In this matter you have written with such
charm, consideration, sense of obligation, and kindness that not only
have I no need to exhort you further, but I could not even anticipate
from you or from anyone else such courtesy and forbearance. So
I consider that my most appropriate response is to write nothing
further on these matters. Once we are together, we shall discuss face
to face any further issue arising from them.

As for your remarks to me about the political scene, your comments 2
reflect both affection and circumspection, and your arguments do not
diverge much from my own thinking, for I must neither forsake my
own high standing, nor entrust myself to another's defences without
supporting forces of my own, since the person you name* in your
letter shows no nobility, no high-mindedness, and nothing which is
not grovelling or 'people-pleasing'.

My strategy, however, though perhaps not without advantage in
securing tranquillity in my life, has indeed been more beneficial to
the state than to myself. I have sought to repel the attacks of unprincipled citizens* upon me, once I had stabilized the vacillating stance
of that man of most exalted status, authority, and influence, and once
I had won him over from the expectations of depraved men towards
praise of my achievements. Had this policy involved me in any lack
of principle, I would not have regarded it as worth the candle. But all
my actions have been directed, not to make me appear less principled
by kowtowing to him, but to make him appear more principled by his
approval of me.

My policy now and in the future will be so conducted that my 3
former actions may not appear to have been a hostage to fortune.

Not only will I never abandon those honourable allies of mine, whom you mention, and the role of Sparta* which you say has fallen to me, but I will adhere to my long-standing principle, even if 'Sparta' were to desert me. But do please realize that since the death of Catulus* I am adhering to that optimate path without any support or associates. As Rhinthon,* I believe, observes, 'Some are of no account, and others show no concern.' As for the jealousy directed against me by our friends of the fish-ponds, I shall either write about it to you on another occasion, or hold it back until we meet. But nothing will tear me away from the Senate House, because that is the right course, or because it accords most closely with my position, or because I have absolutely no complaint about the status I derive from it.

4   As I wrote to you earlier, the Senate offers little hope with regard to the Sicyonians,* for there is now not a single complainant. So you are in for a long wait if you anticipate any action, and you must fight on another front if you can. When it was discussed, people did not realize who were affected, and the rank-and-file rushed pell-mell to support the motion. The time is not yet ripe to rescind the decree, for there are no complainants, and a good number are delighted, some out of ill-will and others because they believe that the motion is fair.

5   Your friend Metellus is an outstanding consul. My only complaint is that he is not greatly pleased at the report of peace from Gaul. I imagine that he is keen to celebrate a triumph. I should have preferred less enthusiasm about this, but otherwise all he does is exemplary. As for Aulus' son,* he behaves in such a way that his consulship is not so much a consulship as *un œil poché* for Pompey.

6   So far as my writings are concerned, I have sent you a polished version of the account of my consulship composed in Greek; I have entrusted the work to Lucius Cossinius. I imagine that you are pleased with my Latin writings, but that as a Greek you look askance at this Greek version. If others have written about it, I shall send their efforts on to you. But, believe me, once they have read this work of mine, somehow or other they hold back.

7   To revert now to my own situation, Lucius Papirius Paetus,* a good man and an affectionate friend, has presented me with books which Servius Claudius bequeathed to him. Since your friend Cincius stated that the Cincian law* allowed me to receive them, I said that I should be delighted to have them if he brought them over.

If you love me and if you know that I love you, do ensure through your friends, dependants, guests, and your very freedmen and slaves, that not one page is lost, for I have urgent need of both the Greek works, which I suspect he left, and the Latin ones, which I know he bequeathed. I relax with such studies more and more every day in the time which my toils in the courts allow. You will do me a supreme favour—I repeat, a supreme favour—if you act in this matter as zealously as you usually do on issues which you think are closest to my heart. I also commend to you Paetus' affairs; he is most grateful for your attention to them. I not merely ask but also urge you to come now to see us.

Letter 17 (*Att.* II 1)

Rome, June 60

CICERO TO ATTICUS

Your lad met me when I was heading for Antium on 1 June, leaving   1
behind me, and gladly, the gladiatorial show* which Marcus Metellus was putting on. The boy handed me a letter from you, together with an account of my consulship composed in Greek. On receiving it, I was pleased that some days before I had entrusted a work on the same theme, likewise written in Greek, to Lucius Cossinius to deliver to you; for if I had read yours first, you could have pronounced me guilty of plagiarism. I read your version with pleasure, for though it seemed somewhat rough and ready,* the very avoidance of embellishment lent it an embellished flavour. As is the case with ladies, what seemed to lend it fragrance was its avoidance of fragrance. My work on the other hand exhausted the entire perfume-casket of Isocrates and all the wee scent-boxes of his pupils, together with some of Aristotle's pigments. At Corcyra, as you indicated in another letter, you scratched the surface of it, but it was later, I think, that you received the copy from Cossinius. I should not have presumed to send it to you if I had not revised it with leisurely and fussy application.

However, Posidonius* has already written back to me from   2
Rhodes, saying that when he read the *mémoire* which I had sent him to encourage him to write on these same events with greater embellishment, so far from being fired to compose an account, he was in

fact totally discouraged. What more can I say? I have thrown the entire Greek world into confusion. Those who in large numbers were urging me to provide them with a record which they could embellish have now ceased to plague me. If you like the work, you must arrange to make it available both in Athens and in other Greek towns, for that may possibly lend lustre to my achievements.

3   I shall send you my speeches, such as they are,* not only those which you request, but others besides, since those which I commit to paper (because urged to do so by the enthusiasm of our tender youths) also give you pleasure. Just as your fellow-citizen Demosthenes had performed with brilliance in the speeches termed *Philippics*, having turned aside from the argumentative type of court oratory practised here, to appear as *un homme d'état plus majestueux*, so it was in my interest likewise to ensure that speeches of mine should be accounted worthy of a consul.

The first of them was delivered in the Senate on 1 January, the second to the citizens on the agrarian law, the third on Otho, the fourth in defence of Rabirius, the fifth on the children of men proscribed, the sixth when I renounced a province before the Assembly, the seventh when I discharged Catiline from the city, the eighth delivered before the citizens the day after Catiline took to his heels, the ninth before the Assembly on the day when the Allobroges laid information, and the tenth made in the Senate on 5 December. Besides these, there are two short speeches,* *petits morceaux*, so to speak, from the agrarian law. I shall ensure that you obtain the whole *rassemblement*, and since both my writings and my achievements give you pleasure, from these works you will get an insight into both my actions and my speeches. Otherwise you should not have requested them, as I am not for submitting myself to you.

4   You ask why I summoned you, and at the same time you indicate that you are hindered by business dealings, but you do not refuse to hasten here, not merely if I need you but even if I should like you to come. There is certainly no real need. However, it did seem to me that you could organize your periods of travel more conveniently. You are too long away from Rome, especially as you live so near at hand. We do not enjoy the pleasure of your presence, and you forgo ours. At the moment peace reigns, but should the mad behaviour of our little Beauty* be enabled to progress any further, I should rouse you at the top of my voice from that abode of yours. But Metellus

nobly bars his way, and will continue to do so. In short, he is a consul *vraiment patriote*, and as I have always regarded him, a naturally honourable man.

But Clodius is not bluffing. He is clearly keen to become a plebeian 5 tribune. When this issue was discussed in the Senate, I tore him to pieces. I rebuked his inconsistency in seeking to become a plebeian tribune at Rome in spite of his repeated claim that he was seeking an inheritance in Sicily.* I said that we should not greatly exercise ourselves, because it would be no more possible for him to bring down the state as a plebeian than it had been for those of like complexion to do so as patricians when I was consul; moreover, that when he stated that he had journeyed from the Straits to Rome in a week, that no one had been available to meet him, and that he had entered the city in darkness (he had boasted before an Assembly about all this), I remarked that this was no new experience for him. 'What?' I said. 'Sicily to Rome in a week, but Rome to Interamna in three hours?* And he had entered the city in darkness? So too on an earlier occasion. And no one had met him?* No, nor on that earlier occasion either, when such an encounter would have been desirable!' In short, I am cutting this wanton fellow down to moderate size, and not merely by oratory of sustained seriousness, but also by this type of witticism.

So now I indulge in friendly banter and joking with him. Indeed, when we were each escorting a candidate down to the Forum, he asked me whether I had been in the habit of awarding Sicilians seats at gladiatorial shows. I said no. 'Well, I am their new patron,' he said, 'and I intend to institute the practice, but my sister,* who has discretion over the consular enclosure, is allowing me one measly foot.' 'Don't complain', I rejoined, 'that your sister offers you only one foot, for you can haul up her other one as well.' You will comment: 'Not a remark worthy of a consul.' True enough, but I abominate that woman, so unworthy of a consul, for she is a trouble maker, constantly at war with her husband. Indeed, not just with Metellus, but with Fabius as well, for he takes it badly* that both are so worthless.

You bring up the agrarian law.* It seems to have utterly fallen flat. 6 As for my friendship with Pompey, you give me a gentle push to rebuke me. But I should not like you to think that my alliance with him is for my own protection. The situation has so developed that if any disagreement chanced to arise between us, the greatest disharmony in the state would immediately ensue. I have taken forethought and precautions against this, not to the point of abandoning my most principled policy-but to ensure that he is better disposed, and abandons some of his 'people-pleasing' instability. You are to realize that he proclaims my achievements (which many induced him to attack), more enthusiastically in fact than his own. He attests that while he has served the state well, I have been its saviour. I do not know how much this attitude of his benefits me, but it is certainly of benefit to the state. Perhaps I may make a better citizen of Caesar* too; his career is now borne on the fairest of winds. I am surely not doing much harm to the public weal if I succeed in persuading the men with power not to adopt an obstructionist policy.

7   No, even if no one bore me ill-will, even if all were well disposed to me as would be just, the healing which restored the health of malignant parts of the state would be no less worthy of approval than any treatment which amputated them. But as things stand, now that the equestrians, whom I had posted under your standard and leadership on the slope up to the Capitoline hill,* have abandoned the Senate, and now that our leaders believe they have come close to heaven if there are bearded mullets in their fish-ponds* which come to them to be fed, and they disregard all else, I surely seem to you to be doing a sufficiently useful job if I ensure that the men in power are reluctant to inflict harm?

8   As for our Cato, your affection for him is no greater than mine. Yet in spite of his exemplary attitude and total integrity, he sometimes inflicts damage on the state,* for he delivers speeches as if he were in Plato's *république* and not in Romulus' cesspit. What decision could be more principled than that those who received bribes for their adjudication in a trial should be brought to court? Cato framed this proposal, and the Senate approved it; the equestrians then declared war on the Senate House, though not on me, as I dissented from the motion. What could be more shameless than for the tax-farmers to renege on their contract? Yet we ought to have borne the financial loss to keep the equestrian order on our side. But Cato registered opposition, and carried the day. So now a consul has been locked up* in gaol, and a sequence of riots has followed. Yet not one of those who used to rally round me when I was consul, and again round the consuls who succeeded me, has lent a hand in defence of

the state. So what is to happen now? You will ask: 'Are we to bribe those supporters of yours to keep them with us?' What else are we to do, if there is no other way? Are we to kowtow to freedmen and even to slaves?* But as you say across the water, *assez de choses sérieuses*.

Favonius* has gained the electoral support of my tribe more hon-   9
ourably than his own, and he has not won that of Lucceius. He made a poor show in indicting Nasica. Though he conducted the case decorously, his speech gave the impression that he had spent his time at Rhodes, not at the feet of Molon, but grinding at the millstones.* He was mildly cross with me for acting as counsel for the defence. He is once again a candidate in the interests of the state. I shall write to you about Lucceius' intentions* once I have seen Caesar, who is to be here in two days' time.

You must blame Cato and his echo Servilius for your ill-treatment   10
by the Sicyonians.* But after all, aren't many decent souls under the cosh? However, if that is how they wanted it, we must approve the decision. Then, once disagreements break out, we are to be left on our own.

My Amalthea awaits you, and misses you. My residences at   11
Tusculum and Pompeii are an absolute delight, except that they have left me, who am the champion of creditors, up to the neck in debt— in Roman, not Corinthian, currency! We are hoping that peace pre- vails in Gaul. You are to expect my version of the *Prognostica*,* together with those trivial speeches, any day now. None the less you must inform me when you envisage your arrival here, for whereas Pomponia told someone to tell me that you would be in Rome in July, the message was at odds with the letter which you sent me about getting yourself on the census list.

As I wrote to you earlier, Paetus* has made me a present of all the   12
books bequeathed by his cousin. That gift of his is now dependent on your concern. As you love me, do ensure their safe-keeping and their dispatch to me. No service can win my appreciation more. Do care- fully ensure the safety of both Greek and Latin volumes, and I shall then consider that this little gift comes from you. I have written to Octavius,* with whom I had not discussed the matter, for I did not think that these affairs of yours were the concern of the province, nor did I regard you as one of those wretched usurers. But I did my duty in writing with all care.

Letter 18 (*Att.* II 3)

?Rome, December 60

CICERO TO ATTICUS

1   To start with, here is what I consider *une bonne nouvelle*. Valerius*
was acquitted after Hortensius defended him. The verdict is
regarded as a concession to Aulus' son, and I nurture the suspicion
that Epicrates has been up to his tricks, as you say. I certainly don't
like the look of his military boots and blancoed puttees. We shall
know the facts when you return.

2   You must realize that your criticism of my narrow windows is criticism of the *Education of Cyrus*.* When I pose the same objection,
Cyrus states that *les vues* of the greenery through broad windows are
not so attractive. For if *le point de vision* is A, and *l'objet qu'on voit is*
AC, and the optical rays are D—you appreciate the rest, for if our
sight were attributable to *l'impact des images, les images* would have
extreme difficulty in narrow confines. But as things stand, *l'émission*
of the rays proceeds pleasantly. If you criticize the other features,
you will not find me mute, unless your objection is in some way
amenable to correction without expense.

3   I turn now to the month of January and *la base de notre politique*,
about which I shall present *comme Socrate, l'un et l'autre*, but finally,
after the fashion of the Socratics, *ma préférence*. The situation certainly demands careful consideration. I must either stoutly oppose
the agrarian law,* which involves a degree of conflict but abundant
prestige, or keep my head down, which virtually spells departure to
Solonium or Antium, or even lending a hand, which people say
Caesar confidently expects of me; for Cornelius has been visiting
me—Cornelius Balbus,* the close ally of Caesar. He maintains that
Caesar will accede to the advice of Pompey and myself in all things,
and that he will see to it that he aligns Crassus with Pompey.

4   What follows from this is that I enjoy the closest alliance with
Pompey, and if desired with Caesar too. I am restored to favour with my
personal enemies, to peace with the world at large, and to tranquillity in
my old age. But I am still animated by *le dernier mot* of the third book:*

> Meanwhile maintain the course which from your early youth,
> And then as consul, you pursued with heart and soul;
> Enhance your glory, gain the praise of honest men.

Since Calliope herself laid down this instruction to me in that book which contains many *sentiments aristocratiques*, I do not think that I should doubt that I must always believe that

> The best, the only omen is defence
> Of one's own native land*.

But let us reserve this topic for when we take our stroll on the feast of the Compitalia.* Keep in mind the day before. I shall order the bath to be heated. Terentia is inviting Pomponia too, and we shall include your mother in the party. Please bring me Theophrastus' *On Ambition** from Quintus' library.

3

DISILLUSIONMENT AND EXILE (59–57 BC)

CICERO's attempt to promote his vision of a traditional republican government buttressed by the alliance between the Senate and the equestrians, which he had hoped to maintain with the support of Pompey, was fatally undermined when Caesar returned from his province in Further Spain in 60, and made an informal alliance with Pompey and Crassus. Having obtained the consulship for 59, Caesar overrode the passive opposition of his colleague Bibulus, and with the support of Pompey and Crassus put through several measures, including the agrarian law, in the Assembly with the threat of violence. He sought to deflect Cicero from active opposition by offering him various commissions, but Cicero refused them. Meanwhile Clodius, following his acquittal on the charge of sacrilege and a year as quaestor in Sicily, returned to Rome, and with Caesar's help in March 59 was transferred to a plebeian *gens*. He subsequently gained election as tribune for 58. A series of bills—choice provinces for the consuls, removal of Cato on a commission to acquire Cyprus, free corn for the common folk—gave him control of the Assembly. In January–February 58 he carried a bill denying fire and water to anyone who had procured the execution of citizens without trial. Though Cicero was not named, he was clearly the target, and on the advice of Hortensius he anticipated condemnation by quitting Rome. Clodius followed up with a second bill which cited Cicero by name, confiscating his property and forbidding him to reside within 400 miles of Rome. Cicero then left Italy via Brundisium, and in May finally reached Thessalonica, where he stayed miserably until November, when he moved to Dyrrhachium. There he stayed till he was formally recalled in August 57.

Letter 19 (*Att.* II 5)

Antium, April 59

CICERO TO ATTICUS

1 I am indeed keen, and have long been keen, to visit Alexandria* and the rest of Egypt, and at the same time to quit the society which has had more than enough of me, and to return when there is some

longing for me. But in view of the times and the identity of those who want me to go,

> I fear the Trojans, and their wives with trailing gowns.

What will our optimates say, if indeed there are any left? Will they think that I have been seduced from my principles by some bribe?

> Polydamas will be the first with his reproach,*

in other words my friend Cato, 'who alone is worth a hundred thousand'* in my eyes. And how will history pass judgement on me six hundred years hence? I am indeed much more apprehensive of that than of the petty gossip of those who are alive today. But I suppose we must await and anticipate what comes, for if some offer is made to me, I shall have some sort of discretion, and I shall then ponder it. There is, after all, some prestige in refusing it. So if Theophanes* chances to make some suggestion to you, do not reject it outright.

I await a letter from you about affairs at your end. What has 2 Arrius* to say for himself, and how is he taking his having been dropped? Who are being groomed to be consuls? Is it to be Pompey and Crassus, as general gossip has it, or as a letter informs me, Servius Sulpicius and Gabinius? Have any new laws been passed? Or is there any new development at all? Who is being offered the augurate now that Nepos* is leaving Rome? That is the only bait with which they can lay a trap for me—what a fickle man I am! But why do these issues preoccupy me, when I am eager to abandon them, and to devote all my energy and attention to *philosophie*? This, I declare, is my intention. I only wish that I had done it from the outset. But now, having learnt by experience how empty are the pursuits I considered glorious, I plan to take account of all the Muses.

None the less, you must reply and give me more definite informa- 3 tion about Arrius, and whether anyone is being groomed in his place. What is being done about Publius Clodius?* Tell me every-thing *à loisir*, as you promise to do. Please let me know on what day you think of leaving Rome, so that I can tell you where I am to be. Write back at once about the matters I have raised with you, for I await your letter eagerly.

Letter 20 (*Att.* II 9)

Antium, April 59

CICERO TO ATTICUS

1 Caecilius the quaestor has suddenly informed me that he is sending
a boy to Rome, so I write this at speed to extract from you those
remarkable exchanges of yours with Publius,* both those which you
mention in your letter, and the one which you keep up your sleeve,
saying that it would be too long to write down what you said in reply.
As for the exchange which has not yet taken place, and which Lady
Ox-eyes* is to report to you on her return from Solonium, do realize
that nothing could be more delightful for me to receive. If the agreement made with regard to me* is not kept, I am on cloud nine at the
thought that our friend from Jerusalem, who converts patricians into
plebeians,* should ascertain the helpful favour with which he has
repaid me for those grovelling speeches of mine. You must anticipate
a retractation of them from on high! Indeed, in so far as I can hazard
a guess, if that scoundrel is to remain popular with those rulers of
ours, he will not be able to crow over this 'ex-consul of the Cynic
school'* or even over your 'Tritons of the fish-ponds',* for once we
are stripped of our influence and of that notorious senatorial power,
we cannot be the recipients of any odium. On the other hand, if he
parts company with them, it will be ridiculous for him to attack me.
None the less, let him attack me!

Take my word for it, how amusingly this wheel of politics has
turned full circle more quietly than I had imagined, and indeed more
quickly than seemed possible! The fault lies with Cato, but also with
the lack of principle of the Three, who have ignored the auspices and
the Aelian as well as the Junian, Licinian, Caecilian, and Didian
laws.* They have disposed of all the healing remedies of the state,
and have bestowed kingdoms on tetrarchs, and massive sums of
money on the few.

2 I see now in what direction the unpopularity is veering, and where
it will lodge. You are to believe that if within a short time you do not
see people pining for the days when I was at the helm, I shall have
learnt nothing from experience, or from Theophrastus.* Granted
that the power of the Senate was loathed, but what do you think the
outcome will be, now that the power has passed not to the people but
to three uncontrolled individuals? So let the Three appoint consuls

and plebeian tribunes at will, let them even clothe Vatinius'* hideous carbuncles with the purple robe *bon teint* of the priesthood, yet soon you will see canonized not merely those who have kept their noses clean, but even Cato the arch-sinner himself!

As for myself, so long as your boon-companion Publius* allows it, 3 I intend *jouer comme sophiste*,* but if he forces the issue with me, to go only so far as to defend myself, and deploying the sophist's native wiles, *je déclare*

> To strike back when a man shows violence first.

I pray that my country may be favourably disposed to me, for she has had from me, if no more than her due, at any rate more than was demanded. I prefer to see her launched on a wayward course under another helmsman rather than to provide sound steering for ungrateful passengers. But it will be more appropriate to discuss these matters face to face.

Listen now to my reply to your question. My plan is to return 4 from my house at Formiae to Antium on 3 May. I intend to leave Antium for my Tusculan estate on 7 May. But once I return from my place at Formiae, where I plan to be till the last day of April, I shall at once inform you. Terentia sends greetings, and *le petit Cicéron salue Tite l'Athénien.*

Letter 21 (*Att.* II 16)

Formiae, April–May 59

CICERO TO ATTICUS

On 29 April I had finished dining and was snoozing when your letter 1 was delivered in which you wrote about the issue of the allotment of Campanian land.* To put it briefly, initially I was so taken aback that it banished all sleep from me, but more in concentrated thought than from irritation. My reflections developed on these lines. What first came to mind, arising from your previous letter, was that you had heard from a friend of Caesar's that there would be a proposal to which no one would object. I had feared that it would be a major announcement, but this does not appear to be on that scale. Secondly— a comforting thought this, for myself personally—all expectation of land-allocation seems to have been concentrated in Campania.

Assuming that the allocations are to be of ten *iugera* each, that land cannot accommodate more than 5,000 settlers, so inevitably the sponsors will lose the support of all the rest of the flood of applicants. What is more, if anything can more emphatically rouse the indignation of the honest men—and I see that they are already worked up—this proposal surely will, and all the more so, since now that customs-duties have been abolished in Italy, and the Campanian land is apportioned out, what internal tax remains except the 5 per cent?* In my opinion that too is likely to go by the board through the raucous demands of our dependants* at one mere Assembly.

2   I have absolutely no idea what my friend Gnaeus* now has in mind.

> No longer does he blow on slender reeds,
> But with blasts uncontrolled, his mouthband off,

since he has been induced to go as far as this. Up to now *il s'armait des sophismes*, saying that he approves of Caesar's laws but that the consul himself must ensure their passage; that he favoured the agrarian law, but that it was no business of his whether it could be vetoed or not; that he approved the settlement at long last concerning the Alexandrian king,* but that it was not for him to investigate whether Bibulus* at that time had his eyes trained on the heavens or not; that he had sought to accommodate the order of the equestrians, but that he could not have prophesied the outcome had Bibulus at that time gone down to the Forum.

But what are you going to say now, dear Sampsiceramus?* That in our interest you have imposed a tax on the Antilibanus mountain-range, and abolished that in Campania? How will you get that to stick? 'I will keep you in order', he says, 'by deploying Caesar's troops.' But by heaven you will not keep me under control so much with that army of yours as with the ungrateful attitudes of the men they call honest.* They have invariably failed to repay me, not merely with material rewards but even with words of thanks.

3   If I were to rouse myself to face these issues, I should certainly now devise some means of opposing them. But as things stand, I have firmly decided, since there is such disagreement between your friend Dicaearchus and my comrade Theophrastus,* with your man preferring *la vie active* and mine *la vie contemplative*, that I shall be seen to

fall in with both. I believe that I have done abundant justice to Dicaearchus, and now I am turning my attention to the other school, which not merely allows me to rest from my labours, but rebukes me for not having remained inactive all this time. So, my dear Titus, I must devote myself to the studies of fair fame, and now at last return to the pursuits which I ought never to have abandoned.

As for your comment on my brother Quintus' letter, I too have 4 received one which was *lion par devant, et par dernière* [lion all before, and the rear end . . .]—well, I don't know how to express it. In the first lines he laments his lengthy stay so bitterly that he would engage anyone's sympathy, but then in turn he becomes light-hearted enough to ask me to correct and publish his historical work. But I should like you to concentrate on the point you mention, namely the tax* levied on goods transported from place to place. He states that, on the proposal of his council, he has referred the issue to the Senate. Presumably he had not then read my letter, in which after careful consideration and enquiry I reported that no tax was due. If any Greeks have already reached Rome from Asia with this brief, please contact them, and if you think it appropriate, tell them my views on this matter. If they can reach an agreement to prevent their excellent case from foundering in the Senate, I shall lend my support to the tax-farmers. But otherwise—I shall speak with candour—in this instance I favour the whole province of Asia and its merchants, for the question is of serious concern to them as well. I do feel that this matter is of great concern to us, but you will see to it.

I ask you, are the quaestors hesitating about paying out even in cistophores?* If there is no other way after we have exhausted every avenue, I shall not despise that as a last resort. We shall see you at our house at Arpinum, and greet you there with rustic hospitality, since you have scorned a welcome at the seaside.

Letter 22 (*Att.* II 18)

Rome, June 59

CICERO TO ATTICUS

I have received a number of letters from you, from which I gather 1 you are on tenterhooks in your anxious longing for news. We are oppressed on all sides. We do not now object to a life of slavery, but we fear death and expulsion as greater evils, whereas in fact they are much the lesser. All with one voice bemoan this situation, but no one raises a finger or voice to relieve it. *L'objectif* of those who hold the reins is, I suspect, to leave no one any wealth to pass on. The one man who speaks out and openly opposes them is young Curio.* The loyalists* accord him the loudest applause, greet him in the Forum with the greatest respect, and bestow on him numerous signs of their goodwill, whereas they pursue Fufius* with raucous shouts, abuse, and whistling. These incidents awake no greater hope, but greater sadness, for one sees that the community's aspiration is free, but its courage is fettered.

2   To save your making possible enquiries *en détail* about particular issues, the whole situation has degenerated to such a point that there is no prospect of freedom at any time, not merely for private citizens but even for magistrates. Yet in spite of this oppression, in social gatherings and at dinner-parties at any rate, speech is freer than it ever was. Resentment is beginning to prevail over fear, but in such a way that the entire scene is one of total despair. The Campanian legislation even incorporates a curse* on any candidates if they suggest in any assembly that possession of land should be on terms other than those that accord with the Julian laws. The rest do not hesitate so to swear, but Laterensis* is reckoned to have made a splendid gesture in withdrawing his candidature for the plebeian tribunate to avoid taking the oath.

3   But I have no desire to write further on the political scene. I am at odds with myself, and it causes me the utmost grief to take up the pen. While all citizens are ground down, I keep my self-respect without stooping to degradation, but, in view of my earlier distinguished record, with insufficient courage. Caesar has most obligingly invited me to act as deputy on his provincial staff,* and I am also offered a roving legation to discharge a vow. But this second offer on the one hand fails to guarantee sufficient protection as regards the propriety of our little Beauty,* and on the other it removes me from Rome on my brother's return. The first option is both safer and does not prevent my being here when I wish to be. I keep the offer open, but I do not think that I shall exploit it. However, no one knows what I have in mind. My inclination is not to take to my heels, for I am eager to fight. Popular support for me is strong. But I make no promises; you are to say nothing.

I am indeed exercised about Statius' manumission* and about a 4
number of other things. But by now I have become quite thick-
skinned. I only wish—indeed, I long for—your presence here, for
then I should not be short of advice or comfort. But do hold yourself
in readiness to hasten here if I call.

Letter 23 (*Att.* II 19)

Rome, July 59

CICERO TO ATTICUS

I have lots of serious worries because of great convulsions in the state 1
and dangers levelled at my person. They are beyond counting, but
nothing irks me more than Statius'* manumission.

> To think that my command—forget command,
> Not even my displeasure wins respect!

I do not know what to do about it, though its effect is not so dam-
aging as the gossip. I cannot even feel angry towards those whom I
love dearly. I am merely saddened, but quite remarkably so. My
other worries are on major issues. Clodius' threats* and the struggles
in store for me affect me only marginally, for I seem able to confront
them, maintaining the greatest self-respect, or to dodge them without much trouble. Perhaps you will say 'Forget your self-respect;
that is *vieux jeu*.* Think of your survival, I beg you.' Poor me! Why
are you not at my side? Nothing would escape your eye, that's for
sure, whereas perhaps *je suis frappé de cécité*, and *je m'adonne trop à la
noblesse* [I am blind, and too attached to what is noble].

You are to realize that the political situation* has never been so dis- 2
graceful, demeaning, and unpalatable equally to all kinds and classes
and ages of citizens as it is now—more so, I swear, than I could have
wished, not merely more than I could have imagined. These 'people-
pleasers' have now taught even moderate men to hiss. Bibulus is
exalted to the skies. I have no idea why. He is praised as if he were

> The one who single-handed saved the state
> By his delaying.

As for my darling Pompey, to my great chagrin he has shot himself
in the foot. The Three retain no adherents by ties of goodwill, and

what I fear is that they may find it necessary to resort to terror. For my part, I do not battle against their programme because of my known friendship with Pompey. But I do not indicate my approval of it, for that could imply condemnation of all my earlier actions. I adopt a middle course.

3   The feelings of the citizens are most blatant in the theatre and at the shows. When the gladiators were on, both the presenter and his supporters were drowned with hisses. At the Games of Apollo* the tragic actor Diphilus launched quite insolently into our dear Pompey. He was made to repeat a thousand times the line

> It is our wretched lot which made you great.

when he declaimed the lines

> A time will come when you will sore lament
> Your valour,

the whole theatre applauded, and the rest of the speech was greeted likewise. Indeed, the lines sound as if they have been written by an enemy of Pompey for this special occasion. The line

> If neither laws nor customs can constrain

and what follows evoked massive din and shouting. When Caesar entered, the applause was tepid, but when the younger Curio followed him in, there was the sort of ovation that used to greet Pompey while the republic was still in being.

    Caesar was affronted. It is said that a letter is winging its way to Pompey at Capua. The pair of them loathe the equestrians, who rose to their feet and applauded Curio. They are at war with everybody. They repeatedly threaten the Roscian law, and the corn law* as well. The situation is certainly chaotic. My own preference would have been to let their plans develop in silence, but I fear that this may not be possible. People will not tolerate their behaviour, yet it seems that we must. All citizens now speak with one voice, but in tones of hatred rather than self-defence.

4   My friend Publius* keeps threatening me and is my personal enemy. Proceedings are looming. Doubtless you will hasten here to confront them. I appear to have behind me my army of all ex-consuls who are loyalists, as well as those who are tolerably loyal. Pompey shows his support for me in no mean measure. He also maintains that

Clodius will not utter a word about me, but when he claims this, he is beguiling himself and not me. Cosconius has died, and I have been invited* to replace him. This would have been an invitation to fill a dead man's shoes, and in the view of the public I should have been the most despicable figure possible. Indeed, nothing could have been more remote from the *sécurité* you talk of, for the Three are out of favour with honourable men, as I am with the dishonourable. So without losing my personal unpopularity, I would have acquired that of others as well.

Caesar would like me to serve on his staff. That would be a more 5 honourable way of avoiding the danger, but I am not shrugging that danger off. So what am I to do? I prefer to fight, but I have made no firm decision. I repeat that I only wish you were here. If needs must, I shall send for you.

What else? Just this, I think: I am convinced that all is lost. *Pourquoi dissimuler* for so long? But I write this in a hurry, and indeed fearfully. From now on, if I have a reliable courier to trust with a letter, I shall put everything down in black and white, or if I write in code, you will get the message. In such letters I shall sign myself 'Laelius', and call you 'Furius'.* All else will be *à mots couverts*. Here in Rome I cultivate Caecilius,* and scrupulously attend on him. I hear that Bibulus' edicts have been forwarded to you. My friend Pompey is blazing with annoyance and anger at them.

Letter 24 (*Att.* II 21)

Rome, July–August 59

CICERO TO ATTICUS

Why should I bother you with details of state affairs? The republic is 1 utterly finished. It is more wretched now than when you left it, for at that time the tyranny with which the state was weighed down seemed to be regarded as agreeable by the common herd, and honourable men found it objectionable but not ruinous. But all of a sudden it has now become hated by one and all, and we are aghast at where it is likely to explode. We have now had a taste of the anger and lack of restraint of the Three. In their fury at Cato* they have brought low the entire state. The poisons they injected seemed so mild that I thought it possible our demise would be painless, but owing to the hissing of the mob, the gossip of decent citizens, and the rumble of disapproval throughout Italy, I fear that the trio are now ablaze with anger.

2   As I would often tell you in conversation as well, I entertained the hope that the political wheel had turned so imperceptibly that we could barely hear its sound or observe the impress of its circular course. This would have been the outcome if people had been able to await the passing of the storm. But after heaving secret sighs for quite a time, they all subsequently began to groan, and finally to give voice and to shout aloud.

3   So now that friend of ours,* who is a stranger to notoriety and has always basked in praise and been awash with glory, is unsightly in body and broken in spirit, at a loss where to turn. He sees the way forward as perilous, and the way back as irresolute. The honourable men are his enemies,* and even the scoundrels are not his friends.

Note how soft-hearted I am. I did not restrain my tears when, on 25 July, I watched him address the public on the edicts of Bibulus.* He had earlier been accustomed to comport himself most majestic- ally in that gathering, as the people's favourite and with the goodwill of all, but on this occasion how abject and downcast he was, and how disappointing his performance, not only to the audience but even to himself! It was a sight which pleased Crassus alone and

4   no one else. Because he had tumbled from the heights of heaven, he seemed to have slipped back rather than moved forward. Imagine if Apelles saw his Venus, or Protogenes* his famed Ialysus, smeared with mud. Each would, I imagine, appear desolated. That was how grieved I was at seeing the man whom with every embellishment of my art I had adorned and polished, suddenly rendered unsightly. Though in view of the trouble involving Clodius no man believes that I owe my friendship to Pompey, my affection for him has been so great that no injustice from him could impoverish it.

The outcome has been that Bibulus' Archilochian* edicts against him are so popular with the public that we cannot make our way past the place where they are posted owing to the crowds reading them. Pompey himself finds them so harsh that he is wasting away with resentment, and in God's truth I myself find them irritating. On the one hand they cause too much pain to a man for whom I have always felt affection, and on the other I fear that, because he is so aggressive, so eager to resort to weapons, and so unaccustomed to insults, the entire prompting of his spirit may lead him to indulge his resentment and anger.

How things will work out for Bibulus I do not know. The present situation finds him extraordinarily popular. When he had the elections postponed until October—this usually alienates the support of the citizens—Caesar thought that a speech of his could rouse the Assembly to visit Bibulus with violence. But for all his most factious talk, he could not elicit a shout from anyone. To put it in a nutshell, the Three feel that they do not have the goodwill of any section of the state, which is why I am all the more fearful of violence on their part.

Clodius is hostile* towards me. While Pompey maintains that the tribune will take no action against me, it is hazardous for me to believe it, and I am preparing to offer resistance. I hope that I shall have maximum support from all classes. I feel the need for your presence, and in view of the crisis the situation also demands it. If I have your timely presence to look to, I shall have the reinforcement of abundant advice, courage, and lastly protection. Varro* is quite helpful towards me, and Pompey's assurances are gifts from heaven. My hope is that at least I shall emerge from the conflict with the utmost credit or indeed without distress.

Do let me have news of your activities, diversions, and negotiations with the citizens of Sicyon.

Letter 25 (*Att.* II 23)

Rome, August–September 59

CICERO TO ATTICUS

Up to now, I think, you have never read any letter from me not written by my own hand. From this you will be able to infer how hectic is the busy life which distracts me, for now I have no time to spare, and I need to walk to restore my poor vocal chords, so I am dictating this as I walk.

Well, now, the first thing I want you to know is that our friend Sampsiceramus* is markedly unhappy with his situation, and he is eager to be restored to the eminence from which he has tumbled down. He confides his wounded feelings to me, and from time to time he openly seeks a remedy, but I believe that there is none to be found. Moreover, the spokesmen of that faction* and their supporters are all losing their vigour, though no one opposes them. There has never been greater unanimity of attitudes and of gossip than there is at present.

3 For my own part, as I am well aware that you are keen to know, I am involved in no political activities. I devote myself entirely to the routine and the toil of the courts.* As you can readily understand, this leads me to dwell a great deal on the memory of my past activities, which I sorely miss. But the brother of our Lady Ox-eyes is issuing threats which inspire no mean apprehension, and though he denies them to Sampsiceramus, he airs them blatantly and flaunts them before the rest of the world.

So if your affection for me is as great as is certainly the case, rouse yourself if you sleep, get moving if you are on your feet, start running if you are on the move, and take wing if you are running. My dependence on you for your advice and practical wisdom, and above all for your affection and loyalty, is beyond belief. The importance of the situation perhaps demands a lengthy explanation, but the unity between our hearts is content with few words. It is highly important for me that you should be in Rome at least once Clodius' appointment is ratified, if you cannot attend for the elections. Look after yourself.

Letter 26 (*Att.* III 4)
Vibo / Brundisium, April 58

CICERO TO ATTICUS

1 I should like you to regard my sudden departure from Vibo,* where I summoned you, as evidence of my unhappiness rather than vacillation, for the bill relating to my undoing has been delivered to me. The emended form of it, as I had already heard, was to the effect that I should journey four hundred miles from Rome, and not reside within that distance. I at once headed for Brundisium, before the day when the bill becomes law, to ensure that my host Sicca* should not be ruined as well, and also because I am not allowed to reside in Malta.

You must now hasten to catch up with me—so long as I get a welcome there. So far I am receiving friendly invitations, but I am fearful of what lies ahead. Dear Pomponius, I am heartily tired of

living, and in these circumstances you have been my greatest
strength. But we can discuss this when we are together; just make
sure that you come.

Letter 27 (*Fam.* XIV 4)
Brundisium, April 58

TULLIUS TO HIS DEAR TERENTIA,
FOND TULLIA, AND CICERO

I write to you less often than I can, both because I am unhappy at   1
every moment, and especially because when I write to you or read
your letters I am so overcome with weeping that I cannot bear it. If
only I had been less eager to go on living! I should at any rate have
experienced no evil, or precious little, in my life. If, however,
Fortune has preserved me to attain some hope of regaining at some
time some benefit from life, my mistake has been of less moment. But
if these ills are irredeemable, I long to see you, light of my life, with
all speed, and to die in your embrace, since neither gods, whom you
have worshipped so devotedly, nor men, whom I have always served,
have favoured us in return.

I have been lodging in Brundisium for thirteen days at the resi-   2
dence of Marcus Laenius Flaccus, best of men, who has disregarded
the danger to his possessions and his person in the interests of my
safety. He has not been deterred by the penalty of a most heinous
law* from observing the rights and obligations of hospitality and
friendship. I pray that I may at some time be able to repay him for
his kindness. I shall always be in his debt.

I commenced my journey from Brundisium on 28 April, and am   3
making for Cyzicus through Macedonia.* Poor me, I am ruined, and
in dire straits! What am I to do? Beg you to join me, when you are a
sick woman, prostrated in body and mind? Or should I *not* beg you,
and as a result be without you? This is the course, I think, that I shall
follow: if there is a prospect of my return, you must strengthen and
assist the process. But if, as I myself fear, the door is closed on me,
then join me in any way you can. Be assured of this one fact: so long
as I have you, I shall not regard myself as utterly lost. But what will
become of my fond Tullia? You must together look to this, for I have
no counsel to offer. However the situation develops, the poor girl's

marriage and fair name at any rate must be safeguarded.* Then again, what is to become of my Cicero?* I cannot write more on this now, for I am choked with grief.

4   How you have been coping I do not know—whether you have kept any possessions or, as I fear, have been stripped of everything.* I hope that Piso,* as your letter states, will always be supportive of us. There is no need for you to be exercised about the manumission of the household. To begin with, your personal attendants were promised that you would treat them individually as each deserved. Up to now Orpheus continues to give loyal service, but apart from him the others are not markedly attentive. The position with the rest of the slaves is that, if I lost the claim to my property, they would become my freedmen, provided they could justify their manumission. But if they continued to belong to me, they would remain slaves, apart from a mere few. But these matters are of minor concern.

5   As for your urging me to be stout-hearted, and to be hopeful of recovering my immunity, I only wish that the situation could offer justified optimism. But in my present wretchedness when shall I now hear from you? Who will deliver a letter from you to me? I would have awaited one at Brundisium if the sailors had allowed it, but they refused to forgo the chance of good sailing weather,

6   For the rest, my dear Terentia, bear up as honourably as you can. I have lived a distinguished life. It was no fault of mine but my integrity which brought me low. My only error was not to have forfeited my life when I lost its distinctions. But if my children are keener that I go on living, I must endure what remains, however intolerable the prospect. Yet even as I afford you strength, I cannot proffer it to myself.

I have sent back my loyal man Clodius Philhetaerus, for his weak eyesight holds him back. Sallustius is the most dutiful of all. Pescennius shows me great kindness. I hope that he will always serve you well. Sicca promised to accompany me, but he has left Brundisium.

Look after yourself as best you can. Believe that I am more troubled by your unhappiness than my own. Dear Terentia, most faithful and best of wives, my darling daughter, and Cicero, my sole remaining hope, goodbye to you all.

From Brundisium, 29 April

Letter 28 (*Att.* III 7)

Brundisium, April 58

CICERO TO ATTICUS

I reached Brundisium on 17 April. Your slaves handed me a letter 1
from you on that day, and two days later others brought me a second
one. You beg and urge me to accept your hospitality in Epirus. Your
invitation is by no means unexpected, and gives me very great pleasure. The idea would certainly be desirable if I could spend all my
time there, for I loathe crowds, I avoid associating with people, and
I can scarcely bear to look upon the light of day. So such solitude,
especially in a friendly abode, would not have been objectionable.
But as a place in which to break my journey, it is out of the way, and
secondly, it is a mere four days' journey from Autronius and the rest
of them.* Moreover, you would not be there. True, a fortified
stronghold would be a help to me if I were resident, but it is hardly
necessary for a bird of passage. If only I dared, I would have made
for Athens, and the course of events would have furthered my inclination. But as things stand there are enemies of mine there, you are
not available, and I fear that the authorities in Rome may claim that
that town too* is not distant enough from Italy. Besides, you do not
in your letter specify on what day I am to expect you.

Your exhortation to me to cling to life provokes the one outcome 2
that I refrain from doing myself harm, but you cannot prevent my
regretting the non-adoption of that course and of staying alive—for
what is there to detain me, especially since the hope that attended me
on my departure from Rome no longer obtains? I shall not list all the
wretched circumstances into which I have fallen because of the
supreme harm and wickedness, inflicted not so much by my enemies
as by those envious of me,* for I do not wish to awaken my grief and
to summon you to share the same distress. What I do claim is that no
one ever sustained a disaster as great as mine, and no one regarded
death as more desirable than I did. I have let slip the most honourable opportunity of embracing it; the opportunities that remain
offer not so much healing as cessation of my pain.

I note that you are gathering from the political scene all the 3
indications which you think can offer me some hope of a changed
situation. Though these are trifling, let us await the outcome of
them, since you so desire.

However, if you make haste you will catch up with me, for I shall either make my way to Epirus or journey in leisurely fashion through Candavia.* My hesitation about Epirus is not attributable to any vacillation, but to my ignorance of where I shall lay eyes on my brother. I have no idea how I am to meet him, or to wave him farewell. This is the greatest and most wretched of all my unhappy misfortunes.

I would write to you more often and at greater length if grief had not robbed me of all my wits, and in particular of the fluency of this type of communication. I am eager to see you. Look after yourself.

Sent on 29 April as I depart from Brundisium

Letter 29 (*Q. fr.* I 3)
Thessalonica, June 58

MARCUS TO HIS BROTHER QUINTUS

1 Dear brother, dear brother, dear brother! Were you actually afraid that some pique constrained me to send slaves to you without a letter, or even to refuse to see you? What, that *I* should be angry with *you*? Could I possibly have been angry with you? As if, I suppose, it was you who brought me low, *your* enemies that assailed me, and men's jealousy of *you* that brought my downfall, and not I who have unhappily caused yours! It was that acclaimed consulship of mine which has deprived me of you, of my children, of my fatherland, and of my possessions. I only wish it had robbed you of nothing but myself alone. What is beyond doubt is that whatever has accrued to me from you at any time has been both honourable and agreeable, whereas my bequest to you has been grief at my disaster, fear of your own,* and feelings of loss, sadness, and desertion.

So was it that *I* was reluctant to see *you*? On the contrary, I did not wish to be seen by you, for you would not have set eyes upon the person who was your brother, the one you had left behind you, the one you knew, the one who attended you as you set out, and to whom you gave your parting greeting as we both wept. Indeed, not a trace or shadow of him would you have seen, but merely a sort of ghost of a living corpse. If only you had earlier gazed on me when dead, or had received tidings of my death! If only I had left you to survive not only my life, but also my distinction!

But I call on all the gods to witness that what summoned me back ₂
from dying was the unanimous assertion of all that some part of your
life was bound up with mine. Therein lay my sin and my crime, for
if I had died, my very death would have readily maintained my
brotherly devotion and affection for you, whereas now I have caused
you to live without me, and to be dependent on others* while I survive, and my voice, which often protected utter strangers, has been
silent at this very time when my family members are endangered. As
for the fact that my slaves visited you without bearing a letter, you
now realize that pique was not the explanation; the reason was
undoubtedly torpor and the apparently unceasing impact of tears and
grief. Can you imagine the tears I shed in writing these very words? ₃
I am sure that you are weeping similarly as you read them. Can I stop
thinking of you at any time, or think of you at all, without shedding
tears? In missing you, do I merely miss you as a brother? No, it is
because you are an engaging brother, almost identical to me in age,*
but also as deferential as a son, and as wise in counsel as a
father. What joy did I ever experience which was not shared with
you, and likewise what joy did you not share with me? Then too
I simultaneously miss my daughter. What filial love she shows, a girl
so unassuming and so talented, so closely reflecting my features, my
speech, my cast of mind! Likewise my most engaging son, so very
sweet in my eyes, whom I cruelly and unfeelingly thrust from my
embrace,* a boy wiser than I would have wished, for the unhappy
child was aware of what was going on. Then again, your son, who
looks so like you, and whom my Cicero both loves and is now
beginning to respect as an elder brother. And in addition that unhap-
piest of women, my most faithful wife, whom I did not allow to
accompany me, to ensure that there would be someone to protect
what survives from our shared disaster and the children whom we
share.

None the less, I did write as best I could, and entrusted a letter ₄
for you to your freedman Philoponus. I believe that the letter was subsequently delivered to you. In it I enclosed the same message of exhortation and the same plea which the slaves reported to you in my own
words, urging you to head for Rome at once with all speed. First of all,
I wanted you to be a bastion in case there are enemies whose cruelty
is not yet sated by my disastrous fall. Secondly, I was apprehensive
of the grief occasioned by our meeting—and as for our parting, I could

not have borne it. Moreover, I feared that you could not be torn from me, as you remarked in your letter. It was for these reasons that the massive deprivation of failing to set eyes on you, apparently the most bitter and wretched experience possible for brothers who are most affectionate and harmonious, was in fact less bitter and wretched than our meeting and subsequent parting would have been.

5   If now you can do what I, though always courageous in your eyes, cannot do, you must hold your head high and brace yourself for any struggle which you must undergo. If my expectation carries any conviction, I anticipate that your probity and the affection in which you are held by the community, as well as pity for my plight, will afford you some protection. Should you emerge unscathed from the danger encompassing you, you will, I am sure, do what you believe it is possible to achieve in my case. Many people in letters to me have made many observations about my situation, indicating that they are hopeful. But for myself, I see no reason for hope, since my foes have such total control, and my friends in some cases have abandoned me and in others have betrayed me, so that if I were to return they would perhaps fear reproaches for their criminal conduct. But I should like you to investigate what things are like, and let me know. None the less I shall go on living for as long as you need me, in the event of your having to undergo some danger. But beyond that I cannot continue in my present existence, for neither practical wisdom nor philosophical teaching is sufficiently strong to be able to endure such great sorrow.

6   I am aware that there was both a more honourable and a more useful time to die, but that was not the only opportunity I have let slip. If I were disposed to lament the past, I would do nothing but increase your grief and expose my stupidity. What I must not and cannot do is to linger in this unhappy and shameful existence longer than either your circumstances or any substantial hope demand. I was once the most blessed man alive by reason of my brother, children, wife, and resources honourably attained. In distinction, authority, repute, and influence my standing was as high as that of any who ever lived. But now my condition is so harrowing and ruinous that I can no longer bear to grieve for myself or for my family.

7   Why then did you write to me about transferring money,* as if your resources at this time were not keeping me alive? Your very mention of this makes me appreciate and realize in my wretchedness the crime which I have committed, now that you and your son are about to make

every sacrifice to clear your debts, and while I have squandered to no effect the money I received on your behalf* from the Treasury. However, both Marcus Antonius and Caepio* were paid the amounts you specified in your letter. The money which I possess is sufficient for my purposes, for whether I am allowed to return, or the prospects are gloomy, I have no need of more. If you happen to be in any difficulty, I suggest that you approach Crassus and Calidius.*

How far Hortensius is to be relied upon I do not know. He has 8 treated me most abominably and most deceitfully, with a most hypocritical pretence of affection, attending me most regularly every day, and taking aboard Quintus Arrius* in this as well. Their counsels, promises, and instructions left me high and dry, so that I have fallen headlong into this disaster. But you must draw a veil over this 9 in case it presents an obstacle. Be on your guard in particular—and because of this I think you should cultivate Hortensius himself, using Pomponius as intermediary—in case the epigram about the Aurelian law* attributed to you, when you were a candidate for the aedileship, becomes firmly attached to you through false testimony. I fear nothing so much as that when people realize how much pity your plea and your immunity will bring to bear on my situation, they may impugn you more fiercely.

I believe Messalla* is favourable to you. I think that Pompey is still playing the hypocrite, but I hope that you do not have to experience the ordeal. I would entreat the gods to bring this to pass, if they had not ceased to heed my prayers. But I do pray that they rest content with these boundless ills of mine. They have not been caused by the notoriety of any wrongdoing of mine, but my resentment lies entirely in the fact that the greatest punishment has been visited on the noblest of activities.

There is no need, dear brother, for me to commend my daughter, 10 who is also yours, and my Cicero into your keeping. On the contrary, I am sad that their being orphaned will bring as much grief to you as to me. But they will not be orphaned as long as you remain unscathed. My tears do not allow me to write on other topics. I swear that this is true, so may heaven grant me a measure of salvation and permission to die in my native land! Please look after Terentia as well. Write back to me on all these matters. Be as courageous as the situation allows.

13 June at Thessalonica

Letter 30 (*Att.* III 15)

Thessalonica, August 58

CICERO TO ATTICUS

1 On 13 August I received four letters from you. In the first, you rebuke me, and beg me to show greater resolution. In the second, you say that Crassus' freedman told you that I was depressed and wasting away. In the third you inform me of proceedings in the Senate, and in the fourth you write that Varro* has assured you of Pompey's good intentions.

2   In reply to the first, I write to say that my depression, far from robbing me of my mental powers, is in fact concentrated upon my having no scope and no companions with whom to exercise their vigour. If you feel somewhat unhappy at being without me, how do you think I feel at being deprived of both you and everyone else? If you in your enjoyment of citizenship feel deprived of my presence, what yearning do you imagine I have for that status? I have no wish to recount the things of which I am deprived, not merely because you are aware of them, but also to avoid reopening the scars of my grief. But I do claim that no one was ever deprived of such great blessings, or was plunged into such great wretchedness. Time does not merely fail to assuage this sorrow, but even intensifies it, for whereas other griefs are softened with lapse of time, this can only increase daily through both present unhappiness and remembrance of past days. I miss not only my possessions and my family, but also my former self, for what am I now? But I shall neither distress your mind with my complaints nor finger my wounds too frequently.

When you sought to justify the men who in my letter I said had envied me, you included Cato. In fact, I believe him so guiltless of that villainy that I regret exceedingly that the hypocrisy of others* outweighed in my eyes his good faith. As for your justification of the rest, they must win my approval if they have yours. But it is late in the day for us to be discussing this.

3   I do not believe that the comment of Crassus' freedman was spoken from the heart. You write that the discussion in the Senate went well. But what of Curio? Has he not read that notorious speech?* I do not know how it got out, but when Axius reported the proceedings of that same day to me, he was not so complimentary about Curio. Mind you, he may have omitted something, whereas

you have certainly set down nothing but the facts. What Varro said leads me to entertain hopes of Caesar. I only wish that Varro would apply himself to my cause, as he will certainly be willing to do, both of his own accord and at your prompting.

If ever at some time Fortune grants me access to you all and to my 4 native land, I shall certainly ensure that you alone of all my friends will have cause for the greatest joy. I shall carry out my obligations and intentions, which I must admit have previously been far from evident, in such a way as to make you believe that I have been restored to you as much as to my brother and our children. Do pardon me if I have wronged you in any way, or rather because I have wronged you. Indeed, I have more harshly wronged myself. I do not write in ignorance of the fact that you have suffered most heart-felt grief at my misfortune. But certainly, if all the affection which you show and have shown ought to be and to have been my due, you would never have allowed me to forgo your extensive advice, nor to be persuaded that the enactment of the law on guilds* was advantageous for me. But you merely bestowed tears of affection at my distress, tears which I too shed. It was my fault, not yours, that you failed to devote days and nights to devising the necessary course of action such as could have been achieved by my meritorious conduct. If not merely you but anyone at all had discouraged me, when I was alarmed by Pompey's less than generous response,* from adopting a most shameful course of action (you alone could have done this), I should either have met my death with honour, or I should today be living flushed with victory. You must pardon me at this point. I am accusing myself much more than you, and you as my second self, because I also need an associate in my guilt. Then if I am restored, my guilt will appear to be of less account, and your affection for me will at any rate be manifest from your kindness to me, since there has been none to you from me.

You write that you have discussed with Culleo the law as applied 5 to an individual.* There is some point in this approach, but it is much better that the law be repealed, for if no one blocks it, this is a more secure course. But if some individual refuses to allow the measure to be passed, he will also veto a senatorial decree. There is no need for anything else to be repealed, for the earlier law did not affect me. If I had decided to speak in support of it when it was proposed, or to ignore it as it deserved, it could not have harmed me at all.

It was then that my strategy was first found wanting, and indeed blocked my progress. I was blind—I repeat, blind—when I put on mourning-garb* and appealed to the people, for this was a fatal step to take unless I had initially been cited by name in the proceedings. But I am harping on the past. My reason for this, however, is so that if the matter is raised, you should not advert to that law, for it contains many features dear to the popular party.

6   But it is the height of stupidity for me to prescribe what action you are all to take, or how you are to take it. If only something is done! Your letters cast a veil over this very possibility, because of your fear of inciting me to bitter desperation. For what do you visualize can be done, or how? Through the Senate, perhaps? But you yourself wrote to me that Clodius posted a clause of the law on the lintel of the senatorial chamber, forbidding any proposal or discussion concerning it. How then did Domitius* claim that he would propose a motion? And how was it that Clodius held his peace when the persons you mentioned both discussed the issue and demanded that a proposal be made? Or perhaps through the Assembly? If that is the plan, will it be possible if it does not have the support of all the plebeian tribunes? What of my possessions and my house?* Will they possibly be restored to me? If not, how then can I return? If you do not see a way to achieving that, what hope do you urge me to grasp? But if there is nothing to hope for, what sort of life is in store for me?

So here at Thessalonica I await the discussions of 1 August. Their outcome will make me decide whether to seek refuge on your estate* and thus avoid the persons I do not wish to see, and, as you write, to meet up with you, and thus be closer at hand on the off-chance of any development, as I gather both you and my brother Quintus favour, or retire to Cyzicus.

7   Pomponius, you applied none of your practical wisdom to ensure my immunity, either because you had decided that my own acumen was sufficient, or that you owed me nothing more than your availability. I was betrayed, deceived, subjected to treachery. I abandoned all my defences, I deserted and forsook the whole of Italy, which was admirably eager to protect me, and I consigned myself and my family to my enemies while you, less apprehensive than I but no more far-seeing, looked on and said not a word. So now you must do all you can to help me rise from my ruinous state and to assist me in my plight. But if every avenue is blocked, acquaint me with the fact,

and now at last cease to reproach me or to console me with vapid generalizations.

If I were indicting your loyalty, I should not entrust myself to your hospitable roof before all others. It is my own foolishness that I condemn for believing that your affection for me was as great as I could have wished. If it had been, you would have exercised the same degree of loyalty, but a greater sense of concern. You would at any rate have held me back* as I leapt headlong to my destruction, and you would not have had to undertake all the toil which you now shoulder because of my shipwreck.

Do be sure to investigate and nose out all developments, and com- 8 municate them to me. Now that I cannot be the person I was and could have been, be still willing to regard me as a person, as in fact you do. Do not let this letter give you the impression that I have been accusing you rather than myself. If there are any persons to whom you think letters should be sent under my name, be sure to write and ensure that they are sent to them.

17 August

Letter 31 *(Fam. XIV 1)*
Thessalonica/Dyrrhachium, November 58

TULLIUS TO HIS TERENTIA, HIS DEAR TULLIA, AND HIS CICERO

Your astonishing courage and bravery, Terentia, are recounted to 1 me in letters by many and in conversation by all. They say that no stress of mind or body exhausts you. How wretched I feel at having landed you in such great afflictions on my account, when you show such courage and loyalty, integrity and decency! And my dear Tullia too, for she used to derive such great pleasure from her father, whereas now he is the cause of such great distress to her. And what am I to say of our Cicero, who has experienced most bitter feelings of grief and unhappiness from the very dawn of his awareness? I could more readily accept this if I thought, as your letter puts it, that it was the work of fate. But all that has happened is my fault. I believed that I had the affection of men who were in fact jealous of me, and I did not attend to those who sought my friendship.

2   If only I had applied my own intelligence, and had not taken so seriously the assurances of those who were either foolish friends or knaves, I should be the happiest person alive. But since my friends now bid me live in hope, I shall ensure that my state of health does not undermine your efforts. I realize what a mammoth task it is for you, and how much easier it would have been to stay put at home rather than get back. However, if we have all the plebeian tribunes with us, and Lentulus* is as supportive as he seems to be, and indeed Pompey and Caesar as well, we need not despair.

3   As regards our domestics, I shall follow the advice of our friends as expressed in your letter. The epidemic has now vanished from this locality, and even while it persisted it did not affect me. Plancius* is most attentive. He is keen to have me with him, and keeps me here. My preference is to reside in some less frequented district of Epirus, unvisited by Piso or his soldiers,* but Plancius insists on my staying here awhile. His hope is that he may leave the province for Italy with me. If I see that day, and I am hugged in the embrace of all of you, and win back both you and my own person, I shall have gained a sufficiently great reward for both your devotion and mine.

4   Piso's generous, intrepid, and affectionate attentions* to all of us cannot possibly be bettered. I pray that this behaviour may be a source of pleasure to him. I envisage that it will certainly bring him esteem. As regards my brother Quintus, I was not being critical of you; I merely wanted all of you to become as close as possible, espe-
5 cially as you are so few. I have expressed my gratitude to those whom you wished me to thank, and I have written that you are the source of my information.

In your letter, dear Terentia, you say that you intend to sell a block of dwellings.* I feel wretched about this. Whatever is to be the outcome, I ask you? If this same misfortune continues to afflict me, what will become of our unhappy boy? I cannot set down the rest of my thoughts owing to a copious flood of tears, and I would not have you weep as well. I say only this: if our friends remain committed to us, money will not be lacking. If they do not, you will be unable to deploy your funds to good effect. I beg you, by the wretchedness of our fortunes, do ensure that we do not ruin our unfortunate boy. If he has enough means to ward off poverty, all he needs is a sufficiency of moral sense and of good fortune to achieve all else.

Look after yourself. Send couriers to me to keep me posted on 6
developments, and on the activities of all of you. The period of suspense is quite short for me now. Pass on my greetings to dear Tullia
and to Cicero. Goodbye to you all.

I have come to Dyrrhachium because it is a free city which affords 7
me help, and since it is closest to Italy. But if the crowds in the place
get on my nerves, I shall retire elsewhere, and write to you from
there.

Dyrrhachium, 25 November

4

RESTORATION AND RECANTATION (57–54 BC)

In July–August 57 the Senate (Clodius alone dissenting) and the Assembly (with the unanimous vote of the centuries) voted for the recall of Cicero. He returned in a mood of exhilaration to begin 'a second life', regaining immediate prominence by proposing a five-year command for Pompey to protect the corn-supply. Disillusionment rapidly set in, especially after the three dynasts renewed their informal alliance at Luca in 56. Pompey and Crassus became consuls for 55 and awarded themselves five-year commands thereafter; Caesar's command in Gaul was renewed for a further five years. Pompey, however, preferred to remain in Italy and to administer his Spanish province through legates. Tensions between him and the extreme optimates were exacerbated. Clodius, increasingly hostile to Pompey following his support for Cicero's restoration, sought to exploit these differences, and also to drive a wedge between Pompey and Crassus. Cicero kept his head down as far as possible, while sedulously promoting good relations with Pompey, and supporting his policies as the sole means of maintaining public order. He also developed cordial relations with Caesar through his brother Quintus, now on Caesar's staff. Caesar showed Marcus every possible courtesy.

Letter 32 (*Att.* IV 1)
Rome, September 57

CICERO TO ATTICUS

1 The moment I arrived in Rome and a courier was available to whom I could appropriately entrust a letter for you, I thought that the first thing I should do was to congratulate you, in your absence, on achieving my return. To tell the truth, I had become aware that you were no more courageous or wise in the counsels you offered to me than I was myself. Moreover, you were not excessively industrious in defence of my immunity, considering the attentive regard I had shown you. But after you shared in my mistake, or rather my madness,

in those early days, and you colluded with me in my unjustified fear,* you then felt our forced separation most bitterly, and you devoted most strenuous activity, zeal, care, and hard work to achieve my restoration.

So I truthfully vouch to you that, in this period of abounding joy 2 and thankfulness so eagerly desired, the one thing which was lacking to enhance my happiness was to have you before my eyes or to hold you in my embrace. When once I have attained this, if ever I relinquish it and fail to demand all the rewards of your charm which have passed me by during these past days, I shall certainly regard myself as insufficiently worthy of the restoration of my happiness.

At this stage in my political standing I have beyond my hopes 3 attained what I believed could be regained only with the greatest difficulty, namely my past prestige at the bar,* my influential position in the Senate, and my favour among the politicians of principle. But you are well aware how my domestic fortunes have been shattered, scattered, and plundered. So I am in dire straits, and to cope with them I need not so much your financial resources, which I regard as my own, as your counsels in assembling and ordering the remnants of them.

I imagine that all the details have been passed on to you by mem- 4 bers of your household, or reported to you as well by messengers or in common gossip. All the same, I shall now set down the facts briefly, for I presume that you wish to be informed of them particularly from my own hand.

I left Dyrrhachium on 4 August, the very day on which the law which named me was passed. I reached Brundisium on 5 August. My dear Tullia was there to meet me; it was actually also her birthday, and by a coincidence the anniversary of the foundation of Brundisium* as a colony, as well as that of the temple of Salus, your Roman neighbour.* The fact was noted by the large crowd of townsfolk of Brundisium, and was greeted with the liveliest celebrations. On 10(?) August, while I was still in Brundisium, I received a letter from my brother Quintus, reporting that the law had been passed in the Centuriate Assembly, amid scenes of remarkable enthusiasm evinced by one and all of all ages and ranks, with an astonishing number of Italians present. I then set out, attended by the most honorific praises of the Brundisians. Deputations flocked to me from all sides to offer their felicitations.

5　　When I reached Rome, there was no individual of any rank whose name was known to my attendant-slave* who did not come out to greet me, except for those personal enemies who could not conceal or deny the fact of their enmity. When I got to the Porta Capena,* the steps of the temples were thronged with the lowest members of society, who offered their congratulations with tumultuous applause. Similar crowds and similar applause attended me up to the Capitol. Both in the Forum and on the Capitol itself there was a surprisingly large gathering. Next day, 5 September, I expressed my thanks in the Senate.*

6　　During these two days the price of grain rose sky-high. Crowds of people assembled first at the theatre, and then at the Senate House. At Clodius' instigation, they shouted that the corn-shortage was my fault.* During those days there was a meeting of the Senate to discuss the corn-supply. Pompey was called on not merely by the common folk but also by honourable men to take responsibility for it. Pompey himself was eager to be entrusted with it, and the crowd called on me by name to propose it. This I did in carefully detailed words. With the exception of Messalla and Afranius, all men of consular rank had stayed away,* claiming that it was not safe for them to express their views. On my proposal, the Senate passed a decree that discussions be held with Pompey to invite him to undertake this task, and to formulate a law. When the senatorial decree was thereupon read out, the crowd greeted mention of my name with applause, following the new and tedious practice. I then addressed the Assembly, a task deputed to me by all the magistrates except one praetor and two tribunes.

7　　Next day the Senate was crowded. All the consulars were there, and Pompey was refused nothing he asked for. He demanded fifteen deputies, naming me at their head. He said that I would be his *alter ego* in all matters. The consuls drafted a law,* granting him total discretion over the corn-supply throughout the world for five years. Messius advanced a second proposal, giving Pompey control over all moneys, and in addition a fleet, an army, and authority in the provinces overriding that of governors. That consular law of ours now seems modest, whereas Messius' proposal is intolerable. Pompey himself says that he prefers the first, but his friends say he prefers the second. Consulars led by Favonius* are muttering. I am keeping quiet, all the more because the Pontiffs have not yet formulated a response concerning my house. If they remove the religious impediment,* I have an outstanding site. In accord with the senatorial decree, the consuls will estimate the value of the building. Alternatively, they will demolish the temple, issue a contract in their name and assess the entire value.

So this is how things are with me,   8

> Unstable in prosperity, but in ill-fortune steady.*

As you know, my domestic finances are in chaos. Then too there are certain family matters,* which I refuse to commit to paper. I tender due affection to my brother Quintus, whose fraternal devotion, courage, and loyalty are outstanding. I await your coming, and beg you to hasten it, to arrive with the intention of not permitting me to forgo your advice. I am embarking on a sort of second life. Some of the men who championed me when I was absent are already beginning to feel covert irritation and to show open jealousy, now that I am present. I am in sore need of you.

Letter 33 (*Att.* IV 3)
Rome, November 57
CICERO TO ATTICUS

I have no doubt that you are keen to hear of developments here, and   1
to get to know of them from myself—not that what goes on before everyone's eyes is more reliably reported by me than by the written or verbal accounts of others. But I should like you to observe from my letter my attitude towards these developments, and my state of mind and the general tenor of my life at this time.

On 3 November the workmen were hustled from my building-site   2
by armed men. The colonnade of Catulus,* which was being restored under contract issued by the consuls in accordance with the senatorial decree, and had almost risen to the roof, was demolished. The house of my brother Quintus was first shattered by a volley of stones directed from my site, and then ignited by firebrands hurled on the orders of Clodius before the eyes of the city. This roused loud complaints and wailing from—I won't say the men of principle, for I doubt if any exist, but from the whole population. Even before this occurred, Clodius was rushing around in a frenzy, but following this

act of madness he contemplates nothing but the slaughter of his personal enemies. He roams round the streets and openly offers slaves the hope of their freedom. Earlier, when he set his face against a trial, he had some sort of case, however hard and clearly bogus it was to defend. He could have denied the charges, or put the blame on others, or even argued that he had acted in some sense lawfully. But following these episodes of destruction, arson, and pillage, he has been abandoned by his followers, and has scarcely retained the support of the mummer Decius, or of Gellius.* He follows the advice of slaves, He considers that if he openly kills all his chosen victims, his lawsuit when it comes to court will be no more difficult than it is at present.

3   So it was that, as I was walking down the Via Sacra on 11 November, he and his followers pursued me. There was shouting and stone-throwing and brandishing of cudgels and swords, all quite unexpected. I stepped aside into the courtyard of Tettius Damio.* Those who were with me easily prevented his hirelings from forcing their way in. Clodius himself could have been killed, but I am beginning to seek a cure with medicines, for I am wearying of surgery. Once he realized that he was being hustled by the universal outcry not to judicial trial, but to peremptory execution, he subsequently made every Catiline a man like Acidinus!* Why, on 12 November he tried to storm Milo's house and to set fire to it; it stands in the Cermalus.* In fact, in broad daylight an hour before midday he led out some men with drawn swords and shields, and others with lighted firebrands. He himself had taken over the house of Publius Sulla* as his base, from which to launch that attack. Then Quintus Flaccus led out his eager followers from the house which Milo inherited* from Annius, and slew the most notorious members of Clodius' gang of bandits. Flaccus was keen to dispatch Clodius, but he was holed up deep within Sulla's house.

When the Senate met the next day, 14 November, Clodius stayed at home. Marcellinus* was quite outstanding, and all present were on their toes. But Metellus* talked out time with ill-founded objections. He was assisted by Appius* and also (for heaven's sake!) by your friend,* whose resolute life you describe most accurately. Sestius* was livid. Clodius later laid threats against the city, should his election not take place.* The motion of Marcellinus had been posted. He had written it out before delivering it, and in it he proposed that the trial should incorporate all the incidents which involved me—the building-site, the arson, the danger to my person—and that the entire proceedings should take place before the elections. Then Milo posted a statement that he would be observing the sky for ill omens throughout the days of the elections.

A series of speeches to the citizens followed, that of Metellus pro-   4 voking disturbances, Appius speaking recklessly, and Clodius totally uncontrolled. The outcome in short was that the elections would be held unless Milo reported hostile omens in the Campus Martius.

Just before midnight on 18 November Milo appeared on the Campus Martius with a huge band. Clodius did not dare to make for the Campus in spite of having his picked body of runaway slaves. Milo remained there until midday to the astonished jubilation of the citizens, winning the greatest esteem. The aggression of the three brethren* became a humiliation, their strength broken, and their wild rampaging despised. Metellus however challenged Milo to announce the impediment of omens to him next day in the Forum. There was no need, he said, to go to the Campus Martius before daylight. He himself would be at the Comitium* at dawn next day.

Accordingly, Metellus made his way to the Comitium just before dawn on 20 November. As he hastened stealthily towards the Campus at first light by a circuitous route, Milo caught up with him between the groves and reported an impediment. Metellus retired, followed by loud and vulgar abuse from Quintus Flaccus, The 21st was market day, so for two days there have been no public assemblies.

I write this account on 22 November in the ninth hour of the   5 night. Milo is already in possession of the Campus. Marcellus, who is up for election, is snoring* so loudly that I can hear him from next door. I am informed that Clodius' entrance-hall is quite deserted; there are just a few ragamuffins without a lantern. His supporters complain that I have arranged it all; they are unaware of the fierce spirit and extensive planning of our hero Milo, whose courage is astonishing. I refrain from mentioning some of his inspired actions of late, but the upshot of them is this. I believe that there will be no elections, and I think that Publius will be indicted by Milo unless he is killed first. If he confronts Milo in a mêlée, I envisage that Milo will kill him with his own hands, for he has no hesitation about doing it, and boasts about it. He has no fear of the fate which befell me, for he has never any intention of following the advice of any jealous or treacherous individual, and of putting his trust in the slothful nobility.

6   As for myself, in mind at least I am flourishing even more than in my prosperous days, but my finances are low. However, with the assistance of friends and in spite of my brother Quintus' protests, I am repaying his generosity in so far as my resources permit without completely bankrupting myself. In your absence I do not know what strategy I am to adopt, so far as my general position is concerned. So do hurry here.

Letter 34 *(Fam. I 2)*

Rome, January 56

MARCUS CICERO TO THE PROCONSUL LENTULUS

1   On 13 January no business was completed in the Senate, because the day was largely spent on a squabble between the consul Lentulus and the plebeian tribune Caninius.* I too spoke at some length that day, and I seemed to make the deepest impression on the Senate by recounting your support for the order. So next day I decided to curtail my proposals, for it was apparent that I had won over the favour of the Senate, since this had become clear to me both in the course of my speech and in my pleas and requests to individuals. What happened was that Bibulus put forward the first proposal, that the restoration of the king should be entrusted to three legates, Hortensius the second, that you should restore him without the backing of an army, and Volcacius the third, that Pompey should restore him. There was a demand that Bibulus' proposal should be subdivided. He obtained agreement for his statement on the religious question,* since there could now be no opposition to this point. But the great majority voted against the commission of three.

2   The motion of Hortensius came next, but then the plebeian tribune Lupus* began to argue that he should have precedence over the consuls in calling for a vote, on the grounds that he had made the proposal about Pompey earlier. His speech aroused fierce opposition from all, for it was both unjust and unprecedented. The consuls neither yielded to his point nor strongly opposed it. They wanted the day to be spent without reaching a decision, which was what happened, for they realized that the great majority would vote for

Hortensius' motion, though many were being openly canvassed to
support Volcacius, for they had wanted the motion of Bibulus to
prevail. The disagreement was prolonged until nightfall, when the
Senate was discharged.

It happened that on that date Pompey was my host for dinner, 3
and this gave me a better opportunity than ever before, because
this had been the most favourable day in the Senate since your
departure. I chatted with him to such good effect that to all seeming
I diverted his mind away from all other considerations towards
safeguarding your high standing. When I listen to him, I exonerate
him totally from all suspicion of selfish ambition, but when I survey
his friends of all classes, I note what is now obvious to all, that
this entire business has for long been unscrupulously exploited by
certain individuals with the complicity of the king* himself and his
counsellors.

I write this letter before dawn on 15 January, the day on which the 4
Senate is to meet. My hope is that I shall maintain my high status in
that body, as far as is possible in such an atmosphere of bad faith and
unfairness. So far as consideration of the commons is concerned, we
seem to have ensured that no debate is possible in that Assembly
without violation of the auspices or the laws, in short without violence. Yesterday a most impressive recommendation* of the Senate
was passed on this subject. Though Cato* and Caninius interposed
their veto, it was none the less recorded. I think a copy has been sent
to you. I shall inform you by letter about other developments, and
I shall deploy all my care, activity, application, and influence to
ensure that things are conducted as appropriately as possible.

Letter 35 (*Q. fr.* II 3)
Rome, February 56

MARCUS TO HIS BROTHER QUINTUS

My previous letter acquainted you with the earlier detail; now hear 1
what happened next. On 1 February the business of the embassies
was postponed till 13 February, so no decision was reached on that
day. On 2 February Milo attended;* Pompey was there and spoke on
his behalf. At my request Marcus Marcellinus spoke. We emerged
with credit; the case was adjourned till 7 February.

Meanwhile the business of the embassies was postponed until 13 February, and there was discussion of the quaestors to be assigned to provinces, and of allowances to praetors. But no decisions were taken, because the business was interrupted by many complaints about the political situation. Gaius Cato proposed a law to recall Lentulus* from his province, and Lentulus' son put on mourning-clothes.

2   Milo appeared to face the charge on 7 February, and Pompey spoke, or rather, tried to speak, for as soon as he rose, Clodius' rowdies* began their uproar, and this continued throughout his speech, so that he was interrupted not merely by the shouting but also by insults and abuse. At his final words (for he continued quite courageously throughout without being put off, and he completed his speech, even achieving silence at times, when his authority prevailed), as I say, at his final words Clodius rose to his feet amid such uproar from our benches (for we had decided to return the compliment) that he could not control his thoughts, words, or features. This performance continued from midday, the time when Pompey had barely reached his close, till two hours later. Every possible insult, and in the end some highly obscene verses, were directed at Clodius and Claudia. He grew wild with rage, and was pale as a ghost. While the uproar continued, he began to question his followers: 'Who is starving the people to death?' 'Pompey,' the rowdies replied. 'Who is itching to go to Alexandria?' 'Pompey,' they answered. And who would they prefer to go? 'Crassus,' they replied.* (Crassus was present at the time, supporting Milo, though not favourably disposed to him.) About three hours after midday, as though at a given signal, Clodius' supporters began spitting at our people. Resentment flared. They tried to dislodge us from our seats, and our supporters launched an attack on them. The rowdies fled. Clodius was ejected from the dais, and I too then made off, fearing some violence in the mêlée. The Senate was then summoned to the Senate House. Pompey went home, and I did not attend it, for I had no inclination to hold my tongue about such outrageous proceedings nor to alienate the men of principle* by defending Pompey, who was being criticized by Bibulus, Curio, Favonius, and Servilius Junior. The debate was adjourned until the next day. Clodius then had the trial put off until the Quirinalia.*

3   On 8 February the Senate met in the temple of Apollo to allow Pompey to attend.* He spoke with high seriousness. No decision was

reached that day. On 9 February the Senate met in the temple of Apollo. A decree of the Senate was passed to the effect that the proceedings of 7 February had been against the interests of the state. That day Cato made an impassioned attack on Pompey, in which from beginning to end he spoke like a prosecuting counsel addressing a defendant. He made many complimentary references to me, which I did not appreciate and in which he denounced Pompey's treachery towards me. He was heard in profound silence by those who are ill-disposed to me. Pompey made a vigorous reply, with allusions to Crassus. He openly stated that he would take greater precautions to protect his life than Africanus did when he was murdered by Gaius Carbo.*

So it seems to me that important developments are in train. 4 Pompey is certainly aware of this, and he gives me to understand that there is a plot to kill him, that Gaius Cato is being backed by Crassus who is supplying Clodius with money, and that both Cato and Clodius have the support of Crassus, Curio, Bibulus, and his (Pompey's) other detractors. He says that he must take the most stringent precautions against being brought down, since those who attend the citizen-assemblies are virtually all against him, the nobility is hostile, the Senate is unfavourable, and the young men are unprincipled. So he is making preparations and summoning men in from country districts. Clodius for his part is reinforcing his rowdies, and assembling a force ready for the Quirinalia. With that occasion in mind, we are much the stronger with the forces of Milo alone, but we are awaiting a huge band from Picenum and Gaul to enable us further to confront the motions proposed by Cato concerning Milo and Lentulus.

On 10 February Sestius* was indicted for bribery by an informer, 5 Gnaeus Nerius of the Papinian tribe, and on the same day for violence by a certain Marcus Tullius. Sestius was ill, so I did my duty and immediately visited him at home, putting myself wholly at his disposal. This gesture of mine was contrary to public expectation, for people believed that I had genuine grievances against him. So I appear both to him and to the world at large as the kindest and most appreciative of men, and that is how I shall act in future. The informer Nerius has also cited two witnesses bound by oath, Gnaeus Lentulus Vatia and Gaius Cornelius of the Stellatinan tribe. The same day the Senate issued a decree that societies and clubs should be disbanded,* and that a law should be passed specifying that those who did not disband them should be subject to the same penalty as those indicted for violence.

6   On 11 February I defended Bestia,* who was charged with bribery. The trial was held before the praetor Gnaeus Domitius in the middle of the Forum, before a huge gathering. In my speech I hit upon the occasion when Sestius sustained several wounds in the temple of Castor, and his life was saved through assistance rendered by Bestia. This provided me with a *bonne occasion de préparer* the defence of Sestius against charges laid against him. I lauded him with praises from the heart; they were received by one and all with great approval. The gesture was profoundly welcome to Sestius. I tell you this because you have often in your letters counselled me to keep in Sestius' good books.

7   I write this before dawn on 12 February. Today I am to dine with Pomponius on the occasion of his wedding.* All else in my affairs is as you assured me when I was close to despair; my prestige and influence have been restored to us both in full measure, thanks to your endurance, courage, devotion, and also your genial character.

A house called 'Licinian' has been rented for you at Piso's Lake,* but I hope that you will move into your own in a few months' time, after the beginning of July. The Lamiae have rented your house in the Carinae; they are tidy tenants.

I have received no letter from you since the one from Olbia. I am keen to know of your activities and your diversions. Above all, I wish to lay eyes on you as soon as possible. Look after yourself, dear brother, and remember that though it is winter, you are living in Sardinia.*

15 February

Letter 36 (*Q. fr.* II 5)

Rome, March 56

MARCUS TO HIS BROTHER QUINTUS

1   . . . as for the *richesses* which you keep mentioning, I am quite keen to have them in a restrained way, that is, to welcome them gladly if they come my way, but without digging them out if they continue

to lie low. I am building in three places,* and refurbishing the rest. My standard of living is necessarily a little more opulent than it used to be. If you were with me, you would have to give place to the workmen for a time. But we shall soon, I hope, be together to discuss these amongst other things.

Affairs in Rome stand like this. Lentulus * makes an outstanding 2 consul, and his colleague does not interfere. The consul, I repeat, is so good that I have not seen a better. He has eliminated all the days for public assemblies, for even the Latin festival is being repeated, and there is no lack of formal thanksgivings. Thus the most 3 destructive bills are being blocked, in particular those of Cato, who has been the victim of a splendid deception by our friend Milo. As patron of gladiators and of those who grapple with wild beasts,* Cato had purchased from Cosconius and Pomponius some of those who battle with beasts, and he never appeared in public without them as armed escorts. He was unable to feed them, and so could hardly keep control of them. Milo got wind of this, and commissioned some outsider to buy the troupe from Cato without raising suspicions. Scarcely had they been taken over when Racilius, the only plebeian tribune worth his salt at present, exposed the situation, saying that he had bought the men for his own use. (This was the prior arrangement.) He then published an advertisement, announcing that he intended to sell Cato's troupe. This has caused great amusement.

So Lentulus has debarred this Cato from proposing laws, and others too who have published outrageous bills concerning Caesar,* with no one vetoing them. The measure which Caninius advocated* concerning Pompey has gone cold, for the proposal itself wins no support, and our friend Pompey's close association with Publius Lentulus* is being criticized. He is certainly not the dominant figure he was. He has alienated the most depraved and down-at-heel dregs of society because of his connection with Milo, and the men of principle find in him much to be desired, and much that is blameworthy. My one complaint about Marcellinus is that he is too waspish towards Pompey, though the Senate does not object to this attitude of his. For this reason I am the more gladly withdrawing from the Senate and from every aspect of public affairs.

My standing in the courts is as high as it was. My house is as 4 thronged as when I was at my peak. Milo's thoughtlessness has

caused one unfortunate circumstance which concerns Sextus Cloelius.*
I opposed his being indicted, for this was not the moment, and the
prosecutors were incompetent. At the hands of that heinous
jury-panel Milo fell short by three votes. So the citizens demand a
fresh trial, and he must be dragged back to court. People refuse to
accept his acquittal, and since he was close to being convicted when
pleading before his own associates, they regard him as found guilty.
In this actual case what has impeded us is Pompey's unpopularity;
the senators acquitted Cloelius by a huge majority, the *equites* were
evenly divided, and the *tribuni aerarii** found him guilty. However,
as consolation for this reverse, there are daily condemnations of our
enemies, among whom to my delight Sevius* has run aground, while
the rest have had their timbers shattered. Gaius Cato in an address
to the citizens has stated that he will not allow the elections to proceed if the days for proposing bills are denied to him. Appius has not
yet returned from his meeting with Caesar.*

5　　I await a letter from you with avid anticipation. I know that the sea
is as yet closed to ships, but people say that some travellers have
reached Ostia who are praising you to the skies, and speak of your
exceptional prestige in the province.* They are also said to report
that you will cross by the first sailing. I am longing for this, but
though I look forward above all to your arrival, I also await a letter
from you first. Farewell, dear brother.

Letter 37　(*Q. fr.* II 6)

Rome / en route to Anagnia, April 56

MARCUS TO HIS BROTHER QUINTUS

1　Earlier I sent you a letter with the information that our Tullia was
betrothed on 4 April to Crassipes.* I also penned the rest of the
news, both public and private. Here are the details of subsequent
events. On 5 April a senatorial decree allocated some forty million
sesterces to Pompey for the grain project. But on the same day
there was a heated discussion on the issue of land in Campania. The
shouting in the Senate almost rivalled that at a public meeting.

2　The shortage of revenue* and the high price of corn made the issue
more bitter. I shall not leave unmentioned the news that the officials

of the Capitoline Games and of the Corporation of Merchants expelled Marcus Furius Flaccus, a Roman knight of dissolute character, in spite of his presence there grovelling at the feet of all and sundry.

On 6 April I laid on a betrothal dinner for Crassipes. Quintus, that splendid boy* of yours and mine, missed the banquet because of a minor upset. I visited Quintus on 8 April, and found him fully restored. He had a long and civilized chat with me about the dissensions between our womenfolk.* In short, it was a most amusing session. Pomponia was complaining about you as well. But we can discuss these matters when we meet.

After parting from the boy I visited your site.* The work proceeds, with many builders. I spoke words of encouragement to the contractor Longidius, who assured me of his desire to give us every satisfaction. The house will be superb; one can now visualize it better than inferences from the plan. My own house too is rising quickly.

That same day I dined at the house of Crassipes. After dinner I was borne on a litter to Pompey at his residence* (I was unable to meet him during daylight, because he was away). I was keen to see him, as I intended to leave Rome next day, and because he is setting out to Sardinia. I got together with him, and asked him to send you back to me with all speed. He said he would do this at once. He intends to leave, he says, on 11 April, planning to embark at Salebro or at Pisae. So, dear brother, do not neglect to make the first crossing as soon as he arrives, provided that the weather is auspicious.

I dictated this part of the letter before dawn on 9 April, and I am writing the rest en route. I intend to lodge at the house of Titus Titius at Anagnia today, and am contemplating staying at Laterium tomorrow. After that I shall stay two days at my place at Arpinum, and then proceed to my house at Pompeii. On my way back I intend to look in on my dwelling at Cumae, and to be back in Rome on 6 May, because Milo's trial is announced for the 7th. I hope, fondest and sweetest brother, to set eyes on you that day. I have decided to delay the building at Arcanum until you arrive. Look after yourself, dear brother, and come as soon as you can.

Letter 38 (*Q. fr.* II 8)

Rome, February 55

MARCUS TO HIS BROTHER QUINTUS

1 I suspected that you would enjoy the second book,* and I am extremely pleased that you like it so very much, as your letter says. As for your admonition about *l'indifférence*,* and your urging me to recall the speech of Jupiter at the close of the book, I do recall it; indeed I wrote the whole passage for myself rather than for anyone else.

2   However, the day after you departed I visited Pompey late at night in company with Vibullius.* After I had discussed with him those buildings of yours and the inscriptions, his most genial response gave me high hopes, He said that he wanted to have a word with Crassus, and he urged me to do likewise. I escorted consul Crassus* back home from the Senate. He took up the issue, and said that there was something Clodius wished to attain at this time through Pompey and himself. He believed that if I did not stand in Clodius' way, I could get what I wanted without any dispute. I left the business entirely to him, and said that I would be guided by him. Young Publius Crassus was present at the conversation; he is, as you know, a great fan of mine. What Clodius is keen to get is an embassy, to be obtained at public expense through the Assembly if not through the Senate, to either Byzantium or Brogitarus* or both. It is a huge money-spinner for him, to which I do not object too much, even if I fail to get what I want. But Pompey has had a word with Crassus, and it seems that they have the business in hand. If they see it through, well and good; if not, we must have recourse to our Jupiter.

3   On 11 February a senatorial decree was passed about bribery on a motion of Afranius. I myself had proposed the measure when you were here. But there were loud expressions of regret in the Senate when the consuls did not forward the proposals of certain senators who, in agreement with Afranius, had added a rider that praetors after their election should remain private citizens for sixty days.* That day they openly rejected Cato.* Enough said. They have total power, and they want the world to know it.

Letter 39 *(Fam.* I 8)

Rome, February 55

CICERO TO THE PROCONSUL PUBLIUS LENTULUS

In all matters that affect you—the discussions, the decisions, 1
Pompey's undertakings—you will be thoroughly briefed by Marcus
Plaetorius.* for he is not merely a participant, but also the guiding
light in them. He has not neglected any obligation towards you
which was appropriate for one who is most affectionate, wise, and
conscientious. He will also acquaint you with the political situation
generally, the nature of which is not easy to set down in writing. It is
certainly subject to the control of our friends,* and to such a degree
that no change seems likely to occur during the lifetime of our
contemporaries.

For myself, I adopt that necessary course of action which you have 2
enjoined on me, and which my sense of duty and practical interests
demand. So I align myself with the politics of the man to whom you
have believed you should be aligned in the strategy which I have
adopted. But you are not unaware of the difficulty involved in abandoning political attitudes which are notably upright and proven.
None the less, I fall in with the intentions of the man with whom
I cannot honourably disagree. In taking this course, I am not being
hypocritical, as some may perhaps think. My attitude and indeed my
affection towards Pompey so dominate my mind that his interests
and aspirations all seem now to be both right and genuine. To my
thinking, even his opponents would not be misguided if they abandoned their opposition to him, since they cannot be a match for him.

What further consoles me is the fact that the world at large would 3
emphatically allow that my status justifies me in being an apologist
for Pompey's aims, or alternatively in lying low, or even in satisfying
my fondest desire to return to my literary pursuits.* This last I shall
certainly do if my friendship with Pompey allows it. The reason for
my saying this is that after I had discharged the most distinguished
offices, and had performed the most taxing labours, I have been
wholly deprived of my prospective role, namely, authoritative
expression of my views, and freedom to participate in political life.
This loss affects not only myself, but all of us. We must either lose

prestige in acceding to the policies of the few, or vainly disagree with them.

4   I communicate this to you above all so that you too can ponder your own course of action. All the processes of Senate, law courts, and the entire mode of politics have changed. What we are to aspire to is a life of leisure, which those who hold the reins of power seem willing to grant us, so long as certain individuals are able to show greater passivity* and to submit to their control. There is no point in aspiring to the lofty consular prestige of the courageous and resolute senator, for this has been lost through the fault of those who deprived the Senate of the allegiance of the most closely associated order, and of the most celebrated individual.*

5   But to hark back to issues more closely relevant to your affairs, I know that Pompey is extremely well disposed towards you. So far as I can see, you will during his consulship obtain all your wishes. He will have me as his close associate in these matters, and I shall not disregard anything in your interest. I have no fear that he will regard me as a nuisance, for he will be pleased also on his own behalf when he sees that I am grateful to him.

6   So please assure yourself that there is not the slightest concern of yours which is not closer to my heart than all my own interests combined. Since such are my sentiments, I could never take sufficient pains to do myself justice, nor can I obtain sufficient satisfaction in the outcome, for I am unable to achieve anything which you deserve, not merely in repaying your favours, but even in contemplating them.

7   Rumour has it that you have waged an extremely successful campaign.* I await the dispatch from you which I have already been discussing with Pompey. Once it arrives, my zealous support will be evident in my canvassing magistrates and senators. So far as your other interests are concerned, though my undertakings will transcend my abilities, my successes will fall short of my obligations.

Letter 40 (*Fam.* V 12)
?Cumae, April 55

MARCUS CICERO TO LUCIUS LUCCEIUS, SON OF QUINTUS

1   I have often tried to discuss with you face to face the subject I am now raising, but a sort of sheepishness, virtually bucolic, has deterred me.

Now that I am away from you, I shall detail it more brazenly, for a letter does not blush. I am consumed with a longing beyond belief, but not, I think, deserving of blame, to have my name lent lustre and distinction by your pen. Though you have often assured me that you will undertake this, do please excuse my urgency, for though I have always eagerly anticipated reading your works, their quality has transcended my expectation. I am so charmed, so fired by them that I long to have my achievements entrusted with all speed to your writings. It is not merely recollection by posterity and a certain hope of immortality which draws me on, but also my desire while still alive to seek enjoyment from the authority of your testimony, your kindly assessment, and the attractive nature of your talent.

I am not unaware, as I write this letter, of the massive burdens of 2 works undertaken and already begun with which you are weighed down. But I note that you have already completed your history of the Italian and Civil Wars,* and you have informed me that you are embarking upon the subsequent events. So I was unwilling to forgo the opportunity of suggesting to you that you contemplate whether you prefer to interweave my history with the other contemporary events, or to do what many Greeks have done, for example Callisthenes on the Phocian War, Timaeus on the war with Pyrrhus, and Polybius* on the Numantine War, for they all separated from their continuous histories the wars which I have mentioned. So you likewise may prefer to detach the civic conspiracy from the external wars fought against enemies. For myself, I do not see that it makes much difference as regards my renown; my desire for haste, however, makes it preferable that you do not await its due place chronologically, but rather that you proceed immediately to get your teeth into the entire episode and crisis. Moreover, if your mind concentrates entirely on the one theme and the one character,* I can already visualize the entire presentation being more expansive and more highly embellished.

However, I am not unaware of my shameless attitude, first of all in my imposing such a great burden on you (indeed, your commitments may cause you to turn me down), and secondly in my asking you to feature me favourably (for what if my achievements fail to strike you as especially praiseworthy?). But once a man has transgressed the 3 bounds of humility, he must be well and truly shameless. So I am asking you openly and repeatedly both to laud my achievements more emphatically even than you perhaps feel, and in so doing to ignore the laws of history.* Do not despise that partiality (if it gains for me more enthusiastic approval in your eyes) about which you write most engagingly in one of your prefaces. There you demonstrate that you could no more be seduced by it than was Xenophon's Hercules* by Pleasure. Be indulgent towards the affection between us, somewhat more even than the truth will allow. Should I induce you to undertake this project, I flatter myself that the subject matter 4 will be worthy of your fluent and eloquent powers. I visualize that a work of moderate size can cover the period from the beginning of the conspiracy to my return from exile. In it you will also be able to exploit your knowledge of changes in the body politic, whether in explaining the causes of the revolution or in expounding solutions for the setbacks. In outlining your reasoning you will both criticize the aspects which you think blameworthy, and express appreciation of those of which you approve. If you follow your usual practice, and believe that you must treat issues more broadly, you will censure the treachery, plotting, and betrayal* of many against me. In addition, my fortunes will afford you a wide variety in your composition, providing abundant pleasure, which can strongly engage the minds of those who read of them in your account. Nothing is more conducive to a reader's pleasure than changes of circumstance and vicissitudes of fortune, for though I found them an unwelcome experience, they will provide enjoyment when read. Recollection of past travails from a safe distance in time is a source of delight.

5 When others have sustained no personal troubles and they contemplate without personal pain the sufferings of others, even a feeling of pity is pleasurable. Which of us does not feel enjoyment mingled with a kind of pity at the death of the famous Epaminondas at Mantinea?* Only finally, when in response to his query he was told that his shield was safe, did he order the javelin to be plucked from his body. Thus even when suffering the pain of his wound, he could meet a praiseworthy death with untroubled mind. Whose enthusiasm is not awakened and held when one reads of Themistocles' exile and return?* Whereas the sequence of historical events exercises only the minor attraction of a calendar-list, the uncertain and varied fortunes of a man who is often outstanding awaken admiration and anticipation, joy and irritation, hope and fear; and if they conclude

with a noteworthy outcome, our minds are sated with the most agreeable pleasure in reading them.

So I shall regard it as preferable if from your continuous narrative, 6 in which you embrace an unbroken history of events, you decide to detach this drama, so to say, of my achievements and experiences. For the drama incorporates different acts, with many changes of both plans and circumstances. I am not afraid to appear to be angling for your favour by a show of modest flattery when I mention that I wish to be lauded and famed by you above all. You are not the type to be oblivious of your standing and you do not fail to regard non-admirers of yours as jealous rather than those who praise you as toadies. I for my part am not so lunatic as to seek to be glorified for eternal fame by one who in recommending me does not himself obtain the fame appropriate to his own genius.

After all, the famous Alexander did not wish to be painted by 7 Apelles and sculpted by Lysippus* above all merely to flatter them; he believed that their skill would be a source of fame both for them and for himself. These craftsmen made representations of persons familiar to men who did not know them. Even if their portrayals did not exist, men of great fame would not be any the less celebrated. The Spartan Agesilaus is no less worthy of note for refusing to have any painted or sculpted representation of himself than are those who were assiduous in seeking such images. The, one brief account by Xenophon,* in his praise of that king, has easily overshadowed all paintings and statues of all artists who ever existed.

If I make my way into your writings rather than into those of all others, that will be a further enhancement of my gratification and of the esteem of my memory. This will be conferred on me not only by your genius, like that of Timaeus upon Timoleon or that of Herodotus upon Themistocles,* but also by your authority as a most famous and highly respected figure, a man recognized and notably proven in the greatest and most momentous affairs of state. As a result, there may be bestowed on me not merely a proclamation of praise such as Alexander on visiting Sigeum* said had been bestowed by Homer on Achilles, but also the weighty attestation of a famous and important man. I am attracted by the words of the celebrated Hector in the play of Naevius,* when he exults not merely in being praised, but adds, 'By a person who is himself praised'.

8   But if you do not accede to my request, in other words, if some circumstance prevents it (for it would not be morally right in my view to fail to obtain any request I make of you), I shall perhaps be compelled to do what a number of people often censure: namely to write a personal account about myself. True, this would be following in the footsteps of many famous men, but it does not escape your notice that there are defects in this genre of writing. Those who write about themselves must necessarily be more modest in handling praiseworthy achievements, and must pass over any actions deserving of condemnation. Again, their reliability and authority are diminished. In short, many criticize them, claiming that heralds at athletic contests* show more modesty; for after crowning victors and loudly announcing their names, when they themselves are crowned prior to closure of the games, they make way for another herald, to avoid proclaiming their own victories.

9   I am anxious to avoid this, and if you accede to my plea, I shall avoid it. Hence my request that you take on the task. Perhaps you are surprised that though you have often indicated to me that you will most scrupulously assign to the written word the policies and outcomes of my times, I now beg you so earnestly and at such length to do this. But what fires this is my eagerness for haste, about which I wrote earlier. I am desirous both that your books make me known to the rest of the world during my lifetime, and that I myself may enjoy my modest fame while I live.

10   So please reply to me about your intention in this matter, if this is not burdensome to you. If you accede to my request, I shall put the final touches to my diary about all the events, but if you postpone my request to you to a later time, I shall discuss the matter with you. In the meantime, do not relax. Put the final touches to the work you have in hand, and keep me in your affections.

Letter 41 (*Att.* IV 6)

Cumae, April 55

CICERO TO ATTICUS

1   As regards Lentulus,* I bear the blow as I ought. We have lost a good and great man, whose outstanding nobility of mind was softened by his abundant graciousness. It is a poor consolation I feel, but it is

none the less some consolation that my grief on his behalf is the slightest. My reaction is not like that of Saufeius* and of those of your school, but I swear that his patriotism was such that it seems to me a sort of divine beneficence that he has been delivered from his country's conflagration. For what could be more degrading than the life we lead, and especially my own? Whereas you, by nature *un homme politique*, share in the general servitude but without personal slavery. I myself am considered as a lunatic if I comment on the political situation as I should, as a slave if I am constrained to say what I do say, and as a prisoner in subjection if I remain silent. So what depression should I be experiencing? Doubtless that which I now feel, and one even more excruciating, because I cannot even grieve for fear of seeming ungrateful to you. Should I perhaps opt to abandon the fray, and seek refuge in the harbour of retirement? By no means; I must go to war, and enlist in the army. So shall I serve as a *simple soldat*, having refused to be a commandant? Yes, that is what I must do, for I see that this is what you recommend. If only I had always followed your advice! All that remains is 'Sparta is your allotted portion; you must adorn it.'* But, heavens, that I cannot do. I absolve Philoxenus* for preferring to be escorted back to gaol. However, I am reasoning with myself in this part of the world to approve the course which you advance, and once we meet you will reinforce this advice.

I note that you have been writing often to me, but I have received all the letters at one time. This further deepened my depression, for I happened to read first the three in which it was mentioned that Lentulus was improving somewhat. But then the fourth letter— what a thunderbolt! But as I wrote earlier, he is out of his misery, and I am steeling myself.

As for your advice that I write the Hortensius treatise,* I have become involved with other works; not that I disregarded your instruction. But heaven help me, just when I was beginning it, I ducked out, afraid that having appeared to have stupidly tolerated my friend's outrageous behaviour, I should again draw glaring attention to his unfair attack in whatever I wrote. I also feared that my *gravité*, so obvious in the spoken word, might lie more hidden in my writing, and that my apologia might appear to contain an element of jocularity. But we shall see. Just write to me as often as is feasible. Be sure to extract from Lucceius the letter I sent him,* a handsome effort in which I asked him to pen the history of my affairs.

Encourage him to hurry on with it, and thank him for his reply to me promising to oblige. Keep an eye on our house as best you can, and give a nod to Vestorius, who is being very generous to me.

Letter 42 (*Att.* IV 9)
Naples, April 55

CICERO TO ATTICUS

1 I should very much like to know whether the tribunes are delaying the census* by invalidating the days, as the local gossip here has it, and what action they are taking and planning about the censorship generally. I have been in Pompey's company here. In conversation with me he had much to say on politics. He is not at all pleased with himself (so he said—this has to be added when we talk of him). He was dismissive of Syria, and jettisoned Spain*—again, so he said. In my view, whenever we mention him we must add, 'This too is according to Phocylides.'* He also expresses his thanks to you for undertaking the arrangement of his statues, and indeed he has been most effusively charming to me as well. He has also visited me at my place at Cumae on the 25th. There is nothing which he seemed to want less than that Messalla* should be a candidate for the consulship. If you have any news about this, I should like to have it.

2 I am grateful for the promise in your letter that you will recommend to Lucceius the theme of my fame, and also for your keeping an eye frequently on our house. My brother Quintus has written to me to say that since you have that most charming young Cicero* staying with you, he will visit you on 7 May. I left my place at Cumae on 26 April, and lodged with Paetus* that day at Naples. I write this letter very early on 27 April, and am on the point of leaving for my place at Pompeii.

Letter 43 (*Fam.* VII 1)
Rome, September 55

CICERO TO MARCUS MARIUS

1 If some physical discomfort or your ill-health has prevented you from attending the theatrical performances,* I attribute this to Fortune, and not to your good judgement. But if you considered as

contemptible these shows which the rest of the world admires, and you refused to come though your state of health permitted it, I am delighted both because you are free from physical ailments, and at the strength of mind shown in your indifference towards what others unjustifiably admire—that is, so long as you have harvested the fruits of your leisure. You have had a marvellous opportunity of enjoying them, since you have been left virtually alone in that beautiful setting. I have no doubt that in that room of yours from which you have opened up a vista of the bay of Stabiae.* by having a window set in the wall, you have been spending the mornings during this period in relaxed reading. Meanwhile those who have forsaken you in that spot have sat half-asleep, watching common-or-garden mimes. And while you spend the rest of the day in the pleasurable activities which you have laid on to suit yourself, we have to endure the shows approved by Spurius Maecius.*

If you are at all interested, the shows have been outstandingly 2 lavish, but not to your taste, as I hazard from my own. In order to grace the occasion, some performers returned to the boards who I thought had quit them to grace the occasion. The performance by your favourite, our dear Aesopus,* was such that the whole world would allow him to retire. When he began to take the oath, his voice tailed off at the words, 'If in full knowledge I deceive . . .'.* Why should I recount to you the rest, when you know about the other shows? They lacked even the charm which we usually get from unpretentious productions. Merely gazing at the display dispels all one's good humour, and I have no doubt that it did not worry you at all to forgo it. What pleasure is afforded by the six hundred mules in the *Clytemnestra*, or the three thousand mixing-bowls in *The Trojan Horse*,* or the range of weaponry wielded by the infantry and cavalry in some engagement? They excited the admiration of the common throng, but they could have caused you no pleasure.

If during these days you have concentrated on Protogenes, so long 3 as he read to you anything other than my speeches, you certainly gained considerably more satisfaction than any of us did. I do not imagine that you pined for the Greek or Oscan shows, especially as you can witness Oscan performances in your city-council.* And you are so far from fondness for the Greeks that you regularly avoid Greek Street on the way to your house. As for the athletes, how can I envisage your pining for them, when you have held the gladiators in contempt?* Why, Pompey himself admits that he has spent 'oil and effort'* on them to no purpose. Beyond these diversions there are the hunts, two a day for five days. No one denies that they are an imposing sight, but what pleasure can a civilized person take in watching some weakling torn apart by a powerful beast, or some magnificent animal transfixed by a hunting-spear? Even if these events are worth witnessing, you have often watched them, and we who have watched them have seen nothing new. The final day was devoted to the elephants, eliciting boundless astonishment but no enjoyment from the common crowd; on the contrary, a feeling of pity* was aroused, and a kind of belief that this species of beast shares some kinship with the human race.

4   During these days, however, of the stage-performances, I myself (I would not have you think that I am not merely content but also as free as air) have almost burst my lungs in speaking at the trial of your friend Caninius Gallus.* If only I found my listening public as compliant as Aesopus did, I swear that I would gladly abandon my profession and spend my life with you and with people of my own sort! Even earlier I was wearying of this way of life, when both my youth and my ambition were incentives, and finally when I could refuse to defend a person if I was disinclined to do so. But these days my life is no life at all, for I anticipate no reward for my labours, and on occasion I am compelled to defend persons who have not deserved thoroughly well of me, at the request of others who are so deserving.

5   So I am looking for every excuse to live at long last as my own master. I both strongly commend and approve you and the pattern of your leisure. I am more reconciled to the greater infrequency of your visits to me, because even if you were in Rome my most troublesome round of activities would not allow me to savour your agreeable presence, nor could you savour mine, such as it is. If I loosen their hold on me*—I am not demanding total freedom from them—I shall certainly tutor you on the nature of civilized living, even though you have practised nothing else for many years. See that you have regard for and nurture your frail health, as you now do, so that you can visit my country houses, and charge around with me in my small litter.

6   My reason for writing to you at greater length than usual (not that I have lots of leisure but I do it out of affection for you) is because in some letter, as you may recall, you gave me a gentle hint to write to you on these lines to prevent you from regretting having missed

the games. If I have achieved this, I am delighted. If not, I console myself with the thought that in future you will attend the games and visit me, and you will not pin any hope of pleasure upon my letters.

Letter 44 (*Fam.* V 8)
Rome, ?January 54

MARCUS CICERO TO LICINIUS CRASSUS, SON OF PUBLIUS

I have no doubt that all your friends have written to tell you of the 1 great enthusiasm I have shown in defending* and even enhancing your high status, for my efforts have not been subdued or furtive, and could not have passed unnoticed or in silence. Indeed, I have grappled with the consuls* and with many ex-consuls in contention greater than I have shown in any previous cause. I have undertaken throughout to champion all your distinctions, and I have abundantly discharged the obligation long owed to our ancient friendship, which has been in abeyance owing to the many vicissitudes of our times.

I swear that there was never any reluctance on my part to cultivate 2 your friendship or to enhance your dignity, but certain plague-ridden individuals, who are aggrieved to hear praise for others, have on occasion both caused you to be estranged from me, and at times affected my attitude towards you. But now the time has come which I have prayed for rather than expected. It allows me, at the peak of your prosperity, to make perceptible both my recollection of our earlier relations and the reliability of our friendship, for I have succeeded in bringing to the notice not only of your whole household but also of the entire Roman community that I am on the closest terms with you. Thus your wife, most outstanding of women, and the Crassi your sons,* men of filial devotion, virtue, and popularity, depend on my counsels, advice, support, and activity, and the Roman Senate and people understand that while you are away, nothing is so available and accessible on all issues pertaining to your interest as my activity, concern, diligence, and authority.

The measures which have been, and are being, undertaken I pre- 3 sume are being reported to you in letters from your household. So far as I am concerned, I should very much like you to believe and to persuade yourself that it is not through some sudden whim or chance event that I have deployed my services to enhance your prestige.

Rather, you must believe that ever since I appeared on the public stage my aim has always been to associate myself with you as closely as possible. Indeed, from those earliest days I recall that my attentiveness towards you, and your supreme goodwill and generosity towards me, have never been withdrawn. If withdrawal of them has been suspected, though non-existent, it must be expunged from our entire recollection and our lives, for it is false and groundless, since you are the kind of man—as I too desire to be—that I hope will ensure that our close alliance and friendship will redound to the praise of us both, since we made our entry into politics at the same time.

4   In view of this, you will assess the esteem which in your judgement you believe is to be allotted to me, and my hope is that you will assign it in accordance with my high standing. I for my part proclaim and promise my pre-eminent and unique support in performance of every kind of obligation relevant to your honour and glory. Even if there are many vying with me in this, I shall easily outrun them all in the judgement of the rest of the world, and especially in that of the Crassi your sons. I feel a special affection for both of them, but while both enjoy my benevolence in equal measure, I am more devoted to Publius, because ever since he was a boy, and above all at this present time, he shows me the regard and the attention owed to a second father.

5   Please regard this letter as one which will have the impact of a solemn alliance rather than that of a mere epistle, and one which binds me most sacredly and most attentively to carry out what I promise and undertake for you. That defence of your prestige which I have undertaken in your absence will be continued by me, in token not merely of our friendship but also of my fidelity. So at this juncture I have thought it sufficient to assure you that I shall pursue on my own initiative anything which I understand accords with your wish or advantage or prestige. Then if I receive from you or from your entourage any instruction, I shall see that you are made aware that no missive dispatched by you or by any person on your staff has reached me to no effect.

So please write to me personally on each and all matters of trifling or momentous or intermediate importance, considering me as a most intimate friend. Instruct your followers to exploit my efforts, advice, authority, and influence in all affairs public and private, political and domestic, which affect yourself or your friends, guests, and dependants, so that as far as possible the unsatisfied longing for your presence may be alleviated by my labours.

Letter 45 (*Fam.* VII 5)

Rome, April 54

CICERO TO IMPERATOR CAESAR

Note that I am convinced that you are my second self, not only in matters pertinent to me personally, but also in those which affect my friends. My plan had been to take Gaius Trebatius* with me to wherever I was going, in order to bring him home fully endowed with all my backing and favours. But because Pompey lingered here* longer than I expected, and owing to a certain hesitation on my own part which was not unknown to you,* my departure has been foreclosed, or at any rate delayed. So note the plan which I have adopted. I have begun to favour the idea that Trebatius should anticipate from you what he had hoped to obtain from me, and indeed my guarantee to him about your favour is no less wholehearted than the regular assurances of my own.

In fact, a surprising occurrence has come into play, as if to attest my belief, or to pledge your kindness. When I was discussing this very man Trebatius in some detail at my house with our friend Balbus,* a letter from you was handed to me, at the close of which were these words: 'You have recommended to me the son of Marcus Curtius.* I will make him king of Gaul, or alternatively if you prefer, pass him on to Lepta,* and send me some other person for privileged treatment.' Both Balbus and I raised our hands to heaven, for the circumstance was so appropriate that it seemed a god-sent rather than a fortuitous intervention. So I am sending you Trebatius, as I had early decided to do on my own initiative, but now later at your invitation.

Dear Caesar, please take him to your heart with all your courtesy. On him alone bestow all the kindnesses which I can persuade you to bestow on my friends. About Trebatius himself I make this pledge to you, but without employing the hoary old expression of mine which you rightly mocked when I used it in writing to you about Milo. Instead I state in the Roman way, which men of some sagacity employ, that there is no man alive who is more honourable, virtuous, or decent. Moreover, he is top of the class in civil law, and is possessed of a remarkable memory and outstanding knowledge.

I do not seek for him a tribunate or a prefecture or any favour with a specific title. What I do seek is your goodwill and generosity, but I do not object to your awarding him some badge of modest distinction, should you be so inclined. In short, I pass him totally, as the saying goes, from my hands to yours, to the hands of a man so eminent in victory and reliability. Allow me to indulge in such affectation, though you scarcely allow it—but I envisage that you will.

Look after yourself, and keep me in your affection.

Letter 46 (*Att.* IV 16)
Rome, June–July 54
CICERO TO ATTICUS

1 This letter has been penned by a secretary, itself a sufficient indication of my heavy commitments. I make no complaint to you about the frequency of your letters, but most of them merely report where you were when they came from you, or they show in addition that all is well with you. The two letters of this kind which you sent from Buthrotum* at about the same time gave me particular pleasure, for I was glad to know that the sea-crossing went well. But the regularity of your letters pleased me more for their frequency than for any detailed comment. However, the one that your guest Marcus Paecius passed on to me was weighty and full of information, so I shall reply to it now and indeed first of all. I have informed Paecius by both word and gesture of the importance which a recommendation from you carries with me, so though previously he was unknown to me, he is now a close acquaintance.

2 Now for the other items. As for Varro,* about whom you wrote to me, I shall fit him in somewhere as long as there is a place for him, but you know the nature of my dialogues. In my work on oratory* which you praise to the skies, no mention could be made by the participants of anyone except individuals known to them, or men to whom they had listened. Likewise in *The Republic*,* which I have begun, I have allotted the discussion to Africanus, Philus, Laelius, and Manilius as spokesmen. I have further incorporated the young men Quintus Tubero, Publius Rutilius, and the two sons-in-law of

Laelius, Scaevola and Fannius. So my thinking is, since I deploy prefaces to individual books as Aristotle does in the works which he terms 'Exoterica',* to set up a situation allowing me to address Varro without irrelevance. I gather that this is what you would like. If only I can complete what I have undertaken. It is a large-scale project which I have undertaken, as you are well aware, and one which requires the abundant leisure which is largely unavailable to me.

As for your remark that in the books which you praise you regret 3 the absence of Scaevola,* I did not remove him capriciously, but my editing was on the same lines as our god Plato's in his *Republic*. There, Socrates visits the wealthy and genial old man Cephalus in the Piraeus. During the initial conversations, the old man is present at the discussion, but after making most apt observations, he says that he intends to leave to attend a religious ceremony, and he does not return subsequently. My belief is that Plato thought it would be scarcely appropriate if he detained a man of that advanced age any longer in such an extended conversation. I for my part thought that I must be all the more circumspect in the case of Scaevola, whose age and frailty you recall, and whose distinctions were such that it seemed hardly fitting to have him attending for several days in Crassus' Tusculan villa. Then too the conversation in the first book was not foreign to Scaevola's interests, whereas the remaining books, as you know, contain *détails techniques*, and I was quite reluctant to have the old man participating in them, for as you know he was a light-hearted soul.

You mention in your letter Pilia's property.* I shall see to it. As 4 you write, the information from Aurelian indicates its value, and it will also allow me to get into the good books of my dear Tullia. I am not deserting Vestorius.* I realize that this is according to your wishes, and I am ensuring that he is aware of this. But you know what he is like. No assignment is more difficult, since the pair of us with whom he is dealing are so compliant.

Now for your queries about Gaius Cato.* You know that he was 5 acquitted on the charge under the Junian-Licinian law, and I declare to you that he will likewise be acquitted on the indictment under the Fufian law, which will leave the prosecutors happier than the counsels for the defence. He has, however, become reconciled to both Milo and myself. Drusus has been indicted by Lucretius,* but the jury on 3 July is to be challenged. The gossip about Procilius does not augur well, but you know what the courts are like. Hirrus has made it up with Domitius.* The senatorial decree on the provinces ('Whosoever henceforth . . .'), which has been promulgated by the present consuls, I do not think will prevail.

6   I do not know what reply to make to your query about Messalla.* I have never seen candidates so evenly matched. You know the resources Messalla has. Scaurus has been indicted by Triarius. If you want to know, there has been no upsurge of sympathy for him, but his aedileship is recalled with some gratitude, and his father's memory carries some weight with country voters. The other two candidates, the plebeians, are running neck and neck, in that Domitius has influential friends and some favour gained by his show (though it was not a very popular one), while Memmius recommends himself to Caesar's soldiers, and depends on Pompey's influence. People believe that if these factors do not ensure him success, someone will push back the elections until Caesar arrives,* particularly now that Cato has been acquitted.*

7   I have now made replies to the letter brought by Paecius; here for your information is the rest. From a letter from my brother I have learnt surprising details of Caesar's affection for me, and they are corroborated by a most flowery letter sent to me from Caesar himself. The outcome of the war in Britain is eagerly awaited, for it is clear that approaches to the island are guarded by 'wondrous walls widespread'.* It has now been further ascertained that there is not a sliver of silver in that island, nor is there any prospect of booty other than slaves, and I do not imagine that you anticipate that any of them are learned in literature or music!

8   Paulus has now virtually completed the roofing of his basilica* in the middle of the Forum. It is supported by the same antique pillars. The other basilica, which he contracted out, he is having built with great splendour. Enough said; there is nothing more pleasing and nothing more ambitious than that commemorative edifice. This has prompted friends of Caesar (I refer to Appius and myself—go on, explode if you like!) not to have turned a hair at the allocation of sixty million sesterces to that memorial which you often extol, namely, the widening of the Forum, and its extension as far as the Hall of Liberty. A smaller sum could not be negotiated with the private owners. The result will be truly magnificent. Then too in the Campus Martius our plan is to build covered marble booths for the tribal assemblies, and

to enclose them with a lofty colonnade a mile in extent. We shall also attach to this structure the state mansion.* You will be asking what benefit this memorial building will bring to me. But why exercise ourselves on that score?

So much for Roman affairs. I don't imagine that you wish to know about the census (it is now regarded as hopeless), or about the legal proceedings under the *lex Clodia*.*

Now brace yourself for a rebuke, if it is justified. In the letter sent 9 from Buthrotum which Gaius Decimius delivered to me, you write that you think you must go to Asia. I don't for the life of me see that there is a lot of difference between acting through agents and conducting business yourself, resulting in your deserting us for so long, so far away. I only wish I had broached this with you before the plan was settled, for I'm certain that it would have had some effect. But now I will restrain my incipient rebuke, in the hope that my earlier words alone may hasten your return.

I am writing to you less often, because of my uncertainty about where you are and where you will be, but I thought I should entrust a letter to this unknown courier, because it appears that he will be seeing you. Since you think you will be heading for Asia, please let me know the approximate date when we are to expect you, and what you have done about Eutychides.*

Letter 47 (*Fam.* VII 7)

Rome, ?June 54

CICERO TO TREBATIUS

I am constantly recommending you, but with what success I am anx- 1 ious to learn from you. My greatest hope rests with Balbus,* to whom I write about you most conscientiously and most frequently. What occasions me frequent surprise is that I do not receive letters from you with the same frequency as those brought to me from my brother Quintus. I hear that in Britain there is neither gold nor silver. If this is the case, my advice is to commission a chariot,* and to hasten back to us with all speed!

If, however, we can attain what we seek, independently of Britain, 2 be sure to install yourself among Caesar's close associates. My brother will do much in the way of helping you in this, and so will Balbus. But believe me, the important thing is your own seemly behaviour and industry. Your commander is a most generous man, you are at the ideal age, and you are exceptionally well recommended. So the only thing you have to fear is that you may seem to let yourself down.

Letter 48 (*Q. fr.* II 16)

Rome, August 54

CICERO TO HIS BROTHER QUINTUS

1 When you receive from me a letter penned by a secretary, you are to assume that I have not a moment's leisure, but when you get one written in my own hand, you can take it that I have a moment's free time. Believe me, I have never been so distracted by court cases* and trials, and this too in the most tiring season of the year, when the heat is greatest. But since you lay this course of action upon me, I am to endure it, for I must not so act as to seem to disappoint your joint hope or strategy.* This is especially so, since even if it proves quite difficult, I shall garner from this toil great influence and great distinction. So in conformity with your wishes I ensure that I alienate no one, win the regard even of those who resent my close connection with Caesar, and gain the enthusiastic attentions and affection of neutrals and of those who incline towards our standpoint.

2 A most furious debate has raged in the Senate for several days on the subject of canvassing, because candidates for the consulship have taken it to quite intolerable lengths. But I have not attended, having decided to propose no cure for the ills of the state in the absence of any solid support.

3 On the day on which I write this, Drusus* has been acquitted of the charge of collusion by the votes of the *tribuni aerarii*. He escaped by four votes, the senators and equestrians having condemned him. This afternoon I shall act as defence counsel for Vatinius,* an easy assignment. The elections have been postponed until September. The trial of Scaurus* will be held immediately; I shall not fail him. I totally disapprove of *The Dinner-Party* of Sophocles,* though I see that you have turned it into a witty sketch.

4 I pass now to what perhaps should have come first. Your letter from Britain I found quite delightful. I was fearful of the ocean,

and again of the shore-line of the island. Not that I disregarded the other hazards, but they give rise more to expectation than to apprehension, and my uncertainty is prompted by anticipation rather than fear. Indeed, I realize that you have an outstanding *sujet* to pen—the landscapes, the nature of objects and places, the customs, the tribes, the battles, and the commander himself. As you request, I shall gladly lend you a hand on any aspects you wish. I send you the verses you ask for,* an owl to Athens!*

But just listen to me, for you seem to be hiding this from me. Tell 5 me, dear brother, how does Caesar react to my verses? Earlier he wrote to me, saying that he had read the first book, and stating that he had read nothing better than the first section, even taking into account Greek works, but that he found the rest, as far as a certain point, *un peu négligé* (his expression). Tell me truthfully whether it is the subject or *la manière d'écrire* that he does not care for. There is no need to be chary, for I shall not abandon my self-esteem one jot. So write to me about this *ouvertement*, and as usual in a brotherly spirit.

Letter 49 (*Q. fr.* III 3)

Rome, October 54

MARCUS TO HIS BROTHER QUINTUS

The hand of my record-clerk is to be an indication of my busy sched- 1 ule, for you are to realize that I have no day free from speaking on behalf of defendants. So virtually all the finishing touches I make and contemplate I leave to the time when I take a walk.

The situation regarding our affairs is this. Family matters proceed according to plan. The boys are thriving, and taking their lessons seriously. They are carefully taught, and relations with me and with each other are genial. Finishing touches to the residences of both of us are in hand, and those at your properties at Arcanum and Laterium* are now close to completion. On the further issues of the water and the road, I wrote to you in one of my letters in careful detail, omitting nothing. But what worries and troubles my mind severely is that for more than forty days not only has no letter arrived from you or Caesar, but no gossip has filtered through from your region. Thoughts of both sea and land in that part of the world are now exercising me, and my mind harps without respite on most unwelcome thoughts, as affection dictates. I am not in fact at this moment asking you to write to me about yourself and your activities, for you never miss doing this whenever you can, but I want you to know that as I write these lines I have almost never awaited anything so anxiously as a letter from you.

2   Now for your information, here is the news on the political front. One by one the election days are being cancelled by daily reports of hostile omens, to the great relief of all honourable men. Such is the odium felt for the consuls* through suspicion of bribes negotiated by the candidates. All four consular candidates are being taken to court. Their cases are difficult to defend, but I shall try hard to rescue our friend Messalla,* though his situation is closely connected with the acquittal of the others. Publius Sulla, with his stepson Memmius, his brother Caecilius, and his son Sulla as junior prosecutors, has indicted Gabinius* for bribery, Lucius Torquatus put in a counter-claim to prosecute, but to universal satisfaction his application was rejected.

3   You enquire about the proceedings concerning Gabinius. We shall know about the charge of treason in three days' time. In that indict-ment he is oppressed by the hatred of all classes, and is damaged above all by the witnesses. The prosecutors are most uninspiring, and the jury are a motley band. The presiding magistrate Alfius is dignified and firm, and Pompey is working energetically on the jurors. I do not know what the outcome will be, but I see no place for Gabinius in the community. My attitude to his humiliation is meas-ured, and I am most relaxed towards the outcome of events.

4   That is more or less the general picture. I shall add one further item. Cicero, your boy and mine, is very much drawn to his teacher of rhetoric Paconius, who in my view is a highly practised teacher and a good man. But as you know, my technique of instruction is a little more learned and *raisonné*. So on the one hand I do not wish the boy's progress and the teaching he is receiving to be impeded, but on the other, the boy himself seems to be closely attracted to, and delighted by, the declamatory type. Since we ourselves have likewise been in that situation, let us allow him to proceed on the path we took. I am confident that he will attain the same goal. None the less, if I take him off somewhere with me in the country, I shall introduce him to my own technique and practice. You have granted me a

sizeable fee, and it will certainly be no fault of mine if I fail to justify it.

Do please write and give me a most thorough account of where you are to spend the winter, and what hopes you entertain.

Letter 50 (*Att.* IV 18)

Rome, October–November 54

CICERO TO ATTICUS

. . . now to give you my view of the situation, we must put up with 1
it. You ask me how I conducted myself.* The answer is 'Resolutely,
and with freedom'. How, you will ask, did Pompey take it? Like a
gentleman; he felt that he should take account of my standing until
I obtained satisfaction. So how did Gabinius secure acquittal?
Le fin mot de l'affaire was the astonishing dumbness of the prosecutors, in other words of the young Lucius Lentulus,* whom the
whole world is loudly accusing of collusion. Then too there was
Pompey's remarkable pestering, and the degrading response of
the jurors. Even so, there were 32 votes for condemnation, against
38 for acquittal. The other trials are still looming, so he is not yet
wholly in the clear.

You will be asking: 'So what is your attitude to it?' Quite positive, 2
I do declare. I'm quite pleased with myself in that regard. My dear
Pomponius, we have lost not merely the sap and lifeblood of the
state, but also its earlier complexion and appearance. The republic
no longer exists to delight and to comfort me. 'So do you bear it dis-
passionately?' Indeed I do, for I recall how attractive it was during
the short period when I was at the helm, and also the gratitude repaid
to me. No grief affects me because of the all-powerful rule of a single
man,* whereas those who resented the modest power I wielded are
now torn apart. Many things bring me consolations without my for-
saking my prestige. I turn back to the life which most accords with
nature, that is, to literature and to my studies. The labour of pleading I mitigate by my delight in oratory. My house and my country
estates give me pleasure. I remind myself, not of the heights from
which I have fallen, but of the depths from which I have risen. So
long as my brother and yourself are with me, these politicians can
be consigned to perdition. I can chat with you *comme un philosophe*.

That place within me where my spleen dwelt has for some time become hardened. So long as my private and domestic affairs give me pleasure, you will find me remarkably untroubled. But I warrant that this is chiefly dependent on your return, for there is no one else on earth whose sentiments correspond so closely with mine.

3   Now here is the news of other matters. Things are drifting towards an interregnum,* and a whiff of dictatorship is in the air. Certainly there is much talk of it, which further inclined the more timorous jurors to favour Gabinius. All the candidates for the consulship are facing charges of bribery. Gabinius too has joined them, for Publius Sulla has indicted him* in the certain belief that he is in deep trouble. Torquatus sought to prosecute him instead, but unsuccessfully. However, they will all be acquitted, for from now on no one will be found guilty unless he has committed murder. This one charge is, however, pursued more vigorously, and accordingly informers are rife. Marcus Fulvius Nobilior* has been condemned. Many other smart operators are not even troubling to acknowledge the charges against them.

4   Is there other news? Why, yes. After Gabinius was acquitted, an hour later another jury, infuriated by the acquittal, pronounced a guilty verdict under the *lex Papia** on Gabinius Antiochus. He is some freedman or other who attends on Gabinius and works in the studio of the painter Sopolis.* So his immediate response was: 'The state by the law against treason . . .'*

Pomptinus* wants to celebrate his triumph on 2 November. He is being confronted at the city-gate by the praetors Cato and Servilius, and the tribune Quintus Mucius, for they claim that no law was passed to ratify his command, and indeed it was certainly presented in a slovenly way. But the consul Appius will support Pomptinus. Cato, however, maintains that as long as he is alive, Pomptinus will not get his triumph. I believe that Cato will sing this song to no effect, like many others of the same kind. Appius plans to go to Cilicia* without awaiting a curial law.

5   On 24 October I received letters from my brother Quintus and from Caesar. They were sent from the south coast of Britain, dated 25 September. Having completed operations in Britain, they have taken hostages but have seized no booty. They have, however, imposed tribute. They are transporting the army back from Britain. Quintus Pilius* has already set out to join Caesar.

As for you, if you have any affection in your heart for me and for your household, any honest feeling, or even the wit and intention to enjoy your blessings, you should already be on your way and close at hand. I do not, I swear, cope with your absence with equanimity. It is hardly surprising that I miss you, since I miss Dionysius so much! Indeed, when the day of your arrival dawns, I and my dear son Cicero will demand him from you.

The most recent letter I have had from you was from Ephesus, dated 9 August.

Letter 51 (*Q. fr.* III 7)
Rome, December 54

MARCUS TO HIS BROTHER QUINTUS

So far as Gabinius is concerned, none of the courses of action 1 which you have been pondering with such affectionate concern were to be adopted—'so may the broad earth swallow me!'* I acted with the utmost seriousness, as everyone thinks, and with the utmost moderation. I neither harassed him nor let him off lightly. I was an outspoken witness, but beyond that I held my peace. Though the outcome of the trial was disgusting and a disgrace, I took it with the greatest forbearance. Now at last—a blessed outcome this for me—these ills of the state and the excesses of reckless men, which previously afflicted me sorely, do not concern me in the least.

There is nothing more depraved than our present politicians and 2 these times, so since no gratification can now be derived from politics, I see no reason for waxing indignant. My writings and my studies, my leisure and my country houses, and above all, my boys, are a delight. Milo* is my sole source of worry, but hopefully the consulship will bring an end to that. I shall work as hard to achieve it for him as I did for my own, and from where you are you will lend a hand, as you are doing. All else with regard to this proceeds smoothly, unless open violence takes over. But I do have fears about his finances, for he is 'insufferable in his mad career'.* He plans to mount a show at exorbitant cost. His imprudence in this one respect I for my part will shore up as best I can, and be sure to do your best among your subject Nervii.*

3   So far as crises in the coming year are concerned, I did not intend you to interpret these as family fears, but as referring rather to the general position in the state. Though I adopt no measures with regard to this, I can hardly remain wholly indifferent. You can infer my wishes for you to be circumspect in your comments from the fact that I do not mention to you even the disturbances openly rampant in the state, in case my letter is intercepted and causes annoyance to anyone.* So I want you to have no worries on the domestic front. I realize that the political scene continually exercises you.

I envisage our friend Messalla as consul—without a trial,* if created through an interrex, and likewise with no danger of impeachment, if through a dictator. He is the object of no hatred. The warm support of Hortensius will exercise a strong effect. The acquittal of Gabinius is considered the criterion of impunity.* *En passant*, no action has as yet been taken about appointing a dictator. Pompey is away, Appius is stirring things up, Hirrus is making his preparations. People are counting the large number of those who will interpose a veto. The people could not care less. The leaders are all against it. I myself hold my tongue.

4   I am most appreciative of your promise of slaves.* As you say in your letter, I am indeed short of them, both at Rome and on my estates. But please, dear brother, do not give a thought to anything related to my interests unless it is wholly convenient to you, and gives you no trouble whatever.

5   The letter from Vatinius* made me laugh, but please note that he is so deferential towards me that I not merely savour those hateful comments but even swallow them whole.

6   You encourage me to complete the *épopée* to Caesar.* I have already done so, and attractively in my own estimation. But I am searching for a competent courier, in case what happened to your Erigona, the only traveller to find the journey from Gaul under Caesar's command a hazard, may befall it. And what would have happened to Erigona if she had not had such a devoted dog?*

7   What, am I to demolish that building?* It gives me more pleasure every day. The lower portico with its rooms looks particularly well. For Arcanum* we need the elegant taste of a Caesar, or indeed of someone even more elegant. Those statues of yours, the palaestra, the fish-pond, and the conduit require an army of men like Philotimus,

not like Diphilus! But I shall visit the site, and send workmen there with instructions.

The will of Felix would cause you to grumble the more if you 8 knew the story. Through an error perpetrated by himself and by his slave Scurra, he failed to sign the document which he thought he was signing and in which you had a most secure place, inheriting a twelfth share. Moreover, he put his signature to a will when he did not intend to do so. But *la peste soit de lui*, so long as we remain in rude health!

Your Cicero I love as you ask, as he deserves, and as I should. But 9 I free him from my supervision so as not to draw him away from his teachers, and also because his mother is taking off. Without her presence here I am apprehensive at the boy's voracious appetite! But none the less we spend a lot of time together.

I have answered all your queries, so goodbye, most delightful and best of brothers.

5

CICERO AS PROVINCIAL GOVERNOR (51–50 BC)

TWO events of great significance, the one external and the other internal, are not detailed in the extant letters. As consul with Pompey in 55, Crassus had negotiated for himself a five-year command as governor of Syria. His aim was to gain military glory against the Parthians, but after minor successes in 54, he was ambushed near Carrhae and met his death there in 53. This enhanced the dominance of Pompey at Rome, where Milo was a candidate for the consulship of 52, and Clodius was running for the praetorship of the same year. The rivalry between them was played out mainly on the streets, and on 18 January 52 Clodius was wounded on the Appian Way and killed, on Milo's orders. In the ensuing violence the Senate House was burnt down. Pompey was appointed sole consul to restore order. Milo was indicted, and, in spite of being defended by Cicero, was exiled.

One of the measures put through by Pompey in 52 was his *lex Pompeia de prouinciis*, which laid down that an interval of five years should elapse between tenure of a magistracy at Rome and appointment to a provincial governorship. This restricted the number of eligible candidates, and Cicero was unwillingly designated as proconsul of Cilicia from summer 51 to summer 50. In a world of widespread exploitation and corruption, his tenure of the governorship was strikingly civilized. His province lay on the southern coast of modern Turkey, flanked by Asia on the west and by Syria on the east. Cicero was responsible also for Cyprus and for the abutting sector of Asia.

Letter 52 (*Att.* V 7)

Tarentum, May 51

CICERO TO ATTICUS

1 Every day or rather one day after another the letters I send you are shorter, for every day I entertain stronger suspicions that you have now set out for Epirus. However, to let you know that I have fulfilled

the instruction discussed earlier, Pompey states that he will appoint five new prefects for each province* to ensure that they are excused from jury service.

Having spent three days with Pompey* at his residence, I am leaving for Brundisium on 22 May. I leave him playing the role of outstanding citizen, fully prepared to withstand those hazards which engender apprehension. I shall await a letter from you to ascertain both your activities and your whereabouts.

Letter 53 (*Fam.* III 3)

Brundisium, May 51

CICERO TO APPIUS PULCHER

When I arrived at Brundisium on 22 May, your prefect Quintus 1 Fabius Vergilianus was on hand to greet me. In accordance with your instructions, he reminded me of the problem which had preoccupied not only myself, whom it directly concerned, but also the entire Senate, namely that your province required a stronger garrison. Almost all the senators voted for additional troops to be levied in Italy for my legions and for those of Bibulus. When the consul Sulpicius* said that he refused to approve this, I complained at length, but there was such vehement unanimity in the Senate that I should set out without delay that I had to comply, which accordingly I did.

Now for the request which I made of you in the letter which I handed to your couriers at Rome. In conformity with our most harmonious relations, I should like you to arrange with due care and diligence the help which a retiring governor can lend to a successor who is closely bound to him in intimate friendship. In this way everyone may realize that I could not be taking over from a more benevolent predecessor,* and that you could not be consigning the province to a more devoted successor.

From the dispatch you wished to have read out in the Senate, a 2 copy of which you sent me, I understood that you had demobilized many soldiers. Fabius, however, pointed out to me that this was your intention, but that when he left you, there was a full complement of troops. If this is the situation, you will oblige me if you reduce as little as possible the slender numbers under your command. I think the senatorial decrees on this matter have been dispatched to you. For my part, in accord with my high regard for you, I shall approve any action you take, but I am sure that you in turn will carry out what you understand to be most convenient for me.

I am awaiting my legate Gaius Pomptinus* at Brundisium. He will arrive here, I think, before the beginning of June. Once he arrives I shall exploit the first opportunity afforded me to set sail.

Letter 54 (*Att.* V 10)

Athens, June 51

CICERO TO ATTICUS

1 I reached Athens on 24 June, and have been awaiting Pomptinus for four days without any definite information about his arrival. Believe me, I am wholly with you in spirit. You are in my thoughts because though personally I find no traces of you, I am more keenly reminded of you through your associations here. I need say no more; indeed you are the only topic of our conversation.

2 But perhaps you would rather hear something about me, so here goes. Up to now neither I myself nor any of my retinue have been recipients of any expenditure, public or private. We have accepted nothing either under the Julian law* or by way of private hospitality. All my staff have been persuaded that I must safeguard my reputation. So far all goes well, for the Greeks have taken note of this, and it has attracted praise and much talk among them. I am taking pains over this for the future. I realize that this wins your approval, but let us applaud it only at the final curtain.

3 For the rest, the situation is such that I often censure my strategy in not having devised some means of evading this assignment. How totally unsuited it is to my character! How true that saying is, *à chacun son métier!** You will say, 'Why lament at this early stage? You are not yet in the job!' I am well aware of that, and I think that more tiresome experiences are in store. Though I am coping with the prospect, and indeed, as I believe and hope, with the most gracious outward show, none the less deep within I am troubled, for so many things are being said and done every day in anger, or arrogance, or every kind of stupidity, crassness, and conceit. I do not refrain from mention of them to hide them from you, but because they

are *indescriptible*. So once I get back, you will admire my *modération*, a virtue for which I am being given *beaucoup d'application* to practise.

So much for that topic as well then, though I have nothing at all in 4 mind to communicate to you, for I have not even a suspicion of what you are up to, or where in the world you are. And indeed I have never been kept so long in ignorance of my own concerns, on what has been done about my finances vis-à-vis Caesar and Milo.* I have no visitor from home, or even from Rome, to inform me of political developments. So if you have any knowledge of issues which you think I am keen to ascertain, I shall be most obliged if you ensure that it gets to me.

Letter 55 (*Att.* V II)
Athens, July 51

CICERO TO ATTICUS

Dear me! To think that I have sent letters to Rome over and over 1 again, and not one to you! From now on I shall opt to send one that fails to reach you, rather than decide not to send one if there is a prospect of safe arrival.

As long as you are in Rome, for heaven's sake take all prior measures to ensure the non-extension of my province. I cannot describe my avid longing for the city, and my virtual inability to cope with the dullness of my present situation.

Marcellus' behaviour* has been disgusting with regard to the man 2 from Comum, for even if he did not hold a magistracy, he was a Transpadane, so as I see it Marcellus seems to have annoyed our friend as much as Caesar. But that is his responsibility.

I too hold the view which in your letter you ascribe to Varro, that 3 Pompey definitely intends to go to Spain.* I totally disapprove of this, and indeed I readily persuaded Theophanes that the best possible course is that Pompey should refrain from departing anywhere. So the Greek must lean on him. His authority carries the greatest weight with Pompey.

I am dispatching this letter as I quit Athens on 6 July, after staying 4 there for ten full days. Pomptinus has arrived with Gnaeus Volusius. My quaestor is here. The only absentee is your friend Tullius.* I have some undecked Rhodian ships and some twin-decked vessels from

Mytilene, together with a few *bateaux à rames*. There is not a peep from the Parthians. As for the future, we are in the lap of the gods.

5   Up to now my progress through Greece has aroused the greatest admiration, and I can vouch that as yet I have no complaints to make against any of my staff. They appear to be aware of my policy, and of the stipulation laid down for their journey. They are assiduous in safeguarding my reputation. If the saying 'Comme *maîtresse* . . .'* holds good, they will continue in this way in the future, for they will observe nothing in my conduct to give them a pretext for misbehaviour. However, if things do not turn out well, I shall adopt a somewhat sterner profile, for up to now I have been gracious in my indulgence, and as I hope with some success. But I am maintaining such *longanimité*, as the Sicilians call it, for just the one year. So use your clout to prevent my tenure of office being extended, in case people find me despicable.

6   I come back now to your commissions. So far as the prefects are concerned, there must be no chickening out; bestow the office on whom you wish. I shall not be so *distrait* as I was with Appuleius. I am as fond of Xeno as you are, and I am quite sure that he realizes it. I have made you highly popular with Patro* and the other blockheads, as indeed you deserve; in fact he told me that you had written to him, saying that following his letter I had taken on that business of his; he was delighted at this. However, when Patro had arranged with me that I should ask the Areopagus to rescind that *décret* which they had passed when Polycharmus was praetor, it seemed to Xeno and later to Patro himself more appropriate that I should write to Memmius,* who had left for Mytilene the day before I came to Athens, asking him to inform his friends by letter that he was happy about the cancellation. This was because Xeno had no doubt that the Areopagus would not accede to the measure, if Memmius was not in favour. (Memmius had abandoned his plan for a building, but he was cross with Patro.) So I wrote a careful letter to Memmius, a copy of which I have sent to you.

7   Do please pass on my condolences to Pilia. I shall let you in on a secret, but you are not to mention it to her. I received a bundle of letters, including one from Pilia to Quintus. I abstracted, opened, and read it. It was worded *d'une manière tres compatissante*. The letters delivered to you from Brundisium without one from me were obviously sent when I was indisposed. Do not accept the excuse that

I was busy. Be sure to let me know all the news. Above all, do look after yourself.

Letter 56 (*Att.* V 16)

Synnada/Philomelium, August 51

CICERO TO ATTICUS

Though the couriers of the tax-farmers are on the point of leaving, 1 and I am making full speed ahead, I feel that I must steal a moment or two so that you do not think me unmindful of your instructions. So I am settled on the road, in order to inform you briefly of events worthy of a longer account.

You are to know that in a fever of anticipation on the last day of 2 July I entered my province, which is godforsaken and evidently permanently run down. I stayed three days at Laodicea, three more at Apamea, and another three at Synnada.* I have heard nothing but men's inability to pay *les capitations*, and the *impôts** put out to contract which are levied on them; also the groans and laments of the communities, and certain atrocities characteristic not of human beings but of monstrous beasts. To put it bluntly, the locals are totally fed up with life.

However, the wretched communities gain some relief from the 3 absence of outlays upon myself, my deputies, my quaestor, and any others. You are to know that we refuse to accept not merely hay or whatever is usually granted by the Julian law,* but even wood; indeed, none of my staff accept anything but four beds and a roof, and in many places not even a roof, as they often bed down in a tent.

So people assemble in astonishing numbers from every farm and village and town, and believe me, all of them on my arrival experience fresh life when they appreciate the justice, restraint, and clemency of your friend Cicero, for these surpass the expectations of all.

When Appius heard that I was on my way, he dashed off to the 4 furthest boundary of the province, all the way to Tarsus,* where he is presiding over a court of law. As for the Parthians, silence reigns, though new arrivals report that some of our cavalry have been cut down by those barbarians. Bibulus is not so much as contemplating arrival in his province, even at this late hour. They say his reason for this behaviour is because he wishes to delay returning from the

province until later. I am hastening towards our military camp,*
which is two days' journey away.

Letter 57 (*Fam.* III 6)

Iconium, August 51

MARCUS CICERO TO APPIUS PULCHER

1   Though I do not claim greater credit for myself than for you in the
preservation of our friendship, when I compare our respective modes
of behaviour, I get much more satisfaction from my conduct than
from yours. At Brundisium I enquired of Phanias (for I thought that
I was aware of both his loyalty to you and the place which he had in
your esteem) which particular region of the province in his view you
wished me as your successor to visit first. His reply to me was that
nothing could be more welcome to you on my part than to sail first
to Side.* Though such an arrival was less dignified and in many
respects less convenient for me, I none the less stated that I would
comply.

2   Likewise when at Corcyra I met Lucius Clodius,* a man so closely
connected with you that in discussion with him I seemed to be con-
versing with yourself. I told him, to begin with, that I would go to
the region requested by Phanias. Clodius first thanked me for this,
but then pressingly begged me to go first to Laodicea, for he said that
you wished to be on the outskirts of the province so as to quit it as
early as possible. Indeed, he added, had I not been the successor you
were anxious to see there, you would have left the province before
your replacement arrived. This was consistent with the letter I
received at Rome, from which I got the impression that you intended
to depart with all haste. My reply to Clodius was that I would
comply, and indeed much more gladly than if I had had to fulfil my
promise to Phanias. So I changed my plan, and also sent you an
immediate letter in my own hand. From your letter I gathered that it
was delivered to you reasonably promptly.

3   This conduct of mine gives me lively satisfaction, for I could not
have behaved more agreeably. Now consider in turn your conduct.
Not only did you fail to appear where you could have met me at the
earliest possible moment, but you departed to a destination where I
could not catch up with you even within the thirty days which I think

were prescribed for your departure by the Cornelian law.* To people unaware of the friendly feelings between us, your conduct seems to be that of a stranger, to put it at its mildest, whereas my behaviour appears to reflect that of the closest and friendliest of associates.

Yet before I reached the province, a letter was delivered to me from 4 you in which you admittedly made it clear that you were leaving for Tarsus, but also indicated to me your sure expectation of meeting me. But meanwhile men who I believe were ill-intentioned (a widespread attitude indulged by many) seized on some plausible topic for gossip, and having no knowledge of my steadfast loyalty, sought to alienate my goodwill from you, for they said that you were conducting court cases at Tarsus, making many decisions, exercising judicial powers at a time when you could have suspected that your successor was already in place. Such activities are not usually conducted by governors even in the belief that they will shortly be replaced.

So far from being troubled by the talk of these individuals, I would 5 have you believe that, if you are indulging in any such activities, I consider myself relieved of those chores, and I am delighted that my year in the province (for it seems to me overlong) has been reduced to virtually eleven months, since one month's labours have been removed from me in my absence. But what does worry me, to speak frankly, is the absence of the three cohorts which are fullest in strength and whose whereabouts I do not know, when the numbers of troops are so few. Yet what irks me most of all is my ignorance of where I shall meet you. For this reason I have been slow in writing, because I await you every day, while in the meantime I have not even received a letter to inform me of your activities, or of where I shall clap eyes on you. Accordingly I have dispatched to you Decimus Antonius, Prefect of Veterans,* a steadfast soldier whom I hold in the highest esteem, so that if you approve you can entrust command of the cohorts to him, and thus allow me to conduct operations at the appropriate time of the year. Both our friendship and your letter induced me to anticipate that I would exploit your advice in this, and even now I am not without hope of it, but obviously unless you write to me I cannot even surmise when or where I am to see you.

I shall ensure that observers both favourable and unfavourable 6 realize that I am wholly well disposed towards you, but you for your part appear to have given to unfriendly critics some scope for believing otherwise about your attitude towards me. If you give the lie to this impression, I shall be most grateful. To allow you to calculate where you can meet me within the period prescribed by the Cornelian law, I entered the province on the last day of July. I am making my way into Cilicia via Cappadocia, and I am striking camp from Iconium on the last day of August. You must now decide, by calculation of the days and of my route, where and when our meeting can most appropriately take place, if you think that you should meet me.

Letter 58 (*Att.* V 18)

In camp near Cybistra, September 51

CICERO TO ATTICUS

1 I do wish you were in Rome, that is, if by chance you are not. I have nothing definite to report, except that I have received your letter sent on 19 July, in which you wrote that you would be going to Epirus at about the beginning of August. But whether you are in Rome or Epirus, the news is that the Parthians have crossed the Euphrates with virtually all the forces under the command of Pacorus, son of Orodes* king of the Parthians. Bibulus* is not yet reported to be in Syria; Cassius* with his entire army is in the town of Antioch. I am in the Taurus region of Cappadocia with my army, near Cybistra. The enemy is at Cyrrhestica, the region of Syria closest to my province. I have written to the Senate about these matters. If you are in Rome, you must see whether you think that the letter should be delivered. You must deal also with many other matters, or rather all of them, *surtout* that no additional burden or extension of my governorship be imposed on me, 'between the slaughter and the offering',* as the saying goes. So far as I am concerned, given the frailty of my army, and the shortage of allies, particularly loyal ones, the most reliable resource is the winter. If it arrives without the Parthians having earlier crossed into my province, my one fear is that the Senate may be reluctant to let Pompey leave Rome because of their apprehension about the state of affairs in the city. However, if once spring comes on they send out someone else, I have no problem with that, so long as the term of my office is not extended.

2 So if you are in Rome, these are my concerns. But if you are elsewhere, or even if you are there, this is the situation with me. We are

in good fettle, and because our strategy seems to be sound, my hope is that our forces are apparently sound too, for we are securely positioned, our corn-supplies are healthy, we are almost within sight of Cilicia, our base can be conveniently moved, and though our army is small, it is, I hope, united in its benevolence towards me. With the arrival of Deiotarus* and his entire force, we shall redouble our strength. I enjoy allies much more loyal than any governor here has had, for my clemency and incorruptibility appear to them beyond belief. A levy of Roman citizens is being held. Corn is being transported from the farms to safe areas. If needs must, we shall defend ourselves by force; if not, in positions of natural strength.

So be of good heart, for I picture you and sense your affectionate 3 *sympathie* as if you were at my side. But I beg you to be in Rome by January, if it can somehow be arranged, and if my standing in the Senate remains unchanged until the new year, for I shall certainly sustain no handicap if you are there. The consuls are friendly,* and one of the tribunes, Furnius, takes my part. But the situation needs your constant attention, practical wisdom, and influence. This is a critical time—but it would be shameful of me to harangue you at length.

Our young Ciceros are with Deiotarus, but should it prove 4 necessary they will be shipped off to Rhodes. If you are in Rome, write to me in your usual most conscientious way; if in Epirus, none the less send one of your men as courier to me, so that you can keep abreast of my activities and I can elicit details of yours, both present and future. I am coping with your friend Brutus' finances* more diligently than he would tend his own. But I am now exposing my ward to action in court, and am refusing to defend him, for they are a dilatory and impecunious lot. However, I shall do justice to your demands, which is harder than satisfying those of Brutus; indeed, I shall satisfy you both.

Letter 59 (*Att.* V 20)

In camp at Pindenissum, December 51

CICERO TO ATTICUS

The inhabitants of Pindenissum* surrendered to me early on the 1 feast of the Saturnalia, the fifty-seventh day after we began to besiege it. You will remark: 'Who the dickens are the Pindenissites?

I've never heard of them.' So what am I to do about it? I couldn't change Cilicia into Aetolia or Macedonia. Just rest assured that this massive operation could be conducted at this time and in this place. Let me inform you *brièvement*, as you allow me in your letter to do.

You are aware of the manner of my arrival at Ephesus;* indeed, you congratulated me on the crowd which welcomed me on that day. Nothing has ever pleased me more. Thereafter I was greeted with remarkable enthusiasm by such towns as existed there. I reached Laodicea on 31 July. I stayed there for two days, being accorded great honour, and the congratulatory speeches obliterated all earlier affronts. I acted in the same way at Apamea, where I stayed for five days, at Synnada in a three-day stay, at Philomelium, where I was for five days, and at Iconium, where I lodged for ten. Nothing was more equable, lenient, and dignified than my jurisdiction.

2   Thereafter I entered the camp on 24 August, and reviewed the army at Iconium on 28 August. Many disquieting reports about the Parthians were reaching me, so from the camp I made my way into Cilicia through that region of Cappadocia which abuts on Cilicia. My purpose was to make Artavasdes of Armenia* and the Parthians themselves assume that they were debarred from entering Cappadocia.

After encamping for five days at Cybistra in Cappadocia, I was informed that the Parthians were far distant from that entry-point into Cappadocia, and that the threat they posed in Cilicia was greater. So I hastily made my way into Cilicia through the gates of Taurus.

3   Having reached Tarsus on 3 October, I made my way from there to the Amanus range, which separates Syria from Cilicia at the watershed. That mountain-range has always been thronged with enemies of Rome. There on 13 October we slaughtered a huge number of them. We captured and set fire to highly fortified strong-points in a night attack launched by the arrival of Pomptinus, and by an early morning assault conducted by myself. I was hailed as *imperator*. For a few days we encamped at Issus,* where Alexander (a considerably better commander than you or I!) had camped against Darius. We remained there for five days, and, having plundered and ravaged the area around the Amanus range, we departed. Meanwhile (you know how people speak of *paniques* and again of *les illusions de la guerre*)

tidings of my approach boosted the morale of Cassius,* who was held fast in Antioch, and struck fear into the Parthians. So as they retired from the town, Cassius pursued them and won a victory. In the course of their flight, Osaces,* general of the Parthians, a man of great authority, sustained a wound and died of it a few days later. My name rides high in Syria.

In the meantime Bibulus has arrived. I believe that he wanted to match me by gaining that meaningless title.* He began to 'hunt for the laurel-leaf in the wedding-cake'* in that same mountain-range of Amanus. Alas, he lost his entire first cohort, and with it the chief centurion Asinius Dento, a man outstanding in his rank, and the other centurions of that same cohort, as well as the military tribune Sextus Lucilius, the son of Titus Gavius Caepio, who is a person of wealth and eminence. This reverse sustained by Bibulus was really ignominious, for it was both serious and untimely.

I myself advanced on Pindenissum, a town strongly defended in the hands of the Free Cilicians. It has been an armed bastion as long as anyone can remember. The inhabitants are barbaric and fierce, ready to offer resistance with all manner of weapons. We encircled the town with a stockade and ditch, and with a massive rampart, penthouses, and a very high tower. We deployed a huge assemblage of artillery and many archers, and after much toil and use of siege-machinery we concluded the operation. Many of our men were wounded, but the army sustained no mortal losses. The feast of the Saturnalia was joyfully celebrated by myself and by the troops, to whom I assigned the booty with the exception of the captives, who are being sold as slaves on the third day of the Saturnalia. At the time of writing, the platform-sale has reached about 120,000 sesterces. I am entrusting the army to my brother Quintus to conduct it from here into winter quarters in a rural area as yet insufficiently pacified, while I myself am making back to Laodicea.

That is the story so far. Let me now revert to earlier matters. Your most emphatic recommendation, and one which overshadows all the rest, was that I should satisfy even the Ligurian Momus.* I'll swear to die if anything can better my elegant behaviour. I do not label it 'restraint', the virtue which is apparently opposed to pleasure, for during the whole of my life I have never experienced such pleasure as my incorruptibility has brought me. It is not so much the glowing reputation which I have gained as my behaviour itself which delights me. To put it bluntly, it has been extremely gratifying. I did not know my own potential, and I was unaware of what I could achieve in this type of activity. So I am right *me rengorger*, for this is a most splendid achievement. Meanwhile — *an accomplissement splen-dide*, this — Ariobarzanes* continues through my intervention to live and reign. *En passant*, through my good judgement and authority, and by making myself inaccessible to the plotters, and not merely incorruptible, I have established a king, and preserved a kingdom.

Meanwhile Cappadocia has not yielded a single bauble. Brutus is down in the mouth, but I have cheered him up as best I could. I have as much affection for him as you have — I almost said 'as I have for you'. However, my hope is that throughout my year of office, my province will not be liable to pay a single copper in expenses.

7   This is the sum of my news; I am preparing to send an official letter to Rome. It will be more comprehensive than if I had sent it from the Amanus range. But to think that you will not be in Rome! My entire future hinges on what will happen on 1 March.* What I fear is that when the question of the province is discussed, I shall be kept here if Caesar digs in his heels. I should have no fear of that if only you were in Rome.

8   Now back to politics in Rome, with which I finally caught up on 16 December from your most delightful letter. Until then I had for long known nothing. Your freedman Philogenes had most carefully ensured the delivery of the letter by taking a circuitous and some-what hazardous route. As for the letter you say you entrusted to Laenius' slaves, I never received it. Both the senatorial decrees and your expectations are reassuring as regards Caesar. If he gives way, we are saved. I am less disturbed by the fact that Laius(?) was singed in Plaetorius' fire. I am keen to know why Lucceius was so outspoken about Quintus Cassius,* and what the outcome was.

9   I am instructed to present your nephew Quintus with his white toga* when I get to Laodicea. I shall keep an eye on him with some care. Deiotarus, whose considerable auxiliary forces I have deployed, will meet me at Laodicea with the two young Ciceros, as his letter promised. I await a further letter from you from Epirus, in order to obtain an account not only of your business activities but also of your leisure hours. Nicanor is diligent in his duties, and I am treating him generously. I am thinking of sending him to Rome with the official dispatch, to ensure that it is delivered with greater care, and also so

that he can bring back reliable information both about you and from you. I am obliged to Alexis for sending me his greetings so frequently, but why does he not write personally, as my own Alexis writes to you? We are searching for a *cor* for Phemius.*

This is all for now. Look after yourself, and make sure that I know when you plan to return to Rome. A thousand farewells. I have most scrupulously recommended your affairs and your people to Thermus,* both personally at Ephesus and now by letter. I gather that he is most solicitous on your behalf. As I wrote to you earlier, please turn your attention to Pammenes'* house to ensure that the boy is not somehow deprived of what he possesses, thanks to your generosity and mine. I think it does credit to both of us. I shall much appreciate what you do.

Letter 60 (*Att.* V 21)

Laodicea, February 50

CICERO TO ATTICUS

I am really delighted that you have reached Epirus safely, and that the voyage was, as you write, to your liking. But I am somewhat upset at your absence from Rome at a vital time for me. However, my one consolation lies in the hope that you are passing a pleasant winter over there in enjoyable relaxation.

You ask me about the purport of the dispatch which Cassius,* the cousin of your friend Quintus Cassius, sent. It was more unassuming than his subsequent missive, in which he writes that by his efforts the Parthian war has been brought to an end. It is true that the Parthians retired from Antioch before Bibulus arrived, but not because of any *coup de main* on our part. Today they are wintering in Cyrrhestica, and massive operations are looming. On the one hand the son of Orodes the Parthian king is in our province, and on the other Deiotarus (his son is betrothed to the daughter of Artavasdes,* and can keep us informed) has no doubt that the king himself will cross the Euphrates with all his forces at the beginning of summer. On 5 December, the very day that Cassius' dispatch announcing victory was read out in the Senate, my own dispatch reported a chaotic situation. Our friend Axius* states that my communication was taken extremely seriously, whereas no credence was placed in his.

None from Bibulus had as yet arrived, but I am quite sure that it will register total alarm.

3   This sequence of events makes me apprehensive. My fear is that since Pompey through fear of revolution is not being sent anywhere abroad, and since the Senate refuses to defer to Caesar, senators may believe that until this dilemma is resolved we should not leave our provinces before our replacements arrive, and that when disturbances are so rife, no single legate should be left in charge of each of the two important provinces. I am aghast at the possibility that in these circumstances my tenure may be extended, and that even a tribune with his veto may be unable to maintain the status quo—all the more so because of your absence, for you could have confronted many contingencies with your advice, influence and support. You will say that I am creating worries for myself. I am bound to do so, and I only hope that this is what I am doing, but I fear every circumstance even though that letter of yours which you sent while still seasick from Buthrotum embodied that splendid *conclusion*: 'I realize and hope that there will be no delay in taking off.' But I'd rather you left it as as 'I realize' without the need to add 'and hope'.

4   The letter which you sent following Lentulus' triumph* I received quite promptly at Iconium, delivered by the couriers of the tax-farmers. In it you confirm your *douce-amère*, that on the one hand there will be no delay affecting me, but on the other you add that if things don't work out, you will come and join me. Your hesitations cause me pain, but at the same time you realize which letters have reached me, for I have not received the one you mention having given to Hermo, the slave of the centurion Canuleius. You frequently mentioned in your letters that you had entrusted one for me to the slaves of Laenius. Laenius finally delivered it to me at Laodicea when I arrived there on 13 February. You had sent it on 21 September. I intimated to Laenius my approval of your recommendation of him personally on the spot, and in the future I shall show my approval in deeds.

5   The rest of that letter was old hat, but one item was new to me, which concerned the Cibyran panthers.* I am most grateful to you for your response to Marcus Octavius to the effect that you did not believe so, but in future you can bluntly say no to all requests of an unsavoury kind. My own native strength of mind and indeed your authority have both fired me to excel all others in restraint, justice,

affability, and merciful treatment. You cannot credit how surprised people have been that during my period as governor there has not been a penny of imposed expenditure upon either the administration or upon any individual, apart from my deputy Lucius Tullius. He is in general an abstemious man, but he has drawn the allowance permitted under the Julian law—just once a day, unlike others who are in the habit of drawing it at every village. But no one else has drawn it, except that one individual once a day. So his practice forces me to exclude him from my claim that not a penny of expense has been imposed. No one other than he has accepted anything. This blemish I have sustained at the hands of our friend Quintus Titinius.*

Now that the summer operations are completed, I have appointed 6 my brother Quintus in command of the winter quarters and of Cilicia. I have dispatched Quintus Volusius, the son-in-law of your friend Tiberius—he is a reliable man and remarkably abstemious— to Cyprus* for a few days, so that the few Roman citizens there on business cannot claim that their cases are neglected (Cypriots cannot be extradited from the island).

On 5 January I left Tarsus for Asia. I honestly cannot describe the 7 enthusiasm of the Cilician townships and especially that of Tarsus. After crossing the Taurus range, I was greeted by a remarkable sense of anticipation from the districts of Asia which lie under my administration. Throughout the six months of my tenure they had received no letter from me, and had never laid eyes on an official guest. Before my arrival here, every year this season was devoted to profiteering of the following sort. Wealthy communities paid out vast sums to avoid having soldiers quartered on them for the winter. The Cypriots disbursed two hundred Attic talents.* While I hold the reins, not a penny will be exacted from the island. This is no *exagération*, for I speak the absolute truth. In return for these benefits, which are a source of wonderment to the islanders, I allow no honours to be decreed to me, beyond verbal compliments. I forbid statues, shrines, *cars* to be dedicated to me,* and I am not a burden on communities in any other way. But perhaps I am burdening you by boasting about myself like this. Bear with it, if you love me, for you were keen that I should behave in this way.

As I was saying, I made my way through Asia in such a way as to 8 make even the famine desirable from my point of view. There is nothing more wretched, and at that time it was widespread in my sector of Asia, for the harvest had failed. Wherever I journeyed, without use of force, legal impositions, or verbal insults, but by my authority and exhortations, I induced both Greeks and Roman citizens who had hoarded their corn to promise to disburse huge amounts to the communities.

9   On 13 February, the day on which I have written this letter, I arranged to hold assizes at Laodicea for the districts of Cibyra and Apamea from 15 March, and likewise at Laodicea for the districts of Synnada, Pamphylia (I shall look out for a *cor* for Phemius then), Lycaonia and Isauria. After 15 May I shall go to Cilicia to spend June there, hopefully without interference from the Parthians. The month of July, if things go according to plan, is to be spent making the return journey through the province. I entered the province at Laodicea on the last day of July, in the consulship of Sulpicius and Marcellus, so I must leave it on 30 July. Initially I shall try to persuade my brother Quintus to allow himself to be put in command, though this will be totally against the inclination of both of us. But no other honourable arrangement can be made, especially as I cannot even now retain that excellent man Pomptinus, for Postumius (and perhaps Postumia* as well) is bearing him off to Rome.

10   You are now abreast of my plans. Let me now inform you about Brutus.* Your friend Brutus is on friendly terms with certain creditors of Cypriot Salamis, Marcus Scaptius and Publius Matinius, whom he has specially recommended to me. I am not acquainted with Matinius. Scaptius visited me in camp. I promised him that I would ensure for Brutus' sake that the citizens of Salamis would pay their debts. He thanked me, and then asked to become a prefect. I said that I did not confer that rank on any businessman. (I acquainted you with this earlier. I justified my practice to Gnaeus Pompey when he made such a request, not to mention Torquatus' plea on behalf of your friend Laenius, and the requests of numerous others.) I told him, however, that if he wished to become a prefect to safeguard the financial contract, I would ensure that he enforced the payment. He thanked me, and left. Our friend Appius had assigned some cavalry troops to this Scaptius to enable him to put pressure on the Salaminians, and he had appointed him prefect. He was harassing the Salaminians. When I ordered the cavalry to quit the island, Scaptius took it badly.

Enough said. When the Salaminians, and Scaptius as well, came to 11
see me at Tarsus, I ordered them, in order to fulfil my promise to
him, to pay over the money. They had a great deal to say about the
contract and about their ill-treatment from Scaptius. I refused to
give ear to them, and I exhorted and even begged them to conclude
the business in return for my services to the community. In the end
I said that I would compel them to pay. The Salaminians not merely
offered no objection, but stated that the money they were paying over
belonged to me, for since I had not accepted what they usually gave
to the magistrate, they were in a sense paying up at my expense.
They further said that the sum owed to Scaptius was somewhat less
than the levy paid to the magistrate. When I praised the Salaminians,
Scaptius remarked: 'Fine, but let us calculate the amount due.'
Meanwhile I had entered into the customary edict that I would
approve a rate of 1 per cent compounded annually, but he demanded
4 per cent, in accordance with the contract. 'What do you mean?' I
said. 'Can I possibly countermand my own edict?' But he produced
a senatorial decree issued in the consulship of Lentulus and
Philippus* to the effect that the governor of Cilicia should pass
judgement on the basis of the contract.

At this I was initially aghast, for it spelt ruin for the township. 12
I ascertained that there were two senatorial decrees issued in that same
consular year, referring to the same contract. When the Salaminians
sought to raise a loan at Rome, they could not do so, because the
Gabinian law forbade it. Then Brutus' associates, relying on his influence, expressed willingness to issue a loan at 4 per cent, provided that
it was protected by a senatorial decree. Through Brutus' influence, a
decree was passed to the effect that neither the Salaminians nor those
who paid over the money should be made liable. Later, however, it
struck the lenders that the senatorial decree did not help them
because the Gabinian law forbade a judicial decision to be made on
the basis of the contract. Then a senatorial decree was passed*
stipulating that the decision should rest on the contract; it did not,
however, make the contract better or worse in law than other contracts, but accorded it the same status. When I had expounded all
this, Scaptius took me aside. He said that he did not dispute those
facts, but that the Salaminians believed that they owed two hundred
talents. He said that he was willing to accept that sum, but that their
debt was a little less. He asked me to increase their payment up to the

two hundred. 'Very well,' I said. I called the Salaminians in to me, excluding Scaptius. 'What is your position?' I asked. 'How much do you owe?' 'One hundred and six talents,' they replied. I put this figure to Scaptius, who reacted indignantly. 'What better solution is there', I asked, 'than to compare your calculations?' They sat together, did their sums, and agreed to the last penny. The Salaminians wanted to put the money down, and urged Scaptius to take it. He took me aside again, and asked me to leave the matter in abeyance. I acceded to his request, and when the Greeks complained and demanded that they should deposit the money in a temple, I did not allow it. All present cried that Scaptius was as shameless as could be for refusing to be satisfied with 1 per cent compound interest. Others saw it as the height of stupidity, but I regarded him as shameless rather than stupid, for he was either dissatisfied with 1 per cent on good security, or he hoped for 4 per cent on doubtful security.

13   I rest my case, and if Brutus does not approve, I see no reason to mollycoddle him. His uncle* at any rate will approve it, especially as a decree of the Senate has now been passed (after your departure, I believe) fixing for creditors the rate of 1 per cent simple interest. If I know your powers of ready reckoning, you have already worked out the difference. *En passant*, with reference to this, Marcus Lucceius' son Lucius complains in a letter to me that there is no greater danger to the state, arising from these decrees—the Senate is to blame— than the possible cancellation of debts. He recalls the earlier damage Gaius Julius* did when he allowed a brief postponement of payments; the state never experienced a more severe blow. But I return to the matter in hand. Think over my case against Brutus, and whether it is a mere case when no honourable argument can be posed against it, especially as I have left the issue and my ruling open.

14   The remaining matters are domestic. So far as *relations intimes*￼* are concerned, my preference is the same as yours for Postumia's son, since Postidia is playing fast and loose. Do not expect any word from Quintus during these months, for the Taurus range cannot be crossed until June owing to the snowfall. As you request, I am sending Thermus frequent letters of support. As for Publius Valerius, Deiotarus states that he is penniless, and that he is maintaining him. Once you know whether there has been an intercalation at Rome or not, please write to inform me of the date of the mysteries. I await letters from you a little less often than if you were at Rome, but none the less I await them.

Letter 61 (*Att.* VI 1)

Laodicea, February 50

CICERO TO ATTICUS

I received a letter from you at Laodicea four days before the 1
Terminalia.* I read it with the greatest pleasure, for it was chock-full
of affection, civility, sense of obligation, and concern. So I shall send
a detailed reply as you demand, following your order of topics rather
than arranging it *à moi*.

You say that the most recent letter you have received from me was
sent from Cybistra on 21 September, and that you would like to
know which of yours I have received. The answer is, almost all of
those which you mention, apart from the one you sent by the slaves
of Lentulus and those which you dispatched from Equus Tuticus
and Brundisium. So your industry was not, as you fear, *inutile*, but
excellently invested, if indeed your motive was to give me pleasure,
for nothing pleased me more.

I am extremely glad that my *modération* towards Appius and my 2
gentlemanly handling of Brutus meets with your approval. I imagined that your reaction would be rather different, for Appius on his
return journey sent me two or three letters *d'un ton plaintif*, because
I had rescinded some of his decisions. It is as though some physician
whose patient had been assigned to another doctor chose to be cross
with his successor for making some changes to what he had prescribed for treatment. Just so, Appius, having governed the province
comme pillard, draining its blood, bearing off all he could, and hand-
ing it over to me half-dead, was not delighted to see her *engraissée*. At
one moment he is furious, but at the next grateful because no action
of mine reflects badly on him. It is just that my different approach
annoys him—for what difference can be so pronounced as that
between a province which was in his governorship drained dry by
outlays and expenses, and one which under me had not to pay out a
penny publicly or privately? Need I mention his prefects, staff members, and his legates too? Or the plunderings, sexual assaults, and
outrageous insults? Whereas now I swear that no private residence is
controlled so prudently and strictly, or is so undemanding as my
entire province. A number of Appius' friends put a ridiculous interpretation on this, claiming that I wish to gain a good reputation so

that Appius may get a bad name, and that I behave in upright fashion, not for my own repute, but to cast aspersions on him. However, if Appius, as the letter which Brutus sent to you revealed, expresses gratitude to me, I am not cross with him. But on the very day on which I write this before dawn, I plan to rescind many of his unjust decisions and enactments.

3   I now pass to Brutus. At your suggestion I have taken him most enthusiastically to my heart. I had begun even earlier to show affection for him, but to put it bluntly I held off to avoid offending you. You are not to think that I sought to do anything other than to do justice to his instructions, or that there is any matter over which I have taken more trouble. He gave me a catalogue of those instructions, and you had already broached the same issues with me. I have most conscientiously discharged them all. First, I induced Ariobarzanes* to give him the talents which he promised to give me. For as long as the king was with me, the negotiations were proceeding well, but subsequently the vast number of Pompey's agents began to put pressure on him. Pompey has more clout than the rest of the world put together, both for all other reasons and because the expectation is that he will come to take over the war against Parthia. Mind you, he is already being paid thirty-three Attic talents a month derived from taxes, which is not enough to meet the monthly interest. However, our Gnaeus is not being extortionate. He is forgoing the principal, and is happy with a reduced rate of interest. The king is neither paying nor can pay anyone else, for he has no treasury and no revenue. He levies taxes following the practice established by Appius, but they scarcely bring in enough to pay the interest to Pompey. The king has two or three wealthy friends, but they guard their money as carefully as you or I. None the less, I send an unceasing flow of letters to the king, requesting and persuading and reproaching him.

4   Deiotarus too has told me that he had sent envoys to the king concerning Brutus' business, and they had reported back to him that Ariobarzanes did not have the money. My emphatic judgement is that the plundering of that kingdom and the poverty of the king is nowhere greater. In consequence, I am thinking of resigning my trusteeship, or of refusing to draw both interest and capital, as Scaevola did for Glabrio.* However, I bestowed prefectures, as I promised Brutus through you, on Marcus Scaptius and Lucius Scavius,

who were supervising Brutus' interests in the kingdom, because they are not engaging in business at present in my province. You remember that in my dealings with him I agreed he should obtain as many prefectures as he wished, provided none was given to a businessman. Accordingly I had granted him two more besides, but the men for whom he sought them had quitted the province.

Now hear the story of the Salaminians,* which I see was news to 5 you as it was to me, for I never heard from Brutus that the money was his own, and indeed I have his notebook containing the words: 'The Salaminians owe money to my friends Marcus Scaptius and Publius Matinius.' He recommends them to me, and to spur me on he adds that he has stood surety for a large sum on their behalf. I had arranged that the debtors should pay interest at 1 per cent per month, to be renewed each year for six (?) years.* But Scaptius demanded 4 per cent. I feared that if he obtained this it would have alienated you, for I would have ceased to apply my own edict, and would have utterly bankrupted the community, which was under the patronage of Cato and of Brutus* himself, and on which I had conferred benefits.

Then at that very time Scaptius pressed a letter from Brutus upon 6 me, which stated that he was the person at risk from the transaction. He had never mentioned this to me or to you. He added a request that I should award a prefecture to Scaptius. But I had already through you stipulated that no businessman should be honoured in this way, and that if any exception had been made, it would not have been made for Scaptius. He had been a prefect under Appius, commanding some troops of cavalry, by deploying which he had enclosed and blockaded the senate at Salamis in their senate house, and in consequence five senators had starved to death. So on the very day on which I set foot in the province, after Cypriot envoys had come to meet me at Ephesus, I dispatched an instruction that the cavalry should immediately evacuate the island. Because of this, I believe, Scaptius had written to Brutus with an unjust allegation against me. But my attitude is that if Brutus imagines I ought to have imposed interest at 4 per cent when I was maintaining a rate of 1 per cent throughout the province, and had issued an edict accordingly which was approved by even the most hard-hearted usurers, and if moreover he will complain that a prefecture has been refused to a businessman (as I refused the request of our Torquatus on behalf of your friend Laenius, and even that of Pompey on behalf of Sextus Statius, and I justified my decision to both), and if Brutus is resentful at the removal of the cavalry, I shall indeed regret that he is cross with me, but shall be much more regretful that he is not the kind of man I thought he was.

7   Scaptius will at any rate admit that my judgement allows him the discretion to bear off all the money in accord with my edict. I add a further stipulation which I fear I may not justify to you: the interest as in my edict was to remain capped. The Salaminians wished to deposit the money, but I prevailed on them not to suggest this. They granted me this favour, but what will be the outcome for them if Paulus* comes here? But I have granted the entire concession to Brutus, who has written to you about me in most friendly terms, but who tends when he writes to me to be abusive and arrogant and *sauvage*, even when making some request. Do please write to him about these incidents to enable me to ascertain how he reacts to them, for you will let me know.

I have penned an account of these matters in some detail in an earlier letter to you, but I wanted you to understand expressly that I have not forgotten your comment in one of your letters that if I bring back from the province nothing but Brutus' goodwill, that will be a fair return. Fair enough, since that is how you would have it, but I think it needs the addition of an unsullied record. So in accordance with my decree, Scaptius obtained the money promptly. But you 8 must be the judge of its fairness. I shall not lodge an appeal even with Cato. But do not think that I have disregarded your *paroles d'encouragement*, which I keep close to my heart. You have tearfully entrusted my reputation to my own safe keeping. Is there any letter of yours which does not mention this? So let any person who so wishes be angry with me, for I shall bear with it, 'for right is on my side',* especially as I have pledged myself in a sense with my six books* as guarantee.

I am delighted that you value them so highly. You raise a *problème historique* in one of them concerning Gnaeus Flavius,* son of Annius. He did not live before the decemvirs, for he was a curule aedile, a magistracy inaugurated many years after them. So what relevance was there in his publication of the calendar? People believe that at one time this record was kept a secret, so that, to elicit the days when business could be conducted, recourse had to be had to a few persons. Several authorities state that the scribe called Gnaeus Flavius published the calendar and assembled a catalogue of the legal processes. So do not imagine that I myself, or rather my spokesman Africanus, invented it all. I take it that the gesture of the actor* did not escape you? Your suspicions are unworthy, for I wrote the passage *sans artifice*.

You write that you have learnt from Philotimus' letter that I was 9 acclaimed *imperator*.* But I imagine that now you are in Epirus you will have received two letters from me with all the details, the first following the capture of Pindenissum, and the second from Laodicea. Both were entrusted to your slaves. I sent an official dispatch to Rome concerning those events, deploying two sets of couriers in view of the hazard of sea-travel.

I agree with you about my Tullia, and I have written to her and to 10 Terentia that I am agreeable. You had already written to me, 'If only you had returned to your old crowd.'* Once the letter of Memmius was corrected, there was no problem, for I much prefer Pontidia's candidate to Servilia's. So you must enrol the aid of our Saufeius, who has always been very friendly towards me, and I imagine that his affection has grown all the more now, because he is under an obligation to bestow the regard of his brother Appius on me as part of his inheritance. Appius showed on frequent occasions how highly he held me, and especially in the matter of Bursa.* You will thereby certainly free me of much anxiety.

I am not happy about Furnius' proposed exception,* because the 11 only circumstance which he regards as exceptional is the one crisis which I fear. But I would write to you on this matter at greater length if you were in Rome. I am not surprised that you pin all your hope of civic tranquillity on Pompey, for that is the reality of the situation, and I think that the charge of hypocrisy on his part should be withdrawn. (If the *ordre des matières* in this letter is rather jumbled, you must take the responsibility, for I am following you *à l'impromptu*.)

Our young Ciceros get on well with each other. They are learning 12 and declaiming together. But as Isocrates reports about Ephorus and Theopompus,* the one needs the rein and the other the spur. I am thinking of investing Quintus with his white toga of manhood on the feast of the Liberalia,* following his father's instruction. I shall observe the feast day as though there has been no intercalation.* Dionysius is in my good books. The boys say that he gets extremely cross, but no man can be more learned, upright, or fonder of us both.

13   The good reports you get of Thermus and Silius are justified, for they behave most honourably. Include with them Marcus Nonius, Bibulus, and myself too if you like. As for Scrofa,* I only wish he had scope for his potential, for he is an impressive character. The rest are reinforcing Cato's *gouvernement*. Your recommendation of my cause to Hortensius pleased me greatly. Dionysius thinks that there is no hope of tracing Amianus, nor have I found any sign of Terentius. Moeragenes* is certainly dead; I journeyed through his native region, in which no living creature survives. I was unaware of this when I discussed it with your man Democritus. I have ordered the Rhosian ware. But ho there, Atticus, what are you thinking of? You usually feed me with cabbage-leaves in dishes patterned with fern-leaves, and in most attractive baskets; what am I to believe you will put before me in earthenware vessels? A *cor* has been commissioned for Phemius, and one shall be found. I only hope he plays something worthy of it!

14   War with Parthia is looming. Cassius sent a foolish dispatch,* and as yet none has been delivered from Bibulus. Once his is read out, I think that the Senate will finally be moved to take action. I myself am greatly troubled. If, as I pray, my tenure is not extended, the months which cause me anxiety are June and July. Fair enough, Bibulus will hold the fort for two months, but what will happen to the person I leave in charge, especially if it is my brother? And what will happen as regards myself if I do not quit the province so quickly? It is a most troubling situation. However, I have made an agreement with Deiotarus* that he and all his forces will be stationed in my encampment. He has 30 cohorts of 400 men each, all equipped with Roman weapons, together with 2,000 cavalry, which will be enough to hold out till the arrival of Pompey, who indicates in a letter to me that this is to be his concern.* The Parthians are wintering in our province, and are awaiting Orodes himself. In short, it is quite a problem.

15   Bibulus' edict contains nothing new except the reservation about which you wrote to me that it represents 'a too oppressive precedent against our order'. But I have a reservation which is equivalent but more guarded, adapted from the edict in Asia of Quintus Mucius,* son of Publius: 'Unless the business has been conducted in such a way that in good faith it should not be endorsed.' I have followed many of Scaevola's injunctions, among them the one which Greeks maintain preserves the independence granted them, namely that the

Greeks themselves conduct internal court-disputes according to their own laws. The edict is short because of the *partage* which I made, for I thought that it should be issued under two separate heads. The first relates to the province, and includes city finances, debt, usury, contracts, and all issues which concern the tax-farmers. The second type, which cannot be satisfactorily settled without an edict, relates to possession of inheritances, ownership of property, appointment of receivers, and sale of possessions which are frequently both demanded and transacted in accordance with an edict. A third type, concerned with judicial administration of other matters, I left *non écrit*. I stated that on this third category I would align my decrees with edicts at Rome, and this is how I handle them, in a way which so far is satisfactory to everyone. In fact the Greeks are happy because they employ jurymen from other communities. You will call them triflers. No matter; the locals believe that they have achieved *autonomie*. Moreover, I suppose, we have such dignified jurymen, like Turpio the cobbler, and Vettius* the dealer!

You ask, I think, about my handling of the tax-farmers. I molly- 16
coddle them, defer to them, praise them, honour them, and ensure that they are a nuisance to no one. And—*très étonnant*, this—the interest-rates adopted in their agreements were maintained even by Servilius!* My procedure is to appoint a date, quite a fluid one, and I announce that if the debtors pay by then, I shall impose an interest-rate of 1 per cent; if not, then the rate in the agreement applies. As a result, the Greeks for their part pay at an adequate rate of interest, and the tax-farmers are well satisfied, for in full measure they obtain both compliments and frequent hospitality. Enough said. They are all such bosom friends of mine that each of them thinks he is especially close to me. None the less, 'Don't let them . . .'; you know the rest.*

Next, about Africanus' statue* (what disjointed topics, but this is 17
just what delights me about your letter!), are you serious? Is this Metellus Scipio unaware that his great-grandfather was never a censor? Yet the statue which stands on high ground by the temple of Ops contains no inscription other than consul. But the statue that stands side by side with the *Hercules* of Polycles bears the inscription 'consul, censor', though the posture, dress, ring, and representation itself clearly specify the same man. But gracious me, when I myself observed the statue of Africanus bearing the subscription 'Sarapio'

among the troop of gilded equestrian statues which the same Metellus erected on the Capitol, I thought that it was a worker's error, but now I realize that Metellus was responsible. What disgraceful *faute de recherche*!

18   As for that observation of mine about Flavius and the calendar,* if it is untrue, it is a misconception generally held. You were justifiably *embarrassé* by it, while I was following a belief virtually sanctioned by the state. There are many such beliefs held by the Greeks. Which of them has not stated that Eupolis, the writer of Old Comedy, was thrown into the sea by Alcibiades when he was sailing to Sicily? Eratosthenes refutes the story by citing plays which Eupolis mounted subsequently. We surely do not mock Duris of Samos,* that careful historian, for making that mistake in company with many others. What commentator has not stated that Zaleucus framed the laws at Locri? So is Theophrastus humiliated because your friend Timaeus* censured that view? But it is disgraceful for a man to be unaware that his great-grandfather was not a censor, especially as no Cornelius became censor in the years which followed the consulship during that forebear's life.

19   Now for your comments on Philotimus and the payment of 20,000 sesterces. I am told that he disembarked in the Chersonese about the beginning of January. As yet I have had no word from him. Camillus* writes that he has received the remainder owing to me, but I have no knowledge of what this sum is, and I am eager to know. But we must discuss this later, and perhaps more appropriately face to face.

20   Your comment, dear Atticus, at the close of your letter caused me some concern. After writing '*Quoi de plus?*', you then most affectionately entreat me not to forget to be vigilant, and to keep an eye on developments. You haven't heard something about someone, have you? But there is nothing of that kind; *il s'en faut de beaucoup*. It would not have caught me unawares, nor will it. But that careful warning of yours seemed to me to indicate something or other.

21   So far as Marcus Octavius is concerned, I write yet again to tell you that your response to him was admirable. I only wish that it had been expressed more emphatically. Caelius* sent a freedman to me bearing a letter, carefully phrased, about panthers and contributions from the townships. In reply to the second request, I said that I was irritated that my activities were so shrouded in darkness that report

had not reached Rome that in my province not a penny had been exacted except for payment of debts. I added that I was not permitted to procure money, nor was he able to accept it. I advised him (for I am quite attached to him) that since he had laid accusations in court against others, his conduct should be more circumspect. As for his first request, it was not in keeping with my reputation to order the authorities of Cibyra to organize a hunt.

Lepta* is absolutely delighted with your letter; indeed it was 22 admirably phrased, and it has made me more popular with him. I am grateful to your fond daughter for instructing you so carefully to send me her greetings. Thanks too to Pilia, but your daughter's greeting is more punctilious, for she has never set eyes on me, though she has been fond of me for a long time now. So you must likewise pass on my greetings to both. The date of your letter, 29 December, agreeably reminded me of that most celebrated oath* which I have not forgotten. On that day I was *magnus*,* though clad in the magistrate's gown.

Now all your points are answered. My replies are not, as you demanded, *or pour bronze*,* but like for like.

Why, another letter has arrived. It is very brief, but I shall not 23 leave it *sans réponse*. Lucceius has certainly been wise to put up his Tusculan house for sale—unless perhaps he is merely sounding off, as he often does. I should like to know what the situation with him is. I hear that our friend Lentulus has advertised the sale of (?) in addition to his Tusculan residence. I am eager to see the two of them unencumbered,* and Sestius as well, and Caelius too, if you like. 'They are ashamed to say no, but afraid to say yes.' I imagine that you have heard that Curio is thinking of having Memmius restored. So far as Egnatius Sidicinus' debt goes, I have some hope, but not a lot. You commend Pinarius to me. He is seriously ill, and Deiotarus is looking after him. So I have now answered your shorter letter as well.

Do please correspond with me by letter as often as possible when 24 I am at Laodicea, that is until 15 May, and especially after your arrival at Athens, for we shall soon know about affairs in Rome, including the allotment of provinces, all of which are decided in the month of March. Be sure to send couriers.

Ho there, Atticus, have you Greeks extracted fifty talents out of 25 Caesar* through the agency of Herodes? I am told that you have all incurred Pompey's deep displeasure because of this. He thinks that you have squandered his coppers, and that Caesar will be paying more attention to his mansion-building in the Grove. I got this news from that dreadful rascal Publius Vedius,* a boon-companion of Pompey's. This fellow Vedius came to meet me with two carriages, a four-wheeler drawn by horses, a litter, and a great horde of domestics. If Curio* gets his bill through, Vedius will have to pay a hundred sesterces a head for these servants. He had a baboon too in one of the carriages, and some wild asses as well. I never set eyes on a more degenerate character. But hark to the end of the story. He stayed at Laodicea at Pompeius Vindillus' house, and dumped his luggage there when setting out to visit me. Meanwhile Vindillus died. As Pompey the Great was believed to have a financial interest in the property, Gaius Vennonius* visited Vindillus' residence, and as he was putting everything under seal, he came upon Vedius' belongings. Among them were discovered five miniature portraits of married ladies, one of them the sister of your friend who is 'brutish' enough to be associated with Vedius.* She is the wife of the man refined (*lepidus*) enough to tolerate that behaviour with such indifference. I wanted to report this to you *en passant*, as we are both such accomplished nosy parkers.

26   There is one further item which I should like you to bear in mind. I hear that Appius is constructing a *porte d'entrée* at Eleusis. Would I be a fool to do the same for the Academy? 'Yes, I think so,' you will reply. Well, then, you must put this down in writing to me. I am extremely fond of Athens, and I want to have some memorial there, and I loathe spurious inscriptions on other people's statues. But I shall fall in with your views. Let me know at what date the Roman mysteries* are celebrated, and how the winter is treating you. Look after yourself. I write this on the 765th day after the battle of Leuctra.*

Letter 62 (*Att.* VI 4)

On the march, June 50

CICERO TO ATTICUS

1   I reached Tarsus on 5 June. There were many problems to vex me there—a large-scale war in Syria, massive brigandage in Cilicia, ticklish problems of administration, for I have only a few days left of my

year of office, and most taxing of all, the need to leave someone in charge in accordance with the senatorial decree. There could be no one appointed less suitable than my quaestor Mescinius. Of Coelius* I get no reports. The most straightforward choice seems to be to leave my brother Quintus with supreme authority, but that solution has many troublesome aspects: our separation, the danger of war, the misbehaviour of the troops, and a thousand other things. The whole situation is so disagreeable. But chance must be the arbiter, since planning can play only a minor role.

Now that, as I hope, you have arrived safely in Rome, you must as 2 usual take a hand in all that you conceive to be relevant to my concerns, especially those affecting my dear Tullia. When you were in Greece, I wrote to Terentia stating my preference in the matter of Tullia's marriage-settlement. Secondly, with regard to my triumph, I fear that because you were away, my dispatch did not receive sufficiently careful attention in the Senate.

A further point I must raise with you is *plus confidentiel*, and you 3 must follow the scent more perceptively. My wife's freedman* (you know the one I mean) seemed to me the other day to have tampered with the accounts relevant to the purchase of the Crotonian tyrannicide's property.* I inferred this from his garbled version. I have my fears—you will understand of what. So investigate this, and wrap up the rest. I cannot put all my fears on the written page. See that your letter comes winging to greet me. I write this in haste on the march. Please greet Pilia and your very beautiful girl Cecilia for me.

Letter 63 *(Fam. XV 6)*

Tarsus, July 50

MARCUS CICERO TO MARCUS CATO

It is, I think, Hector in Naevius* who remarks: 'From you, father, 1 I am pleased to win praise, for you are a man who has won praise.' Praise is especially gratifying when it comes from those whose lives have won praise. For myself, your letter of congratulation and the testimony of your proposal in the Senate make me believe that I have attained all that there is to attain, and what is to me most honorific and gratifying is that you were glad to ascribe to friendship what you would unequivocally have granted to truth. Even if there were many

Catos in our community (I do not say all, for it is remarkable that it has produced one), what triumphal chariot or what laurel crown could compare with praise from you? To my way of thinking, as to the unclouded and refined judgement of your school,* nothing can be more praiseworthy than that speech of yours, which my friends have copied and sent to me.

2 In an earlier letter to you, I explained my willingness (I shall not call it eagerness) to be awarded a triumph. Even if this seemed unjustified to you, the thinking behind it was not that the honour seemed unduly desirable, but that if the Senate awarded it, it should by no means appear to be despised. I hope, however, that in view of the labours I have undertaken on behalf of the state, the senatorial order will consider me not unworthy of the honour, especially as it is regularly bestowed. If such is the happy outcome, my sole request to you—to use your own most friendly formulation—is that having granted me what in your judgement you consider to be the greatest compliment, you should be delighted if my aspiration comes to pass. I see that your actions, your expressed views, your letter to me, and your presence at the drafting of the supplication* show that the honour granted to me met with your approval, for I am not unaware that such decrees of the Senate are usually drafted by the closest friends of the person being honoured. I hope that I shall soon see you, and I pray that the state may be in healthier shape than I fear.

Letter 64 (*Att.* VI 6)

Side, August 50

CICERO TO ATTICUS

1 Whilst here in my province I was showing Appius courteous respect at every turn, I have suddenly become the father-in-law of his accuser!* You respond: 'That's good! May the gods look kindly on it!' That is my fervent wish, and I am sure that you long for it as well. But believe me, it was the last outcome that I expected, for I had sent reliable persons to the ladies apropos Tiberius Nero,* who had been negotiating with me. But by the time they reached Rome, the betrothal was announced. However, I hope that the present settlement is better. I gather that the ladies are quite ecstatic with the

young man's deference and genial manners. For the rest, don't *relever les points faibles*!

But what is this about *blé aux citoyens* at Athens? Do you think it 2 wise? Mind you, my writings at any rate are not opposed to it, for this is not largesse to fellow-citizens, but generosity* to hosts. None the less, you bid me think hard about the *porte d'entrée* to the Academy, though Appius has shown no such hesitation about Eleusis. I am sure that you are upset about Hortensius;* I myself am extremely sad, for I had planned to form a really close link with him.

I have appointed Coelius* to administer the province. 'What?' you 3 will say. 'A mere boy and perhaps a silly ass, lacking sobriety or self-control?' I concede that, but no other course was possible. I was considerably affected by that letter of yours, received some time ago, in which you wrote that you intended *suspendre jugement* on what action I should take about leaving the province. I recognized your reasons for such suspension of judgement, for they corresponded with my own. Was I to consign the province to a boy, when this was detrimental to the public good? Or to my brother, then? That was not in my own interest. Yet there was no one, apart from my brother, whom I could advance above the quaestor without insulting him, especially as he is from a noble family. But for so long as the Parthians seemed to be looming over us, I had decided to leave my brother in charge, or even in the interests of the state to remain myself, in contravention of the senatorial decree. But when by an astonishingly happy chance the Parthians departed, my doubts were removed. I visualized the chatter: 'So he has left his brother in charge? Doesn't this amount to government of a province for more than a year? What of the will of the Senate that provinces should be governed by those with no previous tenure, when this fellow was a governor for three years?'*

So much then for the reactions of the public. How does it strike 4 you? I should be everlastingly unhappy if it provoked more than a hint of anger or insult or negligence, as arises in the usual run of things. Then there is the man's son—a mere boy, and a boy with a fair conceit of himself. What resentment would be felt there? His father was against letting him go, and was annoyed at your suggesting it. As for Coelius, I won't say 'for better or worse', but I am much less exercised. There is also the consideration that Pompey with all his power and resources chose Quintus Cassius without casting lots, and Caesar* similarly chose Antony. Was I to alienate a man assigned to me by lot, and moreover have him spying on the one I had left in charge? I made the better choice, and there are more precedents for it. It is certainly more appropriate for a man of my advanced age. As for yourself, heaven knows I have made you extremely popular with him, and I have read to him that letter composed not by you but by your secretary.

Letters from my friends are summoning me back for my triumph, a celebration which I think is not to be neglected in view of this renaissance of mine. So you too, dear Atticus, must begin to long for it, so that I may not appear so much a fool.

Letter 65 *(Fam.* XIV 5)

Athens, October 50

TULLIUS TO HIS DEAR TERENTIA

1 If you and Tullia, the light of our lives, are well, I and your most delightful young Cicero are likewise well.

We reached Athens on 14 October, after coping with quite contrary winds which made the voyage slow and tedious. As we disembarked, Acastus was at hand with the mail, after completing the journey quite briskly in three weeks. I received your letter, from which I gather that you feared that your earlier ones had not been delivered to me. All of them were delivered, and you included in them all the news, which was most welcome to me. No wonder the letter brought to me by Acastus was so short, for you are expecting me, or rather us, in person, and we are eager to join you both with all speed. Mind you, I am aware of the parlous condition of the state to which I am coming, for I have ascertained from many friends' letters which Acastus brought that the situation looks like war, so that once I arrive I shall be unable to cloak my views. But since we must endure the blows of fortune, I shall ensure that I arrive all the more speedily, the more easily to ponder the entire situation. Do travel to meet us as far as you possibly can,* considering your state of health.

2 The bequest of Precius* is a source of great sadness to me, for I loved him dearly. But please ensure, if the auction is held before my arrival, that Pomponius, or if he cannot attend, Camillus negotiates on my behalf. Once I have arrived safe and sound, I shall myself

conduct the rest of the business. Ensure that this is done even if you have already left Rome. If the gods are kind, we hope to arrive in Italy about 13 November. My most delightful and desirable Terentia, if you love us, take care of yourselves. Farewell.

Athens, 16 October.

Letter 66 (*Att.* VII 1)

Athens, October 50

CICERO TO ATTICUS

I have entrusted a letter to Lucius Saufeius* for you and for you 1 alone, for though I have insufficient time for writing, I do not wish someone who enjoys such close association with you to greet you without bearing a letter from me. But in view of the slow progress of philosophers, I imagine that this letter will be delivered to you first. If, however, you have already received the other one, you are aware that I reached Athens on 14 October; that on disembarking at the Piraeus, I was handed your letter by our friend Acastus; that I was distressed at your having reached Rome with a fever, but that I began to be reassured because Acastus reported the news which I longed to hear of your physical recovery, but that I was aghast at the report in your letter about Caesar's legions, and that I asked you to ensure that I should come to no harm through the *vaine gloire* of you know whom.* I also briefly explained why I had not appointed my brother to administer the province, a subject which I had broached in a letter to you some time ago, but which Turranius misrepresented to you at Brundisium, as I learnt from the letter delivered to me by that excellent man Xeno. These were more or less the contents of that previous letter.

Now hear the rest of my concerns. Do for heaven's sake concen- 2 trate all that affection which you have lavished on me, and all that practical wisdom, which God knows I reckon to be unique in every sphere, upon consideration of my entire position. Unless that same divinity, which delivered me from the Parthian war more providentially than I could have dared to hope, looks with pity on the republic, I seem to envisage a mammoth struggle, one greater than any which ever existed before. I am not, mind you, bidding you take thought for the evil which afflicts me in company with the rest of the world, but I am begging you to concern yourself with my personal *dilemme*. You see, I am sure, that following your advice I have sought the friendship of both these leaders, and I only wish that I had hearkened to your truly friendly admonition from the outset,

> But never did you stir the heart within my breast.*

At last, however, you did persuade me to seek intimacy with the one, because he had deserved particularly well of me, and with the other because he exercised so much power. I acquiesced, therefore, and by total compliance I ensured that no one was dearer than 3 myself to either of them. My thinking was that my close association with Pompey would not compel me at any time to compromise myself politically, and that if I sided with him I should not have to go to war against Caesar, as their alliance was so very close. But now a titanic struggle looms between them, as you for your part indicate, and I for mine envisage. Each of them reckons me as an ally, unless perhaps one of them is indulging in pretence. Pompey has no doubts, for he rightly judges that I enthusiastically approve his present political stance. I have received, at the same time as yours, letters from both of them which suggest that neither seems to regard anyone whomsoever as of greater account than myself.

4 But what should I do? I am not asking about the final step, for if the dispute is settled by warfare, I realize that defeat in company with the one is better than victory with the other. I am thinking of developments on my arrival, that is, of preventing the acceptance of Caesar as candidate in his absence,* and thus compelling him to disband his army. 'Speak up, Marcus Tullius.' But what am I to say? 'If you don't mind, wait until I meet Atticus'? There is no opportunity to fight shy. So am I to oppose Caesar, then? But what of our close-knit handshakes? For I aided him in obtaining that concession when he requested it of me at Ravenna* in connection with the plebeian tribune Caelius. What, requested by Caesar himself? Yes, and not merely by him, but also by our friend Gnaeus, in that third consulship* of his bestowed by heaven. Or am I to take my affections elsewhere? But it is not just Pompey, but 'the Trojans and their ladies that I fear', and 'Polydamas will be the first with his reproaches'.* What Polydamas? Why, you yourself of course, you who laud both my deeds and my written words.

Thus, during the two previous consulships* of the Marcelli I 5 escaped this difficulty when Caesar's province was under discussion, whereas now I am in the throes of the crisis itself. So 'to allow the idiot the chance of making his proposal first',* my strong inclination is to apply for triumph, and thus to have a thoroughly justified reason for remaining outside the city. Even so, the two contestants will seek to elicit my views. You may perhaps smile when at this juncture I only wish that even now I was lingering in my province, for with the crisis looming that was the desirable ploy. Yet what solution could have been so dismal? For *en passant* I would have you know that all those initial postures you lauded so highly in your letters were *tous en surface*.

Virtue is no easy option, and pretence is difficult to sustain for 6 long. I thought it an honourable and splendid thing to bequeath to my quaestor Gaius Coelius a year's expenses out of the year's allowance which had been allocated to me, and to return a million sesterces to the Treasury. But my staff raised a lament, for they thought that all that money should be apportioned among them. Thus I would be regarded as more well disposed to the treasuries of the Persians and Cilicians than to our own! But they did not shift my stance, for on the one hand my reputation counted most with me, and on the other there was no honourable gesture I could have made to anyone which I neglected to make. But to use Thucydides' phrase,* 'let this digression be not without profit'.

But you must give thought to my situation, and advise me first by 7 what artifice I can maintain Caesar's goodwill, and secondly on the triumph, which I envisage as *vraisemblable*, unless the political crisis hinders it. My assessment is made on both the letters of friends and the Supplication itself. The person who opposed it* lent me more support than if he had proposed every conceivable triumph on my behalf. Moreover, only two senators agreed with him, my friend Favonius and Hirrus who bears a grudge against me. Cato in any case turned up to witness the decree, and sent me a most agreeable letter explaining his proposal, and in spite of it congratulating me. Caesar is jubilant about Cato's proposal with regard to the Supplication. His letter does not specify what Cato's proposal was, but only that Cato did not support the Supplication on my behalf.

I come back to Hirrus, whom you had begun to reconcile with 8 me. Now complete the reconciliation! You have Scrofa and Silius* in support. Previously too I wrote to them, and now I have written to Hirrus himself, for he had spoken with them in a conciliatory way, saying that he could have blocked the Supplication, but that he did not wish to do so; he had merely expressed agreement with Cato, an intimate friend of mine, when he made a proposal which showed the utmost respect for me. Moreover, I had sent no letter to him, though I was sending letters to everyone else. What he said was true; he and Crassipes were the only senators to whom I failed to write.

9   So much for public concerns. I must return to domestic matters. I wish to dissociate myself from that fellow.* He is a thorough *fricotteur*, a real Lartidius, 'But let us though sore at heart forget what is done',* for we must deal with what lies ahead. First, that worry which has compounded my depression. Whatever this inheritance is which Precius has bequeathed, I do not want it mingled with my accounts, which he is handling. I have written to Terentia and also to Philotimus himself that I shall consign to you any money which I could raise to meet the expenses of my anticipated triumph. In this way I think that the whole business will be *irréprochable*, but it will wait on his pleasure. You must take on this additional chore of deciding how to extricate me. You indicated your willingness to do this in a letter from Epirus or from Athens, and I shall lend a hand in it.

6

CIVIL WAR (49–46 BC)

CICERO eagerly quitted his province of Cilicia and arrived in Rome in January 49. En route in Campania he held discussions with Pompey, to whom he pledged his support in the hope that he would opt for reconciliation with Caesar. Meanwhile in Rome the Senate had voted in December that both dynasts should lay down their arms, but Cato and his friends were already threatening to indict Caesar on the expiry of his command. Caesar retaliated by marching from his winter quarters at Ravenna across the Rubicon to Ariminum, thereby launching the great Civil War. He marched on Rome in January 49. Pompey left the capital for Luceria, and in mid-March, having avoided a meeting requested by Caesar, he sailed from Brundisium, preceded by the consuls and his senatorial allies. Cicero dithered until June 49, when he finally left to join Pompey in Greece. The cool reception offered by the Pompeians, and in particular by Cato, who berated him for leaving Rome, contributed to the breakdown of his health, which prevented him from leaving Dyrrhachium while the battle of Pharsalus was fought in August 48, and Pompey was subsequently murdered in Egypt. Instead he returned disconsolately to Brundisium, where he was immured for a year from November 48, awaiting Caesar's permission to return to Rome. That permission was duly forthcoming, and he was in Rome when the news arrived of the defeat of the Pompeians in Africa, and the suicide of Cato, refusing to accept Caesar's offer of clemency, in the early summer of 46.

Letter 67 *(Att. VII 4)*

? Cumae, December 50

CICERO TO ATTICUS

I have sent Dionysius to you, for he was fired with longing to see you. 1
Though unhappy at his going, I had to allow it. I have found him not only learned (of which I was already aware), but also honourable, wholly dutiful, jealous for my reputation, economical, and, to avoid seeming to lavish praise on a freedman, a really good man.

2   I saw Pompey on 10 December, and spent something like two hours
with him. He seemed to me to be greatly heartened at my arrival, spoke
encouragingly about my triumph, and undertook to declare his support for it. He advised me not to attend the Senate before I had the
business wrapped up, in case any proposals I advanced might alienate
one of the tribunes. In short, this friendly advice of his could not have
been more detailed. In discussion with me of the political situation, he
intimated that we undoubtedly had a war on our hands; there was
nothing to indicate hope of harmony. He said that though previously
he was aware that Caesar was utterly estranged from him, this impression had recently been confirmed, for Hirtius,* a close intimate of
Caesar, had come from him but had made no contact with himself. He
added that following his arrival on the evening of 6 December, Balbus
had decided to visit Scipio* before dawn on the 7th to discuss the
entire situation. But Hirtius had left at dead of night to join Caesar.
Pompey considered this a *preuve patente* of their estrangement.

3   Enough said. My sole consolation is that I do not think that
Caesar, awarded a second consulship* even by his enemies, and
supreme power by Fortune, is so lunatic as to endanger these concessions. However, if he enters on a headlong course, I do indeed have
many fears which I dare not commit to paper. But as matters are at
the moment I intend to make for Rome on 3 January.

Letter 68 *(Fam.* XVI 11)

Near Rome, January 49

TULLIUS, CICERO, TERENTIA, TULLIA, AND THE
QUINTI TO TIRO

1 Though I miss the convenience of your help at every point, it is not
for my sake but for yours that I am sorry that you are unwell. But
now that the impact of your illness is reduced to quartan fever,* as
Curius has written to tell me, I hope that by taking care you will soon
be stronger. Be sure at this time not to attend in your kindness to
anything other than what is most appropriate to regain your health.
I am well aware how painfully you are missing us, but once you are
well the situation will be entirely eased. I would not have you worried in case you suffer the inconvenience of sea-sickness* while still
an invalid, and the sea-journey which in winter is perilous.

I arrived close to Rome on 4 January. People came out to greet me 2 in such numbers that it could not have been more impressive. But I have stepped right into the blaze of civil discord,* or rather of war, and though I was eager and (I believe) capable of healing the breach, the debased desires of certain men—on both sides there are people eager for a fight—have blocked my way. Certainly our friend Caesar has himself sent a threatening and bitter letter* to the Senate, and is shamelessly still clinging to his army and his province against the wishes of the Senate, and my friend Curio is urging him on. Our friend Antony, and Quintus Cassius* too, though not forcibly expelled, have departed with Curio to join Caesar after the Senate entrusted the consuls, praetors, tribunes, and us proconsuls with the task of ensuring that the state should come to no harm.

Our state has never been in greater danger, and never have unscrupu- 3 lous citizens had a leader better prepared. But at the same time very careful preparations are being made on our side as well, with the authority and seal of our friend Pompey, who has begun to fear Caesar late in the day.

However, in the midst of these disturbances a crowded Senate demanded the award of a triumph to me. But the consul Lentulus, wishing to make it a mark of greater kindness on his part, said that he would formally propose it once he had dealt with business necessary in the interests of the state. I have not sought the eager promotion of the issue, and my authority on that account is the greater. Italy has now been divided into regions so that we each control one of them. I have taken on Capua.*

I wanted you to be aware of these developments. I beg you repeatedly to look after yourself, and to send me letters whenever you have someone to whom to entrust them.

Repeated good wishes.

Written on 12 January

Letter 69 (*Att.* VII 10)

Near Rome, January 49

CICERO TO ATTICUS

On impulse I have decided to quit Rome before daylight, to avoid 1 exchanging looks or words, especially with the laurelled lictors.* For the rest, I have no earthly idea what to do now or in the future.

I am utterly dismayed by the thoughtlessness of our totally mindless strategy. What am I to counsel you to do, when I myself await advice from you? I do not know what plan our Gnaeus has adopted even now or is about to adopt. He is hemmed in and stands paralysed in the Italian townships.* If he takes his stand in Italy, we shall all join him, but if he leaves the country, we will need to consult. Unless I am off my head, up to now at any rate the whole situation is utterly stupid and thoughtless. Do write often to me on anything which comes to mind.

Letter 70 (*Fam.* XIV 18)

Formiae, January 49

FONDEST GREETINGS TO HIS TERENTIA FROM TULLIUS, TO HIS MOST CHARMING DAUGHTER FROM HER FATHER, AND TO HIS MOTHER AND SISTER FROM CICERO

1 Dear hearts, I think that you must carefully consider over and over again what you are to do, whether to stay in Rome, or to join me, or to go to some safe place, for this is for you as well as me to decide. These are the considerations that occur to me. You can remain safely at Rome under the protection of Dolabella,* and this can be a help to me if there is any outbreak of violence or plundering. On the other hand, I am influenced by the sight of all honourable men abandoning Rome and taking their womenfolk with them, whereas this area in which I am staying is one in which both townships and country estates are friendly towards me, so that you can be in my company a great deal, and when you are apart from me you can conveniently stay on our properties.

2 To tell you the truth, I am not yet certain which is the best course. You must take note of what other ladies of your standing are doing, and beware of being unable to leave when you wish to go. Do please take careful and repeated thought about this, discussing it among yourselves and with friends. You must instruct Philotimus* to ensure that the house is securely barred and well protected. I would like you to appoint reliable couriers to ensure that I receive a letter from you each day. Above all, be sure to look after yourselves, as you would have me do likewise.

Formiae, 22 January

Letter 71 (*Att.* VII 17)

Formiae, January 49

CICERO TO ATTICUS

Your letter was welcome and agreeable to me. I did think of sending 1
the boys over to Greece when our flight from Italy seemed on the
cards, for we would have been heading for Spain,* and this would
not have been equally appropriate for them. It seems to me that you
and Sextus can even now justifiably remain in Rome.* The fact is
that you are not under the slightest obligation to show friendship to
our Pompey, for no one has ever brought property values so low at
Rome.* As you see, I am still good for a joke!

You must know by now the response which Lucius Caesar* is 2
carrying back from Pompey, and the letter he is bearing from him
to Caesar, for it was written and sent as if published for general circu-
lation. I mentally criticized Pompey for this, because though he
himself writes with clarity, he entrusted the communication of such
important issues to our friend Sestius* for all the world to lay their
hands on. The result is that I have never read anything more
sestianesque. But Pompey's letter makes it clear that he refuses nothing
to Caesar, and that all Caesar's demands are abundantly met. Caesar
will be wholly insane not to agree to them, especially as the requests
he makes are wholly shameless. Who do you think you are, Caesar, to
stipulate 'Provided that Pompey leaves for Spain', and 'Provided that
he demobilizes his garrisons'? Yet these concessions are granted, less
honourably now that Caesar has violated and made war on the republic than if his candidacy had been granted earlier. I fear, however, that
he may not be satisfied even with these concessions, for after entrusting these instructions to Lucius Caesar, he ought to have indulged in
a little more restraint until replies were brought back, instead of
which he is now said to be at his most incisive.

Trebatius* writes that on 22 January Caesar requested him to 3
write to ask me to be in the vicinity of Rome, and that he would
appreciate this from me more than anything. The request was made
at some length. I realized from calculation of the days that as soon as
Caesar heard of my departure, he had begun to worry that we might
all quit Rome. So I have no doubt that he has written to Piso and to
Servius. What surprises me is that he did not write personally to me,
or communicate with me through Dolabella or Caelius,* though I do

not view a letter from Trebatius with contempt, for I know that he regards me with unsurpassed affection.

4   I wrote back to Trebatius (since Caesar had not written to me, I refused to contact him directly), to say that the request was difficult for me to meet at this time, but that I was residing on my estates, and had undertaken no levy of troops or other negotiations. I shall adhere to this policy for so long as there is hope of peace, but if war breaks out, I shall not fail my duty, or demean my standing, once I have consigned the boys to Greece *à l'abri du danger*, for I realize that the whole of Italy will be ablaze with war, since such great harm has been awakened by citizens, some of them disreputable and others envious. But within a few days future developments will become clearer from Caesar's response to our reply. I shall then write to you at greater length if it is to be war, but if it is peace or even a truce I shall, I hope, be with you in person.

5   Today, 2 February, the day I pen this letter, I await the ladies at my house at Formiae, to which I have returned from Capua. I had in fact written to them to remain in Rome, following the advice in your letter, but I fear that apprehension is rife in the city. I want to be at Capua on 5 February at the consuls' command. I shall at once pass on to you any message which reaches me from Pompey, and I shall await a letter from you on matters at your end.

Letter 72 (*Att.* VIII 8)

Formiae, February 49

CICERO TO ATTICUS

1   What a dishonourable, and, on that account, wretched situation this is! (For I feel that the dishonourable in the final analysis, or rather it alone, is wretched.) Pompey has nurtured Caesar, has of a sudden begun to fear him, has approved no terms of peace, has made no preparations for war, has abandoned Rome, has culpably lost Picenum, has tied himself down in Apulia, and is off to Greece, abandoning us all *en silence*, and leaving us to play no part in his

2   momentous and unprecedented plan. He suddenly receives a letter from Domitius,* and dispatches one to the consuls. As it seems to me, *la noblesse* shone before his eyes, and the man he ought to have been cried out:

> Therefore let both now plot, if plot they must,
> And scheme to do me every harm they can,
> For right is on my side.*

But Pompey is making for Brundisium, *disant adieu à la noblesse*. People are saying that on hearing this news, Domitius and his associates have surrendered. What a dismal situation! So I am choked with grief, and can write no more to you. I await a letter from you.

Letter 73 (*Att.* VIII 13)

Formiae, March 49

CICERO TO ATTICUS

You can regard the handwriting of my secretary as an indication of 1
my eye trouble, and as the reason for the brevity of this note, though in fact I have nothing to write about at present. All my thoughts for the future lie in the news from Brundisium. If Caesar has met our Pompey there,* there is a slight hope of peace, but if Pompey has earlier crossed to Greece, one must fear a destructive war. But do you note what kind of man into whose power the state has fallen, how keen and watchful and carefully prepared he is? I swear that as long as he does not slaughter or rob anyone, he will gain the affection even of those who have most greatly feared him. Many men from towns 2
and country chat with me, and their concern is for absolutely nothing but their fields and little farmsteads and meagre finances. Notice how things have gone into reverse; they fear the man whom they trusted earlier, and favour the man they feared.* I cannot contemplate with untroubled mind the monstrous blunders and faults of ours which have led to this. I have already written to you about what I think lies in store, and I now await a letter from you.

Letter 74 (*Att.* VIII 16)

Formiae, March 49

CICERO TO ATTICUS

I have taken prior thought for everything except a secret and safe 1
route to the Adriatic, for at this time of year I cannot journey by sea on this side.* But how am I to go where my heart longs to be, to

where the action summons me? I must retire speedily, in case I am somehow hindered and fettered. It is not our apparent leader who draws me on, for already I have found him before now the most *incompétent* of statesmen, and now I find him most *incompétent* as general as well. So it is not he who draws me on, but the common gossip about which Philotimus' letters inform me,* for he says that the optimates are cutting me up. Which optimates, for heaven's sake? See how they are streaming out to welcome Caesar, and how they are selling their souls to him. The townships are deifying him, and this is no hypocrisy such as they showed when uttering vows on behalf of Pompey* when he was sick.

2   Clearly, whatever wickedness this Pisistratus* of ours has not committed is as popular with them as if he has prevented some other from committing it. They place their hopes in Caesar as one well disposed, whereas they consider Pompey as one angry. Do you picture the *députations*, and the distinctions bestowed by the townships? You will respond: 'They are fearful.' Yes, I believe they are, but I swear that they fear Pompey more. Caesar's crafty clemency* delights them, whereas they are fearful of Pompey's irascibility. The jurors from the Body of 360,* who regarded Gnaeus as their particular joy—for I see one or other of them every day—are all a-tremble at threats of his; don't ask me which. So my question is: who are these optimates who seek to root me out while they remain at home? But whoever they are, 'I fear the Trojans',* though I realize the forlorn hope with which I am setting out, though I am associating myself with a man readier to ravage Italy than to win a victory, and though I anticipate a future life under a master. Indeed, as I write this letter on 4 March, I am already awaiting some news from Brundisium. But why do I speak of 'some news', rather than that Pompey has ignominiously fled from there, and the return of the victor, his route and destination? Once I hear that he is approaching on the Appian Way, I intend to make for Arpinum.*

Letter 75 *(Att.* IX 6)

Formiae, March 49

CICERO TO ATTICUS

1   No news has yet reached me from Brundisium. Balbus has written from Rome that he believes the consul Lentulus* has already made the crossing without having met up with the younger Balbus,* for

the young man had heard this news at Canusium, and had written to Balbus senior from there. He added that the six cohorts which had been at Alba* had gone over to Curius by the Minucian Way. Caesar, Balbus senior adds, had informed him of this by letter, and had stated that he would shortly be in Rome.

I shall therefore take your advice and refrain from going into hiding at this juncture at Arpinum, though, I should have liked to invest my son Cicero with the white toga* at Arpinum. I intended to leave a message to this effect for Caesar as an excuse, but perhaps he would be irritated by my not choosing Rome for it instead. But if I have to meet him, this place will be best. I shall then address the other issues—where to go, by what route, and when.

I hear that Domitius is in his residence at Cosa.* Indeed, they say 2 he is ready to set sail. If to Spain, I am not critical; if to join Gnaeus, I applaud him. At any rate, anywhere is better than eyeing Curius. Though I was his defence counsel, I cannot bear the sight of him, and likewise of others, but I suppose I must hold my peace out of fear of incriminating myself, for owing to my love of Rome, my native land, and in my belief that a settlement could be reached, my actions have resulted in my being totally isolated and circumscribed.

When I had finished this letter, a missive was delivered to me from 3 Capua. I quote what it says:

Pompey has sailed* across the sea with all the troops he had with him. They comprise 30,000 men, and with them are the two consuls, the plebeian tribunes, and all senators who were with him, together with their wives and children. He is said to have embarked on 4 March, the winds being northerly from then on. They say that all the ships he did not use have been broken up or burnt. A letter about the operation has been delivered to Lucius Metellus the plebeian tribune, at Capua from his mother-in-law Clodia, who has herself made the crossing.

Previously I was worried and deeply disturbed by the pressure of the 4 situation, for I could not solve the dilemma by constructive thought. But now that Pompey and the consuls have quitted Italy, I am not distressed, but blazing with resentment.

My heart does not stand firm, but I am tortured.*

Believe me, I am out of my mind at the deep dishonour which I am seen to have incurred. First of all, to think that I am not with Pompey, however weak the strategy he has adopted, nor secondly, with men of honour, despite their rash handling of our cause, especially as those for whose sake I was more chary of committing myself to fortune—my wife, my daughter, and the young Ciceros—would have preferred me to adopt the other course, and considered my present stance ignominious, and myself unworthy! As for my brother Quintus, he said he believed that whatever I approved was right, and he embraced it, wholly untroubled in mind.

5   I now read those letters of yours written from the outset, and they restore my morale a little. The earlier ones advise and implore me not to commit myself, and those most recent reveal your pleasure that I have stayed behind. When I read them, I consider myself to be less cowardly, but only for so long as I read them. Then my distress resurfaces, and with it *le fantôme de déshonneur*. So I beg you, dear Titus, remove or at any rate relieve this grief of mine by consolation or advice or in whatever way you can. Yet what could you or anyone possibly do? God can scarcely help me now.

6   I am myself trying to achieve what you advise and hope can ensue, namely that Caesar may permit me to be absent when any proceedings are taken against Gnaeus in the Senate. But I fear that I may not obtain this concession. Furnius* has come from him, and reports that the son of Quintus Titinius* is with Caesar. This is to acquaint you with the leaders we are to follow! Furnius also says that Caesar thanks me more profusely than I could wish. What he asks of me, in few words but with the force of *autorité*, you must ascertain from his letter.*

How sad for me that you were under the weather! Otherwise we could have been together, and at any rate we would not have been without a strategy. 'Two heads together . . .'*

7   Let us not rake over the past, however, but plan for the future. Up to now I have been deceived on two counts. To begin with, there was hope of an agreement, and if this had been established I was keen to exploit the popular path,* and free my old age from anxiety. Secondly, I began to realize that Pompey was embarking on a cruel and destructive war. So help me God, I believed it was my higher duty as citizen and man to suffer any punishment whatever rather than not merely preside over, but even participate in, such barbaric behaviour. But it seems that even death would have been preferable to cooperation with the politicians here. So, dear Atticus, think on, or better, think through these issues. I shall endure any outcome more bravely than my present suffering.

Letter 76 (*Att.* IX 9)

Formiae, March 49

CICERO TO ATTICUS

I received three letters from you on 16 March; they were sent on the
12th, 13th, and 14th. So I shall answer each in chronological order,
beginning with the first. I agree with you that I should stay in my
house at Formiae rather than anywhere else. I also agree with you
about the Adriatic, and, as I wrote to you previously, I shall investigate to see if there is any way I can, with Caesar's consent, avoid
taking part in public affairs. You praise me for having written that I
forget the previous actions and misdeeds of our friend.* True, I do
forget them; why, apart from those which you recount, I do not recall
those which he directed against me personally. So much more does
gratitude for kindnesses count with me than resentment at injuries.
So let me act as you propose, and gather my thoughts, for as soon as
I take a trip into the country, I play the role of *sophiste*,* and as I
travel I continually review my *dispositions*. Some of them, however,
are difficult to assess. So far as the optimates are concerned, have it
your own way. But you know the proverb, 'Dionysius in Corinth';
the son of Titinius has joined Caesar. As for your apparent fear that
your counsels irritate me, in fact your advice and letters are my sole
delight. So be true to your opinions, and do not stop writing to me
whatever comes to mind, for nothing can be more welcome in my
eyes.

I pass now to your second letter. You are right to be sceptical
about the number of soldiers, for Clodia has exaggerated* them by
more than half. Her account of the crippling of the ships was also
untrue. As for your praise of the consuls, I too praise their courage,
but I censure their strategy, for their departure has undermined any
peace-initiatives which I was in fact contemplating. So thereafter I
sent back to you Demetrius' work *On Concord*,* entrusting it to
Philotimus.

I have no doubt that a destructive war now looms over us, and it
will be ushered in by famine. Yet I am sorry not to be involved in this
war, in which the impact of lawlessness will be so great, for though it
is an impious thing to deny food to our own parents, our leaders
believe that our fatherland, our most ancient and sacred parent, is to

be killed by starvation. My fear of this is based not on conjecture, but on conversations* at which I was present. That entire fleet is being assembled from Alexandria, Colchis, Tyre, Sidon, Aradus, Cyprus, Pamphylia, Lydia, Rhodes, Chios, Byzantium, Lesbos, Smyrna, Miletus, and Cos, to cut off all supplies for Italy and to control the corn-producing provinces.

Think how angry Pompey will be when he comes, and especially with those particularly devoted to his welfare—as if he has been abandoned by those whom he has abandoned! So as I hesitate, wondering what it is fitting for me to do, it is my friendly feeling towards him that carries great weight with me. If this were laid aside, it would be better to die in my native land than by saving her to overthrow her. What you say about the north wind* is clearly right; my fear is that Epirus may suffer badly. But is there any place in Greece which you think will not be plundered, when he is openly declaring and intimating to his troops that he will prevail over Caesar even in his bestowal of largesse? Your advice that when I meet Caesar I should not be over-gracious but should adopt a dignified tone is splendid, for that is clearly what I must do. I am thinking of visiting Arpinum once I have met him, in case when he arrives I happen to be away, or am dashing here and there on that most unpleasant of roads. As you mention in your letter, I hear that Bibulus came* and went back on 14 March.

3   In your third letter you say that you await Philotimus. He set out from here on 14 March, so my letter, an immediate reply to the earlier one of yours, will have been delivered to you somewhat later. As you say in your letter, I imagine that Domitius* is staying in his residence at Cosa, and his intentions are unknown. As for that most despicable and contemptible individual* who claims that the consular elections can be conducted by a praetor, his political stance is as it always was. So his claim is surely what Caesar is referring to in that letter, a copy of which I sent you, in which he states that he wishes to consult my 'advice' (so be it, for it is available to all), my 'influence' (a stupid suggestion, but I think it is a pretence to gain some votes of senators), my 'standing' (perhaps my vote as a consular), and finally, 'my assistance in general'. I began to suspect from your letter at that time that this was what he was after, or something not much different, for it is very much in his interest that matters do not come to an interregnum. He achieves his aim if consuls are

elected under the presidency of a praetor. But our augural books*
have it that it is illegal not only for consuls, but also for praetors, to
be elected when a praetor is in charge, and that this has never
occurred before. It is unlawful for consuls to be so elected because it
is illegal for the higher power to be proposed by the lower, and for
praetors, because they are proposed as colleagues of consuls, who
possess the greater executive power. Quite soon Caesar will want me
to propose this, for he will not rest content with Galba, Scaevola,
Cassius, and Antony.* 'Then may the broad earth swallow me.'*

But you realize what a massive storm is brewing. I shall write to 4
tell you which senators have crossed to Greece when I know for
certain. Your understanding about the corn-distribution is correct; it
cannot be administered without the revenue from the provinces.
Your fears with regard to Pompey's entourage demanding the earth,
and an impious war, are justified. I should be very keen to see our
friend Trebatius,* in spite of your warning that he is wholly
pessimistic. You must urge him to get a move on, for it will be convenient for him to visit me before Caesar arrives.

With regard to the property at Lanuvium, the moment I heard of 5
Phamea's death* I expressed the hope that one of my friends would
buy it, provided that the republic still survives. But I did not think
of you, though you are my dearest friend, for I know that you usually investigate the yearly produce and the land-value, and I had
observed your distinctive approach not only at Rome but also at
Delos. But though the estate is handsome, my own valuation is lower
than the assessment in the year of Marcellinus' consulship, when I
considered that the modest property would be quite pleasant to have
because of the house I owned at that time at Antium, and it would
have cost less than the refurbishment of my dwelling at Tusculum. I
offered 500,000 sesterces through Precius* as intermediary; he was to
pass it on at that price when he intended to sell it. He refused. But
nowadays I think that the entire property has declined in value,
because money is scarce. It will in fact be more convenient for me, or
rather for us, if you buy it. But be sure not to despise that same
owner's house at Antium. It is most charming, though all such properties in my view seem doomed to desolation.

This is my answer to your three letters, but I expect more from
you, for your letters have been my support up to now.

Written on the feast of the Liberalia

Letter 77 (*Att.* IX 11A)

Formiae, March 49

CICERO IMPERATOR TO CAESAR IMPERATOR

1 On reading your letter delivered to me by our friend Furnius,* in which you requested my presence in Rome, I was scarcely surprised that you wished to exploit my 'advice and standing', but I am pondering what you meant by my 'influence and help'. But hope leads me to contemplate that in accordance with your remarkable and unique wisdom I may believe that you wish to discuss tranquillity, peace, and harmony between citizens, and I regard my nature and image as sufficiently apt for this purpose.

2 If this is the case, and you are at all anxious to uphold our friend Pompey, and to reconcile him both to yourself and to the republic, you will certainly find no one more suited to the cause than myself, for I have always at the first opportunity counselled both him and the Senate to seek peace. Since the recourse to arms, I have taken no part in the warfare, and, in my judgement, in that war you are unjustly treated, for men hostile and jealous of you strive to deny you the distinction* granted by the favour of the Roman people. But just as on that occasion I not merely lent support to your prestige, but encouraged all others to assist you, so now the prestige of Pompey is likewise my urgent concern.

3 It is some years now since I marked out the two of you in particular as persons to cultivate and to engage in the close friendship which I enjoy today. So I ask, or rather beg and beseech you with all my prayers, to devote a little time amid your pressing concerns to consider how by your generosity I can conduct myself as a good, grateful, and devoted person in recalling his outstanding kindness. If this request concerned myself only, I should still hope that you would grant it, but in my opinion it is also the concern both of yourself and the republic that I, the friend of peace and of both of you, should through your agency be allowed to continue as the most appropriate person for maintaining harmony between the two of you and between our citizens.

When earlier I thanked you for being Lentulus' saviour* as he had once been mine, I later read the letter he sent me, in which he most gratefully recalled your generosity and kindness. . . . that

I owed my salvation to you as he did. If you are appreciative of my gratitude towards him, I beg you to allow me to show it likewise to Pompey.

Letter 78 (*Att.* IX 18)

Formiae, March 49

CICERO TO ATTICUS

I followed your advice in both respects, for my discussion with him* 1
was such as to make him think well of me rather than to thank me, and I adhered to my resolve not to go to Rome. But my belief that he would be accommodating was mistaken, for I have never encountered anything less likely. He said that I was adjudging him guilty, and that if I did not attend, the others would be more reluctant. I stated that their situation differed from mine. After several exchanges, he said: 'Then you must come and argue for peace.' 'What, at my own discretion?' I asked. 'Of course,' he replied, 'for am I to tell you what to say?' 'I shall propose,' I replied, 'that the Senate disapprove of any movement into Spain, or of any transportation of armies into Greece, and I shall express', I added, 'at length my regrets about Gnaeus.' He then remarked: 'I do not want these things to be said.' 'I imagined that such would be the case,' I observed, 'but I am reluctant to attend, because I must either speak on these lines or absent myself, and there is a good deal more which I could in no way refrain from saying, if I were present.' Finally, as if he was seeking to foreclose the discussion, he asked me to consider. I could hardly refuse. We parted on that note. So I believe that he is not pleased with me, but I was pleased with myself, and it is some time since this has been my experience.

For the rest—ye gods, what an entourage, or to use your favourite 2
expression, what a *foule*, among them the *héros* Celer!* What an unsavoury occasion, what a crew of desperadoes! Fancy, the son of Servius and the son of Titinius* being in the army which blockaded Pompey! The man has six legions, he is constantly on the qui vive, and he is bold. I see no end to the mischief. Now, if ever, you must proffer your advice. That meeting had to be the last throw.

I almost forgot to mention his *dernier mot*, a distasteful one. He 3
said that if he could not have the benefit of my counsels, he would

adopt the advice of those he could, and that he would stoop to any lengths. So do you recognize the man you described in your letter? You must at any rate have groaned on reading this! You ask what ensued. Well, he immediately left for his estate at Alba, and I am retiring to mine at Arpinum, where I await that swallow's *gazouille-ment** of yours. You will retort: 'I'd rather you didn't rake up the past. Even that leader of ours was mistaken on many counts.'

4   But I await your letter, for we can no longer say, as we said earlier, 'Let us see how things turn out.' My meeting with him was the last straw, in which I have no doubt that I have alienated him. Hence there is need for action all the more speedily. Do please write, and make it *une lettre politique*. I now eagerly await what you have to say.

Letter 79 (*Fam.* IV 1)

Cumae, April 49

CICERO TO SERVIUS SULPICIUS

1   My friend Gaius Trebatius has written to me to say that you have asked him for my whereabouts. He spoke of your regret that ill-health prevented you from seeing me when I was in the neighbour-hood of Rome,* and that at this time you would welcome a chat with me, if I made my way reasonably close to Rome, about the obligations of both of us.

Servius, I only wish that we could have talked together while the state was still intact (we must, alas, speak of the situation in these terms). We would certainly have lent some assistance to the republic as it was collapsing. Already while I was away I realized that you had foreseen these evils long before, and that both during and after your consulship you were defending the peace. But though I approved your strategy and held the same views, I achieved nothing, for I arrived too late. I was a lonely figure, appearing unfamiliar with the situation, and I encountered the lunacy of men bent on fighting. But now, since it means that we can lend no help to the republic, if there is any way by which we can consult our personal interests, seeking not to preserve any feature of our earlier standing, but to lament the course of events as honourably as we can, there is no one in the world with whom I believe I should discuss the situation rather than you. For you are not forgetful of the examples of men of the greatest fame, whom we ourselves should emulate, nor of the precepts of those of greatest learning, whom you have always cultivated. Indeed, I would have written previously to you to suggest that it would be pointless for you to attend the Senate, or rather, the gathering of senators,* but I feared to alienate the attitude of the man who was begging me* to follow your example. When he asked me to attend the Senate, I indicated to him that I would express all that you have said about peace, and with regard to the provinces of Spain.

You are aware of the situation as it stands: a world ablaze with war 2 through division of supreme powers, a city without laws, without courts, without respect for rights and pledges, abandoned to pillage and arson. So I cannot think not merely of anything to hope for, but of scarcely anything to presume even to pray for. However, if you, a man of immense practical wisdom, consider it useful for us to confer, even though it is my intention to retire at some distance from the city whose very name I am now reluctant to hear, I shall make my way to the vicinity of Rome. I have instructed Trebatius not to demur at any request you wish him to send to me. So I should like you to comply with this, or if you prefer, dispatch to me one of your trusted servants, so that you do not have to leave Rome, nor I to approach it. I repose so much confidence in you as I am perhaps claiming for myself, in the certainty that whatever we decide by common agreement will meet the approval of the world at large. Farewell.

Letter 80 (*Att.* X 10)

Cumae, May 49

CICERO TO ATTICUS

How blind I was not to have foreseen this! I sent Antony's letter on 1 to you. I wrote to him that I had no thought of opposing Caesar's plans, that I was keeping my son-in-law in mind,* and also that I was mindful of my friendship with Caesar; that if my affections had moved elsewhere, I would have joined Pompey; but because I was unwilling to rush to and fro accompanied by lictors, I wished to get away from here, though even now my mind was not definitely made up. Now observe his *conseil* which he has sent in reply:

Your plan* is a good one, for the man who seeks to be neutral remains in 2 his native land, whereas if he departs, he appears to be passing judgement on one side or the other. But I am not the person who must rightfully decide who is to depart or not. Caesar has charged me with this role, instructing me not to allow anyone at all to leave Italy. So it hardly matters whether I approve your idea, since I cannot grant you any permission. I think that you should write to Caesar and make this request of him. I have no doubt that you will obtain it, especially as you promise to take account of the friendship you share.

3   *Voilà une dépêche laconienne!** I shall be on the look-out for him none the less. He arrives on the evening of 3 May, that is today, so perhaps he will visit me tomorrow. I shall try him out, and listen to him. I shall say that there is no hurry, and that I shall send a message to Caesar. I shall act in secret, lurk in a hide-out somewhere with very few companions. I shall at any rate take flight from here, wholly against the wishes of these custodians—if only I can reach Curio!* *Écoutez-moi bien!* Deep resentment has reinforced my determination. I shall achieve something worthy of myself!

Your *dysurie** worries me a lot. Treat it, I beg you, while it is *à son début.*

4   I was pleased with the news in your letter about the Massilians;* do let me know anything more which you hear. I should be keen to take Ocella* if I could make the journey openly, as I had negotiated with Curio. I await Servius here at the request of his wife and son, and I think I must oblige.

5   This fellow* here is transporting Cytheris as a second wife in an open litter with him. He has seven litters in train as well, some with mistresses and some with boyfriends in them. Take note of the disgusting circumstances of our final days, and remain sceptical, if you can, whether Caesar on his return as vanquished or victor will indulge in mass slaughter. For myself, I shall escape from the clutches of these murderous assassins by rowing-boat if no ship is available. But once I have met Antony I shall write further.

6   As for our young man,* I cannot withhold my affection from him, but I clearly realize that he has no such feeling for me. I have never seen anyone so *sans scrupule*, so hostile to his family, and so devious in his intentions. What an unbelievable weight of worries! But I shall ensure that he obtains guidance, as indeed he is already receiving it. He is remarkably talented, but *il faut diriger sa caractère.*

Letter 81 (*Att.* X 14)

Cumae, May 49

CICERO TO ATTICUS

How wretched life is! And protracted fear is a greater ill than the 1
object of that fear. Servius,* as I wrote earlier, arrived on 7 May, and
visited me next day in the early morning. To avoid keeping you any
longer in suspense, we found no solution in any plan. I never saw
anyone more aflutter with fear, and indeed each and every one of his
fears merited such fear. Pompey, he said, was angry with him, and
Caesar was unfriendly. The prospect of victory for either was
ghastly, on the one hand because of the cruelty of Pompey and the
recklessness of Caesar, and on the other because of the financial
straits of both, the solution for which could come only from the
property of private individuals. He expressed these views with so
many tears that I was surprised that such protracted unhappiness did
not dry them up! So far as I am concerned, even the ophthalmia
which prevents my writing to you in my own hand does not induce
tears, but it troubles me more often because it keeps me awake.

So gather all the information you can as consolation for me, and 2
commit it to paper, but not philosophical reflections or citations from
books, for I have these at home. Somehow such medicine is not so
strong as the infirmity. Instead, enquire about the Spanish provinces
and about Massilia. The news which Servius brought about these was
quite reassuring, and he also claims that there are reliable sources for
the report of the two legions.* So this and the like is the information I
want, if you have it. You will for sure hear something within a few days.

I come back to Servius. We have put off our entire discussion till 3
tomorrow, but he is reluctant to leave Italy. He says he much prefers
to face whatever the future brings in his own bed. His son's military
service at Brundisium is a troublesome obstacle. The one thing
which he most emphatically maintained was that if the persons condemned are allowed back, he will retire into exile. My riposte to this
was that the restoration would certainly happen, and that the present
developments were no less grave; I assembled several instances. But
they did not inspire courage in him, but further fear. Accordingly,
I now think that I must refrain from divulging my plan to him, rather
than take him aboard. So his presence here has made little difference.
Following your advice I am taking thought about Caelius.*

Letter 82 (*Fam.* XIV 7)

Aboard ship at Caieta,* June 49

CICERO TO HIS DEAR TERENTIA

1 I have laid down and cast aside the troubles and worries which to my profound regret have caused such great unhappiness both to you and to dear Tullia,* who is dearer to me than my own life. The reason for them I understood the day after I left you; that night I vomited *bile pure*, and gained such immediate relief that some god seems to have cured me. You must make devoted and chaste satisfaction to that god in your usual way.

2 I hope we have a really good ship. As soon as I embarked, I got down to writing this, I shall next write a series of letters to my friends, to whom I shall most conscientiously entrust you and my dear Tullia. I would exhort both of you to be more courageous in spirit if I did not already know that you are more courageous than any man. However, the situation is such that it enables me to hope that for your part you are most conveniently settled where you are, and I for mine will at last be defending the republic in company with others of like mind.

3 First and foremost, do safeguard your health. Secondly, if you are so disposed, do take advantage of the country houses furthest away from the soldiery. You will be able to make good use of the farm at Arpinum with our servants from Rome, if the price of grain rises higher. Our most charming young Cicero sends you most affectionate greetings. A thousand farewells.

Sent on 7 June

Letter 83 (*Att.* XI 1)

Epirus, January 48

CICERO TO ATTICUS

1 I have received from you the sealed document which Anteros brought. I could not ascertain from it any information about my private affairs.* I am most painfully exercised about them, because the one who was handling them is not in Rome, and I have no idea where in the world he is. All my hopes of keeping my reputation and my domestic finances rest on your long-attested kindness to me. If you afford that kindness at this wretched and critical time, I shall more

bravely endure the dangers which I share with others here. I beg and beseech you to undertake this commission.

In Asia I possess the equivalent of 2,200,000 sesterces in cisto- 2 phori.* You will without difficulty protect my credit by a bill of exchange for this sum. Had I not believed that I was leaving it readily available (I trusted the person in whom, as you know, I put too much trust long ago), I should have lingered for a short while and avoided leaving my private finances tied up. The reason why I am writing about it rather late to you is because I was late in realizing what I had to fear. I beg you repeatedly to take me totally under your wing, so that if my comrades here survive, I can emerge with them unscathed, and can ascribe my integrity to your kindness.

Letter 84 (*Att.* XI 2)

Epirus, March 48

CICERO TO ATTICUS

I received your letter on 4 February, and on that day I formally 1 accepted the inheritance in accordance with the will. One of the many wretched anxieties has been lifted from my shoulders if, as you write, the inheritance can guarantee my credit and protect my reputation, though in fact I gather that even without the inheritance you would have protected my good name with your own resources.

You mention the dowry.* I beg you by all the gods to take over the 2 entire transaction, and protect my daughter, whose wretched plight is attributable to my guilt and carelessness. Use whatever resources I have, and your own money, so long as it does not embarrass you. You write that she is short of everything. Do not, I beg you, allow this to continue. What expenses are absorbing the returns from my properties? As for the 60,000 sesterces* which you mention in your letter, no one ever told me that this had been taken from the dowry, for otherwise I would never have allowed it. But this is the least of the indignities I have sustained. My chagrin and my tears forbid me to write to you about them.

I have drawn about half of the money which was lodged in Asia. 3 I think that it is more secure where it is* than in the hands of the tax-farmers. You urge me to maintain strength of mind; I only wish you could adduce some reason which would enable me to do so. But if in addition to my other misfortunes there is the further one which

Chrysippus* said lay in store for my house, and which you did not mention, who was ever more wretched than myself? Forgive me, I beg and beseech you, for I cannot write anything more. You are well aware of the depth of sorrow which oppresses me. But if my plight was shared with the rest who appear to embrace the same cause, my fault would appear less blameworthy, and accordingly more easily borne. But as things stand, there is nothing to console me, unless you can contrive something—if even now something can be contrived—to prevent my being visited by some unprecedented disaster and injustice.

4   I have sent back your courier rather late, because I had no opportunity to do so earlier. Your servants have provided me with 20,000 sesterces, and with the clothes which I needed. Please write in my name to any persons you think appropriate; you know who my friends are. If they demand my seal and my handwriting, you must tell them that I refrained from using them because of the guards on watch.

Letter 85 (*Att.* XI 3)

Pompey's camp, June 48

CICERO TO ATTICUS

1 You will be able to ascertain what goes on here from the courier who delivered your letter. I have detained him rather too long, because I expect news every day, and the only item which merits dispatching him at present is that for which you sought a reply, namely my wishes concerning 1 July.* Both courses are problematic; on the one hand the risk involving such a large sum at this hazardous time, and on the other the break in friendly relations (which you mention) when the outcome of events is so doubtful. So as with other matters I leave this problem in particular to your friendship and indulgence, and also to Tullia's judgement and wishes. I would have consulted the poor girl's interests better if some time ago I had discussed with you my security and my finances in person rather than by letter.

2   You state that none of our communal misfortunes overhang me in particular. Though this observation affords some consolation, there are none the less particular misfortunes* of which you are certainly aware. They are most oppressive, and such as I could most easily have avoided. But they will be less oppressive if they are lightened by your management and care, as they have been up to now.

The money is with Egnatius.* I am happy to let it lie where it 3
rests, for it does not appear that the present situation here can continue for long, so I shall soon be able to ascertain what best needs to
be done. Mind you, I am short of everything, for the person I accompany here* is likewise in straitened circumstances. I have lent him a
large sum in the belief that when a settlement is reached my gesture
will further redound to my credit.

I would like you as before to write to anyone you think deserves a
note from me. My greetings to your household, and look after yourself. Above all, take care and ensure by every means, as you say you
will, that the girl on whose account I am as you know most distressed
may not want for anything.

In camp, 13 June

Letter 86 (*Att.* XI 4A)
Dyrrhachium, June 48
CICERO TO ATTICUS

You will be able to learn from Isidorus the answer to your query about 1
recent operations here. What remains to be done does not seem to present
too much difficulty. Do please attend to the task which you know is my
particular wish;* your letters and actions show that you are already doing
this. This worry is the death of me, and it has made me extremely ill. When
I recover, I shall join the person who is directing operations,* and who is
extremely optimistic. Brutus* is my friend; he shows enthusiasm for the
cause. This is as much as I can prudently commit to paper. Farewell.

With regard to the second instalment, I beg you to ponder the
appropriate action with every care, as I wrote in the letter which Pollex
carried to you.

Letter 87 (*Att.* XI 4)
Pompey's camp, July 48
CICERO TO ATTICUS

I have received one letter delivered by Isidorus, and two others dis- 1
patched later. The most recent of these informed me that the farms
have not been sold, so you yourself must ensure that you provide

for her. With regard to the property at Frusino, it will be a convenient purchase, as long as I live to enjoy it.

As for your request for letters from me, I am hindered by lack of topics. I have none that deserve a letter, for neither happenings nor operations meet in any way with my approval. If only I had earlier conversed with you face to face, rather than by letter! I am protecting your interests here as best I can. Celer will give you the rest of the news. Up to now I have myself avoided every commission,* and all the more so because I could discharge nothing appropriate to me and to what concerns me.

Letter 88 (*Fam.* XIV 12)

Brundisium, November 48

CICERO TO HIS DEAR TERENTIA

1 I pray that your joy at my safe arrival in Italy* may continue unabated. But in addition to the worries occasioned by my mental distress and the monstrous injustices suffered by my family, I fear that I am embarked on a course which I cannot readily sort out. So lend me your help, as far as you can, though nothing occurs to me that you can do. There is no point at this time in your making the journey here; the road is long and unsafe. Moreover, I do not see how you can help if you came. Farewell.

4 November

Letter 89 (*Att.* XI 5)

Brundisium, November 48

CICERO TO ATTICUS

1 I cannot without the greatest sorrow write to tell you of the reasons— so bitter, so serious, so unprecedented—which have impelled me to follow my heart's prompting rather than my rational thinking, but their impact has been such that they induced the outcome which you observe. In consequence I can find nothing to write concerning my situation, and nothing to ask of you. You are aware of the facts and the main thrust of the business. I do indeed realize from your letters, both

those written jointly with others and those signed by yourself, what I recognize without prompting, namely that you are shattered by the suddenness of events and are searching for new ways of coming to my aid.

With regard to the suggestion in your letter that I should draw 2 nearer by travelling at night* from one town to another, I have not the slightest notion how that is practicable. I have no lodgings convenient enough to spend all the hours of daylight in the various places, and from what you envisage, there is not much difference between being observed by people in a town and on the road. But I shall ponder this like other suggestions to see how this aim can be most aptly achieved.

I have not been able to pen more letters because of mental distress 3 and physical problems which are unbelievable, so I have replied only to persons from whom I have received letters. I should like you to reply in my name to Basilus and to others who occur to you, including Servilius.* As for my failure to write a single word to you and yours for so long, you can infer from this letter that what is lacking is not good intentions, but topics to discuss.

As for your enquiry about Vatinius,* neither he nor anyone else is 4 remiss with their attentions, if only they can find any means of aiding me. Quintus' attitude towards me at Patrae was most unfriendly. His son joined him there from Corcyra. I think they have now left with the others.

Letter 90 (*Att.* XI 6)
Brundisium, November 48

CICERO TO ATTICUS

I appreciate that you are worried not only for your own fortunes and 1 for those we all share, but above all for myself and my grief, which not merely does not diminish but is intensified when joined by your distress. With your practical wisdom you surely sense the consolation which can above all afford me relief, for you show approval of my decision, and you state that I could not have acted at such a time in a better way. You further say (though this is not so important to me as your own judgement, but it is none the less important) that my action is approved also by others who are of some account. If I thought that such was the case, it would relieve my distress.

2 'Believe me', I hear you say. Indeed I do, but I know how much you long to relieve my depression. I never regretted having steered clear of the warfare; so monstrous was the cruelty involved in it, and so monstrous was the association with barbaric nations,* that a list of the proscribed had been compiled, embracing not individuals but entire classes, and by general assent it was decided that the possessions of all of you would be the booty following that victory. I say 'all of you' expressly. Consideration of your case in particular was never mooted except in the most heartless terms. So I shall never regret my good intentions, but I do regret my strategy. I should have chosen to lie low in some town until I was summoned.* I would have been the object of less talk, and I would have endured less grief. My present situation would not have caused me anguish; to stagnate here in Brundisium is in every way burdensome, but how can I follow your advice to draw nearer to Rome without the lictors* which the people bestowed on me, and which cannot be taken from me so long as I retain my citizenship? Recently, when I was approaching this town, I made them merge for a short time with the crowd, carrying staves in case the soldiers attacked them. Since then I have remained indoors.

3 I have raised this matter in letters to Balbus and Oppius,* in view of their positive reaction to my approaching nearer Rome, to ask them to give thought to it. I believe that they will approve, for their attitude to it is that Caesar will be anxious not merely to preserve my standing, but even to enhance it. Moreover, they urge me to keep my spirits up, and to set my hopes high. This is what they pledge and maintain. I would be more certain of this reception had I stayed in Italy, but this is to harp on the past. So I beg you to take thought for the future, and to investigate the situation with these associates of yours, if you think it advisable and they agree. Let them take on board Trebonius, Pansa,* and any others, and get them to write to Caesar to say that whatever action I take is on their advice. In this way Caesar may approve my action as being done on their recommendation.

4 The illness and physical weakness of my dear Tullia weigh heavily upon me. I realize that you are taking great care of her, and I greatly appreciate it.

I was never in doubt that Pompey would meet his end,* for the 5 hopelessness of his situation had so dominated the attitudes of every king and every nation that I believed that this would be the outcome wherever he went. I cannot but lament his fate, for I knew him as an honest, clean-living, and dignified man.

Am I to console you for Fannius?* He used to make poisonous 6 comments about your staying in Italy. As for Lucius Lentulus,* he had promised himself Hortensius' house, and Caesar's urban gardens and his estate at Baiae. Admittedly this same greed is in evidence among the faction here, but on the other side there was no end to it, for all who had stayed in Italy were accounted enemies. But I should like to advert to this in the future, when I am in a more detached frame of mind.

I hear that my brother Quintus has retired to Asia to offer his 7 apologies from there. I have heard nothing about his son, but you can enquire of Caesar's freedman Diochares, the bearer of the letter you mention from Alexandria. I did not set eyes on him, but they say that he saw Quintus when he was on his way to Asia, or was already there. I await the letter from you which the situation demands. Please ensure that it is brought to me as early as possible.

27 November

Letter 91 (*Att.* XI 7)

Brundisium, December 48

CICERO TO ATTICUS

I welcomed your letter, in which you detailed everything you 1 thought was of concern to me. I shall accordingly do what you tell me accords with your comrades' wishes,* namely, retain these same lictors, as you say Sestius* was allowed to retain his, though I believe that those he was allowed to deploy were not his own but those granted by Caesar. For I am told that Caesar censured the senatorial decrees passed after the departure of the tribunes. So if he wishes to be consistent, he will be able to approve my lictors.

But why do I mention lictors, when I am virtually ordered to quit 2 Italy? Antony* sent me a copy of Caesar's dispatch to him, in which it was stated that Caesar had heard that Cato and Lucius Metellus* had entered Italy to appear openly in Rome, and that he disapproved of this, in case it resulted in disorders. All were barred from Italy, it said, except those whose cases he had investigated personally. The letter was quite vehement on this point. So Antony in his letter to me begged me to excuse him, but he could do no other than obey that dispatch. Then I sent Lucius Lamia to him, to point out that Caesar had told Dolabella to write bidding me enter Italy with all speed, and that I had come as a result of Dolabella's letter. Then Antony issued an instruction exempting myself and Laelius* by name. This was much against my wishes, for the exemption could have been made without citation of names.

3   How numerous and oppressive are these vexations! You try to soften them, and you are not altogether unsuccessful, for in fact you relieve my distress by the heavy labours you apply to relieve it. I hope that you do not find it oppressive to do this so very often. You will most successfully achieve your wish if you induce me to believe that I have not utterly lost the approval of honourable men. Yet what can you achieve in that respect? Clearly nothing. But if the actual situation offers you some scope, that can afford me the greatest consolation. I do in fact realize that this is not the case at present, but the course of events may provide it, as in the recent occurrence.* It was being said that I ought to have set out with Pompey, but his death has diminished the blame for this neglect of my obligation. But of all my failings, nothing is regarded as more regrettable than my failure to go to Africa. The criterion I applied was that the state should not be defended by barbarian auxiliaries of a most treacherous race,* especially against an army which had often been victorious. Perhaps this explanation does not meet with approval, for I am told that many honourable men have made for Africa, and I know that others were there earlier. On this count I am under heavy pressure. Here too I need the support of chance, that some or if possible all of them may put their own survival before all else, for if they stick it out and gain the day, you realize what will become of me. You will comment: 'But what will become of them if they are defeated?' That is the more honourable wound to endure. Such considerations turn the screw on me.

4   You have not explained in your letter why you do not prefer Sulpicius' decision to mine. Though it is not so impressive as that of Cato,* it is at any rate free of risk and pain. Most dismal of all is the

situation of those in Achaia, yet even they are better off than I am, since there are many of them in the one place, and once they return to Italy they will at once repair to their homes. You must continue as you are doing to excuse my decision and to have it approved by as many persons as possible.

As for your apologia for your own position, I am aware of your 5 reasons, and I also believe that it is in my interest for you to be in Rome, for no other reason than to discuss with appropriate people the necessary business that concerns me, as you have done previously. Please be aware particularly of my belief that there are many who have informed Caesar, or intend to do so, that I regret the course I adopted, and that I disapprove of what is happening. Both observations are true, but these persons are making them not because they are aware of the truth of them, but because they are hostile to me. What is vital is that Balbus and Oppius withstand their malice, and confirm Caesar's goodwill towards me by repeated letters. So apply yourself conscientiously to ensure that this is precisely what is done.

A second reason why I do not want you to leave Rome is the 6 remark in your letter that you are being harried.* What a wretched situation! What am I to write or to wish for you? I shall say little about this, for my tears have suddenly welled forth, I leave the matter in your hands; you must decide. Only ensure that nothing can hinder her at this time. Do pardon me, I beg you, for my tears and distress do not allow me to linger longer on this subject. I shall only say that nothing is more appreciated by me than your affection for her.

Your diligence in sending letters to those you think appropriate is 7 most helpful. I met someone who saw young Quintus at Samos, and his father at Sicyon. There is no difficulty in their seeking a reconciliation. I pray that, as they will see Caesar* before I do, they may be willing to support my case with him, as I would willingly help them if I had any influence.

You ask me to take a positive attitude to anything in your letters which may cause me pain. Indeed I do, and in the best possible spirit, and I beg you to write to me as frankly on every topic as you do and as often as possible.

17 December

Letter 92 (*Fam.* XIV 16)
Brundisium, January 47

TULLIUS TO HIS TERENTIA

1 It is good if you are well, as I am.

Though our circumstances are such that I have no reason either to expect a letter from you or to write to you myself, somehow I expect letters from you both, and I write them to you when I have a courier to deliver them.

Volumnia* ought to have been readier than she was to assist you, and she could have carried out what she did with greater care and prudence. However, there are other concerns which preoccupy and grieve me more. These are having the devastating effect intended by the people who have diverted me from my intention. Take care of yourself. Farewell.

4 January

Letter 93 (*Att.* XI 12)
Brundisium, March 47

CICERO TO ATTICUS

1 Cephalio handed me a letter from you on the morning of 8 March. Early on that same day I sent couriers to deliver a letter to you, but when I read yours I thought I should make some reply, especially as you reveal your anxiety to know what reason I shall give Caesar for my departure when quitting Italy. There is no need for me to advance a new reason, for I have often told him by letter, and I have charged many friends to explain to him, that I could not withstand the expectations which people expressed, much though I wanted to, and a good deal more to the same effect. I did not wish him to think that there was any possible explanation other than that I had followed my own convictions in such an important matter. Subsequently a letter which I received from the younger Cornelius Balbus stated that Caesar believed that my brother had 'trumpeted' my departure (this was the expression in the letter). At that time I did not know what Quintus had written about me to many people, though he had directed many bitter words and gestures* against me face to face. None the less I wrote to Caesar as follows:

I am as much concerned for my brother Quintus as for myself, but in 2 my present circumstances I do not presume to commend him to you. But this request at least I shall presume to make of you: I beg you not to believe that any action of his has sought to play down my obligations towards you and my affection for you. I would have you believe that on the contrary he has always prompted our close relationship, and that he has been my comrade rather than my guide on my journey. So in issues that remain you must accord him all the favour that your kindness and our friendship demand. I earnestly and repeatedly beg you not to allow me to prejudice you against him.

So in any encounter with Caesar, my attitude will be as it 3 has always been, though I have no doubt that Caesar will be indulgent towards Quintus, and has already made that clear. But in my view Africa must be my much more strenuous concern. You write that the daily strengthening of forces there encourages the prospect of negotiation rather than victory. I pray that this may be so, but my reading of the situation is far different. I believe that this is your view as well, and that the different judgement you express is intended not to beguile but to boost me, especially as Spain is now combining with Africa.*

With regard to your advice that I write to Antony and the others, 4 if you think that this is advisable, please do what you have often done,* for nothing occurs to me worth putting on paper. As for the report which you have received that I am more broken in spirit, do you find that surprising, when the splendid exploits of my son-in-law* are appended to my earlier anxieties? But do not break your practice of writing as often as you can, even if you have nothing about which to write, for your letters are always of benefit to me.

I have formally accepted the bequest from Galeo. I imagine that my acceptance is straightforward, since no copy has been sent to me.

8 March

Letter 94 (*Att.* XI 14)

Brundisium, April 47

CICERO TO ATTICUS

Though I am weighed down by misfortunes both general and per- 1 sonal, you do not even embark upon your usual consolations; you say that this is no longer possible. But your frank regard for the truth does not irritate me. My situation is not what it was earlier, when I thought I had comrades and allies, if nothing more. All who in Achaia and also in Asia have pleaded for clemency, both those who do not know the outcome of their pleas and those who do, are said to be on the point of sailing for Africa, so I have no one to share my guilt except Laelius, and he is in much better case than I, in that he has already been pardoned.

2   I do not doubt that in my case Caesar has written to Balbus and Oppius, and I would have been informed about it had there been any happier news. They would also have spoken to you. I would like you to have a word with them about this, and to inform me of their reply to you, not because an amnesty awarded by Caesar will be at all reliable, but it will allow some consultation and provision. Though I am aghast at the prospect of meeting everyone, particularly in view of the son-in-law I have,* I find nothing else to which to aspire, being beset by such great evils.

3   Both Pansa and Hirtius* have written, telling me that Quintus prospers, and again that he is said to be making for Africa with the rest. I shall write to Minucius* at Tarentum, and send on your letter. I shall inform you how I get on. I should be surprised if you could go as high as 30,000 sesterces unless there is a healthy return from Fufidius' properties. I see you are detained at Rome, yet I await you here, for the situation demands that I see you if at all possible. We are at the critical stage, the nature of which is harder to envisage here but is easy to contemplate at Rome. Farewell.

Letter 95 (*Att.* XI 15)

Brundisium, May 47

CICERO TO ATTICUS

1   Since you adduce justifiable reasons for my inability to see you at this time, I beg you to consider what I should do. Caesar seems to be held up at Alexandria,* so much so that he is ashamed even to write about operations there. Meanwhile those coming from Africa seem to be on the point of arriving, while those from Achaia and those due to return from Asia are joining them, or are lingering in some region of freedom. So what do you think I ought to do? I see that advice is difficult, for I am a solitary figure apart from one other,* and there is

no prospect of return to my former comrades, yet no indication is forthcoming from the Caesarians here to lend me encouragement. None the less I should be glad to have your view, and this together with other matters was why I was keen to meet with you if that could possibly take place.

I previously wrote to you that Minucius* had arranged for only 2 12,000 sesterces; I would like you to ensure that the remainder is remitted. Quintus has written to me, not merely failing to express conciliatory good wishes, but in the bitterest terms, and his son demonstrates remarkable loathing. There is no imaginable misfortune which does not oppress me, though all these problems are easier to bear than the pain caused by my miscalculation, for that pain is both massive and unremitting. Even if I were to have the associates with whom I expected to share that miscalculation, it would be a feeble consolation, but whereas everyone else has a way out, I have none. Some who were taken prisoner and others who have been cut off do not leave their aspiration in doubt, and their attitude will be no less evident when they extricate themselves and begin to join the others. Even those who of their own accord made overtures to Fufius* can be taxed only with being chicken-hearted. Then there are many who, no matter what their motives are for rejoining their comrades, will be welcomed back. All the more reason, then, why you should not be surprised that I cannot cope with such deep feelings of remorse, for I am the only person whose mistake is irreparable—though perhaps there is Laelius too, but what consolation is that to me? As for Gaius Cassius,* they say that even he has changed his plan of making for Alexandria.

I am writing to you on these matters not so that you can remove 3 these anxieties, but so that I can ascertain whether you can apply a remedy to the ills which afflict me. On top of these are my son-in-law and the other problems which tears prevent me from setting down. Why, even Aesopus' son* is causing me severe pain. There is absolutely no ill the absence of which can relieve my utter wretchedness. But to return to my initial query, what do you think I should do? Should I covertly draw near to some place close to Rome, or cross the sea? It is no longer possible for me to remain here.

On Fufidius' properties, why could nothing be finalized? The terms 4 were of the type on which there is usually no dispute, since the share which seems to be the smaller can be augmented by public bidding.

This query of mine is not unfounded, for I suspect that the coheirs regard my position as uncertain, and for that reason they prefer to leave the situation hanging. Farewell.

14 May

Letter 96 (*Fam.* XIV 11)

Brundisium, June 47

TULLIUS TO HIS TERENTIA

1 If you are well, it is good. I too am well.

Our dear Tullia came to join me on 12 June. Her unsurpassed courage and unique graciousness afflict me with even heavier remorse that through my inadvertence she has been confronted with a situation far different from that which her devotion and high standing deserve. I am thinking of sending our Cicero to Caesar* in company with Gnaeus Sallustius.* I will inform you if he goes. Pay careful attention to your health. Farewell.

14 June

Letter 97 (*Att.* XI 18)

Brundisium, June 47

CICERO TO ATTICUS

1 As yet there is no talk of Caesar's departure from Alexandria, and on the contrary some mention that he is heavily involved there. So I am not sending my son Cicero as I had planned, and I beg you to get me out of this place, for any punishment is milder than detention here. I have written about this to Antony, to Balbus, and to Oppius, for it is wholly inappropriate for me to be here, whether there is to be warfare in Italy or whether the disputants have recourse to naval forces. Perhaps both will occur; one or other certainly will.

2 From the conversation with Oppius you reported to me, I clearly realize how furious these associates of yours* are, but I urge you to allay their anger. I now anticipate nothing at all but wretchedness, but nothing can be more ruinous than my present situation. So I should like you to speak both to Antony and to your contacts in

Rome to expedite matters as quickly as you can. Then write back to me with all speed about all these matters. Farewell.

19 June

Letter 98 (*Att.* XI 20)

Brundisium, August 47

CICERO TO ATTICUS

On 14 August a freedman of Gaius Trebonius arrived from Pierian 1 Seleucia* after a journey of twenty-seven days to say that he had seen Quintus junior with Hirtius* in Caesar's headquarters at Antioch. He added that they had obtained without difficulty the information they sought about Quintus senior. I should be more pleased about this if the concessions we had been granted offered us any hope of certainty in the future. But there are other things to be feared from other people, and in addition concessions from Caesar, since they are those of a master, remain in his power to reverse at will.

He has pardoned Sallustius as well, and is said to be refusing 2 pardons to no one. This gives rise to the suspicion that investigations are merely being postponed. Marcus Gallias, son of Quintus, has restored his slaves to Sallustius. He has come to conduct the legions over to Sicily, where it is presumed that Caesar will proceed directly from Patrae. If he does so,* I shall come to some nearer place, as I would have preferred to do earlier. I urgently await from you a reply to my letter, in which I recently sought your advice. Farewell.

15 August

Letter 99 (*Fam.* XIV 23)

Brundisium, August 47

TULLIUS TO HIS TERENTIA

If you are well, that is good. I am well.   1

At last a letter has been delivered to me from Caesar. Its tone is quite generous. He is said to be coming more speedily than was anticipated. I shall inform you whether I shall go out to meet him or await him here, once I have decided. Please send the couriers back to me as early as possible. Pay attentive care to your health. Farewell.

Sent 12 August

Letter 100 (*Fam.* XV 15)

Brundisium, August 47

CICERO TO GAIUS CASSIUS

1   In our hope of peace and our abhorrence of civic bloodshed, we each sought to withdraw* from the needless continuance of warfare. But since it seems that I was the ringleader in this policy, I should perhaps render an account to you rather than expect one from you. Yet, as I am often wont to recall, the intimate conversations we shared led us both to the view that if not the entire war, at any rate our policy towards it should be dictated by the outcome of a single battle.* This opinion of ours no one has ever censured, except those who believe that it is better for the republic to be entirely destroyed rather than survive in diminished and enfeebled form. By contrast, I obviously envisage no hope from its destruction, but abundant prospects from what remains of it.

2   But the sequel has been such that the possibility of these events occurring was more surprising than our failure to see that they would occur, and than our inability to foresee them, for we are mere men. I myself confess that my guess was that, once what one may call the fatal battle had been fought, the victors would seek to consult the welfare of the community, and the vanquished their personal survival, but I thought that both these outcomes were dependent on the speed shown by the victor. If this had resulted, Africa would have met with the same clemency as Asia experienced, and also Achaia, where you, I believe, acted as delegate to plead for the troops there. But the opportunities, which play a prominent part especially in civil conflicts, were lost. The year that intervened has led some to hope for victory, and others to despise the prospect of defeat. Fortune shoulders the blame for all these ills, for who would have believed that the long delay caused by the fighting at Alexandria would have prolonged this war, or that the little-known Pharnaces* would strike fear into Asia?

But though we two shared a similar outlook, the fortunes we have 3
experienced have been different. The role which you sought to play
enabled you to participate in planning, and to be able to envisage the
future, which most effectively relieves anxiety. I for my part hastened, or so I thought, to encounter Caesar in Italy as he was returning after sparing the lives of many highly honourable men, and thus
to spur a willing horse towards peace. But I both have been and am
a world away from him. My life is spent amid the groans of Italy and
the most wretched plaints of Rome. Perhaps I myself, and you, and
the world at large, each according to his abilities, could have lent
some aid to relieve these laments if only our sponsor* had been present to allow it.

So please, in accordance with your constant goodwill towards me, 4
write to tell me what you envisage, what you feel, and what you think
we are to await and to perform. A letter from you will be of great
value to me. If only I had heeded that first letter of yours, which you
sent from Luceria!* I would then have preserved my authority and
endured no troubles.

Letter 101 (*Fam.* IX 1)
Rome, December 47–January 46

CICERO TO MARCUS VARRO

Your activities and your location I have ascertained from the letter 1
which you sent to Atticus and which he has read to me. But from that
letter I could not glean the slightest suspicion of when I would see
you. I hope, however, that your arrival is near at hand. I pray that it
may console me, though I am hard pressed by so many major problems that only the most obtuse idiot could hope for any relief from
them. But there may be some way in which you can assist me, or perhaps I can assist you.

What I want you to know is that now that I have come to Rome, 2
I am reconciled with old friends, in other words with my books.*
It was not that I abandoned association with them because I was
cross with them, but because they made me feel somewhat ashamed.
It seemed to me that when I plunged into a welter of confusion
with most disloyal associates, I did not sufficiently obey my books'
injunctions. They pardon me, and recall me into our long-standing

friendship, and they say that you are wiser because you remained faithful to their precepts. So since I have appeased them and am intimate with them, it appears that once I see you I should hope I shall more readily endure both the trials which oppress me and those which loom over me. So whether you wish us to meet at Tusculum or at Cumae, at your place or at mine, or at what I would regard as a last resort, namely Rome, I shall certainly ensure that as long as we are together, our rendezvous will be most convenient for both of us.

Letter 102 (*Fam.* XIII 29)

Rome, early 46

CICERO TO PLANCUS

1 I have no doubt you realize that, among the friendly associates bequeathed to you by your father, I am especially close to you,* not merely for those reasons which seek to present the appearance of an important relationship, but also for those maintained by intimacy and friendship. As you know, that friendship which I enjoyed with your father was most cordial, and ran very deep. From such beginnings my affection for you has grown, and enhanced my relationship with your father, the more so because I became aware that as soon as your developing years allowed you to discriminate in the importance which you were to attach to individuals, you began to respect, cultivate, and show affection to myself. In addition, there was the not insignificant bond between us of our pursuits, a bond important in itself especially relating to those pursuits and disciplines which of themselves bind those who have the same inclinations, in close friendship as well.

2 I imagine that you are waiting to see where these preliminaries, recalled from the distant past, are leading. You must realize that this recollection of the past has not been made without great and just cause. I am on most friendly terms with Gaius Ateius Capito.* You are aware of the ups and downs of my career; in every aspect of my distinctions and afflictions, Gaius Capito has made his energy, action, authority, influence, and even his domestic finances available to me, and has put them at the service of my circumstances and fortunes.

3 When Titus Antistius* his kinsman was appointed by lot to the role of quaestor in Macedonia, and no successor appeared,* Pompey

entered the province* with his army. There was nothing Antistius could do. If given the choice, he would have preferred above all to return to Capito, whom he loved as a father, especially as he was aware how highly Capito regarded Caesar, both then and always in the past. But when he was put under pressure, Antistius took on only such activities as he could not refuse.

When money was minted at Apollonia, he was in charge of it. 4 I cannot say that he was not, or deny that he was, but it was for no more than two or three months. Subsequently he steered clear of the army and avoided any involvement. Please believe me when I attest this, for he was aware of my unhappiness about the war, and he shared all his views with me. So he retired into the depths of Maccdonia to hide away, and there he was able to keep the military at arm's length, so that not merely was he in charge of no operations, but he was not even present at any. After the battle, he joined a kinsman, Aulus Plautius,* in Bithynia. There Caesar interviewed him, and with no sharp or bitter word ordered him to proceed to Rome, He immediately contracted an illness from which he did not recover. He retired to Corcyra, a sick man, and died there. Under his will, which he had drawn up at Rome when Paullus and Marcellus were consuls,* Capito became heir to five-sixths of the estate; the remaining sixth was bequeathed to men whose share can pass to the state without complaint from anyone. It amounts to three million sesterces. But Caesar must see to that.

My dear Plancus, I appeal to you by my friendship with your 5 father, by the affection between us, by our shared pursuits, and by the entire course of our whole lives which are so closely identical. I beg you with all possible concern and eagerness to undertake this commission, and to regard it as mine. Strain, strive, and ensure that through my recommendation, your enthusiasm, and Caesar's favour, Gaius Capito may acquire the bequest of his relative. If I obtain this request, I shall believe that you have spontaneously bestowed on me all that I could have obtained from you, with the boundless influence and power which you wield, if I had sought it.

A factor which I hope will assist you, and of which Caesar himself 6 can be the best possible judge, is that Capito has always cultivated Caesar, and regarded him with affection. But Caesar himself can bear witness to this; I know his power of recall. So I have no need to give you any instruction. When conferring with Caesar in speaking on

Capito's behalf, merely take as your brief what you will realize Caesar himself recalls.

7   For my part, I shall lay before you what I have been able to experience in my own case. You must decide how much weight it carries. You are well aware of the party and the cause I have espoused in the field of politics, the individuals and the classes on which I relied, and those in whose eyes I was an enemy. Please believe me when I say that if I have done anything in the current war which was not to Caesar's liking (you are to realize that Caesar himself knows I acted in this way most reluctantly), I did it on the advice, exhortation, and authority of others, and if I have been more moderate and restrained than any other of that party, this has been above all through the authority of Capito. If the rest of my associates had been like him, I should perhaps have been of benefit to the state in some degree, and certainly to myself most handsomely.

8   My dear Plancus, if you execute this request, you will strengthen my expectation of your goodwill towards me, and in Capito himself to your supreme advantage you will enrol among your circle* of tried friends a most welcome, serviceable, and excellent man.

Letter 103 *(Att.* XII 2)
Rome, ?April 46

CICERO TO ATTICUS

1   Here there is nothing but rumours: that Murcus* has perished in a shipwreck, that Asinius* has been consigned alive into the custody of the troops, that fifty ships have been swept by this contrary wind to Utica, that there is no sign of Pompeius,* for he has not appeared at all in the Balearics, as Paciaecus claims. But there is no reputable source for any of these stories. So much for the gossip in your absence.

2   Meanwhile there are games at Praeneste.* Hirtius and all the Caesarians here have gone there. The games are in fact to continue for eight days. What dinners, and what cavortings! Meanwhile the business is perhaps completed. What remarkable men! But Balbus is busy building—*il s'en fiche de tout cela.** If you want the truth, for a man seeking pleasure rather than virtue, *n'a-t-il pas assez vécu?* Meanwhile you are fast asleep. *Le problème** has to be coped with

now, if you are to achieve anything. If you ask for my views, I believe we are reaping the harvest. But enough is enough. I shall see you soon, and my hope is that you will head here straight from the road. Then together we will arrange a day for Tyrannio, and for any other business.

Letter 104 (*Fam.* V 21)
Rome, April 46

MARCUS CICERO TO LUCIUS MESCINIUS

I was pleased to receive your letter. It made me aware of what even without it I presumed was the case, that you are most eager to meet me. But I do not yield to you in this, for I swear by all the blessings that I pray may accrue to me that my earnest wish is to be with you. Though earlier there was a greater number of individuals, good citizens, agreeable persons, men with great regard for me, there was no one whose company I enjoyed more than yours, and few with whom I associated equally gladly. But at this time, when some have died, some are abroad, and some have renounced their allegiance, I swear that I would more gladly spend one day with you than the entire course of my present life with most of those with whom I am obliged to spend my days. Indeed, you are not to think that I do not prefer solitude (though I am not permitted to enjoy it) to the conversation of those who throng my house—with one or at most two exceptions.

So I exploit the refuge which I think you too should exploit, namely, my modest literary work, and beyond that the recollection of my political principles. For as you can most readily imagine, I am a person who has never sought my own interests rather than those of my fellow-citizens. If that person of whom you were never fond* (by contrast with your fondness for me) had not been jealous of me, both he and all honourable men would be happily placed today. I am the kind of person who wanted no man's violence to prevail over honourable tranquillity, but when I realized that those very arms which I had always feared had greater strength than that harmony between honourable men which I myself had achieved, I preferred peace even on unjust terms rather than employing violence in fighting against a stronger adversary. But we shall soon be able to discuss this, and many other matters, face to face.

3   Nothing makes me linger in Rome other than awaiting events in Africa,* for I believe that the decisive stage is imminent. I think it is of some concern to me (though frankly what that concern amounts to I do not understand) not to absent myself from the advice of friends, whatever the news from Africa. For the situation has reached the point at which, in spite of the vast gulf between the causes of the warring sides, I do not believe it will make much difference whichever wins.

But undoubtedly my attitude, which was perhaps too vacillating while the situation was fluid, has hardened considerably now that it is hopeless. Your previous letter further reinforced my attitude. That letter made me understand the courage with which you endured your injustice,* and it has helped me to see that both your highly civilized attitude and your studies were a source of strength, to you. For to tell you the truth, you seem to have been too soft-hearted, like virtually all of us who have lived the lives of men of breeding in a happy and free community.

4   But just as we showed moderation in those times of prosperity, so we must bravely endure our present fortune, which is not merely unhappy but utterly ruinous, so that amidst these monstrous ills we may at last achieve the blessing of death. Even in happy times we are to despise it,* because we will experience no consciousness; in our present circumstances we are not merely to despise it, but even to desire it.

5   As you love me, enjoy your present leisure, and be persuaded that nothing grisly or fear-provoking can befall a person other than guilt and sin,* which have never possessed you and will never do so. I shall visit you soon, if it seems possible and practicable; if something happens which necessitates a change of plan, I shall immediately inform you. However eager you are to see me, do ensure that in your precarious health you do not stir from your residence without first enquiring of me by letter what I would have you do. Do maintain your present affection for me, and safeguard your health and peace of mind.

Letter 105 (*Fam.* IX 7)

Rome, May 46

CICERO TO VARRO

1   I was dining at Seius' house* when letters from you were delivered to each of us. Yes, the time now seems ripe to go.* As for my previous objections, I shall reveal my wilful purpose. I wanted you to be

somewhere close by in the hope of a propitious outcome: 'When two men march in step . . .'.* But now, since all is wrapped up, we must not hesitate, but go full speed ahead by every possible means. When I heard about Lucius Caesar junior,* I said to myself

What then has he in store for me, his father?*

So I do not forgo regular dinners with those who are now our 2 masters. What ought I to do? One must yield to circumstances. But joking aside (especially as there is nothing to laugh at)

The bristling Afric land's a-tremble with tense tumult.*

So there is no *chose indifférente** which I do not fear.

But as for your queries about when and where and to which port of call he is coming, we know nothing as yet. As for your suggestion of Baiae, some are wondering whether he is coming via Sardinia, for so far he has not run his eye over his estate there. It is the poorest one he has, but he does not despise it. My own view at any rate is that he will come via Sicily.* We shall soon know. Dolabella* is on the way. I think that he will be our schoolmaster,

For many pupils are oft better than their teachers.

But once I know what you have decided, I shall adapt my plans most closely to yours, so I now await a letter from you.

Letter 106 (*Fam.* IX 18)

Tusculum, July 46

CICERO TO PAETUS

When I was at leisure in my Tusculan residence (for I had sent my 1 pupils to meet their friend,* so that at the same time they could effect the closest reconciliation between him and myself), I received your most charming letter. It gave me to understand that you approve my strategy by which (like the tyrant Dionysius,* who on being driven from Syracuse is said to have opened a school at Corinth) now that the law courts are abolished and I have lost my forensic kingdom, I have begun to establish a school.

No need to ask; the strategy pleases me as well, for I achieve many 2 ends. To begin with, I am protecting myself against the prevailing circumstances, which is particularly vital at this time. The repercussions of this strategy I do not know. I am merely aware that I approve no other's planned course in preference to this, unless death was perhaps the better option. True, it would have been death in my own bed, but that did not come to pass. I did not stand in the battle-line, where the rest—Pompey, your friend Lentulus, Scipio, Afranius*— met miserable deaths. But Cato's,* you object, was glorious. That in fact will be possible for me when I so wish. I must only ensure that it is not as necessary for me as it was for him, and this is what I am working at. So much, then, for my first objective.

3　　A second consideration follows. I am improving, first in physical health, which had failed when I postponed my exercises,* and secondly, in fluency in public speaking, such as I had, which would have dried up if I had not resumed those exercises. There is a final point which you may perhaps regard as primary: I have already disposed of more peacocks than you have pigeons!* While you find your pleasure where you are in Haterius' legal spices, I am here enjoying Hirtius' gravy.* Come then, if you are a man, and let me teach you *les principes* which you seek to know, though that would be a case of the pig teaching Minerva.*

4　　But as I see it, if you cannot sell your valuations, or fill your pot with denarii, you must relocate yourself at Rome. It is better to suffer indigestion here than starvation where you are. I note that you have lost your property; I expect that the same fate awaits your friends here. So it is all up with you unless you take precautions.

5　　You can ride to Rome on that mule which you say is all you have left, since you have sold your gelding for food. There will be a chair for you in the school here as an assistant master next to mine, and a cushion will be provided!

7

THE DICTATORSHIP OF CAESAR (46–44 BC)

AFTER his victory at Thapsus, Caesar returned to Rome in July 46 to be greeted with fresh honours and powers bestowed by the Senate, including dictatorship for ten years and the right to designate all magistrates. He sought to temper these autocratic powers by pardoning and promoting prominent Pompeians. He embarked upon an ambitious programme of political and social legislation. Meanwhile the surviving Pompeians in Africa sought to reform in Spain. In November 46 Caesar left Rome for Spain, and in March 45 he brought the Civil War to a close by his victory at Munda. This was followed at Rome by the award of further distinctions. A ten-year consulship was added to his dictatorship. Though he rejected the right to designate all magistrates, signs were not lacking of a total despotism. His dictatorship was pronounced perpetual, and religious honours established him virtually as a god. In February 44 he was hailed by some citizens as king. Antony placed a diadem on his head, and though Caesar rejected this gesture, an increasing number of influential citizens were affronted. Hence the conspiracy which led to the assassination on the Ides of March 44.

Cicero initially held out slight hopes of the reinstatement of republican institutions. Caesar treated him respectfully. Cicero prevailed upon many Pompeian associates to resume life in Rome. But as the despotism became more pronounced, he became more and more disillusioned, and retired to set himself a demanding programme of philosophical writing, beginning in late 46 with the publication of *Hortensius* (an exhortation to philosophy), and in 45 composing in rapid succession the *Academica* (on the theory of knowledge), *On Ends* (on the highest good), *The Tusculan Disputations* (on the means to happiness), and *The Nature of the Gods* (on theology and physics). He continued with this programme throughout 44.

Letter 107 (*Fam.* VII 28)

Rome, August 46

CICERO TO CURIUS

1 I remember thinking that you were soft in the head when you preferred to live with your friends over there rather than with us, for life in Rome was much more suited to your civilized and sociable character than that in the whole of the Peloponnese, let alone that at Patrae. But nowadays the opposite is the case. You seem to me to have shown great foresight now that the situation here is virtually beyond hope, and you have taken yourself off to Greece. At this time you are not only wise in absenting yourself from Rome, but also truly content—though what man of rudimentary wisdom can be truly content today?

But what you attained, so far as lay within your power, by moving to the region 'where no mention of the sons of Pelops . . .'* (you know the rest), I am achieving almost identically by other means. Once I have acknowledged the early morning greetings of my friends, a ritual even more crowded than of old because people seem to regard a right-minded citizen as a bird of good omen, I go to ground in my library,* and publish works the importance of which you will perhaps gauge; for in a conversation with you, when at your house you were inveighing against my melancholy and loss of hope, I understood you to say that you missed the vital spark so evident in my writings.

2 But at that time, I assure you, I was grieving for the republic, which was dearer to me than my life, not only because of the benefits it conferred on me, but also those it received at my hands. Again, at this time, though I am consoled not only by reflection,* which ought to exercise the greatest influence, but also by time, which usually provides remedies even to idiots, I none the less lament that the political blessings we shared have so faded away that not even hope survives that things will at some time improve. The fault, mind you, does not lie with him on whom rest all our destinies*—except perhaps that this situation ought never to have arisen. Rather, some events have occurred by chance and others through our own fault, so that we should not complain about what is past. I see no hope remaining, so I return to what I said at the outset: if you have

abandoned life here by design, you have shown wisdom, but if by chance, you are blessed.

Letter 108 (*Fam.* IV 8)

Rome, August 46

MARCUS CICERO TO MARCUS MARCELLUS

I do not presume to advise one of outstanding practical wisdom like 1 yourself, nor to bolster you, since you are a man of the greatest spirit and unique courage, and certainly not to console you, for if you are bearing, as I have heard, the events which have occurred, I must instead congratulate you on your bravery rather than console you in your grief. But if the monstrous ills of the republic are wearing you down, I am not richly endowed with the talent to console you, for I cannot console myself. So what remains is to make myself ready and available to assist you in every way, and to be at the service of your household in all that they seek, in such a way as to consider myself bound not only to do all I can for your sake, but also to attempt to do things beyond my ability.

But there is one thing which you are to believe I offer by way of 2 advice or suggestion, or which I have been unable to suppress because of my goodwill. I urge you to contemplate, as I myself do, the obligation, if some sort of republic survives, of becoming a leader by virtue of the judgement of the citizens and the reality of the situation, yielding to the needs of the time. But if no republic exists, you must believe that Rome is the most suitable place even to live in exile. For if freedom is what we seek, where in the world does this tyranny not exist? But if any abode whatsoever is our goal, what place is more agreeable than one's own homestead? But believe me, even he who controls all shows respect to men of talent, and in so far as conditions and his cause allow, he shows favour to those of noble birth and political standing.

But I have gone beyond my intention, so I return to my sole point: that I am devoted to you and that I shall line up with your adherents as long as they are truly yours. If they prove to be otherwise, at any rate I shall in all circumstances do justice to our close association and affection. Farewell.

Letter 109 (*Fam.* IV 13)

Rome, August 46

MARCUS CICERO TO PUBLIUS FIGULUS

1   I have for some time been pondering on the most suitable topic on which to write to you, but I cannot think of any conventional literary theme, let alone any specific subject. Our times have torn from us one customary motif of these letters which we used to exploit in happy days, and Fortune has ensured the impossibility of my writing, or even at all contemplating, anything of that kind. All that remains is a kind of melancholy and the sad type of letter appropriate to these days, but this topic too fails me, for it ought to contain promise of some assistance or consolation in your distress. No promise is open to me to fulfil, for I myself am afflicted by a like fate, and I endure my own misfortunes by depending on the resources of others. More often it occurs to me to complain of the nature of my life rather than to rejoice at my being alive.

2   Though no signal injustice has afflicted my private life,* and though nothing at such a time as this occurs to my mind which Caesar has not granted unasked, I am none the less so overwhelmed by my present concerns that I regard my remaining alive as sinful. I am deprived of many of my closest comrades whom death has snatched or exile has dragged from me, and also of all those friends whose goodwill was won for me by my defence of the republic long ago, when you were my ally. I now exist amid the shipwreck of those friends and the plundering of their possessions. I am not merely informed of these events, which would be wretched enough, but I actually witness the bitterest sight of all, the dispersal of the posses- sions of men who of old aided me when I quenched those notorious fires.* In the city in which I recently prospered in influence, author- ity, and fame, I am now bereft of all these allies. I do enjoy the supreme kindness of Caesar himself towards me, but that cannot outweigh the violence and the transformation of every event and circumstance.

3   So I am now bereft of everything to which I have become accus- tomed by nature, inclination, and habit, and as I see it, I am an embarrassment both to others and to myself, for though I was born always to achieve something worthy of a man, I now have no recourse

not merely to action but even to contemplation. Whereas previously I could lend assistance* to individuals who were little known or even guilty offenders, nowadays I cannot even graciously promise help to Publius Nigidius, uniquely the most learned and clean-living of men, who at one time was most influential, and is certainly a dear friend of mine.

Since, then, this category of letter-writing is out of the question 4 for me, all that is left is the offer of consolation, and the suggestion of ways by which I can try to divert you from your difficulties. But in fact you have the ability, if anyone ever had, to console yourself or your neighbour. So I shall not embark upon the type of writing based on specialized argumentation* and teaching, but I shall leave it entirely to yourself. You will investigate what is worthy of a brave and wise man, and what is demanded of you by the qualities of seriousness, high-mindedness, the life you have lived, and the pursuits and disciplines in which you have excelled from boyhood. Because I am in Rome, where I carefully monitor events, through my understanding and observation I can assure you that you will not be for much longer plagued by those hardships* which exercise you at present, though you will perhaps be involved for ever in those privations under which I too am labouring.

First of all, I believe that I detect, in the attitude of the person 5 with boundless power,* support for your immunity. I do not write this lightly. The less intimate I am with him, the more scrupulous is my investigation. Up to now he has been slower to free you from your harassment so that he can more easily discourage those with whom he is more angry. His friends, and notably those he finds more agreeable, both speak and think remarkably well of you. This view is enhanced by the goodwill of the common folk, or rather by the unanimity of all. Believe me, even the apparatus of the republic, which to be truthful is now virtually powerless, will inevitably exercise some power at a future time, and will exploit such power as it has to obtain immunity in your case from those who hold it in subjection.

So I revert to the point of even promising you now what initially 6 I forbore to promise. I shall closely cultivate Caesar's particular friends who now show me affection, and are often in my company. I shall also wheedle my way into friendship with him, which up to now has been foreclosed to me by my sense of shame. I shall for sure pursue every means by which I believe I can attain the purpose we seek. In this entire mode of activity I shall act more vigorously than I presume to mention here. The other modes of help which I am sure have been afforded you by many are more readily available to you from me. None of my domestic possessions I would regard as mine rather than yours. I refrain from writing at greater length about this and all else of this kind, because I would rather that you hope for what I am sure you will obtain, namely the enjoyment of your own possessions.

7   My final request is to beg and beseech you to be of truly good heart. Recall not merely the injunctions which you have imbibed from other great men, but also those which you have activated from your own intelligence and studies. If you assemble them, you will have the best of hopes all round, and you will bear with wisdom all that comes to pass, whatever it will be. But you have a better understanding of this than myself, and indeed better than that of all the world. For myself, I shall give most earnest and careful attention to what I apprehend is your concern, and I shall preserve the recollection of your kindness to me during these most melancholy days of my life.

Letter 110 (*Fam.* IX 17)

Rome, September 46

CICERO TO PAETUS

1   What a joker you are, seeing that after our friend Balbus* has visited you, you ask for my views on the townships and estates in your area! As if I knew anything which Balbus does not know, or as if whatever at any time I do know isn't usually learnt from him! On the contrary, as you love me, do tell me what is to happen in my case, for you had him in your clutches, and from him, whether he was sober or at any rate under the influence, you could obtain the information. But, my dear Paetus, I do not enquire about these matters, first of all because to live on for almost the past four years* is a positive gain—if indeed it is a gain, or if surviving the demise of the republic is a life; and secondly, because I think I know what is in store for us. The future will correspond with the wishes of those who will be in power, and that power will always rest with armed force, so whatever is granted us

must suffice for us, and whoever could not bear this should have chosen death.

The powers that be are surveying the lands of Veii and Capena,* 2 not far from those of Tusculum. But I am not apprehensive, for I enjoy my possessions while I can, and I pray that I can always do so. But if things turn out otherwise, brave man and philosopher too that I am, I have opted for living as my finest possession, so I cannot but be benevolent towards the man through whose kindness I have gained it. Even if he were eager for a republic such as he perhaps desires and we should all long for, he has no means of achieving it, for his hands are tied by his numerous associates.

But I am taking this too far. After all, it is you to whom I am 3 writing. But do realize that not only I, who am not privy to his plans, but even our leader himself does not know what the future brings. We are his subjects, but he is subject to circumstances. Hence he does not know what the circumstances will demand, and we cannot be privy to his thinking.

I did not send this reply earlier, not because I am usually a 4 dawdler, particularly in letter-writing, but because I have nothing definite to impart, and I did not wish my hesitation to cause you anxiety, nor my assurances to bring you hope. But I will add what is God's truth, that so far at this time I have heard nothing of the danger you mention, But wise man that you are, you must pray for an outcome that is best, but contemplate what is most arduous, and endure whatever will be.

Letter 111 (*Fam.* IV 7)
Rome, ?September 46

CICERO TO MARCUS MARCELLUS

I am aware that your course of action has been such that I do not pre- 1 sume to criticize it. But this is not because I myself agree with it, but because I respect you as a person of such wisdom that I do not rate my own course of action as preferable to yours. None the less our long-standing friendship and your unique goodwill towards me, which I have experienced since you were a boy, have encouraged me to write to you in terms which I think are conducive to your own immunity, and which I regard also as not incompatible with your standing.

2   I have outstanding recollections of you as one who long previously foresaw the beginnings of these ills, and who handled the consulship* in the most splendid and outstanding way. But I also saw that you disapproved of the tactics employed in the civil war, and of the forces and the kind of army led by Gnaeus Pompey, and that you totally distrusted them throughout. I think that you recall that I too was of the same opinion. In consequence you were not at all prominent in the military operations, and I myself always succeeded in avoiding them, for in the fighting we failed to exploit the attributes by which we could have been influential, and in which we excelled, namely, policy, authority, and justice of the cause. We relied instead on the brute strength in which we were inferior. So we were worsted, or if our lofty values cannot be worsted, we were at any rate battered and laid low. No one could fail to accord the highest praise to your conduct throughout, for when you surrendered hope of victory, you also relinquished your eagerness for the contest, and you showed that the prudent and sound citizen embarks on civil war unwillingly at the outset, but is happy not to see it through to the end.

3   I observe that those who did not adopt the course which you followed are sharply divided into two categories. Some tried to renew the war, and took themselves to Africa. Others like myself entrusted themselves to the victor. Your conduct took a different path from these, for perhaps you considered that the second course smacked of pusillanimity, and the first of obduracy. I concede that most people, or should I say the world at large, regarded your decision as prudent, and indeed some pronounced it worthy of a great and courageous mind. But in my view your course of action has a certain limitation, especially as nothing hinders you from gaining possession of all your properties except your inclination. This is especially the case as my understanding is that there is nothing to cause the man who exercises power to have any hesitation except his fear that you would totally reject the notion that his gesture was a kindness. On this there is no need for me to express a view, since my action makes it clear.

4   However, even if you had already decided that you preferred permanent withdrawal to contemplation of what you did not wish to witness, you should none the less reflect that, wherever you were, you would be subject to the power of the man you seek to avoid. Even if he readily allowed you to live in tranquillity and freedom by forgoing your native land and possessions, you would still have to

ponder whether you preferred living at Rome in your own home, whatever the political situation, or at Mytilene or Rhodes.* But since the power of the person we fear extends so widely that it has embraced the whole world, you must surely prefer to reside without danger in your own home rather than hazardously in some foreigner's dwelling. For myself, even if I had to seek death, I should prefer to face it in my own home and native land, rather than in some alien region abroad. All who have regard for you feel the same way, and they number many by reason of your outstanding and widely celebrated qualities.

I am also taking into account your family possessions, for I do not 5 want them to be dispersed. Though they will come to no enduring harm, for neither the personage who wields power over the state nor the state itself will permit it, I am unwilling to contemplate assaults of brigands* on your properties. I would not hesitate to identify them by name if I were not sure that you know them.

Here in Rome the anxieties and the abundant and unremitting 6 tears of one person, Gaius Marcellus,* your cousin and the best of men, are interceding on your behalf. I come very close to him in my concern and distress, but I am somewhat behindhand in entreaties, for as one needing intercession myself I have no right of approach. My influence is confined to that of one of the conquered, but in advice and support Marcellus does not find me wanting. Your other relatives do not seek my assistance, but I am ready to offer help in any way.

Letter 112 (*Fam.* VI 12)

Rome, September 46

CICERO TO AMPIUS

I congratulate you, dear Balbus,* I sincerely congratulate you. I am 1 not so stupid as to have you relish the enjoyment of a spurious happiness, only to have it followed by a sudden bruising and a tumble so low that nothing could in consequence restore your equilibrium. I have pleaded your case more openly than my position warranted, for my affection for you, and the undying fondness which you have most attentively fostered, have prevailed over the unhappy circumstance of my limited influence. All that was promised has been confirmed;

the proceedings relating to your return and immunity are fixed and ratified. I have witnessed, ascertained, and attended the arrangements.

2   Indeed, I have satisfactorily involved all Caesar's intimates in friendship and goodwill towards me, so that, Caesar apart, they regard me as their closest ally. Pansa, Hirtius, Balbus, Oppius, Matius, and Postumus* behave so demonstrably in this way that their regard for me is unsurpassed. Had I been forced to achieve this through my own efforts, I should not regret having taken such pains, if one takes account of the times. But I have indulged in no time-serving.* My long-standing friendship with all those men does the interceding, and I have never stopped discussing your case with them. Pansa has been my chief contact. A most keen supporter of yours and an eager friend of mine, he is influential with Caesar as much by his authority as by his genial ways. Tillius Cimber* has been most obliging to me. With Caesar, petitions based on friendship carry more weight than those involving special pleading. Because Cimber had such a connection, it had more effect than he could have achieved on behalf of someone else.

3   A certificate of immunity has not been immediately granted because of the extraordinary ill-will of some people who would have been more bitterly resentful of a pardon granted to you which they call 'the trumpet of civil war'.* They use many such expressions which suggest that they are not happy that the war took place. So it seemed advisable to proceed with some secrecy, and in no way to divulge that your case has already been approved. But the delay will be brief, and I have no doubt that by the time you read this letter the process will be completed. In fact Pansa, a sober and reliable person, not merely confirmed this to me, but also guaranteed that he would bear off the document with all speed. But I decided to give you notice of this, for the comments of your Eppuleia and the tears of Ampia* indicated that you are less stout-hearted than your letters suggest. They believe that you will be more downcast now that they are not with you. So I thought it extremely important, so as to relieve your depression and melancholy, to confirm by letter to you as definite what is in fact definite.

4   You are aware that previously it has been my custom to write more in consolatory vein as to a courageous and wise man than to flaunt an assured expectation of immunity. My sole reservation was that

I thought we should live in hope for the future of the republic at a time when the zeal for war had been stifled. You must keep in mind those letters of yours in which you invariably revealed to me a spirit both lofty and resolutely ready to endure all that comes to pass. This did not surprise me, since I recalled your involvement in public life from your earliest days, the tenure of your magistracies in the face of those dangers to the safety and the fortunes of the community, and your attitude when engaging in this war itself, when you were ready to be not merely an exultant victor, but if need be also philosophical in defeat.

Thereafter, since you now apply your energies to recording the 5 deeds of courageous men,* you must reflect that there is no reason why you should not aim to show yourself to be closely similar to those whom you praise. But this exhortation would be more appropriate to the circumstances from which you have now withdrawn. You must now merely brace yourself to endure in my company our present plight. If I could devise a remedy for it, I would share it with you. Our sole refuge is our learning and our literary activity, which we have always practised. In happy times they seemed to afford us merely pleasure, but now they are also our salvation. But to revert to my initial point, you must take it as certain that all arrangements have been completed for your immunity and your future.

Letter 113 (*Fam.* VI 14)

Rome, November 46

CICERO TO LIGARIUS

Do realize that I am directing all my efforts, assistance, care, and 1 enthusiasm to achieving your immunity. On the one hand I have always felt the utmost affection for you, and on the other the unique devotion and fraternal love of your brothers, to whom with the greatest goodwill I am as equally attached as I am to you, permit me to forgo no duty or occasion demanded by my obligation and support for you. But I would rather that you learn of my present and past actions on your behalf from your brothers' letters than from mine. I wish rather to report to you my hope, or rather my conviction and certainty, of your immunity, for if anyone is apprehensive in important and hazardous operations, and is always more fearful of unhappy outcomes than optimistic of successes, I am that man, and if this is a fault, I confess that I am not free from it.

2   None the less, I can inform you that on 26 November at your brothers' request I visited Caesar in the early morning, enduring all the humiliation and trouble which approaching and meeting him involves. Your brothers and relatives prostrated themselves at his feet, and I spoke as demanded by your case and the occasion. It was not merely Caesar's words, which were emollient and friendly, but also his looks, demeanour, and several other indications I could more easily observe than describe, which gave me the parting impression that your immunity was not in doubt. So be of good heart and courage. You have borne the stormiest days with philosophic resignation, so now rejoice in calmer weather. But for my part, I shall be on hand to cope with your problems as if they were most taxing, and I shall most happily plead on your behalf, as I have done up to now, not merely to Caesar, but also to his intimates, whom I have found most friendly to me. Farewell.

Letter 114 (*Fam.* IV 10)

Rome, ?December 46

CICERO TO MARCELLUS

1   Though there is nothing new about which to write to you, and I am instead beginning to await a letter from you, or better still your arrival here, none the less since Theophilus is now setting out, I could not but give him a letter to you. So do ensure that you come as soon as possible.* Believe me, your coming is awaited not only by us your friends, but by absolutely everyone. I tell you this because I am visited by the slight fear from time to time that you are taking

2 pleasure in delaying your departure. If your eyes were your only organs of perception, I should certainly forgive you for refusing to train them on certain individuals. But since the accounts you hear offer not much more relief than the objects of your sight, and my suspicion would be that it would greatly benefit your private property for you to come here with all speed (this observation holds good in all respects), I thought that I should nudge you to this effect. But now that I have made clear my own view, for the rest you must take thought as your prudence dictates. But do please inform me when I am to await you.

Letter 115 (*Fam.* XIII 16)

Rome, December 46–January 45

CICERO TO CAESAR

Of all members of the nobility, I had the greatest affection for the   1
youthful Publius Crassus.* Though from his earliest days I had high
hopes of him, I began to think particularly well of him when I learnt
of the glowing assessments which you formed of him. I already had
a high opinion and strong approval of his freedman Apollonius*
during Crassus' lifetime, for he showed great consideration to his
patron, and was highly suited to assist him in his excellent researches,
in consequence of which Crassus was really fond of him.

After Crassus' death he seemed to me to be even worthier of   2
admission to my patronage and friendship, for he believed that those
who had been recipients of Crassus' regard and affection, and had
reciprocated them, were men he should respect and cultivate. So he
joined me in Cilicia, and his reliability and practical wisdom were
extremely useful to me in a host of activities. Moreover, I believe that
he did not fail you during the war in Alexandria, in so far as his support and loyalty could achieve this.

Since he hoped that you too were of the same opinion, he has set   3
out for Spain to join you, chiefly on his own initiative, but also at my
suggestion. I did not promise to give him a recommendation—not
that I did not think that you would take it seriously, but I considered
that he had no need of such advocacy, because he had participated in
warfare with you; and since he was faithful to the memory of
Crassus, he was one of your supporters. Moreover, I thought that if
he wished to exploit recommendations, I well understood that he
could effect them through others. But I have gladly given him an
attestation of my judgement of him, because he considered this valuable, and I have found in practice that you accord it due weight.

I know him, then, to be a scholarly man, devoted to studies of the   4
best kind, as he has been from boyhood, for from his early days he
spent much time at my house with the Stoic philosopher Diodotus,*
who in my view was a man of the greatest learning. He is now fired
with enthusiasm for your exploits, and desires to embody them in a
memoir in Greek. I think he is capable of this, for he is talented
and experienced, and has for long concerned himself with this kind

of literary pursuit. He is extraordinarily keen to do justice to the immortality of your praises,

Here you have an attestation of my opinion, but in view of your unique wisdom, you will make your own assessment much more readily, and in spite of my previous denial I do recommend him to you. I shall be particularly grateful for any favour which you bestow on him.

Letter 116 (*Fam.* IV 14)

Rome, December 46 – January 45

CICERO TO PLANCIUS

1 I have received two letters from you sent from Corcyra. In the first of them you offered me your felicitations because you had heard that I was preserving my standing as of old, and in the second you expressed your good wishes that my 'proceedings'* may have a good and happy outcome.

For myself, if 'standing' means having the proper political attitude supported by decent men, I am maintaining my standing. But if the word implies the ability to translate that attitude into action, or at any rate to defend it in open discussion, not even a trace remains of my standing, and it is a notable achievement to be able to control oneself to endure with sangfroid events partly already with us and partly overhanging us, and this is difficult in a war of this kind, when its outcome signals massacre on the one side, and slavery on the other.

2 Confronted by this danger, I am somewhat consoled by the recollection that I foresaw this outcome, when I feared not merely defeat on our part but also success, and I realized the immense danger which armed dispute presented to constitutional law. I was aware, if by use of arms the party prevailed which I had joined in the hope of peace and not in zeal for war, how cruel that victory would be, administered by men who were enraged and greedy and arrogant, and on the other hand, if our party were defeated, how widespread would be the deaths of citizens, some of the greatest eminence, and others our finest men. When I foretold this outcome, and showed the most prudent concern for their safety, they preferred to regard me as too cowardly rather than sufficiently far-sighted.

As for your felicitations on my 'proceedings',* I am quite certain 3
that your remarks are genuine, but at so wretched a time I would not
have adopted any new course, if on my return I had not found my
domestic affairs in no better state than the political situation. When
I realized that owing to the wickedness of those to whom my safety
and my fortunes ought to have been most dear, in view of the constant kindnesses that I had shown them, I had no security and no
refuge from ambush within my own walls, I thought that I must protect myself against the treachery of my long-standing relationships
by seeking the loyalty of those which were new. But that is enough
of private affairs, or even too much.

So far as you are concerned, I beg you to show the necessary atti- 4
tude, which is that you must not think you have anything special to
fear. If there is to be any political structure of the community, I foresee that there will be no hazards to which you are subject, whatever
form that structure takes, for I know well that some are now reconciled, and that others have never been at odds with you. As for my
own attitude towards you, do please take the view that in spite of my
awareness of my present position and limited capability, I shall make
myself available in whatever ways I regard as necessary with action
and advice, or at least with support, to defend your properties, your
reputation, and your immunity. Please keep me most scrupulously
informed of your activity and future plans. Farewell.

Letter 117 (*Fam.* IX 13)
Rome, January–February 45

CICERO TO DOLABELLA

Gaius Subernius of Cales is a friend of mine and a close connection 1
of Lepta's,* who is a particularly intimate associate of mine. He set
out to Spain with Marcus Varro* in order to avoid hostilities. This
was before warfare broke out. He intended to stay in the province in
which, following Afranius' defeat,* none of us believed that there
would be any fighting. But he became involved in the very ills he had
sought so earnestly to avoid, for he was overtaken by sudden warfare
initiated by Scapula,* and intensified thereafter by Pompeius* so
fiercely that he could devise no means of extricating himself from
that unhappy circumstance.

2   Marcus Planius Heres* is in virtually the same case. He too is from Cales, and is a close friend of our dear Lepta. So I am recommending both these men to you with all the concern, support, and anxiety that I can muster. I seek this for their sakes, and friendship and decency spur me on profoundly in this matter. Indeed, since Lepta is in such straits that his finances appear to be running into danger, I cannot refrain from involving myself closely or even equally with him. So though I have often experienced the measure of your regard for me, I should like to persuade you to show it to me especially in this case.

3   So I am asking, or if you allow it, begging you to guarantee the immunity of these unhappy men, whom Fortune (which no one can avoid) rather than guilt has plunged into disaster. Make it your wish that through your agency I may confer this gift not only upon these men who are my friends and also on the township of Cales with which I have a close relationship, but also on Lepta, whom I rank above all other friends.

4   The words that follow I do not regard as closely relevant to the matter in hand, but there is no reason for me to suppress them. The finances of one of these men are very precarious, and those of the other scarcely qualify him for equestrian status. So since Caesar in his generosity has granted them their lives, and there is nothing further of any account which can be taken from them, grant the two men leave to return here, if your regard for me is as great as I am sure it is. There is no obstacle facing them other than the long journey, from which they do not shrink in their desire both to live with their families and to die in their own homes. I beg you earnestly and repeatedly to strive and struggle to achieve this, or rather to expedite it, for I am persuaded that it is within your power to do so.

Letter 118 (*Fam.* VI 18)

Rome, February 45

CICERO TO LEPTA

1   As soon as I received the letter delivered by your courier Seleucus, I immediately wrote to Balbus to enquire about what the law specified.* He replied that auctioneers are excluded from membership of city-councils, but that such exclusion did not apply to

past practitioners. So friends of both you and myself can be of good heart, for it would have been intolerable if those who had at one time been auctioneers could not be councillors in townships, whereas present-day diviners were open to selection for the Roman Senate.

There is no news from the Spanish provinces, but it is certain that 2 Pompeius has a large army, for Caesar himself has sent a copy of a letter from Paciaecus to his followers in which it is stated that there are seven legions* under him. Moreover, Messalla* has informed Quintus Salassus by letter that his brother Publius Curtius by order of Pompeius has been executed in full view of the army for having conspired with certain Spaniards to arrest Pompeius if he entered some town or other to obtain corn-supplies, and to escort him to Caesar.

So far as your business as guarantor for Pompey goes, once your 3 fellow-sponsor Galba* returns (he is quite careful with his finances!) I shall keep raising the question with him in the hope that some solution can be found. I got the impression that he was confident of this.

I am thoroughly delighted that you approve enthusiastically of my 4 *Orator*.* I am certainly convinced that I have committed to that book all the discernment I possess about public speaking. If the book is as good as you say you find it, then I too count for something. But if that is not the case, I concede that my reputation for sound judgement suffers commensurately with the value of the book. I am keen that our dear young Lepta now finds pleasure in such works. Though he has not yet reached maturity, there is some point in his having oratory of this kind dinned in his ears.

My dear Tullia's child-bearing has wholly preoccupied me at Rome, 5 and though now, I hope, she is sufficiently strong, I am still detained here until I extract the first payment* from Dolabella's agents. But to tell the truth, I am not now the regular traveller of former days. My residences and my leisured life give me pleasure. My house at Rome yields to none of my country-dwellings. The tranquillity here is greater than that in any unpopulated region. So even my literary activities are unhindered, and I am immersed in them without interruptions. So I expect that I shall see you here before you see me in your part of the world. Your most charming son Lepta must take his cue from Hesiod,* and have on his tongue 'Sweat before excellence' and the words that follow.

Letter 119 (*Att.* XII 14)

Astura, March 45

CICERO TO ATTICUS

1   I sent you a letter yesterday asking you to make my excuses to Appuleius.* I imagine that there is no problem. No one will refuse, no matter whom you call on. But get in touch with Septimius, Laenas, and Statilius, for we need three. But it was Laenas who took on the whole business for me.

2   You write that you have been asked for payment* by Junius. Cornificius is quite wealthy. However, I should like to know when I am said to have acted as guarantor, and whether it was for the father or the son. But all the same, as you write, you must see Cornificius' business-managers and Appuleius the estate-agent.

3   Your wishes for my recovery from grief are in keeping with all your kind gestures. But you are my witness that I have been true to myself, for there is no work written on the alleviation of grief which I have not read in your house. Grief, however, prevails over all consolation. Why, I have even done something which I am sure no one has ever done before me, for I have written a literary consolation* to myself. I shall send you the work once the scribes have copied it. I claim to you that there is no consolation to match it. I spend whole days in writing; not that I feel any benefit thereby, but it distracts me for that length of time, not indeed sufficiently (for the thrust of grief presses hard), but it makes me relax, and I make every effort, if possible, to compose my features, if not my mind. In the course of doing this I sometimes think that I am sinning,* and at other times that I shall sin if I do not do it. Being alone is of some help; none the less it would be much more helpful if you were here. That is the sole reason for my departing from here, for it helps to confront my misfortunes. Yet this is for me a reason for grieving, for you will be unable to remain unchanged towards me, since what you liked about me is no more.

4   I wrote to you earlier about Brutus' letter to me. It was tactfully composed, but contained nothing to raise my spirits. I wish he were here in person, as he says in his letter to you that he would be. That at any rate would be a help to me, for he is extremely fond of me. Please write to me if you get any more news, particularly about when Pansa is setting out.* I am sorry about Attica, but I put my trust in

Craterus.* Tell Pilia that she is not to grieve, for it is sufficient that I do the mourning for all.

Letter 120 (*Att*. XII 19)

Astura, March 45

CICERO TO ATTICUS

Yes, this is indeed a pleasant spot, right on the sea, visible from both 1
Antium and Circeii. But I must ponder the means by which through every change of owner (such changes can be innumerable in the indefinite future, as long as our world survives) it can remain as what we can call consecrated ground. I myself am in no need of revenues, and can remain content with a little. From time to time I contemplate the purchase of some property across the Tiber, and precisely for this reason, because I visualize none which can become so well known. But we can decide on the purchase when we get together, as long as the shrine* is set up during the summer. You must negotiate with Apella the Chian for the pillars.

I approve your comments about Cocceius and Libo, and particu- 2
larly about my liability for jury-service. I should be pleased to know what you have ascertained about the guarantee, and what Cornificius' agents* are saying. But I would not want you to devote much effort to this business, when you have so much on hand. Balbus jointly with Oppius has also written to me about Antony;* they say that you had requested this to prevent my being worried. I thanked them, but please note, as I have already written to you, that this news does not trouble me, and indeed that none ever will.

If, as you believe, Pansa has set out today, from now on you 3
must start to keep me informed about your expectations of Brutus' arrival,* in other words about the approximate date. You will readily make an informed guess about this if you know his whereabouts.

As for your letter to Tiro about Terentia, I beseech you, my dear 4
Atticus, to take over the whole business. You realize that on the one hand I had a certain obligation with regard to it of which you are aware, and on the other, as some believe, young Cicero's interests* are involved. The first of these is of much greater concern to me, for in my eyes it is more sacrosanct and important, especially as I regard the second claim as neither genuine nor substantial.

Letter 121 (*Fam.* IV 6)

Nomentum, April 45

CICERO TO SERVIUS SULPICIUS

1   As you say, Servius, I could indeed wish that you had been with me
at the time of my most crushing loss. From the fact that reading your
letter helped me to relax a little, I readily realize how much your
presence would have assisted me with words of consolation and of
grief almost equal to my own. For the words you wrote were such as
could lighten my sorrow, and in consoling me you yourself indicated
your not inconsiderable grief of mind. But your dear son Servius, by
rendering all the dutiful help which could be bestowed in these
circumstances, indicated both his deep regard for me and his belief
that the attitude he showed towards me would be welcome to you.
The obligations he paid to me were doubtless more pleasant in the
past, but never more welcome than now.

It is not merely what you say and what amounts to your comrade-
ship in my distress which console me, but also your authority.
I regard it as ignoble not to bear my misfortune as you who are
endowed with such wisdom think it should be borne. But from time
to time I am oppressed and can scarcely withstand my grief, because
I do not have recourse to the consolations which others whom I cite
to myself as precedents did not lack. Examples are Quintus
Maximus, who lost his son, an ex-consul of fame and great achievements; Lucius Paullus, whose two sons died within a week; your
kinsman Galus; Marcus Cato,* who lost a son of outstanding talent
and valour. But these losses occurred at times when they were
consoled by the high standing which the state bestowed on them.

2   But as for myself, I have forfeited the distinctions which you mention, and which I gained through the greatest exertions, and now the
sole consolation I retained has been torn from me. My thoughts are
not hindered by the business of friends or by the administration of
the state. I have no desire to plead in the courts, and I find it impossible to train my gaze on the Senate House. I reflect on the truth that
I have lost all the rewards for both my hard work and my success.
But on recalling that these deprivations were shared with you and
with certain others, as I now restrained and forced myself to endure
these ills with patience, I had a refuge in which to seek rest, a person

in whose conversation and friendly demeanour I could lay aside all my cares and griefs.

But now, under the impact of this oppressive blow, even those scars which seemed to have healed reopen. In earlier days my family welcomed me to lighten my discomfiture in politics, but I cannot now take refuge in politics to find comfort in its blessings from my domestic melancholy. So I am an absentee from both family and Forum, for my household cannot now console me in my political dejection, and politics cannot alleviate my domestic pains.

This is why I await you all the more, and long to see you with all 3 speed. There is no greater relief that I can experience than the affinity of your friendship and conversation. However, I hope that your arrival is at hand, as I hear it is. I long to set eyes on you for many reasons, but especially to rehearse together beforehand how we are to see through these days which are to be wholly adapted to the will of one man. He is both shrewd and generous, and I think I have divined him to be not unfriendly to me and most cordial to you. In these circumstances we none the less need careful deliberation on what strategy we are to adopt—not for positive action, but for lying low by his permission and favour. Farewell.

Letter 122 (*Fam.* IX 11)

Nomentum, April 45

CICERO TO DOLABELLA

I should have preferred that your being deprived of letters from me 1 was attributable even to my death than to the calamity* which has most oppressively befallen me. I should at any rate have borne it with greater restraint if you had been at my side, for both your wise words and your unrivalled affection would have greatly relieved me. But since, as I believe, I am soon to see you, you will find my condition such that I can obtain great help from you, not because I am so shattered that I have forgotten that I am a man, nor because I believe that I must surrender to Fortune, but because my cheerful and agreeable disposition, which gave more pleasure to you than to all others, has been snatched from me. But you will recognize the same strength and resolution, if at any time I possessed them, as when you left me.

2   You write that you are involved in battles on my behalf. My anxiety that you are having to repel some of my detractors is not as strong
as my eagerness to acknowledge (as I certainly do) your affection
for me. I repeatedly beg you to continue as you have done, and to
pardon the brevity of this letter, for I imagine that we will be together
soon, and I have not yet recovered sufficiently to take up the pen.

Letter 123 (*Att.* XII 40)

Astura, May 45

CICERO TO ATTICUS

1   I have a clear picture of what Caesar's censure* in countering my
eulogy is like from the pamphlet which Hirtius has sent me.* In it
Hirtius assembles Cato's faults—combined, however, with resound-
ing praise of myself. So I have sent the pamphlet to Musca to pass on
to your scribes, for I want it to be circulated widely. Please instruct
your staff to ensure that this is done more readily.

2   I often attempt a *Lettre de Conseil*,* but without success, though I
have at my elbow the letters of Aristotle and of Theopompus to
Alexander.* But what similarity is there between them and me?
They were praising what they thought creditable to themselves and
welcome to Alexander. Do you see anything comparable in my role?
Nothing at all occurs to me.

     You write that you fear my popularity and authority are affected
by this mourning of mine, but I do not know what people are censur-
ing and demanding. Do they want me not to grieve? How can that
be? Or not to lie prostrate? Who ever did it less? While residing
in your house lightened my spirits, whom did I keep out, and
what visitor had cause to complain? I left you to go to Astura. Those
jovial people who censure me cannot read as many pages as I have
written.* Their quality is irrelevant; that kind of writing was such as
no one in low spirits could have undertaken. I spent thirty days on
your estate; did anyone have to forgo meeting me or chatting infor-
mally with me? At this very time my reading and writing is such that
my companions find it more difficult to cope with leisure than I do
with my work!

3   If anyone enquires why I am not in Rome, my answer is that this
is holiday-time. If the question is why I am not staying on my small

estates as would be appropriate at this time of year, the answer is that I find it hard to brave the crowds there. So I am staying where the owner of the finest estate in Baiae* usually stays at this time every year. Once I return to Rome, neither my features nor my conversation will give rise to rebuke. The cheerfulness with which I used to spice the melancholy of these days is gone from me for ever, but no one will look in vain for the perseverance and resolve in my thought and speech.

So far as Scapula's estate* is concerned, thanks in part to your 4 influence and in part to mine, it seems feasible to have it put up for auction. If this does not take place, I shall be out of the running. But if I am admitted to the sale, my enthusiasm will prevail over Otho's wealth. As for your mention to me of Lentulus,* it does not lie with him; as long as the situation with Faberius is definite, and you work hard at it as you are doing, we shall achieve our objective.

You ask how long I shall be here. It will be for a few days, but I 5 have not decided. As soon as I do so, I shall write to you, and you must inform me how long you will stay in your suburban villa. Today as I send you this letter, I have learnt both by post and by word of mouth the same news about Pilia and Attica as you have written.

Letter 124 (*Att.* XIII 27)

Tusculum, May 45

CICERO TO ATTICUS

So far as the letter to Caesar* goes, my decision was absolutely right 1 that your friends should read it beforehand. Otherwise it would have been discourteous to them, and, if it was likely to offend him, a source of virtual danger to me. Your friends have responded frankly, and I was pleased that they did not conceal their reactions. Best of all, they suggested so many changes that I have no incentive to write it afresh.

However, on the subject of the Parthian War,* what should I have borne in mind but what I thought Caesar intended? What other theme did my letter have except *flatterie*? If I had wished to urge upon him the course I thought best, would words have failed me?

So the entire letter is pointless, and therefore what need is there *courir un risque*, when no great *avantage* would be achieved, and an *insuccès* however slight would cause embarrassment? This is especially so since it strikes me that he would think that, as I had written nothing previously, I would not have composed anything had the whole war not been concluded. However, I fear that he may believe that I wanted it to be a *tranquillisant* after my *Cato*. In short, I very much regret having written it, and nothing in this business could have occurred to please me more than that my *effort* did not pass muster. Moreover, I should have fallen into the clutches of those hostile people, including your relative.*

2   But to come back to the gardens.* I am wholly against your going there unless it is very convenient for you, as there is no hurry. Whatever the outcome, we must work on Faberius. Let me have the date of the auction if you are in the know. I am immediately sending to you the courier who has come from my house at Cumae, for he has excellent news of Attica's health, and says he has a letter for you.

Letter 125 *(Fam.* XIII 15)

Tusculum, May–June 45

CICERO TO CAESAR

1   I particularly recommend to you Publius Precilius,* the son of an associate of yours and of a very close friend of mine, an excellent man. I feel remarkable affection for the young man for his unassuming and kindly nature, and for his attentive and remarkable affection for me. I have also come to realize and learn by experience that his father has always been most friendly to me. Mind you, he has been most prominent among my critics for his frequent derision and railing at me for not joining you, especially as you did me the greatest honour of inviting me.

> But never did he win the heart within my breast.*

For I hearkened to the cries of my leaders:

> Be brave, to win the praises of posterity.
> At these words grief's black cloud encompassed him.*

None the less, the father consoles me. Though I am a burnt-out case, 2
even now they seek to fire me with desire for fame with words like
these:

> May I not die ignobly and ingloriously,
> But do some mighty deed, which men to come may learn.*

But as you see, they fail to rouse me nowadays. So I turn from the
sublime language of Homer to the true precepts of Euripides:

> I hate the wisdom-teacher who himself's not wise.*

Old Precilius heaps lavish praise on this verse above all, and remarks
that a man can look both forward and backward,* but none the less
should

> strive to be best, and rise superior to the rest.*

But to return to my initial point, you will do me an outstanding 3
favour if with that unique graciousness of yours you take this young
man in hand, and if you add my recommendation to crown the
benevolence which I believe you entertain for the Precilii in their
own right. I have used a novel form of letter to you to help you realize that this is no common-or-garden recommendation.

Letter 126 (*Att.* XIII 7)

Tusculum, June 45

CICERO TO ATTICUS

Sestius* has been with me, and Theopompus* came yesterday. He 1
announced that a letter had arrived from Caesar to the effect that he
had decided to remain in Rome, the reason being that which
appeared in my letter* addressed to him, namely the fear that in his
absence his laws would be disregarded, as his sumptuary law had
been. His reaction is *logique*, and I had suspected that this would
happen. But I must bow to those friends of yours, unless they want
me to follow through with that proposal.

Theopompus further reports that Lentulus has definitely divorced
Metella.* Your knowledge of these matters is greater than mine, so
do reply to this note with any topic you like, as long as you write
something. At the moment I can think of nothing about which you
can write back, except perhaps Mustela, or if you see Silius.*

Letter 127 (*Att.* XIII 19)

Tusculum, June 45

CICERO TO ATTICUS

1 My secretary Hilarius had just left on 28 June with a letter for you which I had given him, when a courier arrived with a letter from you written the day before, which contained the most encouraging news that our Attica begs you not to be depressed, and you write that she is *sans danger*.

2 I note that your authoritative voice has issued an outstanding recommendation of my speech the *Pro Ligario*,* for Balbus and Oppius have written that they enthusiastically approve of it, and for that reason they have forwarded the unpretentious speech to Caesar. So this was the outcome which you predicted in a letter to me earlier.

3 As regards Varro, the argument you advance that I may appear *prétentieux* would not have swayed me, for I had decided to introduce no living person into my dialogues. But because you wrote that Varro both wanted it and regarded it as a real privilege, I completed the work and polished off the whole topic of the Academy* in four books. I cannot vouch for its competence, but it is as carefully written as can be. In these books I assigned to Varro the arguments admirably assembled by Antiochus against the *dénégation des certitudes*. I myself counter these arguments and you play the role of third speaker in our conversation. If I had depicted Cotta* and Varro arguing against each other, as you advised me in your last letter, I myself would have played a *rôle muet*.

4 Such an effect is charming when the characters belong to former times, as Heraclides* portrayed them in many works, and I myself did in the six books of *De republica*. Likewise in the three books of my *De oratore*,* which I regard highly. In that work too the participants were such that I was obliged to keep silent, for the speakers were Crassus, Antonius, the elder Catulus, Gaius Iulius the brother of Catulus, Cotta, and Sulpicius. This conversation is mounted in my boyhood, so that I could play no role in it. But the works I have written in recent days are in the Aristotelian mode,* in which the contributions of the others are introduced in such a way as to lend the leading role to the author himself. Thus in the five books which I have written in *On Ends*,* I entrusted the Epicurean case to Lucius Torquatus, the Stoic to Marcus Cato, and the Peripatetic to

Marcus Piso. I thought that this would arouse no *jalousie*, since they were all dead. The *Academica*, as you know, I entrusted to Catulus, 5 Lucullus, and Hortensius.* Admittedly the subject matter did not suit the characters, for the subject was too *raisonné* for them ever to have seemed to dream of it. So when I read your letter about Varro, I seized upon it as a *bienfait du ciel*, for nothing could be more appropriate to that branch of philosophy in which he seems to me to take particular pleasure, and his role is such that I have not succeeded in making my case appear the stronger. Indeed, the arguments of Antiochus are extremely *convaincants*, I have presented them with care, so that they have the penetration of Antiochus combined with the elegance of my language, if I possess any such faculty. But you must repeatedly reflect whether you think these books should be allocated to Varro. I envisage certain objections,* but we can discuss these face to face.

Letter 128 (*Fam.* IX 8)

Tusculum, July 45

CICERO TO VARRO

Even the common folk do not demand the treat of a show unless they 1 are roused to it, even if someone has dangled it before them. None the less I am so avid in the expectation of your promise* as to remind you, though not to demand it. But I am sending you four reminders* of a less bashful type; you are certainly acquainted with the cheek of the younger Academy!* So I have solicited these from her bosom and sent them to you. I fear that perhaps they may make demands of you, though I have instructed them merely to make a request. I have been waiting for quite a time, and restraining myself from addressing something to you before receiving anything, so that I could repay you with a gift as close to yours as possible. But since you have been proceeding rather slowly—in other words, as I interpret it, rather scrupulously—I could not restrain myself from proclaiming the close link between our studies and our affection for each other by means of the literary genre which lay within my competence.* So I have created a conversation between us held on my estate at Cumae, when Pomponius was with us. I have allotted to you the arguments of Antiochus, of which I have the impression that you approve, while

I have adopted the standpoint of Philo. When you read the treatise, I imagine that you will be surprised at our exchanging views which we have never actually exchanged, but you are aware of the conventions of dialogues.

2   Later on, my dear Varro, if you are agreeable, we must meet as frequently as possible, and discuss with each other the interests we share. Perhaps it is late in the day to do this. But the Fortune of the republic must shoulder responsibility for the past, and we ourselves must take in hand the present. If only we could pursue in peaceful times the studies we share, and in a settled if not ideal political community! Yet in these circumstances there would be other issues which allotted to us honourable responsibilities and activities. But as things stand, what motivation for living would we have without these studies? So far as I am concerned, even with them life is scarcely bearable, and without them not even that. But we shall discuss these matters together more frequently.

I hope that the change of house and its purchase turn out well. I applaud your intentions in this respect. Look after yourself.

Letter 129 (*Att.* XIII 47A)

Astura, July 45

CICERO TO ATTICUS

1   Lepidus* sent me a letter yesterday evening from Antium, for he is staying there. He owns the house which I sold him. He begs me pressingly to attend the Senate* on the 1st, saying that both he and Caesar would be greatly obliged if I did. My own view is that it is without significance, for otherwise Oppius would perhaps have said something to you, Balbus being ill. However, I prefer to make a wasted journey rather than to be missed if I am needed and to regret it later, so I am staying at Antium today, and I shall be at home in Rome before midday tomorrow. I'd be glad if you and Pilia will come to dinner on the 31st, unless you are booked up.

2   I hope that you have concluded the business with Publilius.* I shall hurry back to my place at Tusculum on the 1st, but I prefer that the whole business with these people should be conducted in my absence. I have passed on my brother Quintus' letter to you, a not

particularly gracious reply to mine, but it will satisfy you, I imagine, though you must judge.

Letter 130 (*Att.* XIII 46)

Tusculum, August 45

CICERO TO ATTICUS

Pollex promised to be with me about 13 August, and duly appeared 1 before me at Lanuvium on the 12th, but clearly as a Tom Thumb, and not an index finger.* You will get the news from the man himself.

I met Balbus—Lepta took me along to him, for he was having 2 problems in his supervision of the entertainments*—in the residence at Lanuvium which Balbus had assigned to Lepidus. Balbus' first words were: 'A short time ago I received a letter from Caesar, in which he emphatically makes it clear that he will arrive before the Roman Games.'* I read the letter. It contained a lot about my *Cato*. He says that by reading it very frequently he has become more fluent in expression, whereas after reading Brutus' *Cato** he considered himself eloquent!

Secondly, I ascertained from him the terms of acceptance of 3 Cluvius' will. How negligent Vestorius* has been! There must be free acceptance in the presence of witnesses within sixty days. I feared that I should have to summon Vestorius, but now I must send someone with my instructions to accept. So this will be Pollex again. I also discussed with Balbus the issue of Cluvius' estate. He was quite forthcoming, and said that he would write at once to Caesar. He also said that Cluvius in his will left a legacy of 50,000 sesterces to Terentia, with instructions that this plus the cost of his tomb and many other items should be defrayed from Titus Hordeonius' share, and none of it from mine. Please administer a gentle rebuke to Vestorius, for is there anything more galling than that the perfumer Plotius should through his slaves have informed Balbus of the whole arrangement so long ago, while Vestorius failed to report it to me through mine?

I am sad to hear about Cossinius,* for I was fond of him. I shall 4 make over to Quintus any money which remains after payment of my debts and my purchases, as a result of which I suppose I must incur further debt! I know nothing about the house at Arpinum.

5   There is no need for you to rebuke Vestorius, for after I had
sealed this letter, my courier arrived after darkness fell, and
brought a carefully drafted letter together with a copy of the will
from him.

Letter 131 (*Att.* XIII 50)

Tusculum, August 45

CICERO TO ATTICUS

1 In certain letters of yours you recommended that I should write more
copious letters to Caesar. So when Balbus on the estate at Lanuvium
told me recently that he and Oppius had written to Caesar, telling
him that I had read his books against Cato* and had strongly
approved of them, I composed a letter to Caesar on those very
books, intending that it should be submitted to Dolabella. But
I sent a copy to Oppius and Balbus, and in a letter told them that if
they approved it, they should then order it to be delivered to
Dolabella. They sent me a reply, intimating that they had never read
anything better. They have ordered my letter to be passed to
Dolabella.

2   Vestorius has written asking me to give instructions that my share
in Brinnius' farm* should be entrusted to his slave so that it could be
passed by conveyance to a certain Hetereius. Then he, Vestorius,
could duly present it by conveyance to Hetereius at Puteoli. If you
approve, you must send the slave to me, for I believe that Vestorius
has written to you as well.

3   Oppius and Balbus have sent me the same message as you did
about Caesar's arrival.* I am surprised that you have not yet met up
with Tigellius. I am very keen to know how much he got, though
I don't give a damn!

4   You asked for my thoughts about going to greet Caesar. Where, do
you imagine, other than Alsium? In fact, I have written to Murena
with a request for hospitality, but I think he has set out with Matius,
so your friend Silius will have to bear with me.

5   Just after I wrote that last line, Eros tells me that Murena has sent
him a most generous reply. So I must exploit him, for Silius has no
soft mattresses! But Dida, I believe, has opened his entire house to
guests.

Letter 132 (*Fam.* IX 12)

In one of his country-houses, December 45

CICERO TO DOLABELLA

I felicitate that dear Baiae* of ours, if it is true as you write that it has 1
suddenly become salubrious—unless perhaps in its affection it fawns
on you, and as long as you are there it forgets what it is like. If this is
the case, I am not at all surprised that even the climate and the soil
abandon their offensive properties to please you thereby!

You ask for my unpretentious speech, the *Pro Deiotaro*.* I had not 2
realized that it was here, but I did have it and have accordingly sent
it off to you. Please read it as a trifling and impoverished case, hardly
worthy of publication. But I wished to send it to my long-standing
host and friend as an unpretentious gift, thin-spun from coarse
thread, as his own gifts usually are.

I pray that your thoughts may be wise and brave, so that your
restraint and sober demeanour may bring obloquy upon the injustice
of others.

Letter 133 (*Att.* XIII 52)

?Puteoli, December 45

CICERO TO ATTICUS

What a guest,* so weighty but not *mal venu*, for it was really quite 1
pleasant! When he arrived at Philippus' residence,* in the evening of
the second day of the Saturnalia, the house was so teeming with soldiers that there was scarcely a free dining-room where Caesar could
have dinner, for the troops numbered 2,000. I was greatly exercised
as to what was to happen next day, but Cassius Barba* came to my
rescue and provided guards. A camp was pitched in the open country and the house was guarded. On the third day of the Saturnalia he
stayed in Philippus' house until an hour after noon, and he let no
one in. I think he was working over the accounts with Balbus. After
that he took a walk on the shore. After two o'clock he had a bath. It
was then that he heard about Mamurra,* but his features remained
impassive. After being rubbed down with oil, he reclined at table.
He was following a routine of emetics, which allowed him to eat

and drink *sans apprehension*, lavishly and sumptuously. Not merely that, but

> On food well cooked and garnished,
> Good conversation; if you ask, a pleasant meal.*

2   Moreover, the members of his entourage were entertained most lavishly in three dining-rooms. The less refined freedmen and the slaves enjoyed the full range; as for the more sophisticated, I offered them refined fare. In short, I behaved as a civilized host should. But my guest was not the sort to whom you would say 'Do please drop in on me again, when you return to these parts.' Once is enough. Our conversation did not broach *questions sérieuses*, but was largely *littéraire*. In short, he was delighted, and all went well. He said that he would spend one day at Puteoli, and a second at Baiae.

This, then, is the account of the hospitality or *cantonnement** which I described as distasteful but not troublesome. I shall stay here for a short time, and then repair to my place at Tusculum.

As he passed the residence of Dolabella, and at no other point, all his armed troops posted themselves on the right and left of his horse. I have this from Nicias.*

Letter 134 *(Fam. VII 30)*
Rome, January 44

CICERO TO CURIUS

1   For my part,* I neither urge nor beg you to return home. On the contrary, I myself am eager to fly away and land somewhere,

> where neither names nor deeds of Pelops' sons I hear.

It is beyond belief how ashamed I feel at my presence in the situation here. You certainly seem to have foreseen long ago what was in store, when you decamped from here. Though even hearing of these events is bitter, hearing of them is easier to bear than witnessing them. At any rate, you were not in the Campus Martius when at the second hour of daylight elections to the quaestorship began. The chair of Quintus Maximus,* whom the Caesarians called 'the consul', was set in place. Then, when his death was announced, the chair was removed.

Then the great man, who had taken the auspices for the election by tribes, held the elections by centuries, and at the seventh hour declared the election of a consul to hold office until 1 January, which was the following morning. So I am to inform you that during the consulship of Caninius* no one had lunch, and that no crime was committed while he was consul. His wakefulness was beyond belief, for during his entire consulship he never slept a wink!

This seems comic to you, for you are not here. But if you were to 2 witness it, you could not restrain your tears. What, then, if I recounted the rest, for there are countless instances of the same kind, which I could not endure if I had not retired into the haven of philosophy,* and if I did not have our dear Atticus as associate in my studies? As for your comment that you are his as slave and bondsman, but mine by usufruct, I am happy with that formulation of yours, for what a man enjoys and exploits belong to him. But this we can discuss another time at greater length.

Acilius,* who has been dispatched with legions to Greece, is under 3 the greatest obligation to me, for I have defended him twice in court on capital charges in which he was acquitted. He is a man who is not ungrateful and who pays me earnest attentions. I have written to him most scrupulously on your behalf, and have attached a copy of that letter to this. Please write to inform me how he has greeted the letter, and what promises he has made to you.

8

THE LAST STAND FOR THE REPUBLIC (44–43 BC)

THE Liberators had assassinated Julius Caesar without formulating any strategy for the restoration of republican rule, and in the face of popular resentment they were forced to quit Rome, and eventually Italy, to gather forces and funds in the eastern provinces. Meanwhile Mark Antony, as the surviving consul, showed skill, and initially moderation, in exploiting the popularity of the murdered Caesar to gain the support of the veterans and to seek the loyalty of the legions. But in mid-April 44 the youthful Gaius Octavian, great-nephew and designated heir of Julius, crossed to Italy to claim his inheritance. Cicero sought to take him under his wing and to establish him and the support which he gathered as a bulwark for the Senate against the developing despotism of Antony.

Cicero became increasingly despondent for the future of the republic, seeking refuge in philosophy, and even deciding to quit Italy for Athens, but he was beaten back by contrary winds. A meeting with Marcus Brutus at Velia, and the realization that his departure was being criticized, led him at the end of August 44 to return to Rome, where on 2 September he launched the first of his 14 *Philippics* against Antony. They provide detailed evidence of the political scene between this time and April 43.

Earlier in June Antony had secured for himself the governorship of Cisalpine Gaul, which was held by Decimus Brutus as the senatorial nominee. Towards the close of the year Antony blockaded Decimus Brutus in Mutina. The Senate ordered him to remove his forces from the province. When he refused, he was defeated in two engagements by forces under the new consuls, supported by Octavian. But both consuls fell, Octavian refused to cooperate, and Decimus Brutus was slow to exploit the victories. Antony at the end of May 43 was able to persuade the wily Lepidus, governor of Narbonese Gaul, and his seven legions to unite with him. Cicero vainly pleaded with Marcus Brutus to return to lead the campaign against Antony.

———

Letter 135 (*Att.* XIV 1)

Near Rome, April 44

CICERO TO ATTICUS

I went out of my way to visit the person whom we were discussing*   1
this morning. It was totally depressing, for he claims that the situation is irredeemable. 'If such a talented man as he could not find a
solution, who will find one now?' What more can I say? He claims
that it is all up with us, and perhaps it is, but he was pleased about it.
He maintained that there will be disorders in Gaul within twenty
days. Since the Ides of March, he said, he had held discussions only
with Lepidus.* In short, his view is that things cannot continue as
they are. How worldly wise Oppius is, for he misses Caesar just as
much, but says nothing to alienate any honourable man. But enough
of this.

Do not, I beg you, be slow to inform me* of any news. I anticipate   2
that there are several items, among them whether the report
about Sextus is reasonably certain, and above all any word of
Brutus.* The man whom I broke my journey to see told me that
Caesar used to say of Brutus: 'What he wants matters a lot, but
whatever he wants, he wants a lot.'* Caesar, he told me, had noted
this when Brutus spoke on behalf of Deiotarus* at Nicaea, for he
seemed to speak forcefully and freely. He further mentioned—I'm
happy to jot down any remarks that occur to me—that recently,
when I was visiting Caesar's house at Sestius' request,* and took a
seat while waiting to be summoned, Caesar commented: 'I cannot
doubt that I am the object of the greatest hatred, for Marcus Cicero
is seated there, and cannot join me when he finds it convenient.
If anyone is kindly disposed, Cicero is, but I am in no doubt that
he loathes me.' This is what that person said, and much else in the
same vein.

But to return to the relevant point. Do please inform me about
anything that happens, whether important or trivial. I myself will not
take a break from writing to you.

Letter 136 (*Att.* XIV 10)
Cumae, April 44

CICERO TO ATTICUS

1 Has it come to this? Did Brutus, my friend and yours, act as he did so as to skulk at Lanuvium?* And so that Trebonius* should depart to his province by devious routes? And so that all Caesar's actions, writings, speeches, promises, and designs should be more effective than if he were still alive? Do you recall my crying out on that first day* of the occupation of the Capitol that the praetors should summon the Senate to the Capitoline temple? Ye gods that live for ever, what measures could be taken then, when all men of honour and even those of some decency expressed their joy, while the brigands were broken in spirit! You blame the feast of the Liberalia,* but what could have been done then? It had been all up with us for some time. Do you recall your own cry, that the cause was lost if Caesar was given a public burial? Yet his corpse was even cremated in the Forum and addressed in a pathetic panegyric. Slaves and paupers with torches were launched against our houses. And what was the outcome? Why, they had the gall to say, 'Are you defying Caesar's will?' I cannot endure these scenes and others like them, so I plan to go to *terre au delà de terre,** but your land is *abritée contre le vent*.

2 Has your nausea finally cleared up? I imagine so, judging from your letter. I hark back to men like Tebassus, Bassus, Scaeva, and Fango.* Do you realize that they are confident of keeping their spoils while we remain safe? They believed we had more spirit than they found in us. These no doubt are your peace-lovers, and not sponsors of brigandage! But when I wrote to you about Curtilius and about Sestullius' farm, I cited Censorinus, Messalla, Plancus, Postumus, and all that type.* It would have been better to die when Caesar was murdered—though that could never have been the outcome—than to witness the present scene.

3 Octavian* landed at Naples on 18 April. Early next day Balbus met him there, and the same day he joined me at my residence at Cumae. As you say in your letter, he is about to seek his inheritance, but he fears a big *confrontation* with Antony.

I am coping with your Buthrotum problem,* as is right, and I will continue to do so. As for your enquiry whether the Cluvian property* amounts to 100,000 sesterces a year, it seems to be approaching that figure. In the first year I have cleared 80,000.

Quintus senior* has written some stern words to me about his son, 4 chiefly because the boy is more gracious towards his mother, whereas previously, though she deserved well of him, he was hostile. If you have knowledge of his activities, and if you have not yet left Rome, please write to me about this and about anything else. I get such lively pleasure from your letters.

Letter 137 (*Att.* XIV 12)
Puteoli, April 44

CICERO TO ATTICUS

My dear Atticus, I fear that the Ides of March have gained us noth- 1 ing beyond joy and revenge for our loathing and sufferings. What grim reports reach me from your vantage-point in Rome, and what scenes I witness here!

> Oh, what a splendid deed, but left half-done!*

You know how I love the Sicilians and the great respect I attach to my position as their patron.* Caesar granted them many concessions to which I was not averse, though the award of the Latin franchise* was intolerable, but still . . . But now here comes Antony. He has pocketed a huge backhander, and has resurrected a law allegedly put through the Assembly by the dictator, by which Sicilians become Roman citizens. There was no mention of it in Caesar's lifetime! Then again, is not the case of Deiotarus similar? Yes, he deserves to gain any kingdom, but not when bestowed by Fulvia.* There are countless similar instances, but I come back to the issue of Buthrotum.* Our position will surely to some extent be strong on so celebrated, so well attested, and so just a case? The more such cases as that appear, the stronger our position will be.

Octavian is staying with me. His attitude is most respectful and 2 most friendly. His supporters hail him as Caesar, though Philippus* does not, and accordingly neither do I. He cannot in my view be a good private citizen, for he is surrounded by so many who repeatedly threaten our followers with death and say that the present situation is intolerable. So what do you suppose will ensue when the boy arrives in Rome, where our deliverers cannot live in safety? They will indeed be famous for ever, and also happy in the knowledge of what they have done, but unless I am mistaken we shall be left prostrate. So I am eager to get away, in the words of the poet, 'Where neither names nor deeds of Pelops' sons . . .'* I am not at all keen either on the consuls-designate,* who have in addition compelled me to practise speech-making, so that I am not even allowed to take my ease by the waters here. But this is because I am too easygoing. At one time my oratory seemed vital, but now no matter the situation, it is not what it was.

3   For a long time I have had nothing about which to write to you. But I continue writing to you, not to delight you with my letters, but to elicit those from you. Keep me posted on any other matters, but especially anything on Brutus. I write this on 22 April, at table in Vestorius' house.* He is a stranger to logic, but a quite practised mathematician!

Letter 138 (*Att.* XIV 13B)
Puteoli, April 44

CICERO TO THE CONSUL ANTONY

1 With regard to your communication* to me by letter, I should have preferred you to conduct it with me face to face, for this one reason: you could have gleaned not only from my words but also from my features, eyes, and brow, as the saying goes, my friendly feeling towards you, for I have always regarded you with affection— initially when challenged by your zealous interest in me, and subsequently by your kind attentions; and now in recent times the body politic has recommended you to me in such terms that I regard
2 no one with greater affection. Now your letter, couched in such affectionate and honorific terms, has made such an impact upon me that I appear not to be conferring a kindness on you, but to be receiving one from you, for you make your request in such a way that you are reluctant to come to the aid of my enemy and your friend against my wishes, though you could achieve that end without difficulty.

3   My dear Antony, I grant you this request of yours, and I consider that you have broached it most generously and honourably by

writing in such terms. I believe that whatever the circumstances, you should be granted it in its entirety. I am also bestowing it on my own sense of decency and on my native character, for not only has there never been any bitterness in my make-up, but I have never even in the slightest degree shown more sternness or harshness than the needs of the state demanded. Moreover, there has never been on my part any conspicuous hatred even for Cloelius. My policy has always been that friends of my enemies, particularly those of the lower classes, should not be hounded, and that I should not in this way strip myself of such support.

With regard to young Clodius,* my view is that it is your role, as 4 you write, to imbue his innocent mind with such opinions that he does not consider that any enmities continue to exist between our families. My struggle with Publius Clodius took place when I was defending the interests of the state, and he was championing his own. It was the state that delivered the verdict on the disputes between us. If he were still alive, there would now be no continuing discord between us.

Accordingly, since in making this request of me you state that 5 you will not deploy your powers against my wishes, you will also if you are agreeable offer my assurance to the boy; not that at my advanced age I ought to suspect any danger from his youth, nor that my eminence should be apprehensive of any disputes, but so that we should be more closely associated than we have hitherto been. For while these enmities lay between us, your attitude towards me has been more amenable than your house. But enough has been said on this.

One final word.* Without any hesitation and with the greatest enthusiasm I shall do what I believe to be what is your wish and in your interest. I should wholeheartedly like to assure you of this.

Letter 139 (*Fam.* XII 1)

Pompeii, May 44

CICERO TO CASSIUS

Believe me, Cassius,* I never stop thinking of you and of our Brutus, 1 in other words of the entire republic. Its whole hope rests on the two of you and on Decimus Brutus.* My own hopes are now more optimistic, in view of my dear Dolabella's quite outstanding political coup.* Corruption in the city was spreading, and was becoming so much stronger day by day that I was indeed losing confidence in the city and its freedom from disturbances. But the corruption has been so effectively contained that it seems that we shall be safe at least from that most unsavoury hazard from now on.

But important and numerous tasks remain; all of them rest on your collective shoulders. Let us, however, tackle each issue as it first occurs, for in what has been achieved so far we seem to have been delivered from the king, but not from the kingship; for though the king has been killed, we are upholding every command of his regal nod, and not merely that, but also others which if he had lived he would not have issued. We approve these as if he had planned them, and I see no end to this process. Decrees are posted, exemptions granted, massive sums allocated, exiles restored, and spurious senatorial decrees recorded, so that it appears that merely the loathing for that impious man and our resentment at slavery have been purged, while the state still lies prostrate in the upheavals into which he cast it.

2   All these problems you must together disentangle. You are not to think that the republic has already received sufficient aid from you. She has indeed received as much as would never have occurred to me to desire, but she is not content with that, for she longs for great achievements commensurate with the greatness of your spirit and your service. Up to now she has avenged through your agency by the death of the tyrant the injustices sustained, but she has attained nothing further. Which of her distinctions has she regained? Obedience to the man now dead whom she could not endure in life? Do we show allegiance even to his handwritten directions, when we ought to have remedied those he engraved in bronze? You may say that we approved those decrees. True, but we were yielding to the times. Circumstances play the greatest part in politics, and some people exploit our good nature without restraint or gratitude.

But we shall discuss these and many other matters soon, when we meet. Meanwhile please be assured that your high standing is of the greatest concern to me, both for the sake of the republic, which has always been most dear to me, and for our affection for each other. Look after yourself, and farewell.

Letter 140 (*Fam.* IX 14)

Pompeii, May 44

CICERO TO HIS FRIEND THE CONSUL DOLABELLA

Though the glory you have gained,* dear Dolabella, leaves me 1
happy, and though I obtain a sufficiency of abundant joy and pleasure from it, I cannot refrain from admitting that I am overwhelmed
with the greatest happiness because the general belief of all the world
associates me with your praises. Every day I am in touch with a host
of people (for many excellent men come to this region for health
reasons, and friends of mine come in great numbers from local
townships), but I have met not one who in lauding you to the skies
in most glowing praises does not also at once bestow the greatest
gratitude on me. They state that they have no doubt it is through
falling in with my principles and plans that you show yourself to be
a most outstanding citizen and an exceptional consul.

Though I am able with total truth to respond that your actions are 2
prompted by your own judgement and initiative, and that you stand
in need of no man's counsel, in fact I neither agree with them wholeheartedly in case I detract from your praise if it all appears to be the
outcome of my advice, nor do I vehemently deny it, for my greed for
fame is never satisfied. However, it does not detract from your high
repute to have a Nestor in the framing of your counsels, just as it was
becoming for Agamemnon,* the king of kings. It is truly a proud
boast for me that a young consul* like you should blossom in praises,
when you have, so to say, graduated by my teaching.

When I visited Lucius Caesar* on his sickbed at Naples, his whole 3
body was racked with pain. None the less, before formally greeting me,
he said: 'My dear Cicero, I congratulate you on your great influence
over Dolabella. Had I had as much influence over my sister's son, we
would now be unscathed. I both congratulate and thank your
Dolabella, for he is the only one since your consulship whom we can
truthfully call a consul.' He continued at length to expatiate on your
actions and achievement, saying that no deed was more splendid,
outstanding, and salutary for the state. This is the unanimous view
of us all.

I beg you to allow me formally to acknowledge this spurious inher- 4
itance of a glory not my own, and to permit me to have some share

of your praises. That request is of course a pleasantry. Indeed, my dear Dolabella, I should more gladly transfer to you all my own praises, if only there are some credited to me, than to drain off any part of yours. My regard for you has always been such as you were able to appreciate, but these recent deeds of yours have so fired me that no zeal was ever warmer in its affection—for believe me, nothing is more handsome, more beautiful, and more lovable than virtue.

5   As you know, I have always loved Marcus Brutus for his outstanding intellect,* his most engaging character, and his unique honesty and resolve, but on the Ides of March he so enhanced my affection as to surprise me that there was room to increase what had for long seemed to me to be full to the brim. What person could possibly believe that there could be any enhancement to the affection which I feel for you?* Yet it has grown to such a degree that it is only now that I seem to experience affection, whereas before it was dutiful regard.

6   In view of this, what point is there in my urging you to safeguard your high worth and fame? Why should I, like men who often resort to exhortation, set before you the example of famous figures? I know no one more famous than yourself. You must set yourself up for imitation, and vie with yourself. After such great achievements, you are not permitted to fail to match your own standard. No exhortation is necessary, and congratulation must be the order of the day.

7   It has been your lot, shared with virtually no other, to find that the supreme severity of the punishment which you imposed not merely attracted no odium, but was generally welcomed as most acceptable, not only to honourable citizens, but also to the lowest stratum of society. If this experience had been attributable to mere chance, I would have congratulated you on your good fortune, but it is the outcome of your greatness of spirit, and also of your intellect and your judgement, for I read the speech you delivered to the Assembly, and its wisdom was unsurpassed. Your gradual approach, step by step, forwards and backwards, towards the reason for your action was such that the issue itself, as all admitted, provided you with the opportune moment for dispensing punishment.

8   So you delivered both the city from danger and its community from fear. You have not merely performed a most important service for the moment, but also set an example for the future. You must become aware that through this action the state is entrusted to your

hands, and that you must not merely protect but also honour those men from whom the beginning of freedom has emerged. But we shall discuss these matters at greater length face to face, and I hope soon. So ensure, dear Dolabella, that you protect yourself with the utmost care, for you are keeping alive both the republic and myself.

Letter 141 *(Att.* XV 11)
Antium, June 44

CICERO TO ATTICUS

I reached Antium before midday. Brutus welcomed my arrival, and 1 then in company with several listeners, including Servilia, Tertulla, and Porcia,* he asked what in my view he should do. Favonius* was also there. My advice, which I had pondered en route, was that he should take up the Asiatic corn-commission, for there was no action left for us to undertake unless he remained unscathed. Moreover, the defence of the republic lay in his hands. After I had embarked on this discourse, Cassius' arrival interrupted me. I repeated the same message, and at this point Cassius, with quite combative gaze (you would have said that he was breathing warfare), affirmed that he would not be going to Sicily.* 'Would I have swallowed that insult as though it were a favour?' he asked. I enquired: 'So what do you propose to do?' He replied that he would go to Achaia. 'And, Brutus, how about you?' I asked. 'If you approve, I shall go to Rome,' he replied. 'I totally dissent,' I said, 'because you will not be safe.' 'But if I could be safe, would you approve?' 'Indeed I would, and I would be wholly opposed to your going to a province, either now or after your praetorship. But I am not in favour of your entrusting yourself to Rome.' I then explained the reasons (which will certainly occur to you) why he would not be safe there.

They then voiced complaints at great length, with Cassius taking 2 the lead. They argued that chances had been lost, and laid heavy charges against Decimus.* My response was that it was pointless to lament the past, though I agreed with their views. Then I launched into what should have been, saying nothing new but repeating what everyone is saying every day. I did not make the point that another person ought to have been dealt with,* but said that they should have summoned the Senate, roused more vehemently the citizens who were fired to eager support, and taken control of the entire state. At this your lady friend* cried out: 'I never heard this said by anyone!' I held my peace. However, Cassius for his part seems likely to go (indeed, Servilia promised* to ensure that the corn-commission would be deleted from the senatorial decree), and our friend Brutus was quickly dissuaded from his pointless talk of intending to go to Rome. He therefore decided that the games would be held in his name,* but in his absence. It seems that he intends to leave for Asia from Antium.

3   To cut a long story short, in my having made that journey, nothing pleased me except salving my conscience, for it would not have been in order for Brutus to quit Italy before we got together. Once this duty of affection and obligation had been discharged, all that was left for me was to say to myself; 'Prophet, what profit is there in that journeying now?'* I found our ship of state totally wrecked, or rather in fragments widely scattered. There is no strategy, no rational thought, no system in place. So though even before I had no doubts, I am now still less reluctant to fly from here with all speed, to where

Neither names nor deeds of Pelops' sons I hear.*

4   But here's something for you! On 3 June Dolabella appointed me as his legate. This was reported to me yesterday evening. You did not favour a votive commission* either, and it would have been ridiculous for me to discharge vows made for the survival of the republic when it had been overthrown. Moreover, free commissions are, I believe, limited in time by the Julian law, and it is not easy to append to that type of commission the right to undertake or to abandon it when one wishes. I have now been granted this additional discretion. Freedom to exercise this right for five years is a bonus. But why should I be pondering a period of five years? The enterprise seems to me to be short-lived. But away with *mots de mauvais présage*!

Letter 142 (*Fam.* XI 29)

?*Anagnia, July 44*

CICERO TO OPPIUS

1   As our friend Atticus knows, I was doubtful about my entire plan of departure,* for many considerations both for and against occurred

to me. But your judgement and advice have exercised great additional weight in removing my hesitation, for on the one hand your letter expressed your view explicitly, and on the other Atticus reported to me your conversation with him. My judgement has always been that you possess both supreme practical wisdom in formulating your advice, and honesty in offering it. I experienced this above all at the outset of the civil war, when I sought your counsel by letter on what action you thought I should take, whether to join Pompey or to remain in Italy. You persuaded me to take thought for my reputation, which made me aware of your view, and won my admiration for your honesty and conscientiousness in offering advice, for though you believed that your closest friend* preferred otherwise, your obligation to me counted for more with you than his wishes.

Even before then I held you in affection, and I was aware that you 2 always reciprocated this. I recall that when I was away from Rome,* experiencing great dangers, you showed both care and protection to both myself in my absence and to my household here. Then, following my return, all who observe these matters can attest your close friendship with me, and my sentiments and utterances concerning you. But the weightiest judgement which you expressed concerning my honesty and resolve came after the death of Caesar,* when you entrusted yourself wholly to my friendship. If I do not justify this discernment of yours by the utmost goodwill towards you, and by every meritorious service, I shall not count myself truly human.

Dear Oppius, for your part you must preserve your affection for 3 me—I write this more from custom than from any belief that you need to be reminded—and lend your assistance to all my concerns. I have instructed Atticus to ensure that these are not unknown to you. You can expect a more extensive letter from me once I have a little leisure. Look after yourself; nothing which you can do is more welcome to me.

Letter 143 (*Att.* XVI 7)
Off Pompeii, August 44

CICERO TO ATTICUS

I set out from Leucopetra* on 6 August, as I intended to cross from 1
there. I had sailed out for some thirty-odd miles when a strong south

wind bore me back again to Leucopetra. As I waited there for a favourable wind (my dear Valerius has a country-house there, which provided a friendly and congenial base), some distinguished men arrived. They were natives of Rhegium, and had arrived quite recently from Rome. Among them was a friend of our Brutus, whom he had left at Naples. These men reported the edict* of Brutus and Cassius, a full meeting of the Senate scheduled for the 1st,* and letters addressed by Brutus and Cassius to former consuls and former praetors requesting their attendance. These visitors stated that there was the fairest prospect that Antony would give way, that agreement would be reached, and that the men of our persuasion were returning to Rome. In addition they stated that my presence was missed and that I was being criticized.

Once I heard this, I abandoned my plan to leave Italy without hesitation. Even earlier this prospect had afforded me little pleasure.
2 Then, when I read your letter, I was surprised that you had so emphatically changed your view, but I believed this was not without good reason. Though you had not advised and urged my departure, at any rate you approved the plan so long as I was in Rome at the beginning of January. The consequence of this would have been that I was absent when there was less prospect of danger, and that I would have returned into the firing line.* But even though such advice was hardly prudent, it was not *digne de reproches*, first because the plan was adopted as a result of my own decision, and secondly, even if I had acted on your advice, what service should an adviser offer but good faith?
3   What caused me the greatest surprise was the comment which you wrote: 'Very well, then, since you wish *mourir noblement*. Very well, leave your native land!' So I was abandoning my native land, or at that time I seemed to you to be abandoning it, yet not merely did you not seek to prevent me, but you even approved of it. Your further comment is more injurious still: 'What I should like is for you to polish up for me *un opuscule*, explaining why you had to do this.' Is this, then, what you want, my dear Atticus? Does my action need an apologia, in your eyes above all, though you gave it your ringing approval? Very well, *je publierai une justification*, but addressed to one of those who opposed and counselled against my departure. Yet what need is there now of *une explication*? If I had persevered in my departure, there would have been such a need. You counter: 'You did not

show consistency in this matter.' But no man of learning—and there are many writings of this type—has ever stated that a change of plan shows irresolution.

So then you state: 'If you belonged to our Phaedrus' school,* an 4 explanation would be at hand, but as things stand, what explanation can we give?' So was my action such that I cannot justify it to Cato?* No doubt it is utterly wicked and shameful. I only wish that this had been your view from the beginning, for then you would have played your usual role as a Cato.

Your final comment is the most infuriating: 'As for our Brutus, he 5 holds his tongue.' In other words, he does not presume to offer advice to me at my age. I cannot think of any other interpretation to put on your comment, and you are absolutely right. When I arrived at Velia* on 17 August, Brutus got wind of it, for he was with his ships three miles beyond Velia on the river Hales, and he at once walked over to meet me. Ye immortal gods, what great delight he showed at my return, or rather at my turning back! He poured out all the words that he had stifled, which made me recall that comment of yours: 'As for our Brutus, he holds his tongue.' My absence from the Senate on 1 August was what pained him most. He praised Piso* to the skies, and expressed his delight that I had avoided two severe criticisms. I was aware that by making the journey I had laid myself open to the first, namely my despair and my desertion of the republic, for those to whom I did not signal that I would speedily return were tearfully complaining to me in droves. The second criticism was one which Brutus and his numerous associates were pleased at my escaping: it had been thought that I was going to watch the Olympic Games,* a most despicable motive at any crisis in the state, but at this juncture *impardonable*. Indeed, I owed profound thanks to the south wind for having delivered me from such monstrous disgrace.

You now know the plausible reasons for my turning back, and 6 indeed they are worthy and compelling, but none of them is worthier than that contained in another letter of yours: 'If you owe anyone any money, make provision to ensure that I have enough to settle the account. Fear of armed conflict makes borrowing money remarkably difficult.' I read this letter in mid-course on the sea, so that I had no notion how to make provision, except by being present to protect my reputation. But enough of this; we can discuss the rest of it when we meet.

7   I have read Antony's edict, which was sent to me by Brutus and Cassius, and their admirable reply,* but frankly I do not see what point these edicts have, and what their purpose is. Nor am I, as Brutus proposes, now coming to Rome to play an active political role, for what can be done? I doubt if there is any support for Piso; I don't suppose he turned up again next day. But people say that at my time of life one must not roam far from the grave.

8   But what is this I hear from Brutus, for heaven's sake? He says that you have written that Pilia has suffered *une congestion cérébrale*. I am extremely exercised by the news, though he added that you wrote that the prospects are better. I certainly hope so. Do please pass on to her and to your sweetest Attica my fondest greetings. I am writing this aboard ship on my way to my residence at Pompeii, on 19 August.

Letter 144 (*Fam.* X 1)
Rome, September 44

CICERO TO PLANCUS

1   I have been absent embarking on a journey to Greece, and ever since the voice of the republic summoned me back from mid-course, I have never been left in peace* by Mark Antony. His arrogance—or better, since that vice is widespread, his monstrous behaviour—is such that he cannot tolerate a man's independence, not merely in speech, but even in the look on his face. So my chief preoccupation is not concern for my own life (for I have done justice to it in terms of length of years, and activities, and, if indeed it is relevant, fair fame), but anxiety for my native land, and in particular, dear Plancus, for the prospect of your consulship, which is so distant* that I must pray rather than hope that I continue to draw breath until that moment in the life of the state; for what hope can there be in a state entirely ground down by the arms of a most headstrong and unrestrained individual, a state in which neither the Senate nor the people wield any power, a state in which there are no laws, no courts, nor any appearance or trace whatever of a community of citizens?

2   But since I imagine that all the present proceedings are being sent to you, there is no need to write on individual matters. But my affection for you, which I embraced from the time of your boyhood

and have not merely maintained but also enhanced, is concerned to advise and encourage you to devote yourself to the republic with all your thought and attention. If it continues to exist till the time of your office, it will be easy for you to steer your course. But it needs both great attention and good fortune to ensure that it survives.

However, we shall have you here, I hope, some time before you 3 undertake the office, and apart from my obligation to consult the interests of the state, I am so supportive of your prestige that I devote all my advice, enthusiasm, service, activity, toil, and attention to your high standing. In this way I am aware that I will most readily do justice both to the republic, which is most dear to me, and to our friendship, which I believe we should most devotedly cultivate.

I am not surprised but delighted that you appreciate our friend 4 Furnius* as much as his civilized and worthy ways demand. I want you to believe that any judgement you make of him, and any service you bestow on him, I regard in the same light as if I believed you have bestowed this on myself.

Letter 145 *(Fam.* X 2)

Rome, September 44

CICERO TO PLANCUS

The distinction* voted to you could not have lacked support from me 1 appropriate to our friendship, had I been able to enter the Senate safely or honourably. But no one with independent political views can appear there without danger, for swords are wielded with total immunity. Nor does it apparently accord with my standing to express my sentiments on any political issue in the place where armed men are better and more closely positioned to listen than are the senators.

So though you will never lack my services or support in private 2 matters (nor indeed, if anything arises in public matters for which my participation proves necessary, will I ever fail to support your reputation, even if it spells danger to myself), on business which can be conducted equally well in my absence I beg you to allow me to take account of my personal safety and prestige.

Letter 146 (*Fam.* XII 2)

Rome, September 44

CICERO TO CASSIUS

1 I am absolutely delighted that you approve my motion and my speech.* Had I been able to exploit my oratory more often, the recovery of our freedom and of the republic would have afforded no difficulty. But that lunatic and depraved individual, who is much more wicked than the man you labelled 'the most wicked man ever killed',* is seeking the first opportunity for bloodshed. He accuses me of having been the sponsor of Caesar's murder, for no other reason than to rouse the veterans against me. I have no fear of this danger, so long as he allots to my credit a share in the glory of your deed. In consequence of his attitude, entry into the Senate is unsafe for Piso,* the first man to attack him but without receiving support, for myself, for I followed suit thirty days later,* and for Publius Servilius,* who emulated my example. That gladiator is seeking bloodshed and planned to make a start with me on 19 September.* He was ready for action against me, having spent several days in Metellus' house* practising his speech. But what sort of speech could be prepared in that den of vice and drunkenness? So, as I wrote to you earlier, he appears to all not to be declaiming, but to be vomiting as usual.*

2 So as regards your written comment that you are sure some progress can be made through my authority and eloquence, some progress *has* been made, considering the great evils that encompass us; for the Roman people realize that the three consulars who voiced their opinions freely because their political views are sound cannot enter the Senate in safety. One cannot expect more than this, for your kinsman,* who is pleased with his new family connection, has now no enthusiasm for the games, and is fit to burst at the unstinting applause which your brother* receives. That other family-connection* of yours has likewise been mollified by new diaries of Caesar. Such attitudes as this are easily borne, but what is intolerable is that a certain individual* believes his son will become consul in the year projected for Brutus and yourself, and for this reason he is making no secret of his humble allegiance to that brigand.*

3 As for my close friend Lucius Cotta,* he attends the Senate less often because, to use his own phrase, of 'a sort of desperation imposed

by fate'. Lucius Caesar,* best and most courageous of citizens, is dogged
by ill–health. Servius Sulpicius,* who wields immense authority and
holds the soundest views, is away from Rome. As for the others,
pardon me for not regarding them as consulars, with the exceptions
of the consuls-designate.* So such are the men who initiate state-
policy. They were few in number in better days, so you can guess
their number now that things are desperate.

So all our hopes rest on you two. If the reason for your absence
from Rome is your personal safety, no hope remains even in you. But
if you plan something worthy of your fame, I only wish that I may
survive to witness it. If I do not, the republic through your agency
will soon regain its rights.

Now and in the future I shall not fail to aid your family. Whether
they turn to me or not, my goodwill and loyalty to you will be in
evidence. Farewell.

Letter 147 (*Fam.* XII 3)

Rome, October 44

CICERO TO CASSIUS

Your friend's madness* increases day by day. To start with, on 1
the statue which he has set up on the rostra, he has inscribed the
words 'To the father who deserves so well of us'. So now you are
adjudged not merely assassins but also parricides! But why should
I say 'you', when it should rather be 'we'? For the madman states that
I am the ringleader in this most splendid deed of yours. If only I had
been! He would not now be a thorn in our flesh. But that is your concern, and since it is past history, I only wish I had some advice to
offer you. But I cannot devise a necessary course of action even for
myself, for what can be achieved against violence without the use of
violence?

The entire strategy of that faction is to avenge Caesar's death. 2
Thus on 2 October, Antony was introduced to the Assembly by
Cannutius.* True, he left the dais in utter humiliation, but he spoke
of the saviours of our fatherland in terms applicable to its traitors. He
claimed explicitly that all that you and your allies did, and what
Cannutius is now doing, was at my prompting. You can assess
what the rest of the business was like from the fact that they stripped

your legate* of his travelling-expenses. What do you make of their reasoning when they do that? They doubtless regard the money as being paid to an enemy of the state!

What a sad state of affairs! We could not tolerate a master, and now we are in thrall to a fellow-slave. Yet even now a gleam of hope shines out from your courage, though I am supportive rather than optimistic. But where are your troops? For the rest, I would rather that you commune with yourself than take note of words of mine. Farewell.

Letter 148 (*Fam.* XII 23)

Rome, October 44

CICERO TO CORNIFICIUS

1 Tratorius has acquainted me with the entire situation of your command* and of the condition of the province. How many insufferable events are occurring everywhere! But the higher your standing, the less you should tolerate the experiences which have befallen you, for you should not fail to exact punishment for the indignities which your magnanimity and high talent bear with moderation, even if they are not irksome. But we can revert to this later.

2 I am quite sure that reports of events at Rome are being sent to you. If I thought this was not the case, I myself would pen them. Especially notable is the plot of Caesar Octavian.* The common belief is that this charge has been fabricated by Antony to allow him to lay hands on the young man's money, but shrewd observers and likewise honourable men believe that the attempt was made, and they approve of it. In short, people are pinning great hopes on him. Their view is that there is nothing he will not do in pursuit of praise and fame. Our friend Antony for his part realizes that he is the object of such great hatred that, though he arrested the would-be assassins in his house, he does not dare to publicize the incident. So on 9 October he departed to Brundisium to meet the four Macedonian legions.* He intends to win them over with money, to bring them to the city, and to set them over our necks.

3 So this is the shape of the republic, if a republic can exist in a military camp. I often lament your situation, for your youth has

not allowed you to enjoy the flavour of any aspect of a healthy and secure state. Earlier it was at least possible to live in hope, but now even that has been snatched from us, for what hope is there when Antony has dared to declare to the Assembly that Cannutius* is seeking for himself a position among those who could claim no place in the community, as long as he, Antony, remains unharmed?

For my part, I cope with these and all other things that can befall a man, so long as I have the great blessing of philosophy,* which not merely withdraws me from anxiety, but also equips me against all the attacks of Fortune. I counsel you to take the same course, and to account as evil nothing which is not culpable, But with this doctrine you are better acquainted than I am.

Though I have always approved of our friend Tratorius, I particularly acknowledge his outstanding loyalty, care, and wisdom with regard to your affairs. Safeguard your health; it is my dearest wish that you do so.

Letter 149 (*Att.* XVI 8)

Puteoli, November 44

CICERO TO ATTICUS

Once I know the day of my arrival, I shall let you know. I have to 1 await my baggage which is coming from <. . .>, and there is sickness in my household. On the evening of 1 November a letter came to me from Octavian. He is embarking upon ambitious projects. He has won over to his allegiance the veterans at Casilinum and Calatia.* This is hardly surprising, since he is presenting them with 500 denarii each. He contemplates visits to the other colonies. Clearly he envisages waging war as commander against Antony. So I foresee that within a few days we shall be at war. But who is to be our commander? Observe his name and his age. Moreover he now requests me to hold a secret meeting with him first, at Capua, or somewhere in the vicinity. This is a childish request, if he thinks a meeting can be held in secret. I informed him by letter that such a meeting was unnecessary and impracticable.

He sent to me a certain Caecina from Volaterrae, a friend of his, 2 who reported that Antony was marching on Rome with the legion of the Larks,* imposing financial levies on the townships, and leading the legion under the standards. Octavian sought to consult me on whether he should make for Rome with 3,000 veterans, or hold Capua and keep out Antony as he approached, or go to join the three Macedonian legions* as they marched along the Adriatic coast. He hopes to win their allegiance. Caecina states that they rejected a bounty from Antony, abused him fiercely, and deserted him as he was addressing them. In short, Octavian claims he is our leader, and thinks we should not let him down. I myself urged him to proceed to Rome, for I think he will gain the support of both the city-mob and the honourable citizens too, if he gains their confidence. But Brutus, where are you?* What an *occasion magnifique* you are missing! Though I did not foresee this, I did believe that something of the kind would happen.

Now I seek your advice. Should I come to Rome, or remain here, or take refuge in Arpinum, which affords a *lieu sûr*? I prefer Rome, to avoid being missed if some development is thought to have occurred. So resolve this dilemma, for I was never in a greater *impasse*.

Letter 150 (*Att.* XVI 9)

Puteoli, November 44

CICERO TO ATTICUS

1 Two letters from Octavian have reached me on the same day. He now asks me to make for Rome at once. He states that he wishes to conduct business through the Senate. To this I have replied that the Senate cannot meet* before 1 January, which I believe in fact is true. He adds: 'with your advice'. In a word, he is pressurizing me, *et je dissimule*. I do not trust his youth, nor do I know his intentions. I do not wish to do anything without your friend Pansa.* I'm afraid that Antony is growing strong. I have no desire to quit the sea-coast, but I fear that if I am not in Rome, someone else will show his *valeur*. Varro* disapproves of the boy's strategy, but I approve. His forces are strong and he can take Brutus aboard. He is openly at work allocating recruits to centuries at Capua, and paying out bounties. I envisage war breaking out at any moment. Do send me your observations on this; to my surprise, my courier left Rome on the 1st without a letter from you.

Letter 151 (*Att.* XVI 15)

Arpinum, November 44

CICERO TO ATTICUS

Do not imagine that indolence prevents me from writing in my own   1
hand—but indeed it is indolence, for I have no other excuse to offer.
But then I seem to recognize Alexis' hand in your letters!

But to matters in hand. If Dolabella* had not treated me so very
scurvily, I should perhaps have hesitated whether to take a gentler
line or to assert my rights to the utmost. But I am now quite pleased
that the chance has come my way to make both him and everyone
else aware that I am estranged from him, and that I shall make public
both this fact and that my loathing is also on political grounds. For
after initially defending the republic at my instigation, he has not
only been bribed to abandon the republic, but he has also sought to
overthrow it in so far as this lay in his power.

As for your query about how I should like the business to be con-   2
ducted when the day of reckoning comes, I should first of all prefer
it that it does not make my presence in Rome unwelcome. I shall
follow your advice in this as in all other matters. But so far as the
amount is concerned, I want the proceedings to be thoroughly
demanding and stringent. Though calling on the guarantors may
seem somewhat *honteux*, I should like you to note the fact that without calling on them we can bring to court the agents, who will not
contest the case. If they do, I realize that the guarantors are freed
from liability. But I think it would be shameful for him if his agents
do not discharge his legally acquired debt, and it would better befit
my dignity to vindicate my rights without bringing the utmost shame
on him. Do please write back to express your view on this. I have no
doubt that you will handle this entire matter quite gently.

Now back to politics. On issues of *la politique*, your advice has   3
indeed often been wise on many matters, but never more so than in
this letter. For though the boy* is doing well in keeping the pressure
on Antony at the present time, we must await the outcome. But what
a speech to the Assembly that was! A copy of it was sent to me. He
swore that he might 'be allowed to attain the distinctions gained by
his father', and at the same time he extended his right hand towards
the statue. So I pray that my safety may not depend on a man such

as this. But as you say in your letter, I realize that the decisive point will be the tribunate of our friend Casca.* As I said to Oppius on this very matter, when he urged me to embrace the young man, his entire cause, and his band of veterans, I could certainly not do this unless I was convinced that not only would he not be a foe to the tyrannicides, but would indeed be their friend. When Oppius said that this would come to pass, I asked: 'So what is the hurry? He has no need of my support before 1 January, whereas we shall get an insight into his intentions before 13 December in the case of Casca.' He emphatically agreed with me, so we leave it at that.

A final point. You will have couriers every day, and I imagine that you will have something to write about each day. I am sending you a copy of a letter from Lepta, from which it appears that our famous Stratyllax* has sustained a reverse. But you will assess the report when you read it.

4   After I had sealed this letter, I received communications from you and from Sextus.* Nothing could have been more agreeable or amiable than that from Sextus. Yours was brief, but your earlier one was rich in detail. Your advice that for preference I should stay in these parts until we hear the outcome of the present disturbances is both prudent and kind.

5   However, dear Atticus, it is not affairs of state which preoccupy me at present—not that there is, or ought to be, anything closer to my heart. But even Hippocrates forbids healing treatment for hopeless cases. So goodbye to politics! My private finances are what concern me. Do I say 'finances'? It is rather my reputation which is at stake, for though I have a healthy balance of debts due to me, there is not enough ready cash even to pay to Terentia. Do I say to Terentia? You know that I decided some time back to release 25,000 sesterces on behalf of Montanus.* My son Cicero had very decently begged me to pay this on his credit. I promised to comply on the most generous terms (you too were agreeable to this), and I instructed Eros to lay this sum aside. Not only did he fail to do this, but Aurelius was compelled to raise a loan at a most unfavourable rate of interest. So far as Terentia's claim is concerned, Tiro has written that you say that the money will come from Dolabella. I believe that his understanding was at fault—if anyone can have faulty understanding—or rather that he did not understand at all. For you mentioned Cocceius' response* in your letter to me, and Eros says the same thing in virtually identical words.

So I must come to Rome even if it means braving the flames, for 6
private insolvency is more dishonourable than public disgrace. In my
distress of mind I am accordingly unable to reply as usual to the
other questions which you raise so very agreeably. Show your fellow-
feeling in this embarrassment of mine to help me clear myself of
debt. Ideas present themselves about the means to achieve this but
I cannot reach a clear-cut decision until I see you. Why should I not
be able to live as safely in Rome as Marcellus? But this is not the
immediate problem, nor is it my chief concern. You realize what my
problem is. I shall be with you soon.

Letter 152 (*Fam.* XI 5)
Rome, December 44

CICERO TO DECIMUS BRUTUS

When our friend Lupus had arrived after leaving you, and was 1
spending a few days in Rome, I was in the region in which I thought
I was safest. In consequence Lupus returned to you without a letter
from me, though he had ensured that yours was to be delivered to
me. I came to Rome on 9 December, and regarded it of primary
importance to meet Pansa at once.* From him I ascertained the
details about you which I was especially keen to learn.

The information makes it clear that you need no more exhortation
now than you did from anyone in that exploit which was the greatest
in the recollection of mankind. Yet it seems necessary briefly to indi- 2
cate to you that the Roman people centres all its expectations on you,
and places on you its entire hopes of recovering its future freedom.
If day and night you recall, as I am sure you do, the great exploit
which you performed, you will certainly not be unmindful of the
magnitude of the tasks which even now you must accomplish. For if
a province is obtained* by the person with whom I was always
friendly before I became aware that he was waging war on the republic not merely openly, but also with relish, I can see no hope of salvation remaining.

For this reason I beseech you (my pleas are identical with those of 3
the Senate and Roman people) to deliver the republic from regal despotism for ever, so that the outcome may be in harmony with the
beginning. This is your task, your role; this is what the community,

or rather the entire world, not merely anticipates but also demands of you. Yet as my letter stated earlier, you need no exhortation, so I shall not spell it out in too many words. I shall carry out my role, which is to promise you all my services, support, attentions, and thoughts for every project which redounds to your praise and glory. So do please be persuaded both for the sake of the republic, which is dearer to me than my own life, and because I am well disposed to you and desire the enhancement of your prestige, that I will at no stage fail to further your most impressive plans, your distinction, and your glory.

Letter 153 *(Fam.* X 5)
Rome, January 43

CICERO TO PLANCUS

1   I have received from you two copies of the same letter, itself a proof to me of your conscientiousness, for I realize you are ensuring that your most eagerly anticipated letter is delivered to me. I derived twin benefits from it, making it difficult for me to decide by comparison whether I thought I should esteem more highly your affection for me or your devotion to the state. Love for one's native land in my judgement ranks highest, but affection and the bond of goodwill between us is surely sweeter. So your mention of your father's close association with me, and of that friendliness which you say you extended to me from boyhood, together with the other sentiments relevant to that declaration, brought me pleasure beyond belief.

2   In its turn, the declaration of your loyalty to the state,* which you say you show and will continue to show, is a source of the greatest gratification to me, and this joy is all the greater for being additional to that earlier happiness. For this reason, dear Plancus, not merely do I urge you, but I unreservedly beg you, as I did in the letter which elicited your most civilized reply, to devote yourself to the republic with your whole intellect and the entire thrust of your mind. There is nothing which can bring you greater reward and glory, and of all things human there is none more splendid or more outstanding than to deserve well of the state.

3   Up to now (your supreme generosity and sagacity allow me to express my feelings openly) you appear to have achieved the greatest

success with the support of Fortune. Though this could not have
been achieved without personal merit, the advantages which have
been gained are to be assigned for the most part to Fortune and to
circumstances, whereas any aid which you lend to the state in these
supremely difficult times will be credited entirely to you alone. The
loathing felt for Antony by all citizens except lawless men is beyond
belief. Great hope and great expectation rest on you and your army.*
Be careful, by the gods I beg you, not to lose the opportunity of gaining popularity and fame. I extend to you this advice as to a son.
I offer my support to you as to my second self, and I entreat you both
on behalf of our land and as an intimate friend.

Letter 154 (*Fam.* XII 4)
Rome, February 43

CICERO TO CASSIUS

I only wish that you had invited me to the dinner on the Ides of   1
March; there would have been nothing left over!* But as things
stand, what you and your associates left unfinished is a source of anxiety, and to me indeed more than to the rest. Our present consuls*
are outstanding men, but the former consuls are utterly worthless.
We have a stalwart Senate, but the greatest stalwarts are those who
are least distinguished. Nothing is braver or better than the Roman
people and all Italy, but by contrast nothing is more disgusting and
more criminal than Philippus and Piso,* for when they were sent as
ambassadors to Antony with a message issued by the Senate in no
uncertain terms, and he yielded to none of its instructions, they
brought back to us of their own accord intolerable demands* from
him. As a result people are flocking to me, and I have now become a
'people-pleaser' on this issue of the safety of the state.

But I have no knowledge of your activities now or in the future, or   2
even of your location. Rumour has it that you are in Syria,* but no
one vouches for this. As Brutus is closer to us,* reports about him
appear to be better founded. There is severe criticism of Dolabella*
by men of some wit because he is seeking to replace you so quickly
when you have been in Syria for barely thirty days, and accordingly
there is general agreement that he ought not to be allowed entry into
Syria. Both you and Brutus have won high praise because both of

you are believed to have recruited an army contrary to expectation. I would write in more detail if I knew the facts and their motivation, but as things stand, my comments are based on popular opinion and rumour. I look forward eagerly to hearing from you. Farewell.

Letter 155 (*Fam.* X 28)

Rome, February 43

CICERO TO TREBONIUS

1 How I wish that you had invited me to that most attractive feast on the Ides of March! We would have had no left-overs.* But as things stand, the left-overs have caused such complications! That sacred service you rendered to the state is arousing some complaints. Indeed, since you, excellent man that you are, took that plague-ridden man aside* and through your kindness he is still alive, this induces me from time to time to feel irritated with you (an attitude verging on impiety), for you have bequeathed to me more troubles than to all others.

As soon as a meeting of the Senate* could be held in freedom following Antony's most disgraceful departure, I restored that attitude of old which you, in company with your father, that most incisive
2 citizen, always proclaimed and loved. For when the plebeian tribunes summoned the Senate on 20 December and were raising another issue, I took up the topic of the entire political situation, and discussed it in most incisive terms. Thus by force of conviction rather than by rhetorical skill I rallied the Senate, which was by now dispirited and weary, back to its traditional moral stance and practice. That day, and that conviction expressed in my speech, brought hope for the first time to the Roman people of the recovery of their freedom, and indeed thereafter I have neglected no opportunity not merely to dwell upon, but also to pursue actively, the good of the state.
3   If I did not believe that the affairs of the city and all the proceedings were being reported to you, I would detail them, in spite of my being hindered by business of the greatest importance. But others will acquaint you with these matters, so I summarize just a few of them. We have a Senate of courage, but of the consulars, some are chicken-hearted, and others are ill-intentioned. With the death of

Servius* we have sustained a great loss. Lucius Caesar* has admirable views, but because he is Antony's uncle, he does not express them very incisively. Our consuls are outstanding. Decimus Brutus is brilliant, and the young Caesar is also first class. Indeed, I repose great hopes for the future in him. You can take it as certain that if he had not quickly recruited veteran troops, and if two legions of Antony's* had not transferred to his authority, so that Antony was confronted with this threat, there is no crime and no cruelty which Antony would have failed to perpetrate.

I was keen that these facts should be better known by you, though I believe that you have heard of them. If I have more leisure, I will write at greater length.

Letter 156 *(Fam.* XII 5)

Rome, February 43

CICERO TO CASSIUS

I believe that up to now winter has prevented us from obtaining 1
information about your activities and above all about your location,* though everyone says (their wish, I fancy, being father to their thought) that you are in Syria, commanding troops there. This is more readily credited because it seems probable. As for our Brutus, he has won outstanding praise, for he has achieved such important and such unexpected results that they are both welcome in themselves and more highly esteemed because they have been performed so speedily. If for your part you control the area which we think you do, the republic is buttressed by considerable resources, for we shall be defended by the supreme commands and forces of the most reliable citizens* from the nearest shore of Greece as far as Egypt.

Yet if I am not mistaken, the situation is such that the whole 2
decisive stage of the entire war seems to hinge on Decimus Brutus.* If, as we hope, he succeeds in breaking out from Mutina, it seems that the war will be completely over. He is at present blockaded by quite small forces, because Antony is deploying a large garrison to hold Bononia. On our side Hirtius is at Claterna and Caesar at Forum Cornelium;* both have strong armies. Pansa has assembled huge forces at Rome by a levy throughout Italy. Up to now, winter has prevented any fighting. It seems that Hirtius intends to operate

only circumspectly, as he informs me in several letters. With the exception of Bononia, Regium Lepidum, and Parma, we control the whole of Cisalpine Gaul, which supports the republic most enthusiastically. Moreover, your dependants beyond the Po* are remarkably attached to our cause. The Senate is most resolute, if we exclude former consuls, of whom Lucius Caesar alone is committed and upright.

3   We have lost a doughty defender with the death of Servius Sulpicius.* Of the rest, some are sluggish, and others are dishonest. A number of them are envious of the praise of those whom they see gaining popular approval. But there is remarkable unanimity among the Roman people and the whole of Italy.

These are pretty well all the facts I wished to pass on to you. My prayer now is that the light of your courage may shine forth from the eastern regions where you are active. Farewell.

Letter 157   (*Fam.* XII 25)

Rome, March 43

CICERO TO CORNIFICIUS

1 I received your letter on the feast of Liberalia. Young Cornificius handed it to me. By his computation it was twenty-two days after you wrote it. The Senate did not meet on that day nor on the next. On the feast of Quinquatrus* I pleaded your case at a crowded meeting of the Senate. Minerva showed no reluctance because on that very day the Senate decreed that my statue of Minerva,* guardian of the city, which had been brought crashing down by a storm, should be restored.

Pansa read out your letter. It was greeted with loud approval by the Senate, which afforded me the greatest pleasure and affronted the Minotaur* (I refer to Calvisius and Taurus). You were the subject of a congratulatory decree of the Senate, and this was followed by a demand that those two men be censured, but Pansa showed them greater clemency.

2   On 20 December*—the day on which I first entertained hope of freedom, and whilst all others held back I laid the foundations of the republic—on that very day, dear Cornificius, I made careful provision for and justified your high standing, for the Senate supported my proposal on the tenure of the provinces. In fact, since then I have

never ceased to undermine the position of the man who sought to govern your province in his absence,* thereby inflicting injustice on you and disgrace on the state. In consequence, he ceased to sustain my frequent—indeed, daily—rebukes, and accordingly he retired unwillingly to Rome. Through my censure of him, which was thoroughly merited and proper, he was dislodged not merely from his expectation but also from the appointment, his possession of which had seemed cut and dried. I am absolutely delighted that you have retained your worthy office through your signal merit, and that you have been honoured with the most exalted distinctions of your province.

I accept the excuse with which you seek to clear yourself in my eyes in the matter of Sempronius,* for that was a period of slavery which blinded us. I had inaugurated your plans and promoted your status, but I lost patience with the times, and abandoning hope of liberty I made headlong for Greece,* when the Etesian winds like good citizens refused to follow me as I abandoned the republic, and the south wind blew with the greatest force in my face, and bore me back to your fellow-tribesmen at Rhegium. From there I made all haste with both full sail and oars to reach my native land, and next day* I took my stand there as the lone free man, while all around me were totally enslaved.

I launched such an attack on Antony that he could not brook it, and on me alone he poured out all his drunken rage. At one time he sought to lure me into the open to find an excuse to kill me, and at another he tried to ambush me. As he belched and vomited, I drove him into the nets of Caesar Octavian, for that outstanding youth has raised a protective force for himself and for me, and then for the entire state. If he had not been at hand, the return of Antony from Brundisium would have plagued our land. I imagine that you are well aware of what ensued.*

But to return to the matter from which I diverged, I accept your explanation concerning Sempronius, for you were unable to take any principled step at a time of such great upheaval. But now, in the words of Terence,

> The day now brings fresh life, demands fresh ways.*

This is why, dear Quintus, you must embark with me, and indeed take your position at the helm. All good citizens are now aboard a single ship. I strive to keep it on course, and I pray that our journey may be prosperous. But whatever the winds that blow my skill as steersman will not be wanting, for what other way can virtue proffer? So show a lofty and elevated spirit, and consider that your entire standing must be linked with the good of the state.

Letter 158 (*Fam.* X 27)

Rome, March 43

CICERO TO LEPIDUS

1 Since my exceeding goodwill towards you leads to my great concern that your prestige should be as distinguished as possible, I was unhappy that you did not thank the Senate when that body had bestowed the highest honours* upon you. I am glad that you are eager to promote peace between citizens. If you will distinguish such peace from subjection, you will consult the interests of both the state and your own status. However, if your 'peace' is to restore to an abandoned individual his tenure of a wholly unbridled tyranny, you must realize that all men of sense take the view that death is preferable to slavery.

2 So it is my judgement at least that you will be wiser not to get involved in peace-making which meets with the approval neither of the Senate nor of the people, nor of any right-thinking person. But you will hear these sentiments from others, or letters will inform you of them, and in accord with your practical wisdom you will decide on your best course.

Letter 159 (*Fam.* X 12)

Rome, April 43

CICERO TO PLANCUS

1 Admittedly the interests of the community should cause me to rejoice that you have conferred on it such great protection and assistance when it was virtually on its last legs. Yet I pray that once the republic is restored I may embrace you as victor, for my happiness stems in large part from your distinction, which I visualize as most outstanding, both now and in the future. Please do not imagine that

any letter ever read out in the Senate was more welcome than yours, the outcome both of the surpassing greatness of your meritorious service to the state, and of the high seriousness of your words and sentiments. It was by no means a novel experience for me, in view of my acquaintance with you and my recollection of the undertakings made in your letters to me; moreover, I have ascertained in detail your plans from our friend Furnius.* But the Senate regarded them as more important than had been expected, not because they ever doubted your goodwill, but because they had sufficiently investigated neither the extent of your ability nor the limits to which you were willing to go.

So when Marcus Varisidius on the early morning of 7 April deliv- 2 ered to me your letter and I read it, my spirits rose with joy beyond belief, and when a large crowd of our most right-thinking men together with other citizens escorted me from my house, I at once shared my pleasure with all of them. Meanwhile our friend Munatius* visited me as usual, and I passed your letter on to him. He knew nothing of the content, for Varisidius had come to me first, saying that this was your instruction to him. A little later the same Munatius passed to me to read the letter which you had sent him, together with your official dispatch.

We decided to pass the letter immediately to Cornutus,* the urban 3 praetor, who in the absence of the consuls according to tradition exercises their role. The Senate was at once convened, and assembled in great numbers because of the rumour and anticipation aroused by your letter. After it was read out, Cornutus was confronted by a religious impediment. The guardians of the sacred chickens warned him that he had not heeded the auspices with sufficient care, and our college of augurs authenticated this warning. For this reason the business was postponed until the following day. On that day I engaged in a fierce dispute with Servilius* in defence of your prestige. Servilius used his influence to ensure that his proposal was advanced first. The Senate left him high and dry, and voted en masse against him. Then my proposal, the second to be put forward, was supported by the Senate in large numbers, but it was vetoed by Publius Titius at the request of Servilius, and the discussion was postponed till next day.

Servilius arrived, ready to confront Jupiter himself, in whose 4 temple the issue was under discussion. I would rather that you learn from other people's letters how I manhandled him, and disposed of

Titius and his veto. From my letter you can learn just one thing: the Senate could not have been more serious, resolute, and well disposed to your praises than it was then—and indeed the Senate is no more well disposed to you than is the entire citizen-body, for the whole Roman people, with the general accord of all classes and orders, has united in a remarkable way to set the republic free.

5   So continue on your present course, entrust your name to immortality. Despise all present-day features bearing the appearance of the glory which has been gathered in by worthless marks of distinction. Think of them as short-lived, counterfeit, and transient. True distinction lies in virtue, and this is manifest above all in meritorious service to the state. You possess that ability in the fullest sense, and since you have grasped it, you must hold it fast. Ensure that the republic is indebted to you as much as you are to the republic. You will find that I not merely uphold your distinction, but even augment it. I regard this as my debt both to the republic, which is dearer to me than my own life, and to the affinity between us. Moreover, in these concerns which I have shown for your high status, I have gained great pleasure from having seen the practical wisdom and loyalty of Titus Munatius. It was already known to me, but now it is even more manifest in his astonishing goodwill and attentions towards you.

Written on 11 April

Letter 160 (*Brut.* I 3)
Rome, April 43

CICERO TO BRUTUS

1 Our situation seems to have taken a turn for the better.* I am sure that you have been informed by letters of the developments. The consuls have shown themselves in their true colours as I have often described them to you. Young Caesar's native merit is remarkable. At present he is awash with distinctions and popularity. I only wish that I can guide and restrain him as easily as I have done so far. It will certainly be difficult, but I am not pessimistic, for the young man has been persuaded, especially by me, that our salvation is his doing. At any rate, if he had not diverted Antony from Rome, all would have been lost.

Three or four days before this most happy development,* the 2 whole community was afflicted by a species of panic, and was preparing to pour out with wives and children to join you. But now on 20 April they have recovered their poise, and prefer to have you come to Rome* rather than set out to join you. On that day indeed I gained the greatest reward for my heavy labours and many sleepless nights, if in fact substantial and authentic glory begets some reward, for as huge a crowd as our city contains gathered at my house, escorted me to the Capitol, and with tumultuous shouting and applause set me on the rostra. There is no vanity in me, nor should there be, but none the less the general agreement of all classes, the formal thanksgiving, and the felicitations move me, for it is a notable thing to win popular favour by ensuring the safety of the people.

But I would rather have you hear this from others. I should be 3 grateful to be more closely informed about your activities and plans. Please take thought that your generous nature does not make you appear too easygoing. The Senate and the Roman people take the view that no enemies have ever merited all forms of punishment as much as these citizens who have taken up arms in this war against the fatherland. In every formal motion I exact revenge and harry them with the approval of all honourable men. It is for you to assess your attitude in this regard. For myself, the situation of the three brothers* is one and the same.

Letter 161 (*Brut.* II 5)
Rome, April 43

CICERO TO BRUTUS

I believe that your friends have reported to you that the letter from 1 you was read out in the Senate on 13 April, at the same time as that from Gaius Antonius. I regard myself as one of those friends as much as anyone, but there is no need for all of us to report the same details. What I must communicate to you are my feelings about the whole situation of this war, my judgement of it, and my proposals concerning it.

My sentiments towards the supreme affairs of state, Brutus, have always been identical with yours, though perhaps my policy on some issues, but not of course on all, is somewhat more drastic. You are aware that it has always been my view that the state should be delivered not only from a king but also from kingship, whereas you take a milder attitude, which is wholly to your eternal credit. But what to our great sorrow we realized would have been the better course, we now realize to our great danger. In those recent days you sought to adopt every means to achieve the peace which could not be gained by discussion, whereas I used every means to attain liberty, which has no existence without peace. I imagined that peace itself could be gained by war and arms. There was no lack of enthusiasm on the part of those demanding arms, but we restrained their aggression and quenched their zeal.

2   Thus things had reached the point at which, if some god had not prompted the thoughts of Caesar Octavian, we would of necessity have fallen into the clutches of Mark Antony, that most wicked and degenerate man. If he had not then been preserved from death, we would certainly at this very time not have to engage in conflict, the like and extent of which you observe. But I leave that unsaid, for the memorable, almost divine deed which you performed repels all words of blame,* for no terms of praise are sufficiently adequate to address it. Of late you have emerged with uncompromising gaze, and within a short time and by your own efforts you have assembled an army, auxiliary forces, and legions fit for the task. Ye immortal gods, to think of the letter and dispatch which you sent,* the delight of the Senate, the eager reaction of the citizen body! Never have I witnessed any action lauded with such universal unanimity. There was eager expectation about the fate of the remnants of Antonius' army, for you had stripped him to a great extent of his cavalry and legions. That expectation had a further desirable outcome, for your dispatch* recited in the Senate emphasized the valour of both commander and soldiers, together with the busy activity of your staff officers, among them my son Cicero.* If your friends had decided to demand an official response to the dispatch, and if it had not arrived at a most troubled moment following the consul Pansa's departure,* an appropriate and deserved honour would have been decreed to the immortal gods.

3   Suddenly, in the early morning of 13 April, Pilius Celer* came rushing in. Ye blessed gods! What a man of high seriousness and integrity he is, a true representative of the honourable party in the state! He brought two letters with him, one from you and the other

from Antonius. He handed them to Servilius, the plebeian tribune, who passed them to Cornutus.* They were read out to the Senate. The signature 'Antonius Proconsul'* caused as great astonishment as if 'Dolabella Imperator'* had been read out. In fact, couriers had arrived from Dolabella, but none with the bearing of a Pilius with confidence to proffer a letter or to deliver it to the magistrates. The letters were then read out. Yours was short, and not at all hard on Antonius. The Senate was extremely surprised. I was uncertain of my course of action. Was I to denounce it as a forgery? But what if you had approved it? Or was I to authenticate it? That would not have served your prestige.

So on that day I held my tongue. Next day, after much discussion, 4 and after Pilius had looked men challengingly in the eye, I was the very first to initiate the debate. I spoke at length on 'Proconsul Antonius'. Sestius followed me,* and did not let the matter drop. He stated that his son, and mine too, would be in considerable danger if they had taken up arms against a proconsul. You know what Sestius is like; he did not let the side down. Others spoke as well. Our friend Labeo* stated that your seal was not on the letter, and that it carried no date. He added that you had not written to your supporters as you usually did. By this he sought to demonstrate that the letter was forged, and if you wish to know, he proved it.

Now, Brutus, you must devise a strategy for the entire character 5 of the war. I see that you find moderation attractive, and that you regard this as most efficacious. This attitude is impressive, but the role of clemency is, and should be, apt for different circumstances and different times. But, Brutus, what is the situation now? The temples of the immortal gods are threatened by the expectations of indigent and wicked men. In this war what is being decided is nothing other than whether we continue to exist or not. So whom do we spare,* or what is our course of action? Are we consulting the interests of men who if they prevail will leave no trace of us? What difference is there between Dolabella and any of the three Antonii? If we spare any of the three, we have been rough on Dolabella. It was chiefly owing to my strategy and authority that the Senate and people of Rome were persuaded of this, even though the situation itself demanded it. If you do not approve of this policy, I shall defend your view, but without abandoning my own. People do not anticipate from you either lax or cruel behaviour. A temperate approach is easy to adopt, to be tough wth leaders, but generous towards the soldiers.

Dear Brutus, please keep my son Cicero with you as much as possible. He will get no better schooling in virtue than by observing and imitating you.

16 April

Letter 162 (*Brut.* I 3A)
Rome, April 43
CICERO TO BRUTUS

1 We have lost our two consuls,* good men, or at any rate good consuls. Hirtius fell at the very moment of victory; a few days earlier he had been victorious in a great battle. As for Pansa, he had sustained wounds which he could not bear and had quitted the field. Decimus Brutus and Caesar are chasing the remnants of the enemy. All who joined Mark Antony's bloc have been declared public enemies, and consequently many people interpret the senatorial decree as applying to those under your guard as well, whether prisoners or hostages. But when I myself cited by name Gaius Antonius,* I was not proposing drastic punishment, for I had decided that the Senate should hear from you the investigation of his case.

Written on 27 April

Letter 163 (*Fam.* XII 8)
Rome, June 43
CICERO TO CASSIUS

1 I imagine that you have heard of the heinous activity of your kinsman Lepidus,* his utter fickleness and lack of principle, from the city gazette, which I am sure is sent to you. The outcome is that the war which we believed had been wrapped up has been renewed, and we are waging it with all our hopes pinned on Decimus Brutus and Plancus,* or if you want the truth, on yourself and Marcus Brutus, not merely as a refuge for the moment, should anything untoward and undesirable occur, but also to underpin our freedom for ever.

Here in Rome we are hearing the reports of Dolabella* which we 2
hoped for but we have no reliable sources for them. As for yourself,
be assured that you are regarded as a great man on both contemporary assessment and on anticipation for the future. With this
incentive before you, you must strive to achieve the highest aims.
There is no goal so lofty that the Roman people does not judge you
able to reach and maintain it. Farewell.

Letter 164 (*Brut.* I 10)

Rome, June 43

CICERO TO BRUTUS

As yet we have had no communication from you, not even a rumour 1
to report that you have been made aware of the Senate's authoriza-
tion, and that you are bringing your army over to Italy. The political
situation urgently needs you to do this with all haste, for every day
the internal canker intensifies, and we are suffering as much from
enemies within as from those outside. It is true that they have been
with us from the very beginning of the war, but earlier they were
more easily repressed. The Senate was more assured, being roused
not only by my proposals, but also by my exhortations. Pansa in the
Senate was a quite outspoken and incisive figure, inveighing against
the rest of that ilk but especially against his father-in-law.* As consul
he has shown spirit from the outset, and his loyalty was not wanting
in the end.

In the fighting waged at Mutina, Caesar was not at all blame- 2
worthy, but Hirtius merited some censure.* In this way Fortune has
been

Unstable in success, but friendly in adversity.*

The republic was victorious; Antony's forces were slaughtered, and
he himself was driven out. Then Decimus Brutus was guilty* of so
many errors that somehow the victory slipped from our grasp. Our
leaders did not hound the terrified, unarmed, wounded enemy, and
Lepidus was granted a respite to allow us to experience in times of
greater ills the fickleness* which we had often noted. The armies led
by Brutus and Plancus are loyal but untrained; and their Gallic
auxiliaries are utterly reliable and massive in numbers.

3   But Caesar, who up to now has been guided by my strategy and is himself outstanding in character and shows remarkable resolution, has been inveigled into the most confident expectation of the consulship by the most wicked and deceitful letters from certain individuals.* As soon as I became aware of this, I never ceased to advise him by letter in his absence, nor did I hesitate to accuse face to face those friends of his who seemed to be furthering his ambition, nor to expose in the Senate the provenance of this most reprehensible advice. I do not in fact recall the Senate or the magistrates ever before taking a more responsible stance on any issue, for never before has it happened with regard to the extraordinary appointment of a powerful individual (or rather, of a most powerful individual, since power now lies in force of arms) that no plebeian tribune or other magistrate or private individual has emerged to sponsor such a proposal. Yet in maintaining this resolute and courageous attitude, our community remains nervous. The reason, Brutus, is that we are made a laughing stock by the self-indulgence of the troops* and the arrogance of their generals. Each of them demands power in the state commensurate with the force he wields. Reason, moderation, law, custom, obligation—all are of no account, and likewise the judgement and repute of citizens, and respect for posterity.

4   I foresaw this situation long ago, and I was fleeing from Italy when the report of your edicts called me back. Indeed, Brutus, at Velia you were the moving spirit in this. Though it depressed me to head back to the city which you were fleeing after having liberated it, a fate which had likewise once befallen me* when confronted by a similar hazard and a grimmer fortune, I none the less continued the journey, returned to Rome, and though without protection shook up Antony. Against his impious arms I strengthened the defences provided by Caesar's strategy and authority. If he stands firm in loyalty and follows my lead, we shall seemingly have sufficient protection. But if the counsels of evil men prove stronger than mine, or if the frailty of his youth cannot sustain the weight of affairs, all our hope lies in you. So I beg you to take wing, and with your army to free the republic which you liberated by your courage and magnanimity more than through the course of events. The entire body of citizens will rally as one to you.

5   Encourage Cassius by letter to do the same. Our hope of freedom resides in the headquarters of your two camps, and nowhere else.

Both our leaders and our armies in the West are undoubtedly robust. I myself am still confident that the protection afforded by the young Caesar is reliable, but many are seeking to undermine him in such a way that from time to time I fear that he may shift his allegiance.

You now have the entire situation of the republic as it stands, as I write this letter. I pray that things may later improve. But if they turn out differently (may the gods avert such a prediction!), I shall lament the lot of the republic which ought to continue for ever. As for myself, how little time remains!

Letter 165 (*Brut.* I 15)
Rome, July 43

CICERO TO BRUTUS

As Messalla* is with you, what letter can I write with such care as to 1 be able to explain the developments and the political situation more precisely than he will expound them to you? He has outstanding awareness of the entire position, and he can explain and report it to you with consummate elegance. Though it is unnecessary to inform you, Brutus, of what you already know, I cannot pass over in silence such outstanding excellence in all qualities deserving of praise. Hence you are not to imagine that any comparison can be made with Messalla in moral worth, resolve, attentiveness, and patriotism. In consequence the eloquence in which he excels to an extraordinary degree seems scarcely to need any claim for commendation. Yet in that eloquence a greater degree of wisdom is perceptible, for he has schooled himself with sober judgement and abundant skill in the most disciplined category of oratory. He is so hard-working, and commits himself so sleeplessly to study, that the natural talent he possesses to the full does not appear to be regarded as claiming the greatest commendation.

But my affection takes me too far, for it is not the purpose of this 2 letter to praise Messalla, and in particular to you, for you are as aware of his merits as I am, and the qualities which I am praising are better known to you than to me. Though I was upset at bidding him goodbye, my one consolation is that he is setting out to my alter ego in performance of his duty, and in pursuit of the highest praise. But enough of this.

3   I come now after quite a time to a letter in which you paid me
many tributes, but censured one fault, namely that I am too prone
and over-generous in the conferment of honours. While you criticize
this tendency, another person may perhaps condemn me for being
too harsh in votes of censure and punishment. But perhaps you disapprove of both. If that is the case, I am anxious that you should be
wholly aware of my criteria in both. I do not merely adopt the saying
of Solon, who was one of the Seven Sages,* and the only one of the
seven to inscribe laws. His dictum* was that a state is held together
by two things, rewards and punishments. There is of course a due
limit in both as in other things, and a golden mean in each of them.

4   But it is not my intention to hold forth here on this important
subject. Yet I do not regard it as irrelevant to explain the strategy
which I have followed in proposals advanced with regard to this
war. You have not forgotten, Brutus, my remarks following the
death of Caesar and your memorable Ides of March. I spoke of the
action which you and your comrades failed to take,* and of the great
storm which loomed over the republic. You had dispelled a great
plague, and expunged a great stain from the Roman people. You had
earned undying fame for yourselves, but the apparatus of kingship
had been passed down to Lepidus and Antony, the first of whom
was more fickle, and the second more vile. Both feared peace, and
were foes of tranquillity. We had no protective force with which
to confront these men, who were inflamed with the desire to desta-
bilize the state. The citizen-body had roused itself, and was unani-

5   mous in seeking to preserve its freedom. But at that time we were too
impulsive, and the pair of you perhaps showed greater wisdom
in quitting the city which you had liberated, and in releasing Italy
from involvement when she demonstrated to you her enthusiastic
support. So when I saw that the city was in the hands of its
murderers, that neither Cassius nor yourself could remain safely in
it, and that it was subject by force of arms to Antony, I thought that
I too should depart,* for a city downtrodden by wicked men in which
the ability to lend aid is curtailed is a dismal sight. However, my
heart was always steeped in affection for my native land, and
could not bear to desert her in her perils. So when I was in mid-
course for Greece, during the season of the Etesians, and the south
wind, as if dissuading me from my intention, bore me back to Italy,
I set eyes on you at Velia and was profoundly unhappy, for you were

retiring (I say 'retiring' because our friends the Stoics state that the wise man does not flee).

On reaching Rome, I at once confronted Antony's criminal 6 lunacy. Once I had roused him against me, I began to devise a truly 'Brutine' policy to set the republic free (I call this policy 'Brutine'* because it is the preserve of those of your blood). The outcome is a long story, and I must pass over it since it concerns myself. I merely state that the youthful Caesar, to whom, if you are willing to admit the truth, we owe our continuing existence, has developed as a result of my counsels. The sole distinctions* which I have bestowed on him, 7 Brutus, have been both due and necessary, for when we first began to summon back our freedom at a time when not even the heaven-sent courage of Decimus Brutus had bestirred itself to be known to me, and our protection depended solely on the boy who had shifted Antony from our necks, what distinction ought not to have been decreed to him? Yet though at that time in restrained terms I bestowed a verbal accolade on him, I also voted him the military authority which seemed an honorific title for one so young, but was vital for the commander of an army, for what is an army without a supreme authority? Philippus voted him a statue, and first Servius proposed that his age as a candidate for office be advanced,* and this was later extended by Servilius. None of these honours seemed excessive at the time.

But for some reason people are found to be more readily well 8 disposed in time of fear than grateful in the hour of victory. For example, when that day of Decimus Brutus' deliverance dawned, which was most auspicious for the city and also happened to be his birthday, I proposed that his name be enrolled in the calendar against that day. By this gesture I was following the example of our ancestors, who bestowed that distinction on the woman Larentia, at whose altar on the Velabrum* you pontiffs regularly offer sacrifice. When I proposed this for Brutus, my intention was that the calendar should contain an enduring record of a most welcome victory.* That day I became aware that there were in the Senate considerably more who were ill-disposed than who were thankful. During these days I rained down (if that is how you would have it) distinctions on Hirtius and Pansa following their deaths, and on Aquila as well.* Who will censure this gesture, except one who once the fear has been dispelled has forgotten the past danger?

9   In addition to the grateful recollection of the benefit they had
received, I had a further motive which I intended to be salutary for
future generations. I wanted memorials to survive for ever of the
public hatred directed against most cruel enemies. I suspect that you
are less approving of a further gesture of which your friends, the best
of men but politically naive, disapprove. I proposed that Caesar be
permitted to enter the city in ovation.* My own view (perhaps I am
wrong, and I am not the sort of man to take pleasure in my own
actions) is that there was no attitude in the war which was more far-
sighted. I must not reveal the reason for this for fear of appearing to
be more prophetic than grateful. But I have dwelt too long on this
topic, so let me turn to other issues.

I proposed distinctions to Decimus Brutus and to Lucius Plancus.
Minds enticed by the prospect of glory are indeed outstanding, but
the Senate too showed wisdom in employing any means, so long as it
was honourable, by which they believed that an individual can be
induced to aid the republic. You may say that we deserve censure in
the case of Lepidus. True, we erected a statue for him on the rostra,
but we also demolished it.* We were eager to divert him from his
mad course by honouring him, but the lunacy of that most fickle man
prevailed over our practical wisdom, and less harm was done in
erecting that statue of Lepidus than the greater benefit which came
from its demolition.

10   That is quite enough about honours, for I must now say a little
about punishment. Your letters have often given me the impression
that in the cases of men you have conquered, you prefer praise of
your clemency. I indeed regard every action of yours as wise, but
neglect of punishment for crime (for that is what you are calling
pardon), though tolerable in other circumstances, I consider to be
execrable in this war. In our state there has been no civil war of all
those within my recollection in which, irrespective of the victorious
party, some sort of shape of a republic did not emerge. But in this
war I could not readily dogmatize about what sort of state we shall
have if we win, and if we are defeated there will certainly never be a
republic again. This was why I proposed harsh measures against
Antony and against Lepidus, not so much to take vengeance on
them, as for the moment to deter by terror wicked citizens from warring on our native land, and also for the future to post a warning, so
that no one would seek to imitate such lunacy.

Yet this proposal was not just mine, but was universally 11 supported. The feature of it which seems cruel is that the punishment extends to children who have not deserved it. But this stipulation is both long-standing and applies to all communities. Even the children of Themistocles* were reduced to poverty, and if the same penalty is applied to citizens condemned by the courts, how could we be more lenient towards our enemies? How can anyone lay a complaint against me when he must of necessity admit that, had he prevailed, he would have treated me more harshly?

You are now apprised of my proposals of this kind, at any rate as they apply to honours and punishments. As for other issues, I think that you have heard of my attitudes and proposals.

These issues, however, are not of vital importance. What is truly 12 crucial, Brutus, is that you make for Italy with all speed, together with your army. Your arrival is awaited most eagerly. If you set foot in Italy, the whole citizen-body will flock to you. If we are victorious (and we would have won a most handsome victory if Lepidus had not sought to create universal havoc, and to bring down himself and his family), we have need of your authority to establish the state on some formal basis. But if even now further conflict awaits us, our greatest hope lies in your authority and in the strength of your army. But for heaven's sake make haste. You know the importance of timing and of speed.

I hope that you will learn from the letters of your mother and 13 sister how conscientiously I consult the interests of your sister's children. In this matter I appear in some people's eyes to pay greater attention to your wishes, which lie very close to my heart, than to my regular practice. But I prefer to be, and to seem to be, more faithful to my affection for you than to anything else.

Letter 166 (*Brut.* I 18)

Rome, July 43

CICERO TO BRUTUS

Following my frequent letters of exhortation, in which I urged you 1 to come to the aid of the republic with all speed by bringing over your army to Italy, when I was under the impression that your nearest and dearest had no doubts on the wisdom of this course,

I was invited by your mother,* that most far-sighted and scrupulous lady, whose preoccupations are wholly centred upon and absorbed in you, to visit her on 25 July. I carried out this obligation without delay. When I arrived there, I found Casca, Labeo, and Scaptius* present. Your mother broached the question: What was my opinion? Should we send for you? Did we think that this was in your interest or was it better for you to linger and delay?

2   In reply I expressed my conviction that what most befitted your standing and reputation was that you should at the earliest possible moment afford protection to a faltering republic virtually on its last legs. For what misfortune do you think has not attended us in this war, in which our victorious armies have been unwilling to pursue the fleeing enemy, and in which our army commander,* whose life was in no danger, who was adorned with the most splendid distinctions and boundless wealth, and with a wife and children related to you and to your brother-in-law,* has declared war on the republic? There would be no need for me to add, 'When the Senate and the citizen-body are emphatically at one', except that monstrous evil continues to exist within our walls.

3   What grieves me particularly as I write this is that, having stood surety to the republic for the youth who is virtually a boy, I seem scarcely able to redeem my promise. To be responsible for another's disposition and opinion, especially on matters of the greatest moment, is more oppressive and taxing than a financial commitment. Money obligations can be met, and the loss of personal funds can be borne, but how do you discharge your promise to the republic if the person for whom you have stood surety* happily allows you to foot the bill for the pledge? Still, I hope to keep him aboard in spite of the opposition of many. He seems to have the right disposition, but he is at an impressionable age, and there are many who are ready to corrupt him. They are confident that the keen vision of his virtuous intellect can be blinded by the bright prospect of spurious advancement. So this laborious task has been imposed on me in addition to all the others, in that I am to deploy every engine at my disposal to preserve my hold on the young man, so as not to incur the charge of rash judgement.

4   Yet what sort of rash judgement is it, seeing that I have bound not myself, but him for whom I have stood surety? The republic can at any rate not regret my standing surety for the man who in political

activity is both outstanding in natural ability and more reliable by reason of my pledge.

But unless I chance to be mistaken, our most perplexing problem 5 is shortage of money. Honourable men dig in their heels more and more every day at mention of a financial levy. The entire proceeds of the 1 per cent tax,* owing to the shameless self-assessment by the wealthy, are spent on payment to the two legions. Spiralling costs overhang us, both for the armies which now protect us, and for yours. As for our friend Cassius, it seems that he can emerge sufficiently endowed. But I am keen to discuss both this and other problems with you as early as possible face to face.

Dear Brutus, I did not wait for your letter to act with regard to 6 your sister's children. Since the war will drag on, time itself will reserve the case unchanged for you to deal with. But from the very beginning, since I could not predict the length of the war, I pleaded the case of the children in the Senate, as I think you were able to ascertain from your mother's letters. Indeed, there will never be any issue on which I will not speak or act in ways which I think are your wish or your concern, even if such conduct endangers my life.

27 July

CONCORDANCE OF THE LETTERS
WITH THE STANDARD COLLECTIONS

EXPLANATORY NOTES

Letter 1 (*Att.* I 5)

1 *the death of my cousin Lucius*: cf. *On Ends* 5.1, where Cicero describes their studies together in Athens: 'Though he was actually a cousin, I loved him as a brother.'

2 *your sister . . . my brother*: the stormy partnership between Quintus and Pomponia ended in divorce in 45.

3 *Epirus*: Atticus had recently purchased an estate on the coast there, near Buthrotum.

4 *Aemilius*: the nature of his complaint is unknown.

5 *a certain person*: probably Lucceius; see Letter 2.1.

6 *Tadius . . . uninterrupted possession*: it seems that Atticus had inherited property, and sold it to Tadius. Uninterrupted tenure for a year was in Roman law recognized as ownership.

7 *Terentia:* see the Introduction, p. xxii.

Letter 2 (*Att.* I 11)

1 *Sallustius*: this non-political friend of Cicero later accompanied him in exile as far as Brundisium. See Letter 27.6, and *On Divination* 1.59.

Lucceius: this ally of Pompey was a noted historian whom Cicero later tried to persuade to write a eulogy of his career; see Letter 40.

that arbitration: Atticus seems to have acted as arbitrator in a private suit, and to have found against Lucceius.

2 *my election . . . already sewn up*: Cicero was strongly favoured for election to the praetorship of 66. He had made his name by his prosecution of Verres in 70, when he overshadowed the eminent defence counsel Hortensius, who was the consul elect for 69 and the leading orator of the day. Cicero headed the poll. The harassment mentioned here was attributable to C. Cornelius, a reforming tribune whose attempt to stem electoral bribery led to the elections being postponed twice.

my Academy: this was Cicero's gymnasium (lecture hall) on his estate at Tusculum.

Letter 3 (*Att.* I 1)

1 *17 July*: this was the day on which tribunes were elected, the first magistrates appointed for the following year.

Antonius, and Quintus Cornificius: after a chequered earlier career, C. Antonius attained the praetorship and later the consulship in the same years as Cicero. Thereafter he governed Macedonia. Cornificius, like Cicero, was a 'new man', the addressee of Catullus 38, who later served with distinction under Julius Caesar.

Caesonius: Cicero regarded him as a weak candidate, though he had obviously attained the praetorship.

Aquilius: C. Aquilius Gallus, an eminent jurist (hence his 'kingship of the courts' here) was a colleague of Cicero in the praetorship.

Catiline: L. Sergius Catilina (praetor 68) had been governor of Africa. An indictment for extortion there had prevented him from standing for the consulship of 65; see Sallust, *Catiline* 18.1.

2 *Caesar*: this is Lucius Caesar (consul 64), later a respected friend; see Letter 140.3.

Silanus . . . Turius: Silanus became consul in 62; Turius was 'a man of meagre intellect, but very assiduous' (Cicero, *Brutus* 237).

Piso: C. Calpurnius Piso, consul 67 and thereafter governor of Cisalpine and Narbonese Gaul. He was defended by Cicero in 63 when indicted for extortion.

3 *Caecilius . . . Varius . . . Satyrus*: only Caecilius in this mini-drama is at all well known. He is depicted by Nepos (*Atticus* 5.1) as an equestrian friend of Lucullus, and 'an awkward character'.

Lucullus, Publius Scipio, and Lucius Pontius: the celebrated general Licinius Lucullus, recently returned from his operations in the east, was awaiting his triumph. P. Scipio and Pontius the prospective receiver, are little known.

Lucius Domitius: L. Domitius Ahenobarbus (consul 54), ally and brother-in-law of Marcus Cato, was important for Cicero's prospects because of his optimate connections.

4 *'for the prize . . . oxhide'*: Homer, *Iliad* 22.150, in description of Achilles' pursuit of Hector round the walls of Troy.

5 *your Hermathena*: a squared stone pillar surmounted by a bust of Athena.

Letter 4 (*Fam.* V 2)

Q. Caecilius Metellus Celer had served as a legate of Pompey before becoming praetor in Cicero's consulship. He played a prominent role in the suppression of the Catilinarian conspiracy (see Sallust, *Catiline* 57). Cicero here replies to Celer's extant letter of complaint (*Fam.* V 1). Celer attained the consulship in 60.

1 *many who were resentful*: there was a deep vein of hostility towards Cicero among a section of the Senate, following upon the execution of the conspirators without a trial. His self-glorification deepened this hostility among some aristocrats against a 'new man'.

3 *I renounced the province . . . the drawing of lots*: the Senate had assigned Macedonia and Cisalpine Gaul as provinces for the retiring consuls. Cicero yielded Macedonia (the more profitable prospect) to Antonius, while he himself preferred to stay in Rome to play the role of elder statesman, renouncing Cisalpine Gaul, which was then allocated by lot to one

of the eight praetors. The lottery was, it seems, managed to allow Celer to become governor.

4 *the senatorial decree*: this decree appointed Celer in October 63 to raise forces at Picenum against the conspirators; see Sallust, *Catiline* 30. He had by now (January 62) taken over his province.

6 *your brother Metellus*: Q. Caecilius Metellus Nepos had like his brother served as legate under Pompey. When elected tribune in December 63 he caused mayhem in the Senate and Assembly by proposing that Pompey be summoned with his army to crush the conspiracy, thus antagonizing Cicero, Cato, and the entrenched nobility. He susequently fled to the protection of Pompey at Rhodes.

your wife Claudia and your sister Mucia: Claudia (Clodia), second of the three sisters of Clodius Pulcher, is persuasively identified with Catullus' Lesbia. In April 56 she was bitterly excoriated by Cicero in the extant *Pro Caelio*. Mucia Tertia, half-sister of Celer and wife of Pompey, was divorced by him on his return to Rome for infidelity during his absence in the East.

7 *to take the oath*: on demitting office, Roman magistrates swore that during their tenure they had complied with the laws.

8 *punished others unheard*: following the condemnation of the conspirators in the Senate, Cicero immediately had five of them executed without trial; see Sallust, *Catiline* 55.

Letter 5 (*Fam.* V 7)

Pompey: Cicero addresses him formally as 'Gnaeus Pompeius Magnus, son of Gnaeus, Imperator'.

1 *former enemies . . . recent friends*: Pompey had earlier served as Sulla's lieutenant, but after his consulship in 70 he sided with the *populares* in their struggles against the entrenched nobility. This letter signals the abandonment of this stance, as becomes evident on his return (see Letter 17.6).

2 *only the merest suggestion*: Pompey initially visualized Cicero as a rival to be kept at arm's length.

3 *My achievements*: no recognition of Cicero's achievement in crushing the conspiracy was forthcoming from Pompey, for he had hoped to be requested to deal with it. See the previous letter, § 6 and n.

some individual: doubtless Caesar, who had opposed the execution of the conspirators; see Sallust, *Catiline* 51.

Laelius . . . Africanus: the friendship between Scipio Aemilianus (who obtained the title Africanus after his destruction of Carthage in 146) and Gaius Laelius (consul 140) was proverbial, commemorated by Cicero in his *On Friendship*.

Letter 6 (*Fam.* V 6)

Sestius served as Cicero's fellow-consul Antonius' quaestor in 63, and was at this time serving in the same capacity in Macedonia, a post he wished temporarily to retain. An active supporter of Cicero, he later helped to secure his restoration from exile. With Milo he organized street-gangs to confront Clodius, and when indicted for violence in 53 was defended by Cicero in the extant *Pro Sestio*.

1 *Cornelia . . . Q. Cornelius*: Sestius' wife was the daughter of L. Cornelius Scipio Asiaticus (consul 83). Cornelius was presumably a freedman and client of the same family.

2 *my purchase of Crassus' house*: though far from being the costliest at Rome (see Letter 9.6), this purchase of the house on the Palatine overlooking the Forum evoked sardonic comment on Cicero's pose as *grand seigneur*.

I am keen to join a conspiracy: behind the extended joking, there is a hint of embarrassment here, for Cicero took a loan from P. Sulla (whom he had recently defended on a charge of bribery), whose name was linked with the conspirators. He also sought a loan from Antonius, whose disdain for Cicero is recorded here (§ 3), and whose conduct in Macedonia led to indictment and exile; he too had been linked with Catiline. See the next note.

Letter 7 (*Fam.* V 5)

C. Antonius Hybrida, the son of the noted orator Antonius, had been suspected of complicity with Catiline prior to his consulship shared with Cicero in 63. His conduct as governor of Macedonia (62–60) led to condemnation for extortion. This letter reflects the cool relations between the two men.

1 *Titus Pomponius*: more familiarly called Atticus.

2 *'ascertained'*: *comperisse* was the word used by Cicero to describe the discovery of evidence of the conspiracy (see Letter 10.5); his opponents implied that he had doctored this evidence.

3 *the demands that remain*: Antonius' misconduct was being so widely condemned that Pompey in the East was allegedly pressing for the governor's recall. See Letter 8.1.

Pomponius' concerns: Antonius was being delicately requested to put pressure on the town of Sicyon to repay moneys owed to Atticus.

Letter 8 (*Att.* I 12)

1 *Teucris . . . Cornelius*: Teucris (? a pseudonym) was a go-between arranging a loan from Antonius to Cicero to help defray the cost of his new house (see Letter 6.2). That letter mentions a Q. Cornelius, presumably a freedman in the household of Cornelia, wife of Sestius, who was serving on Antonius' staff in Macedonia.

Considius . . . Axius . . . Selicius . . . Caecilius: all money-lenders, the first two (or three) senators, the fourth an equestrian.

Pompey: he had recently returned to Rome. The threat to unseat Antonius accords with his changed political stance, also demonstrated by his warmer attitude towards Cicero mentioned in § 3 below.

2 *Antonius when extorting money*: this report, emanating from Cn. Plancius, serving as military tribune in Macedonia, is probably associated with the loan Cicero was seeking from Antonius.

3 *his divorce of Mucia*: see Letter 4.6 and n. Caesar was said to have been her seducer (Suetonius, *Julius* 50).

Publius Clodius . . . at Gaius Caesar's house: this was the notorious episode of the Bona Dea ritual, held at the house of the Pontifex Maximus. Clodius allegedly sought an assignation with Pompeia, wife of Caesar, who divorced her because his household had to be 'above suspicion' (see Plutarch, *Caesar* 10).

Letter 9 (*Att.* I 13)

1 *in the shrine of your Amalthea*: Atticus' shrine on his Buthrotum estate was dedicated to the nymph who nursed the infant Zeus. Cicero playfully suggests that Atticus played the military man by performing ritual sacrifice before launching an 'attack' on Sicyon, the town which owed him money. The projected visit to Antonius was to seek the governor's aid in recovering the debt.

2 *not asked to initiate the debates*: the pecking order was decided by the presiding consul, Pupius Piso Frugi. Cicero speaks of him more positively at *Brutus* 236 and *On Ends* 4.23. 'The man who pacified the Allobrogians' was C. Calpurnius Piso (consul 67)—clearly a sarcastic reference, hinting that Piso's governorship of Narbonese Gaul in 66–65 was oppressive. Catulus and Hortensius, both eminent consulars, are cited as third and fourth speakers to underline Cicero's high standing.

His fellow-consul: M. Valerius Messalla Niger, a staunch optimate.

3 *a state ritual*: Cicero here records the aftermath to the Bona Dea scandal described in the previous letter.

Cornificius: see Letter 3.1 n. As a mere praetor, not a consular, he was not 'one of our number'.

a veritable Lycurgus: not the Spartan law-giver, but the fourth-century Athenian orator, celebrated especially for his relentless role as prosecutor.

4 *That friend of yours*: Pompey, towards whom at this time Cicero was at best ambivalent; compare Letter 16.2.

5 *the praetors*: Cicero's brother Quintus was among them; there was a two-month delay in the allocation of provinces in this year.

in my speech: this speech being prepared for publication is unknown.

6 *Teucris*: see Letter 8.1 n.

Letter 10 (*Att.* I 14)

1 *I wrote to you previously*: this letter has not survived.

Fufius: Q. Fufius Calenus later became prominent as a Caesarian; he became consul in 47, and thereafter supported Mark Antony.

selection of the jurymen: they were normally chosen by lot; hence Cicero's explanatory note about the Senate's instruction, which Fufius was implicitly challenging.

2 *Pompey then gave answer*: his reply further signalled his switch of allegiance to the optimates, including Cicero.

3 *Crassus*: M. Licinius Crassus had been supplanted by Pompey in the suppression of Spartacus in 73–71. Following their joint consulship in 70, the bitter rivalry continued. Crassus opposed Pompey's extraordinary commands. Caesar brought them together in an informal triumvirate in 60.

Aristarchus that you are: Aristarchus of Samothrace, head of the Library at Alexandria in *c.*153, was regarded in antiquity as a consummate critic in all branches of literature.

5 *a veritable Areopagus*: the advisory council at Athens still retained its prestige in Cicero's day. This paragraph and the next name Cato, Hortensius, Favonius, Lucullus, Calpurnius Piso, Messalla, and Cornutus as the stalwart optimates he has in mind.

that dear little girlie: Scribonius Curio the elder served with distinction as consul (76) and censor (61), but the son, pilloried here and elsewhere as a homosexual, was an ally of Clodius. He later supported Caesar. *Fam.* II 1–7 are addressed to him.

I 'ascertained' all the facts: see Letter 7.2 n.

6 *That other consul*: for earlier abuse of Piso, see Letter 9.2.

7 *Lucceius*: see Letter 2.1 n.

Letter 11 (*Att.* I 15)

1 *Quintus . . . has obtained Asia*: Cicero's younger brother was praetor in 62, and governed the province from 61 to 58. Asia (roughly modern Turkey) was constituted as a Roman province in 133, and was divided into eleven districts by Sulla. In a lengthy letter (*Q. fr.* I 1), Cicero counsels his brother on the task of governing civilized Greek subjects and Roman tax-farmers and businessmen.

'summon all the courage you can': Homer, *Iliad* 22.268.

Letter 12 (*Att.* I 16)

1 *the outcome of the trial*: the indictment of Clodius; see Letter 9.3.

as Homer does: in the *Odyssey*.

2 *the composition of the jury*: the consular bill had proposed that the presiding praetor should select the jurors in place of selection by lot; see Letter 10.1.

3 *like a kindly gladiator-trainer*: he would exempt the more civilized gladiators from the bloody combat.

tribunes . . . as their title implies: the *tribuni aerarii*, eligible as jurors, derived their name from their original role as paymasters in the army. Cicero suggests that *aerarii* means 'handling money'.

4 *Xenocrates . . . Metellus Numidicus*: both were proverbial examples of incorruptible men. Xenocrates headed the Academy after Plato; Metellus was consul in 109, censor in 103. The two anecdotes are similarly cited in close proximity by Valerius Maximus (2.19).

5 *Our distinguished Areopagites*: a sarcastic label for the jurymen.

'Ye Muses . . . descended': Homer, *Iliad* 16.112.

old Baldhead of the Nanneian household: family predecessors of Crassus bore the surname Calvus ('Baldy'). He had obtained the property of a certain Nanneius during the Sullan proscriptions.

Catulus: Q. Lutatius Catulus (consul 78) was an acknowledged leader of the optimates.

6 *Talna and Plautus and Spongia*: disreputable jurors.

8 *I deprived him of the province of Syria*: the Senate designated provinces for retiring consuls. When Piso was deprived of this office, L. Marcius Philippus continued as governor of Syria for a further year (Appian, *Syrian Wars* 51).

9 *Lentulus . . . Catiline*: P. Lentulus Sura (consul 71) was indicted for peculation in 81, and was one of 64 senators expelled for corruption in 70. He became Catiline's lieutenant, and was executed. Catiline was prosecuted for extortion in 65, and for murder in 64.

to be imprisoned . . . to deprive you of . . . exile: Cicero threatens Clodius with summary execution.

10 *Our fancy little fellow*: rendering *pulchellus*, diminutive of Clodius' surname Pulcher.

lurking under cover: after the Bona Dea scandal Clodius went into hiding.

your defence counsel: The word *patrono* suggests that the elder Curio defended Clodius in the trial. Curio had acquired a villa formerly belonging to Marius of Arpinum.

a king . . . Rex: Q. Marcius Rex, brother-in-law of Clodius, had excluded him from his will.

11 *the unchallenged affection of . . . Pompey the Great*: a further sign of Pompey's changed allegiance, and of his popularity at Rome.

12 *Aulus' son*: this was L. Afranius, formerly legate of Pompey in Spain and in the East. He was duly elected consul for 60.

Philip used to say: the epigram of Philip II referring to his 'purchase' of Olynthus in 348, is echoed in Horace, *Odes* 3.16.13 f., and in Juvenal 12.47.

the consul: Piso.

13 *both Aelian and Futian laws*: these second-century statutes restricted proposals by tribunes during election periods. Hence the postponement of
elections mentioned here.

14 *the outcome may be less pleasant*: Quintus' appointment as governor of Asia
is reported in Letter 11. Marcus had hoped that Atticus would join his
staff or offer general support.

15 *those epigrams of yours*: Atticus, a fluent versifier in both languages, wrote
poems on the achievements of outstanding Romans (see Nepos, *Atticus*
18.5, with additional mention of a Greek work on Cicero's consulship).

Archias: Cicero successfully defended his claim to citizenship in the *Pro
Archia* of 62. 'A Caecilian drama' jokingly depicts Archias as a second
Caecilius (the second-century dramatist), contemplating a poem lauding
his patrons, the Caecilii Metelli.

Letter 13 (*Att.* I 17)

2 *by several designing persons*: perhaps Quintus' wife Pomponia and his
influential freedman Statius (on the latter, see Letters 22.4 and 23.1).
Pomponia may again be obliquely referred to in § 3 ('where the blame . . .
lies').

5 *opportunities for advancement*: business opportunities rather than social
and political advantages.

8 *received money for jury-service*: this decree, if approved by the Assembly,
would have deprived equestrian jurors of their immunity from
prosecution. See *Pro Cluentio* 145.

9 *Metellus . . . Cato*: for Metellus Celer, see Letter 4 above. Cicero implies
that Cato would also have opposed the measure had time allowed.

10 *another path*: with Cicero's central policy of harmony between Senate and
equestrians under threat, he proposes to enlist the support of Pompey to
have these grisly concessions approved.

11 *Lucceius*: for his unsuccessful political ambitions, see Letter 10.7. Bibulus
was elected with Caesar. Though elsewhere (e.g. *Fam.* I 14.7), Cicero
claims cordial friendship with Bibulus, his attitude towards him is
frequently hostile, as in the barbed comment here.

Letter 14 (*Att.* I 18)

1 *Metellus*: the reading is dubious, since 'Metellus' must refer to Celer, the
new consul, whom Cicero at § 5 below and elsewhere regards with respect.
The quotations which follow are speculatively assigned to the *Philoctetes*
of the second-century dramatist Accius.

3 *A consul*: Afranius; see Letter 12.12 n.

a decree on bribery and the courts: see Letter 13.8 and n.

Juventas . . . Memmius: Juventas was the goddess of initial manhood; her
temple in the Circus Maximus was dedicated in 191 by C. Licinius

Lucullus (Livy 36.36.5). The Luculli were therefore associated with the ritual, and the adultery of the wife of Marcus Lucullus, brother of the famous general, caused the postponement of the ritual. The adulterer Memmius was hostile to the Luculli, having prosecuted Marcus in 66, and delayed the triumph of Lucius. Cicero satirically equates Memmius with Paris, Marcus with Menelaus, and Lucius with Agamemnon.

4 *Herennius*: not otherwise known.

Clodius: as a patrician, he was not eligible for election to the tribunate.

5 *Metellus . . . issued the same proposal*: when Herennius' proposal was vetoed, Celer thus mollified his brother-in-law, being confident that his bill would likewise be vetoed.

6 *Flavius . . . an agrarian law*: nothing is known of the previous Plotian bill. Flavius, a supporter of Pompey, sought to provide land for Pompey's veterans and the urban poor. The proposal for agrarian reform, traditionally a red rag to senatorial conservatives, was strongly opposed by Cato, Lucullus, and Metellus Celer. Pompey's reticence behind his embroidered toga (awarded him in 63 to commemorate his triumph) reflected his ambivalence, for he was eager to reward his veterans without alienating his new allies.

7 *forced to refrain from passing decrees*: presumably they would have been vetoed by hostile tribunes.

Letter 15 (*Att.* I 19)

2 *fear of war in Gaul*: the Romans at this date envisaged Transalpine Gaul as divided between the Province (the southern region which had passed into Roman control in the late second century) and Gallia Comata ('Long-haired Gaul'). The Province was important as providing a secure land-route into Spain. The Aedui in Comata, occupying the area around Lyons (Lugdunum), had obtained from the Romans the honorific title of 'Brothers' after soliciting Roman protection in 121. They had recently been worsted by Ariovistus, king of the Suebi. The Helvetii, occupying the area between lakes Constance and Geneva, posed a separate difficulty.

Creticus . . . Flaccus . . . Lentulus: Metellus Creticus (consul 69) was the senior figure; Flaccus was praetor in 63. 'Perfume on lentils' (perhaps a citation from the fourth-century poet Strattis, indicating a valuable commodity wasted on something worthless) is probably an ironical comment punning on the name Lentulus and alluding to his junior status; he became praetor in 59. Cicero would have led the embassy if the Senate had not withdrawn him from the post (§ 3).

4 *The agrarian law*: see Letter 14.6.

the consulships of Publius Mucius and Lucius Calpurnius: they held office in 133. The land had not been allocated following Tiberius Gracchus' bill of that year.

citizens of Volaterrae and Arretium: they had been proscribed by Sulla. Cicero (*Pro Caecilio* 97) defended their right to citizenship, and hence their claim to their land.

the windfall: the new taxes were raised from the provinces established in the East by Pompey.

the backbone of my army: the joke contrasts Cicero's support with the veterans of Pompey.

that other consul: Afranius; see Letter 12.12 n.

5 *Herennius*: see Letter 14.4. Cicero underestimated the importance of Clodius' aspiration for the tribunate.

6 *that historic Fifth of December*: the date of the execution of the conspirators.

the fish-pond owners: Macrobius (*Saturnalia* 3.15.6) speaks of 'very well-known Romans, Lucullus, Philippus, and Hortensius, whom Cicero calls *piscinarii*'. All three were senatorials.

8 *Epicharmus*: this Sicilian comic dramatist (fl. *c*.480 BC) was famous for his maxims, an anthology of which circulated in antiquity.

9 *that business of yours*: this refers to the loan advanced by Atticus to the township of Sicyon. Atticus had tried without success to recover his money. The senatorial decree, otherwise unknown, contained a clause rejecting compulsory repayments by free communities. Servilius Isauricus (consul 48), a supporter of Cato, was probably a mere tribune at this date.

10 *an Atticist*: Cicero puns on his friend's *cognomen*; for his fluency in Greek, see Nepos, *Atticus* 4.

what I believe Lucullus said: the famous general was renowned for his knowledge of Greek, in which he wrote a history of the Social War; see Plutarch, *Lucullus* 1.

'Who will praise his father?': the Greek proverb in full reads: 'Who but an ill-starred child will praise his father?', a criticism of those who rely on ancestral achievements for their fame.

Letter 16 (*Att.* I 20)

2 *the person you name*: this is Pompey, whose leading position in the state is acknowledged later in this section.

unprincipled citizens: Clodius and his associates.

3 *the role of Sparta*: at Letter 41.2, Cicero quotes in full the citation in Atticus' letter: 'Sparta is your allotted portion; you must adorn it.' In this quotation from Euripides' lost *Telephus*, 'Sparta' symbolizes the brave resistance of the optimates.

the death of Catulus: Lutatius Catulus, an acknowledged leader of the optimates, died in 61.

Rhinthon: this Syracusan dramatist of the early third century wrote 'cheerful tragedies', comic versions of the themes of Euripides in particular.

4 *the Sicyonians*: see Letter 15.9 n.

5 *Metellus . . . Aulus' son*: for Metellus Celer and Afranius, see Letter 14.5. Pompey had backed the election of Afranius, but he was a sore disappointment. Hence the reference to 'the black eye' (*œil poché*) here.

7 *Paetus*: this Neapolitan friend of Cicero received twelve surviving letters (*Fam.* IX 15–26; see Letters 110 and 106 in this selection) from him. His cousin, Servius Claudius, had retired abroad in disgrace after filching one of his father-in-law's writings (see Suetonius, *De grammaticis* 3). Claudius was one of the pioneers in the composition of commentaries in Latin; hence his possession of Greek and Latin works.

the Cincian law: the original law, promoted by Cincius Alimentus in 204, forbade advocates in the courts to accept payments beyond a certain limit. Cicero cites the law jokingly, because Atticus' agent, called Cincius, had noted the bequest with approval.

Letter 17 *(Att.* II 1)

1 *leaving . . . the gladiatorial show*: under the republic, such shows were mounted by ambitious individuals, usually in honour of dead relatives. Cicero's aversion to them is detailed at Letter 43.3 and elsewhere.

rough and ready: the implicit criticism of Atticus' slapdash production is accentuated by Cicero's description of his own highly rhetorical account.

2 *Posidonius*: the celebrated Stoic philosopher and historian (*c.*130–41) had lectured to Cicero at Rhodes in 77. Cicero's claim to his acquaintance did not result in the testimony from the great man which he anticipated.

3 *my speeches, such as they are*: (translating the diminutive *oratiunculae*). The first two are *Contra Rullum* I–II, also known as *De lege agraria*, delivered to Senate and Assembly respectively in January 60. The speech on Otho (now lost) concerned that tribune's law, which allotted the first 14 rows in the theatre to the equites in 67; this led to disorder in the theatre in 63, the year of Otho's praetorship. Cicero in this speech admonished Otho's critics. The speech *Pro Rabirio* (63 BC) defended Rabirius on a charge of treason. The fifth speech mentioned opposed a tribunician proposal that disabilities imposed by Sulla on children of his proscribed enemies should be lifted. The sixth declined the award of Cisalpine Gaul as his consular province in 62. The remaining speeches mentioned are all against Catiline, delivered on 5 November and 3 and 5 December 63.

two shorter speeches: one of them has survived as the third speech *Contra Rullum*, or *De lege agraria*.

4 *our little Beauty*: playing on Clodius' *cognomen* Pulcher.

5 *seeking an inheritance in Sicily*: following his acquittal in the Bona Dea trial, Clodius went to Sicily as quaestor in 61. Cicero affects surprise at his

returning in haste to Rome rather than remaining in Sicily to claim the inheritance.

Rome to Interamna in three hours?: in the Bona Dea trial, Clodius used the defence of alibi, claiming to have been in Umbria on the night in question. But Cicero pricked the bubble by disclosing that he had seen him in Rome on that very night.

in a week . . . in darkness . . . no one had met him?: Clodius was emphasizing the urgency with which he was seeking election.

my sister: the second of Clodius' three sisters was married to the consul of 60, Metellus Celer, and was thus in a position to allocate the seats. Cicero's quip refers to the reputation for incest levelled against Clodius and his sister (cf. *In Pisonem* 28).

Fabius . . . takes it badly: Q. Fabius Maximus Sanga was allegedly Clodia's lover; 'both' refers to Clodius and Clodia.

6 *the agrarian law*: see Letter 15.4.

Pompey . . . Caesar: Cicero here offers the most detailed account of his motive in seeking friendship with Pompey. Caesar's career, 'borne on the fairest of winds', had risen to the praetorship in 62, and to the governorship of Further Spain in 61 (enabling him to wipe out his debts there). He was to become consul in 59.

7 *posted . . . up to the Capitoline hill*: on 4–5 December 63, the equestrians gathered on that road to protect the Senate (see *Pro Sestio* 28; *Philippics* 2.16, but with no mention of Atticus' role).

mullets in their fish-ponds: see Letter 15.6 n.

8 *Cato . . . inflicts damage on the state*: the linchpin of Cicero's policy was *concordia ordinum*, harmony between Senate and equestrians. He concedes that Cato's stance was principled, but regards it as disastrous for the cohesion of the republic.

a consul has been locked up: Metellus Celer was imprisoned by the tribune Flavius, but because of his opposition to the agrarian bill and not because of the agitation of the tax-farmers. See Letters 14.6, 15.4.

to freedmen and even to slaves?: without the support of the equites, Cicero implies, the optimates will be at the mercy of the lower elements in the Assembly.

9 *Favonius*: a candidate for the tribunate; the reason for his indictment of Scipio Nasica (consul 52) is unknown.

Molon . . . at the millstones: Apollonius Molon of Alabanda was a famed rhetorician at Rhodes. He taught Cicero at Rome in 87 and 81. Cicero puns on Molon and *molae* (millstones).

Lucceius' intentions: he was aspiring to the consulship of 59 with Caesar, but Bibulus was elected with the support of the optimates.

10 *your ill-treatment by the Sicyonians*: see Letter 16.4.

11 *the Prognostica*: this was a rendering of the second part of the *Phaenomena* of Aratus, the third-century Greek poet; the first part discussed the constellations, and the second, weather-signs. Cicero's version has not survived.

12 *Paetus*: for this friend of Cicero and his gift, see Letter 16.7.

Octavius: C. Octavius, father of the future emperor Augustus, had succeeded Antonius as governor of Macedonia.

Letter 18 (*Att.* II 3)

1 *Valerius*: probably M. Valerius Messalla Rufus (consul 53), a leading Caesarian, nephew of Hortensius, and a personal friend of both Cicero and Atticus. The suspected support of the consul Afranius ('Aulus' son'), who was Pompey's protégé, and of 'Epicrates' ('the Powerful One', a nickname for Pompey) may reflect the incipient alliance between Pompey and Caesar.

2 *the Education of Cyrus*: Cicero jokingly labels the advice of his architect Vettius Cyrus the *Cyropaedia* of Xenophon.

3 *the agrarian law*: as had been widely anticipated, one of Caesar's first acts as consul in January 59 was to reintroduce the bill for the agrarian law. It was duly carried, but proved inadequate, and was supplemented in April; see Letter 21.1 n.

Cornelius Balbus: this freedman had received the citizenship after service with Pompey against Sertorius. He became Caesar's agent and financial adviser, and attained the suffect consulship in 40.

4 *the third book*: the citation is from Book III of Cicero's lost poem, *De consulatu suo*. Calliope was the Muse of epic poetry.

The best, the only omen . . . land: Homer, *Iliad* 12.243.

the Compitalia: this feast of the crossroads was celebrated in late December or early January, following the Saturnalia.

Theophrastus' On Ambition: the successor of Aristotle as head of the Peripatetic school wrote on various aspects of social behaviour, notably in *The Characters*. This work *On Ambition* has not survived.

Letter 19 (*Att.* II 5)

1 *I am indeed keen . . . to visit Alexandria*: no letters survive to document Cicero's reaction to the first measures of Caesar's consulship in January 59, but this mention of a possible visit to Egypt suggests that Caesar was seeking to mollify him with the offer of a legation to install Ptolemy XII Auletes as king of Egypt and friend of the Roman people. Caesar and Pompey were to share the bribe of 6,000 talents in return for this appointment.

I fear the Trojans . . . Polydamas will be the first with his reproach: these quotations from Homer (*Iliad* 22.105 and 100) describe how Hector decided not to retreat from Achilles for fear of incurring the charge of cowardice.

Cicero feared similar reproaches if he accepted the offer of this commission.

'who alone is worth a hundred thousand': from Heraclitus, frag. 49 Diels.

Theophanes: this historian from Mytilene accompanied Pompey in 62 on his return to Rome, where he acted as his agent.

2 *Arrius*: Q. Arrius had promoted himself as a candidate for the consulship of 58. Cicero's low opinion of him is reflected at *Brutus* 242 f. In the event, Calpurnius Piso, Caesar's future father-in-law, and Pompey's henchman Gabinius were elected.

the augurate . . . Nepos: for Metellus Nepos, see Letter 4.6 n. The augurate had been held by his brother Metellus Celer, whose recent death had made Nepos a likely successor. But he was leaving Rome to govern a province, and Cicero was casting a hopeful eye on the priesthood. He finally attained it in 53/52.

3 *Publius Clodius*: he had now been enrolled in a plebeian tribe, and was eligible for election as a plebeian tribune. Cicero had good reason to fear this development.

Letter 20 (*Att.* II 9)

1 *exchanges . . . with Publius*: Atticus was on sufficiently friendly terms with Clodius to allow Cicero to keep abreast of his plans.

Lady Ox-eyes: Clodia's striking gaze earned her this title of Hera's (see Homer, *Iliad* 1.551, etc.).

the agreement made with regard to me: Pompey ('our friend from Jerusalem') promised Cicero protection against Clodius; see *Att.* II 20.2: 'Pompey claims there is no danger; he even adds that Clodius will have to kill him before he lays a finger on me.'

who converts patricians into plebeians: Caesar had actually overseen Clodius' enrolment as a plebeian, but Pompey sponsored it.

'ex-consul of the Cynic school': the insult directed at Cicero by Clodius attacks his aggressive oratory ('cynic' means 'canine') rather than his philosophical stance.

'Tritons of the fish-ponds': see Letter 15.6 n. for these leading optimates. Tritons are supernatural marine creatures.

the auspices and the . . . laws: these all sought to restrain the disruptive activities of the tribunes.

2 *Theophrastus*: see Letter 18.4 n. for this authority on human foibles.

Vatinius': this *popularis* was a close adherent of Caesar. As plebeian tribune in this year 59, he proposed the bills which gave the dynast his provinces and which ratified Pompey's eastern settlement. Cicero defended him in 56 under pressure from the Three when he was indicted for bribery. The passage here suggests that he has been advanced to the augurate.

3 *your boon-companion Publius*: see § 1 above.

jouer comme sophiste: Cicero refers to the technique of sophists, who respond to the arguments of others rather than initiate a discussion. The quotation that follows is from Homer, *Iliad* 24.369.

Letter 21 (*Att.* II 16)

1 *the allotment of Campanian land*: this bill, proposed in April as a supplement to the agrarian law passed in January, incorporated land which had been state-owned since the revolt of Capua in 211. It was then leased to tenants 'to provide revenues for the upkeep of the state' (so Suetonius, *Julius* 20.3). Caesar's measures divided it among '20,000 settlers with three or more children each' (so Suetonius), not the 5,000 estimated by Cicero here. The honest men (*boni*) were indignant at the loss of revenue, and also doubtless because of connections with existing tenants.

customs-duties have been abolished . . . the 5 per cent: the two sources of state-revenue (*uectigalia*) in republican Italy were customs-duties (*portoria*) the 5 per cent tax on manumitted slaves. Caesar temporarily abolished the first in 60.

our dependants: freedmen and slaves who dominated the Assembly.

2 *my friend Gnaeus*: Pompey's ambivalence here towards Caesar's legislation is noteworthy. The initial quotation in this paragraph is from Sophocles (frag. 268 Pearson).

the Alexandrian king: see Letter 19.1 and n.

Bibulus: M. Calpurnius Bibulus had been elected consul with Caesar for 59, thanks to the lavish bribery of the optimates. He sought to block Caesar's measures by 'watching the heavens'; the *lex Aelia* and the *lex Fufia* of a century earlier had made it illegal to transact business in the Assembly if a magistrate announced unfavourable omens (*obnuntiatio*).

Sampsiceramus: the name of the ruler of Emesa in Syria is applied satirically to Pompey, who had established Syria as a Roman province in 64. The Antilibanus range, east of Mt. Lebanon in that province, is likewise cited for satirical effect.

the men they call honest: translating *boni*, on which see the Glossary of Terms. As often, Cicero throws doubt on the suitability of the epithet for men who he claims have failed to come to the aid of the republic.

3 *Dicaearchus . . . Theophrastus*: both these fellow-students under Aristotle wrote on a variety of subjects, but Dicaearchus was especially famed for his political writings, while Theophrastus (see Letter 18.4 n.) was more concerned with social behaviour.

4 *the tax*: Cicero was anxious not to alienate the tax-farmers, and hoped that they would reach agreement with the Asians, though he regarded their demands as iniquitous.

even in cistophores: in *Att.* II 6.2, Cicero reported that he had written to the urban quaestors about payment of Quintus' expenses as governor of Asia.

Payment in denarii would have been preferable, but the Asian currency would be acceptable as a last resort.

Letter 22 (*Att.* II 18)

1 *young Curio*: earlier (Letter 10.5) Cicero speaks disparagingly of him as a supporter of Clodius. Here he warmly approves his overt opposition to Caesar, but in 49 he emerges as his supporter.

loyalists: again translating *boni*.

Fufius: see 10.1 n. He is already a staunch Caesarian.

2 *a curse*: Caesar compelled senators to swear to uphold the agrarian law passed in January (Dio 38.7). This letter indicates that candidates for office were required to swear to the April legislation as well.

Laterensis: M. Iuventius Laterensis, a staunch optimate, was active in the restoration of Cicero from exile in 58. He became praetor in 51.

3 *as deputy on his provincial staff*: that is, when Caesar took up his province of Cisalpine and Transalpine Gaul in 58. Caesar was anxious to save Cicero's face with this and the following offer of a roving legation to discharge a vow, which would have removed Cicero temporarily from the political scene.

our little Beauty: Cicero signals his growing apprehension at the menace of Clodius Pulcher ('Beautiful'), soon to be tribune.

4 *Statius' manumission*: Quintus' confidential freedman was heartily disliked by Cicero because Quintus preferred his advice to that of his brother. See further the next letter.

Letter 23 (*Att.* II 19)

1 *Statius*: see the previous letter. The quotation which follows is from Terence, *Phormio*, 232 f.

Clodius' threats: the comments here and in § 4 below indicate Cicero's mounting anxiety, in spite of Pompey's reassurances.

vieux jeu: a free rendering of the Greek proverb, 'Enough of the oak', which recalls the primitive era when acorns were the staple diet.

2 *the political situation*: Cicero expresses dismay at the passivity of the optimates in the face of the alliance of the three dynasts. He is particularly distressed at Pompey's role. His claim that he has 'shot himself in the foot' refers to his loss of popularity. The criticism of Bibulus here echoes that in *Att.* II 15.2: 'What does Bibulus' noble attitude . . . achieve except expression of his own view, with no improvement in the political situation?' The satirical quotation, inviting comparison of him with Fabius Cunctator, is from Ennius, *Annals*, frag. 360 Warmington (see the Loeb edition of *Remains of Old Latin*, vol. i).

3 *the gladiators . . . the Games of Apollo*: the 'presenter' of the gladiatorial show was Gabinius, henchman of Pompey and consul designate. The Games of Apollo were mounted on 7–11 July; actor and play from which

the quoted lines come are alike unknown. For the younger Curio, see Letter 22.1 and n.

the Roscian law . . . the corn law: the law introduced in 67 by the tribune Roscius Otho assigned the front fourteen rows of the theatre to the equestrians; its abolition would have been highly unpopular with that body. A threat to the corn law (probably the *lex Terentia Cassia* of 73, regulating the distribution and price of Sicilian corn) would have been equally unpopular with the commons.

4 *My friend Publius*: an ironical allusion to Clodius.

Cosconius . . . I have been invited: C. Cosconius (praetor 63) was a member of the Board of Twenty appointed in 60 to distribute land to Pompey's veterans and to the deserving poor. Cicero regarded the invitation as demeaning; moreover, the bill had been opposed by senatorial conservatives, and acceptance would have led to unpopularity with them.

5 *'Laelius' . . . 'Furius'*: C. Laelius Sapiens and L. Furius Philus were members of the cultured circle of Scipio Aemilianus. Laelius gained proverbial fame as the friend and political adviser of Aemilianus.

Caecilius: uncle of Atticus.

Letter 24 (*Att.* II 21)

1 *their fury at Cato*: in Cicero's view, Cato's obstruction of their plans as the leading figure in the Senate made the dynasts regard him as their most formidable enemy.

3 *that friend of ours*: Pompey.

The honourable men are his enemies: Pompey's alliance with Caesar had made his reconciliation with the optimates short-lived.

the edicts of Bibulus: Bibulus remained shut up in his house for the eight months of his consulship (so Plutarch, *Pompey* 48). His edicts blocked or sought to rescind the legislation passed by Caesar and approved by Pompey.

4 *Apelles . . . Protogenes*: Apelles of Colophon was the court painter of Alexander the Great. He painted several portraits of Aphrodite, the most celebrated of them depicting her rising from the foam. Protogenes of Caunus, contemporary with and rival of Apelles, was famed for his depiction of the Rhodian hero Ialysus. Cicero modestly compares his own rhetorical portrayals of Pompey with the masterpieces of these Greek celebrities.

Archilochian: the seventh-century Greek poet Archilochus was famous for his stinging wit.

5 *Clodius is hostile*: see Letter 23.1 and 4.

Varro: M. Terentius Varro is in this context relevant politically as a distinguished adherent of Pompey. After the Civil War his wider fame as scholar, poet, and antiquarian made him a boon-companion of Cicero.

Letter 25 (*Att.* II 23)

2 *Sampsiceramus*: see Letter 21.2 n.

that faction: the three dynasts.

3 *the routine and toil of the courts*: only the *Pro Flacco* is dated to this period among the 58 extant speeches, but Cicero will have been kept busy with others which have not survived.

Letter 26 (*Att.* III 4)

1 *my sudden departure from Vibo*: in late March 58, on the night before Clodius presented his first bill indicting those who had executed citizens without trial, Cicero anticipated condemnation by hastily quitting Rome. On reaching Vibo, which lies on the coast of the toe of Italy, he received the emended version of the law of his exile, forbidding him to stay within 400 miles of Rome. This excluded him not only from Sicily, but also from Malta. In early April he therefore made for Brundisium to travel eastward.

Sicca: a close friend of Cicero, who at *Att.* XVI 6 remarks that staying in his house is like being in his own home.

Letter 27 (*Fam.* XIV 4)

2 *Flaccus . . . a most heinous law*: this Flaccus is otherwise unknown. Anyone harbouring a convicted person was liable to be exiled.

3 *making for Cyzicus through Macedonia*: Cyzicus lay in the province of Asia on the coast of the Propontis. Cicero in fact called a halt at Thessalonica in Macedonia.

the poor girl's marriage . . . must be safeguarded: Tullia was married to C. Calpurnius Piso Frugi, an alliance which Cicero strongly approved. But he was to die early in 57.

my Cicero: Cicero's son was six years old, born in 65 (*Att.* I 2.1).

4 *stripped of everything*: Cicero's condemnation entailed the confiscation of his property. His house on the Palatine was burnt down.

Piso: See n. at § 3 above.

Letter 28 (*Att.* III 7)

1 *Autronius and the rest of them*: Autronius had been a prominent figure in the Catilinarian conspiracy (Sallust, *Catiline* 17.3, 18.5, etc.), and was living in exile in Athens after being indicted for bribery. It was rumoured that he sought to assassinate Cicero.

that town too: in fact, the distance from Rome via Brundisium and Dyrrhachium was well over the 400 miles specified in the decree.

2 *by those envious of me*: in his letters Cicero repeatedly condemns Hortensius and other optimates for urging him to anticipate condemnation by retiring into exile.

3 *Candavia*: the district of Macedonia immediately north of Epirus.

Letter 29 (*Q. fr.* I 3)

1 *fear of your own*: Quintus as retiring governor was likely to be indicted for extortion, and if this occurred, Marcus' disgrace might loom large in the court-case.

2 *to be dependent on others*: as spokesmen for the defence, if Quintus were indicted.

3 *almost identical . . . in age*: Quintus was in fact four years younger.

I . . . thrust from my embrace: with reference to the hurried parting when Cicero quitted Rome. At six years old, young Marcus was thirteen years younger than Tullia.

7 *about transferring money*: Quintus was offering to arrange a bill of exchange so that Marcus could draw on it in Thessalonica, where he had taken up residence in May.

the money I received on your behalf: Marcus had negotiated with the Treasury to draw Quintus' expenses as governor of Asia. See Letter 21.4 n.

Marcus Antonius and Caepio: Mark Antony and Brutus, adopted in 59 by his uncle Servilius Caepio, were both to loom large as successor and assassin respectively of Caesar in 44.

Crassus and Calidius: both were prominent money-lenders. Crassus was one of the wealthiest men in Rome. Calidius (praetor 57) was active in helping to achieve Cicero's restoration from exile.

8 *Hortensius . . . Arrius*: in spite of Hortensius' power and influence as a leader of the optimates, and his friendship with Crassus, Arrius failed to attain the consulship (see Letter 19.2 n.). Both had advised Cicero to flee rather than to face Clodius' indictment.

9 *the epigram about the Aurelian law*: this legislation of 70 BC, sponsored by Pompey and Crassus, broadened the panel of jurymen to include *tribuni aerarii* as well as senators and equestrians. The epigram criticized the change, and Hortensius doubtless took a similar attitude.

Messalla: probably the consul of 61; his weighty support would be welcome to Quintus if needed.

Letter 30 (*Att.* III 15)

1 *Varro*: for his allegiance to Pompey see Letter 24.5 n. Connection with Caesar is indicated at § 3 below.

2 *Cato . . . the hypocrisy of others*: by a bill proposed by Clodius, Cato had been sent to annex Cyprus. In his absence Hortensius and Arrius had urged Cicero to quit Rome rather than remain and confront Clodius.

3 *Curio . . . that notorious speech*: immediately following the Bona Dea scandal, when Curio was supporting Clodius, Cicero had published a speech *Against Clodius and Curio* (it has not survived). Now that Curio was defending the optimate cause against the dynasts, Cicero was distressed that the speech had leaked out. Axius, senator and money-lender, was a friend of Cicero; see Letter 8.1.

4 *the law on guilds*: Clodius had carried a law to reinstate guilds or clubs, which had been forbidden by legislation passed in 64. Cicero's motives in first supporting and later opposing the bill are unknown.

Pompey's less than generous response: when a group of senators visited Pompey to beg him to intercede on Cicero's behalf, he pleaded his inability to block the tribune's bills.

5 *the law as applied to an individual*: the second of Clodius' bills cited Cicero specifically. The Twelve Tables forbade laws to be directed against individuals (see Cicero, *The Laws* 3.11). In *Pro Sestio* 65, Cicero complains that he was exiled by such a law. The senator Culleo hoped that Cicero's exile could be rescinded on the grounds that Clodius' second bill was illegal.

I put on mourning-garb: when Clodius proposed that anyone executing citizens without trial (but without as yet naming Cicero specifically) should be indicted, Cicero not only donned mourning-clothes but also went round 'day and night' soliciting support (Dio 38.14.7).

6 *Domitius*: L. Domitius Ahenobarbus, an optimate and brother-in-law of Cato, as praetor for this year proposed to ignore the veto.

What of my possessions and my house?: these were forfeited when Cicero was condemned. His houses in Rome and at Tusculum and Formiae were destroyed.

on your estate: in Epirus, from where the crossing to Italy would be easy if the condemnation were rescinded.

7 *You would . . . have held me back*: that is, from his precipitate departure from Rome.

Letter 31 (*Fam.* XIV 1)

2 *Lentulus*: P. Cornelius Lentulus Spinther was an ally of Pompey and consul-designate. He was to propose on 4 August 57 to the Assembly that Cicero should be restored.

3 *Plancius*: Cn. Plancius, an acquaintance from the Arpinum area, was a quaestor in Macedonia at this time. He met Cicero on landing, escorted him to Thessalonica, and lodged him in his official residence.

Piso or his soldiers: L. Calpurnius Piso Caesoninus was consul in 58. Clodius had gained his support by having the province of Macedonia assigned to him. He governed there from 57 to 55.

4 *Piso's . . . attentions*: this Piso is Cicero's son-in-law, C. Calpurnius Piso Frugi, lauded in earlier letters; see Letter 27.4.

5 *to sell a block of dwellings*: Terentia was wealthy in her own right (see Plutarch, *Cicero* 8.2). Cicero's reaction to the proposed sale is not a rebuke, but an expression of regret at leaving his family in financial straits through the forfeiture of his possessions.

Letter 32 (*Att.* IV 1)

1 *my unjustified fear*: Cicero alludes to the panic which led him to quit Rome rather than oppose Clodius' proposals.

3 *my . . . prestige at the bar*: *forensem* here probably refers to his repute as advocate, for his political eminence is covered by mention of his influence in the Senate.

4 *the anniversary of the founding of Brundisium*: it was founded as a Latin colony in 204; see Velleius 1.14.8.

the temple of Salus, your Roman neighbour: the temple of Safety was dedicated on 5 August 302 BC by C. Iunius Bibulcus (see Livy 10.1.9). It was built on the Quirinal, close to Atticus' house (*Att.* XII 45.2). The Brundisians note the aptness of the anniversary for Cicero's restoration.

5 *my attendant-slave*: the *nomenclator* announced to his master the identity of individuals encountered.

the Porta Capena: the gate leading into the city from the Appian Way, the highway from Brundisium.

my thanks in the Senate: both this speech, *Post reditum in senatu*, and the subsequent address in the Assembly, *Oratio cum populo gratias egit*, are extant.

6 *the price of grain . . . was my fault*: Clodius claimed that the rise in price resulted from crowds flocking into the city to greet Cicero.

all men of consular rank had stayed away: they feared violence if they opposed powers for Pompey. The two who appeared, Messalla and Afranius, were staunch supporters of his.

7 *The consuls drafted a law*: Pompey energetically undertook the commission, and 'with the help of good fortune, he filled the markets with grain' (Plutarch, *Pompey* 50).

Favonius: he was 'Cato's ape', a supporter of the optimates.

the religious impediment: when Cicero was condemned, Clodius demolished his Roman house and erected on the site a temple to Liberty. Cicero addresses the religious question in his extant speech *De domo sua*. Here he surveys the possible outcome. If the pontiffs nullify the impediment, he will be able to replace his house with the compensation granted for the demolition of the previous house. Alternatively, the temple when demolished will be replaced. He will then obtain compensation for both the site and the house.

8 *Unstable . . . steady*: the source of the quotation is unknown.

certain family matters: this is perhaps the first indication of the rift with Terentia. See *Att.* IV 2.7 (October 57): 'I am loved by my brother and my daughter', with significant omission of mention of his wife.

Letter 33 (*Att.* IV 3)

2 *The colonnade of Catulus*: this was the portico erected by Q. Lutatius Catulus (consul 102). Clodius dismantled it and replaced it with one which extended onto Cicero's site (*Att.* IV 2.3 and 5).

Decius . . . Gellius: supporters of Clodius (see *De domo sua* 50; *Pro Sestio* 110 f.).

3 *Tettius Damio*: otherwise unknown.

a man like Acidinus: the proverbial type of good citizen; see e.g. Cicero, *De oratore* 2.260.

the Cermalus: an area of the Palatine hill.

Publius Sulla: P. Cornelius Sulla was elected consul for 65, but rejected when impeached for bribery. When indicted in 62 for complicity in the Catilinarian conspiracy, he was successfully defended by Cicero in the extant *Pro Sulla*.

Quintus Flaccus . . . from the house which Milo inherited: this henchman of Milo based himself in Milo's house on the Palatine hill, close to the Cermalus. Annius Milo (tribune in 57) was a redoubtable supporter of Cicero, and was responsible for Clodius' death in street-fighting in 52.

Marcellinus: Cornelius Lentulus Marcellinus, consul-designate for 56, was a keen supporter of Cicero (see *Att.* IV 2.4).

Metellus: Metellus Nepos, supporter of Pompey and consul in 57. As tribune in 62, he had been hostile to Cicero, but in spite of his connection with Clodius, he had not opposed his restoration.

Appius: Appius Claudius Pulcher, brother of Clodius.

your friend: probably Pompey.

Sestius: the tribune for 57 supported Cicero's recall, and opposed Clodius in gang-warfare on the streets. In 53 Cicero successfully defended him in the *Pro Sestio*, when he was indicted for violence.

should his election not take place: Clodius was a candidate for the aedileship of 56. The elections, normally held in July, had been postponed until November. They were eventually held in January, when Clodius was duly elected.

4 *the three brethren*: the brothers Claudii, Clodius being the third.

the Comitium: the meeting-place of the Assembly, at the foot of the Capitoline hill.

5 *Marcellus . . . is snoring*: C. Claudius Marcellus, consul in 50, was at this time a candidate for a lesser office. He obviously did not believe that the elections would take place.

Letter 34 (*Fam.* I 2)

P. Lentulus Spinther (see Letter 31.2 n.) was now governor of Cilicia. *Fam.* I 1 also addresses him on this topic of the restoration of Ptolemy Auletes to the Egyptian throne.

1 *Lentulus . . . Caninius*: for Lentulus Marcellinus, see Letter 33.3; he had endeared himself to Cicero by his opposition to the three dynasts. Caninius Gallus was a supporter of Pompey.

the religious question: Gaius Cato had produced an oracular pronouncement which forbade use of an army to restore Ptolemy.

2 *Lupus*: for his proposal favouring Pompey, see *Fam.* I 1.3.

3 *with the complicity of the king*: Ptolemy was in Rome at this time, having been expelled by his subjects. He was attempting to regain his throne by bribing the dynasts.

4 *a most impressive recommendation*: the Latin term *auctoritas* is employed when a proposed decree is vetoed by a tribune.

Cato: C. Porcius Cato (tribune 56, to be distinguished from M. Cato Uticensis) was at this time favouring Crassus against Pompey (see Letter 35.3).

Letter 35 (*Q. fr.* II 3)

1 *Milo attended*: i.e. appeared in court, to defend himself on a charge of violence.

Gaius Cato proposed a law to recall Lentulus: for Lentulus Spinther, governor of Cilicia, see salutation of the previous letter and n.; for Cato, see § 4 of that letter and n.

2 *Pompey . . . Clodius' rowdies*: Pompey was now estranged from Clodius owing to his support for Cicero's restoration.

'Crassus,' they replied: by this support of Crassus, Clodius was seeking to exploit the rift between the two dynasts.

the men of principle: *boni* in fact refers to the entrenched nobility listed here.

the Quirinalia: this festival on 17 February honoured Quirinus, the Sabine god associated with the Quirinal hill, and originally the god of male citizens (*Quirites*). He is increasingly identified with Romulus in the later republic as the founder-god of Rome.

3 *to allow Pompey to attend*: Pompey's five-year appointment with *imperium* to ensure the grain-supply debarred him from entry within the pomerium. The temple of Apollo Medicus, outside the *pomerium* between the Circus Flaminius and the Forum Holitorium, often served as the meeting-place for the Senate on such occasions.

Africanus . . . murdered by Gaius Carbo: Scipio Africanus (Aemilius) died in 129. His approval of the murder of Tiberius Gracchus and his agrarian policy made him unpopular, which led to the suspicion that he was murdered (the suspects included Carbo and also Gracchus' mother and sister). But Laelius insisted that his death was natural.

5 *Sestius*: see Letter 33.3 n. The 'grievances' are unknown.

a decree that societies and clubs be disbanded: they were a frequent recruiting-ground for agitators. They were earlier forbidden, but Clodius had recently introduced a bill to restore them.

6 *Bestia*: as tribune in 62, he had been a scourge of Cicero by condemning the execution of citizens without trial. Cicero was doubtless defending him under pressure from one of the dynasts. The speech has not survived.

7 *Pomponius . . . his wedding*: Atticus late in life (he was 54) made a harmonious marriage with Pilia.

Piso's Lake: unknown.

you are living in Sardinia: Quintus served for a year there as Pompey's legate ensuring the grain-supply. The climate there in summer was notoriously unhealthy.

Letter 36 (*Q. fr.* II 5)

1 *I am building in three places*: when he was exiled, his houses at Rome, Tusculum, and Formiae were burnt down. The consuls awarded compensation of two million sesterces for the Roman house, half a million for the Tusculan, and a quarter-million for that at Formiae (see *Att.* IV 2.3).

2 *Lentulus*: Lentulus Marcellinus, a vigorous opponent of Clodius, exploited repetitions of festivals and public thanksgivings to prevent formal meetings of the Assembly to pass laws. His quietist colleague was L. Marcius Philippus.

3 *those who grapple with wild beasts*: the *bestiarii*, often recruits from those condemned in the criminal courts, were matched against leopards, lions, and bears. So they made formidable minders.

bills concerning Caesar: while Caesar was engaged in his Gallic provinces, his enemy L. Domitius Ahenobarbus, who aspired to the consulship of 55, was threatening to have him recalled and indicted. Attempts were also being made to detach him from Pompey, but Crassus kept him abreast of events.

which Caninius advocated: should this be Volcacius? See Letter 34.1.

Pompey's close association with Publius Lentulus: Lentulus Spinther, not Lentulus Marcellinus.

4 *Sextus Cloelius*: this supporter of Clodius (later in 52 he was to superintend Clodius' funeral-rites) was prosecuted by Milo with Pompey's support.

senators . . . equites . . . tribuni aerarii: by the *lex Aurelia* of 70, the juries were drawn equally from these three classes; the third had the same property-qualification as the *equites*, but were of a lowlier status.

Sevius: otherwise unknown.

Appius . . . Caesar: Appius, brother of Clodius, had opposed Cicero's recall which Caesar approved. He may have been seeking Caesar's support for his candidature for the consulship, which he obtained in 54.

5 *your exceptional prestige in the province*: for his presence in Sardinia as Pompey's legate, see Letter 35.7.

Letter 37 (*Q. fr.* II 6)

1 *betrothed . . . to Crassipes*: After the death of her first husband, Calpurnius Piso Frugi, who died shortly before Cicero's return, Tullia married Furius Crassipes in 56. He divorced her in 51.

2 *shortage of revenue*: the public land in Campania had been rented to settlers, and this income was lost to the Treasury by Caesar's land-bills of 56.

Quintus, that splendid boy: now 10 years old, he was supervised by his uncle Atticus during the absences of his father.

dissensions between our womenfolk: doubtless between Quintus' mother Pomponia and Terentia.

3 *I visited your site*: in November 57 Clodius' ruffians had damaged Quintus' house; see Letter 33.2.

Pompey at his residence: his villa (*horti*) lay in the Campus Martius.

Letter 38 (*Q. fr.* II 8)

1 *the second book*: this was the second section of Cicero's poem *De temporibus* ('My Vicissitudes'). It has not survived.

L'indifférence: *adiaphora* is the Stoics' technical term for all things other than virtue or vice. The 'speech of Jupiter' must have centred on the theme of virtue as the only good, dismissing Cicero's privations as 'things indifferent'.

2 *Vibullius*: he later served as Pompey's Prefect of Engineers (see *Att.* VII 24, etc.).

consul Crassus: he and Pompey became consuls for 55.

an embassy . . . to either Byzantium or Brogitarus: Clodius hoped by this visit to gain financial profit in return for earlier aid to Byzantine exiles, and for appointing Brogitarus as high priest of Cybele at Pessinus.

3 *private citizens for sixty days*: the elections for 55 had been delayed until February. Praetors could then assume office at once, and thus avoid indictment for electoral bribery.

they openly rejected Cato: Marcus Cato was a candidate for the consulship, but Pompey and Crassus ensured their own election. Cato was, however, elected consul for 54.

Letter 39 (*Fam.* I 8)

This letter is important as revealing Cicero's increasing adhesion to the person and policies of Pompey.

1 *Plaetorius*: though a trusted confidant of both Pompey and Spinther, he is not prominent elsewhere in the letters.

our friends: Pompey and Crassus, consuls in this year.

3 *to return to my literary pursuits*: Cicero's epic poem, *De temporibus* (see Letter 38.1) was published early this year, and he completed the *De oratore* in November.

4 *certain individuals . . . greater passivity*: Cicero refers to Cato, now back from Cyprus, and other intransigent optimates.

the most closely associated order . . . the most celebrated individual: Cato's principled objections to the renegotiation of the tax-farmers' contract in 61–60 had caused a breakdown in the alliance of Senate and equestrians; see Letters 13.9 and 14.7. The 'most celebrated individual' is Pompey.

7 *an extremely successful campaign*: this must refer to Spinther's operations against the Free Cilicians, whom Cicero himself as governor was to seek to suppress.

Letter 40 (*Fam.* V 12)

Lucius Lucceius, an ally of Pompey, was urban praetor in 67, prosecuted Catiline for murder in 64, and aided Cicero against that revolutionary in 63. His hope of sharing the consulship with Caesar in 59 was dashed when the optimates backed Bibulus instead. His role as historian of contemporary events is outlined in § 2. There is no evidence that he acceded to Cicero's plea.

2 *your history of the Italian and Civil Wars*: these lost works covered the Social War between Rome and the Italians in 91–87, and the ensuing struggle between Sulla as leader of the optimates and Marius as champion of the *populares*, which came to a head with Sulla's bloody victory at the Colline Gate in 82.

Callisthenes . . . Timaeus . . . Polybius: Callisthenes wrote *c*.336 a monograph on the Third Sacred War; Timaeus wrote as an addition to his history of Sicily an account of the war with Pyrrhus; Polybius appended to his universal history an account of the Numantine War of 133 which has not survived.

the one character: Cicero himself.

3 *to ignore the laws of history*: ironically enough, Cicero attaches great importance to these in his *De oratore* (2.62), completed in this year.

Xenophon's Hercules: in Xenophon's *Memorabilia* (2.1.21), the sophist Prodicus describes how Hercules in the wilderness observed two paths, one of Pleasure and one of Virtue, and pondered which to take.

4 *the treachery, plotting, and betrayal*: Cicero censures those optimates who failed to support him when he was threatened with exile, and especially those who urged him to anticipate exile by retiring from Rome.

5 *Epaminondas at Mantinea*: the Theban leader, having crushed the Spartans at Leuctra, was killed in the moment of a second glorious victory at Mantinea in 362 (Xenophon, *Hellenica* 7.18 ff.).

Themistocles' exile and return: but the Athenian statesman, after being ostracized in 470, defected to Persia and became governor of Magnesia, where he died in 450 without returning to his homeland. Cicero may have been misled by Aristotle, who depicts him in Athens in 462–461 (*Constitution of the Athenians* 25).

7 *Alexander . . . Apelles . . . Lysippus*: Horace, *Epistles* 2.1.239 ff., records the tradition that Alexander would permit only the famous painter of Colophon and the noted sculptor of Sicyon to portray him.

Agesilaus . . . Xenophon: the extant biography by Xenophon lays great emphasis on the virtues of Agesilaus II of Sparta (*c.*445–359). Cicero aspired to similar treatment.

Timaeus upon Timoleon . . . Herodotus upon Themistocles: according to Polybius (12.23.4), Timaeus canonized Timoleon, the fourth-century scourge of Sicilian tyrants, as 'one greater than the most celebrated gods'. A similar claim could hardly be made for Herodotus' portrayal of Themistocles, whom he depicts as self-seeking, cunning, and greedy for gain.

Alexander on visiting Sigeum: the anecdote of Alexander's visit to Troy, where he remarked on Achilles' debt to Homer, is recounted by Arrian (1.12) and Plutarch (*Alexander* 15).

Hector in the play of Naevius: the dramatist Naevius, who during the Second Punic War composed many plays in the tradition of New Comedy, also wrote at least six tragedies, including *Hector's Departure*, from which this line with its tribute to Priam is taken.

8 *heralds at athletic contests*: there was great rivalry among heralds and trumpeters at Olympia, and crowns were awarded to those pronounced the victors.

Letter 41 (*Att*. IV 6)

1 *Lentulus*: the dead man is L. Lentulus Niger, probably one of the three Lentuli who indicted Clodius in 60. He was an unsuccessful candidate for the consulship of 58. He was a senatorial stalwart, opposed to the dominance of the Three.

Saufeius: he shared with his friend Atticus an attachment to the Epicurean school, which recommended retirement from public life.

2 *'Sparta is your allotted portion . . . adorn it'*: this line from Euripides' lost *Telephus* had been quoted by Atticus to Cicero. 'Sparta' represents Cicero's present role, willing subservience to the domination of the Three.

Philoxenus: the poet of Cythera (*c.*435–386) was condemned to the quarries for criticizing the tragedies of Dionysius I of Syracuse. When offered his freedom if he praised them, his response was to request a return to his punishment (Diodorus 15.6.2 ff.).

3 *the Hortensius treatise*: this was perhaps to be the *De oratore*, published towards the close of 55, dedicated, however, not to Hortensius but to Cicero's brother Quintus. The 'outrageous behaviour' of Hortensius refers to his advice to Cicero to quit the capital in 58. Hortensius made amends in 53 by nominating Cicero for the augurate. The lost treatise *Hortensius*, published in late 46, was so named as a tribute to his former enemy after his death in 49.

the letter I sent him: this is Letter 40.

Letter 42 (*Att.* IV 9)

1 *delaying the census*: The censors were due to be replaced in 56, but the disorders of that year and the renewal of the alliance of the Three at Luca, had delayed elections. When Pompey and Crassus became consuls in 55, they promised that censors would be duly elected, but certain tribunes were threatening postponement.

dismissive of Syria, and jettisoned Spain: the tribune C. Trebonius was proposing a bill giving the consuls five-year commands in Syria and Spain. Pompey affected to be disdainful of the proposal.

Phocylides: a sixth-century Milesian who wrote a poem in hexameters embodying maxims each introduced with the phrase 'This too from Phocylides'.

Messalla: as an intimate of Hortensius and friend of Cicero and Atticus, M. Valerius Messalla Rufus was cool towards the Three. He became consul in 53.

2 *that most charming young Cicero*: Quintus' son

Paetus: for L. Papirius Paetus, see Letter 16.7 and n.

Letter 43 (*Fam.* VII 1)

Marcus Marius, regular correspondent of Cicero, was an invalid who steered clear of the political scene.

1 *the theatrical performances*: Pompey as consul in 55 mounted these games to dedicate his magnificent stone theatre, the first permanent home of plays to be permitted at Rome. It was part of a complex which included a temple of Venus Victrix, and lay in the Campus Martius. See Pliny, *Natural History* 8.2.1.

Stabiae: modern Castellamare on the Bay of Naples.

Spurius Maecius: Pompey entrusted him with the selection of dramas to be performed. Horace (*Satires* 1.10.38; *Ars Poetica* 387) regarded him more highly than Cicero apparently does.

2 *Aesopus*: Clodius Aesopus was the leading tragic actor of the day. Quintus regarded him as Marcus' friend (*On Divination* 1.80).

'If in full knowledge I deceive': possibly declaimed as part of a play, but more probably a declaration by the actor at the outset. Cicero suggests that the audience interpreted it as self-criticism.

Clytemnestra . . . The Trojan Horse: Accius was the author of the first of these tragedies; the second was by either Livius Andronicus or Naevius, both of whom wrote dramas with this title. Clearly both plays were presented as lavish spectacles.

3 *Oscan shows . . . in your city-council*: the Oscan or Atellan farces were crude shows popular with unlearned audiences. They had stock characters, like Maccus the glutton and Pappus the old fool. Hence the joke about the city-council.

you have held the gladiators in contempt: perhaps a withering comment on the street-fighters led by Clodius and Milo.

'oil and effort': this proverbial description of scholarly activity at dead of night is wittily adapted to operations in the arena.

a feeling of pity: this hint of a popular protest at the massacre of noble beasts is confirmed by the Elder Pliny (*Natural History* 8.21).

4 *Caninius Gallus*: as tribune in 56, he had sought to have Pompey appointed to install Ptolemy XII Auletes on the Egyptian throne. It was presumably at Pompey's request that Cicero defended him. The case was apparently lost.

5 *If I loosen their hold on me*: he refers to the dynasts.

Letter 44 (*Fam.* V 8)

1 *great enthusiasm . . . in defending*: Crassus had recently left for his consular province of Syria. This letter, sententious and insincere, attempts a reconciliation with a man with whom he had frequently been at odds. See *Fam.* I 9, where Cicero reveals that both Caesar and Pompey had tried to achieve warmer relations between Crassus and himself.

the consuls: the newly elected consuls were L. Domitius Ahenobarbus (hostile to the dynasts) and Appius Claudius Pulcher.

2 *your wife . . . and . . . your sons*: Crassus' wife Tertulla was alleged to be one of Julius Caesar's many sexual conquests (Suetonius, *Julius* 50.1). Of Crassus' two sons, Marcus was serving with Caesar as quaestor, while Publius had accompanied his father to Syria, and in 53 was killed with him at Carrhae.

Letter 45 (*Fam.* VII 5)

Though only three letters to Caesar survive (*Fam.* XIII 15–16 are the others; see Letter 115 in this selection), they reflect the warmth of the relationship, and the remarkable courtesy shown to Cicero by Caesar, who at this time was in Cisalpine Gaul.

1 *Gaius Trebatius*: this jurist and protégé of Cicero is the recipient of seventeen surviving letters from Cicero, fourteen of them dating to

this year 54–53 (*Fam.* VII 6–19; see Letter 47 in this selection). After a restive beginning in Caesar's entourage, he became a valued supporter of the dynast.

because Pompey lingered here: in 55 Pompey had received a five-year command in Spain, and Cicero was to accompany him as legate, but in the event neither went.

hesitation on my own part . . . not unknown to you: Cicero was apprehensive about Clodius' machinations, and in any case Caesar was urging him to stay in Rome (*Q. fr.* II 14.2, 15.2).

2 *Balbus*: L. Cornelius Balbus, a Spaniard, received the citizenship from Pompey in 72, but in 56 his status was challenged by opponents of the Three. He was defended in court by Crassus, Pompey, and Cicero (see Cicero's *Pro Balbo*). After his acquittal he remained in Rome as Caesar's confidential agent.

the son of Marcus Curtius: Cicero had requested that he should be appointed a military tribune; see *Q. fr.* II 14.3, III 1.10.

Lepta: Q. Paconius Lepta became Cicero's Prefect of Engineers in Cilicia, but little is known of his earlier career.

Letter 46 (*Att.* IV 16)

1 *Buthrotum*: see Letter 1.3 n.

2 *Varro*: see Letter 24.5 n. As the first 17 leaves of the *De republica* are lost, it is uncertain whether Cicero fulfilled the promise made in this section to include him in the preface.

my work on oratory: Cicero completed his *De oratore* in late 55. Set in the year 91, it is dominated by the two great orators of that generation, Licinius Crassus and M. Antonius, supported by younger contemporaries and by the aged Scaevola (consul 117).

The Republic: this dialogue, composed in 55–51, was set in the year 129, the year of the death of Scipio Aemilianus, the leading statesman of the period and the dominant figure of the dialogue. Other participants include the Scaevola who appeared also in the *De oratore*.

Aristotle . . . 'Exoterica': these 'popular' treatises, as opposed to the more abstract topics such as logic, physics, and metaphysics, included the works on rhetoric and politics, which were expounded in a more popular way.

3 *the absence of Scaevola*: he appears only in Book 1 of the *De oratore*, as the aged Cephalus does in Plato's *Republic*. Scaevola was about 70 in the year 91.

4 *Pilia's property*: Pilia, the young wife of Atticus, was a friend of Tullia (see *Att.* IV 4A.2).

Vestorius: This business associate of Cicero was a personal friend of Atticus (cf. *Fam.* VI 11.2).

5 *Gaius Cato*: see Letter 34.4 and n. His turbulent activities as tribune in 56 led to his incurring a flurry of indictments, especially as he was

supporting Pompey and Crassus at this time. The Junian-Licinian law of 62 required that copies of proposed legislation should be deposited in the Treasury. The *lex Fufia* regulated the conditions under which magistrates could delay business by citing unpropitious omens. The prosecutors would be happy at his acquittal because they had been pressurized to prosecute by Pompey or Crassus.

Drusus . . . Lucretius: Livius Drusus Claudianus (praetor 50) was accused of collusion with the defence when prosecuting Gaius Cato. The identity of this Lucretius is unknown.

Hirrus . . . Domitius: Lucilius Hirrus was to become tribune in 53 as a supporter of Pompey. Domitius Ahenobarbus was consul in this year (54). The reconciliation doubtless indicated more cordial relations between Pompey and the optimates. The senatorial decree sponsored by the two consuls Domitius and Appius Pulcher is unknown.

6 *your query about Messalla*: this was in connection with the consular elections of 53. By the *lex Licinia* one of the two consuls had to be a plebeian. The two patrician candidates were Valerius Messalla Rufus and Aemilius Scaurus (currently being indicted for extortion in Sardinia by Triarius). The plebeian candidates were Domitius Calvinus and C. Memmius. Messalla and Domitius were elected, but not until July, following much controversy.

until Caesar arrives: he was now preparing his second invasion of Britain.

now that Cato has been acquitted: he and his colleagues could propose postponement of the elections.

7 *'wondrous walls widespread'*: the alliterative description of the cliffs of Dover is a citation (or a take-off) of an unknown source.

8 *Paulus . . . his basilica*: Plutarch (*Caesar* 29.3) states that Aemilius Paulus beautified the old basilica with money donated by Caesar. The second basilica became in due course the *basilica Iulia* (see *Cambridge Ancient History* IX' (Cambridge, 1994), 476).

the state mansion: the Villa Publica was used mainly for official functions and for accommodating foreign ambassadors.

the lex Clodia: in 58 Clodius sponsored a bill depriving censors of the right to depose senators without prior consultation of the Senate.

Eutychides: Eutychides had recently been awarded his freedom by Atticus, and was now 'T. Caecilius', having acquired Atticus' adoptive name.

Letter 47 (*Fam.* VII 7)

For Cicero's young jurist friend Trebatius, see Letter 45.1 n.

1 *Balbus*: see Letter 45.2 n.

to commission a chariot: the quip presupposes the knowledge that the Gallic war-chariot (*essedum*) was much in use in Britain. It could be adapted as a light travelling-carriage.

Letter 48 (*Q. fr.* II 16)

1 *court cases*: in addition to those mentioned in § 3, the *Pro Plancio* and the *Pro Rabirio Postumo* are assigned to this year.

your joint hope or strategy: Cicero's use of *uestrae* rather than *tuae* indicates that Quintus had spoken for Caesar as well as for himself. They were pondering some sort of distinction for Cicero, perhaps the augurate he was awarded in 53–52.

3 *Drusus*: see Letter 46.5 n.

Vatinius: as tribune in 59, he sponsored Caesar's appointment to Cisalpine Gaul and Illyricum, and Pompey's eastern settlement. In 56 he testified against Sestius, which provoked Cicero's *Invective against P. Vatinius*. But pressure from the dynasts compelled Cicero to defend him in this year 54.

The trial of Scaurus: Aemilius Scaurus (praetor 56) was indicted for extortion as governor of Sardinia. Cicero secured his acquittal on that occasion, but not later when he was accused of bribery as a candidate for the consulship of 53.

The Dinner-Party of Sophocles: this was a satyr-play performed after the close of a tragic trilogy. It will have contained libidinous elements which Cicero found undignified.

4 *the verses you ask for*: A section of Cicero's autobiographical poem *De temporibus suis*, detailing his varying fortunes from the glories of his consulship to the humiliation of his exile.

an owl to Athens!: the proverbial equivalent in the scholarly context of 'coals to Newcastle'.

Letter 49 (*Q. fr.* III 3)

1 *Arcanum and Laterium*: these properties of Quintus both lay close to Arpinum. Marcus visited them regularly; see *Q. fr.* II 6.4, III 1.1, III 17.7; Letter 37.4.

2 *the consuls*: Domitius Ahenobarbus and Appius Claudius Pulcher.

Messalla: see Letter 46.6 n.

Sulla . . . Gabinius: On his return from his province of Syria, Gabinius faced various charges. While in Syria, in return for a massive bribe, he had illegally installed Ptolemy XII Auletes on the Egyptian throne. In a letter sent three days after this, Cicero reports that he was acquitted by 38 votes to 32. The Sulla now intent on indicting him for extortion is the man defended by Cicero in 62 under pressure from Pompey.

Letter 50 (*Att.* IV 18)

1 *how I conducted myself*: the first lines of this letter are lost, so that the precise occasion referred to is uncertain. But the encounter with Pompey must have included discussion of Cicero's relations with Gabinius, whose behaviour in illegally installing Ptolemy on the Egyptian throne

prompted Cicero to threaten to indict him. Pompey smoothed over the disagreement.

Lucius Lentulus,: the son of Lentulus Niger, whose death in 55 is recorded with sorrow in Letter 41.1.

2 *a single man*: Pompey.

3 *towards an interregnum*: the prognostication was justified. The new consuls did not take up office until July 53 because of the scandal arising from the elections.

Publius Sulla has indicted him: see Letter 49.2. If the prosecution had succeeded, Sulla could have been restored to the Senate in Gabinius' place.

Marcus Fulvius Nobilior: possibly the Catilinarian cited by Sallust (*Catiline* 17.4).

4 *lex Papia*: this law of 65 expelled aliens from Rome.

the painter Sopolis: on this celebrated artist, see Pliny, *Natural History* 35.147 f. Gabinius Antiochus was doubtless a pupil.

'The state by the law against treason . . .': the text that follows is hopelessly corrupt. Antiochus doubtless contrasted Gabinius' acquittal on a serious charge with his own conviction on a minor one.

Pomptinus: as governor of Narbonese Gaul in 62–59, he had suppressed a rising of the Allobroges, and had awaited a triumph following his return. Since his *imperium* would lapse when he entered the *pomerium*, a law was necessary to authorize its continuance. It was put through at dawn before the legal hour; hence the controversy. Marcus Cato's opposition would be overridden by the dynasts.

Appius plans to go to Cilicia: he became governor there following his consulship. In disreputable bargaining with the consular candidates for 53, the consuls lent their support to these candidates, who in return pledged to fabricate proof of a *lex curiata* approving their appointments.

5 *Pilius*: this kinsman of Atticus' wife Pilia was a devoted Caesarian.

Letter 51 (*Q. fr.* III 7)

1 *'so may the broad earth swallow me!'*: Homer, *Iliad* 4.182 (Cicero cites only the first three words of the Greek passage).

2 *Milo*: he was bidding for the consulship of 52, but the continuing disorders in Rome led the Senate to authorize Pompey to restore order, and he was appointed sole consul in February 52.

'insufferable in his mad career': so Homer's description of Hector at *Iliad* 8.255.

among your subject Nervii: I translate Watt's emendation *Neruiorum* for *neruorum*. Quintus, serving with Caesar, was wintering among the Belgic Nervii; Marcus hopes that he will raise funds from booty.

3 *annoyance to anyone*: in particular, to Caesar.

Messalla as consul—without a trial: it was now December 54, and elections for 53 held under an interrex would be delayed until the new year. Messalla duly became consul then, and could not be indicted until demitting office.

the criterion of impunity: since Gabinius, though clearly guilty, had been acquitted, argues Cicero, so will everyone else be.

4 *your promise of slaves*: they would be brought from Gaul or Britain.

5 *The letter from Vatinius*: Cicero had attacked this creature of the dynasts at the trial of Sestius in 56, but had been pressurized to defend him in the *Pro Vatinio* of 54. No love was lost between them at this time.

6 *the épopée to Caesar*: this epic poem has not survived.

Erigona . . . a devoted dog: for various versions of the Erigone myth, see the *Oxford Classical Dictionary* (3rd edn.). Her dog Naera was proverbially faithful. Quintus' poetic version was lost en route from Gaul.

7 *that building*: see *Q. fr.* III 1 for this acquisition of Quintus near Arpinum. Diphilus as worker is criticized there, while Philotimus is highly regarded.

Arcanum: see Letter 49.1.

Letter 52 (*Att.* V 7)

1 *for each province*: that is, for each of the two Spains.

three days with Pompey: the senatorial decree that Pompey should levy troops to restore public order had Cicero's strong backing. He flaunts here his close relations with the sole consul.

Letter 53 (*Fam.* III 3)

1 *Sulpicius*: Servius Sulpicius Rufus (consul 51) was an eminent lawyer. His refusal to support the application for additional troops for Syria and Cilicia, which was motivated by fear of Parthian attacks, stemmed from the disorders at Rome which required a levy of additional troops by Pompey.

a more benevolent predecessor: Appius Claudius Pulcher, the corrupt governor of Cilicia, is the recipient of 13 extant letters from Cicero (*Fam.* III 1–13; see Letter 57 in this selection). Those addressed to him in the province reflect the dislike between the two men, but the final letters addressed to Appius at Rome indicate a partial reconciliation. Appius indeed dedicated a work on the augurate to Cicero.

2 *Pomptinus*: see Letter 50.4. He had been praetor in the year of Cicero's consulship; here he appears as the governor's senior legate.

Letter 54 (*Att.* V 10)

2 *under the Julian law*: the *lex Iulia de repetundis*, sponsored by Julius Caesar as consul in 59, remained for centuries the statute governing treatment of provincials, protecting them from extortion.

3 *à chacun son métier*: a free rendering of Aristophanes, *Wasps* 1431.

4 *my finances vis-à-vis Caesar and Milo*: in this year Cicero secured a loan of half a million sesterces from Caesar. For his financial support of Milo, see Letter 51.2.

Letter 55 (*Att.* V 11)

2 *Marcellus' behaviour*: after Caesar founded the colony of New Comum in Transpadane Gaul, the consul Marcellus registered his contempt for the new franchise by flogging a citizen there; see Plutarch, *Caesar* 29. Any ex-magistrate of the Latin colony would have enjoyed full citizenship. 'Our friend' here is Pompey.

3 *Pompey . . . intends to go to Spain*: after his consulship of 55, Pompey obtained a five-year command over the two Spains, with the right to administer them *in absentia* through legates. Up to now he had remained in Rome. For his Greek adviser Theophanes, see Letter 19.1 n.

4 *Pomptinus . . . Volusius . . . my quaestor . . . Tullius*: for Pomptinus, see Letter 53.2 n. Volusius and Tullius were lesser members of Cicero's staff. His quaestor was L. Mescinius, who was regarded unfavourably by Cicero during his period as governor.

5 *'Comme maîtresse . . .'*: the Greek proverb means 'like mistress, like dog'.

6 *Appuleius . . . Xeno . . . Patro*: Appuleius is probably the estate-agent of Letter 119.2. Xeno is an Athenian friend of Atticus. Patro is head of the Epicurean school; hence the jocular 'and other block-heads', referring to other members of the school.

Memmius: this Roman exile owned a site on which were the ruins of a house once owned by Epicurus. He had obtained permission from the Areopagus to clear the site and build on it. But Patro, in piety to the founder, was attempting to have the permission rescinded.

Letter 56 (*Att.* V 16)

2 *Laodicea . . . Apamea . . . Synnada*: these were the chief towns in the three Phrygian dioceses attached to the province of Cilicia.

les capitations . . . impôts: these were poll taxes and revenues from local taxation conceded to the tax-farmers.

3 *the Julian law*: see Letter 54.1 and n.

4 *Tarsus*: this leading city of Cilicia, the birthplace of St Paul, had been transferred to Cilicia from Syria by Pompey.

our military camp: not the main camp, which was at Iconium in Lycaonia, but a transit camp at Philomelium in Isauria.

Letter 57 (*Fam.* III 6)

1 *Side*: this harbour town had earlier been the centre of piracy until Pompey settled the pirates inland.

2 *Lucius Clodius*: he was Appius' Prefect of Engineers and adjutant to the commander in the field.

3 *the Cornelian law*: this law of Sulla, *De provinciis ordinandis*, specified the period when the departing governor had to make way for his successor; see § 6 below.

5 *Prefect of Veterans*: the Veterans were an elite force eligible for discharge, but retained or re-enlisted as valuable volunteers.

Letter 58 (*Att.* V 18)

1 *Pacorus . . . Orodes*: following the disastrous defeat of Crassus at Carrhae in 53, the Parthians crossed the Euphrates in a large-scale cavalry-raid under Pacorus. But he was quickly recalled by his father Orodes II, and by 51 the Parthians had withdrawn across the Euphrates. See M. A. R. Colledge, *The Parthians* (London, 1967), 39 ff.

Bibulus: Cicero reports his tardy arrival as governor of Syria, and his military reverse, in Letter 59.4.

Cassius: C. Cassius Longinus, the future tyrannicide, had survived the debacle at Carrhae, and led back the pitiable remnants of the Roman army to organize the defence of Syria.

'between the slaughter and the offering': the proverbial phrase is adopted from the practice at sacrifices of allowing a brief delay between the slaughter of the animal and the offering of the entrails. Cicero fears a sudden decision to extend his period as governor.

2 *Deiotarus*: the tetrarch of western Galatia had been a loyal ally of Pompey, and remained a firm friend of Rome.

3 *The consuls are friendly*: the consuls for the coming year were L. Aemilius Paullus and C. Claudius Marcellus.

4 *your friend Brutus' finances*: Brutus had lent money at interest to Ariobarzanes; see Letter 61.3 below. Cicero had brought from Rome a document of formal recognition of the young king (*Fam.* II 17.7); hence 'my ward'. In the next letter (59.4) Cicero boasts of rescuing the young king from a conspiracy.

Letter 59 (*Att.* V 20)

1 *Pindenissum*: a stronghold in the Amanus mountains, close to 'Alexandria called Issus' in south-east Cilicia. The Saturnalia was 17 December.

my arrival at Ephesus: for his enthusiastic reception there, see *Att.* V 13.

2 *Artavasdes of Armenia*: Artavasdes II had been Rome's ally until Crassus' invasion of Parthia, when he changed sides.

3 *Issus*: the site of the celebrated victory of Alexander over Darius III of Persia in 333 BC.

Cassius: see Letter 58.1 n.

Osaces: though Pacorus was nominally in command of the Parthian force, Dio (2.28.3) states that the true leader was Osaces.

4 *that meaningless title*: Cicero was acclaimed *imperator* by his troops (see § 3).

He began to 'hunt for the laurel-leaf in the wedding-cake': that is, he sought the status of victor (the laurel) without effort. For wedding-cakes baked on laurel-leaves, see Cato, *De re rustica* 151.

6 *the Ligurian Momus*: in Greek literature, Momus is the fault-finding god. The epithet 'Ligurian' may satirically connect the deity with Aelius Ligus, tribune in 58, or some other Ligus.

Ariobarzanes: for what follows, see Letter 58.4 n.

7 *what will happen on 1 March*: on that day the consular provinces would be allotted. Caesar's command was due to expire in 50, and his decision whether to demobilize his troops was awaited; he hoped to become consul in 49. Cicero feared that the crisis would lead to postponement of other provincial appointments, including that of Cilicia. See Letter 60.3.

8 *Laius . . . Quintus Cassius*: nothing is known of these incidents.

9 *his white toga*: Quintus, now 15, resident with Deiotarus, was to receive the toga of manhood.

Alexis . . . Alexis . . . Phemius: the first Alexis is Atticus' secretary, the second is Cicero's counterpart Tiro. Phemius is a talented musician in Atticus' household.

10 *Thermus*: Q. Minucius Thermus was at this time governor of Asia.

Pammenes': a rhetorician, formerly Brutus' tutor (Cicero, *Brutus* 332), now resident in Athens.

Letter 60 (*Att*. V 21)

2 *Cassius*: see Letters 58.1, 59.3. His cousin, Quintus Cassius, became tribune in 49, and joined Caesar, meeting an ignominious end in Spain in 47, where he drowned in the river Ebro.

Orodes . . . Deiotarus . . . Artavasdes: see the nn. to Letters 58–9.

Axius: Q. Axius, a senatorial friend, kept Cicero informed on Roman affairs.

4 *Lentulus' triumph*: Lentulus Spinther, governor of Cilicia 56–53, had waited until now to celebrate his triumph.

5 *the Cibyran panthers*: M. Octavius, curule aedile, was requesting these for his forthcoming games.

Lucius Tullius . . . Quintus Titinius: Titinius, a wealthy friend of Cicero, and a senator, had pressed Tullius as legate upon him.

6 *Volusius . . . to Cyprus*: at Letter 55.4, a Cn. Volusius is mentioned as a member of Cicero's staff. This must be the same man, with one or other *praenomen* incorrectly attributed. He will have held assizes in Cyprus.

7 *two hundred Attic talents*: a considerable sum, equivalent to almost five million sesterces.

I forbid . . . cars to be dedicated to me: these were bronze chariots, which incorporated a statue of the person honoured.

9 *Postumius . . . Postumia*: Postumius cannot be identified with certainty. Postumia was notorious as one of Caesar's sexual conquests (Suctonius, *Julius* 50.1) and as the president of a drinking-party in Catullus (37.1: 'more tipsy than the tipsy grape'). Hence the hint of malice in the implied association with Pomptinus.

10 *Brutus*: the future tyrannicide's financial dealings have figured in Letter 58.4. The account here of his dealings with the Salaminians through the unscrupulous Scaptius puts him in a similarly unfavourable light.

11 *the consulship of Lentulus and Philippus*: 56 BC.

12 *the Gabinian law . . . a decree was passed*: the upshot was that contracts agreed between the parties were legal but had no more validity than the magistrate's edict.

13 *His uncle*: Marcus Cato.

Gaius Julius: presumably Julius Strabo, curule aedile in 90.

14 *relations intimes*: this refers to negotiations concerning Tullia's third marriage. Neither candidate mentioned here, Postumia's son Servius Sulpicius Rufus nor Postidia's candidate (see Letter 61.10), was successful.

Letter 61 (*Att.* VI 1)

1 *the Terminalia*: this festival honouring the god of boundaries was celebrated on 23 February.

3 *Ariobarzanes*: see Letter 58.4 n.

4 *resigning my trusteeship . . . Glabrio*: Cicero wishes to cease acting for Brutus, refusing to squeeze money out of the unfortunate king. He intends to leave the task to the prefects whom he has appointed. The precedent cited of Scaevola's action is not elsewhere attested.

5 *the Salaminians*: see Letter 60.10–11.

for six(?) years: if the text is sound, the debt was contracted in 56.

under the patronage of Cato and of Brutus: they had become its patrons following the annexation of the island, and its incorporation into the province of Cilicia.

7 *Paulus*: L. Aemilius Paulus, a kinsman of Brutus, was consul in this year and a possible successor to Cicero as governor, though he would have had to circumvent Pompey's law prescribing a five-year interval between his magistracy at Rome and a governorship.

8 *'for right is on my side'*: a fragment of Euripides (frag. 918 Nauck).

my six books: these are the books of *De republica*, which Cicero had recently published to general acclaim.

Gnaeus Flavius: mention of him in *De republica* is lost, but Livy (9.46) reports his aedileship in 364, whereas the decemvirs had revised the calendar in 454 (Livy 3.31). Cicero's lame explanation is that the college of pontiffs ('a few persons') had kept the details secret until Flavius published them.

the gesture of the actor: the mention of this in the *De republica* is lost.

9 *I was acclaimed imperator*: see Letter 59.3.

10 '*If only you had returned . . . old crowd*': this evocation of Terence, *Eunuch* 1084, is qutoed in connection with Tullia's future betrothal; see Letter 60.14. Reference to the letter of Memmius remains obscure.

Saufeius . . . Appius . . . Bursa: Bursa was a supporter of Cicero's enemy Clodius, and was implicated in the rioting which followed Clodius' death; Cicero prosecuted him on a charge of violence. Appius, Saufeius' brother, presumably supported Cicero in the indictment.

11 *Furnius' proposed exception*: as tribune, this supporter of Cicero was willing to block proposals for extension of Cicero's tenure unless there was a Parthian invasion.

12 *Isocrates . . . Ephorus . . . Theopompus*: Cicero recounts this anecdote in *De oratore* 3.36 and *Brutus* 204. Isocrates (436–338), the outstanding rhetorician of the day, numbered among his students the celebrated historians Theopompus (author of *Hellenika* and *Philippics*) and Ephorus, who compiled a universal history. The fact that they were fellow-pupils makes the comparison with the young Ciceros appropriate.

the Liberalia: the festival honouring the Italian deities Liber and Libera was held on 17 March.

intercalation: responsibility for adjusting the calendar by adding a month every second year lay with the college of pontiffs, who at this time were so remiss that in 46 the calendar was two and a half months behind the seasons. Caesar extended that year by three months, and inaugurated the Julian calendar in 45.

13 *Thermus . . . Silius . . . Nonius . . . Bibulus . . . Scrofa*: governors of eastern provinces, Thermus of Asia, Silius of Bithynia, and Bibulus of Syria. Nonius and Scrofa presumably governed Macedonia and Crete respectively.

Amianus . . . Terentius . . . Moeragenes: runaway slaves.

14 *Cassius sent a foolish dispatch*: cf. Letter 60.2.

Deiotarus: see Letter 58.2 n.

Pompey . . . his concern: a long-term intention.

15 *Bibulus' edict . . . the edict . . . of Quintus Mucius*: Atticus' criticism suggests that Bibulus' edict restricted the activities of the tax-farmers. Quintus Mucius Scaevola (consul 95) was the most famous legal authority of the late republic.

Turpio . . . Vettius: provincial juries, Cicero suggests, are not inferior to those in Rome.

16 *even by Servilius!*: P. Servilius Isauricus, consul in 79 and thereafter governor of Cilicia, was regarded as a man of probity.

you know the rest: the saying has not survived, but presumably a phrase such as 'hoodwink you' is to be supplied.

17 *Africanus' statue*: Metellus Scipio incorrectly identified the three statues of Scipio Aemilius Africanus (consul 147, censor 142) as those of his great-grandfather Nasica Sarapio (consul 138). The third statue, erected by Metellus Scipio himself, was wrongly inscribed with the name of his great-grandfather.

18 *Flavius and the calendar*: see § 8 above.

Eupolis . . . Eratosthenes . . . Duris of Samos: the anecdote about Eupolis being drowned by Alcibiades is nowhere else attested. Eratosthenes (*c*.285–194) was the celebrated scholar and head of the Alexandrian library. The historical writings of Duris of Samos (*c*.340–*c*.260), which have not survived, were frequently criticized for sensational and tragic effects.

Zaleucus . . . Theophrastus . . . Timaeus: see Cicero, *The Laws* 2.15.

19 *Philotimus . . . Camillus*: Philotimus, a freedman of Terentia closely concerned with family finances, is frequently criticized by Cicero in his letters (see e.g. Letter 62.3). Camillus is a friend of Cicero who is well versed in business law.

21 *Marcus Octavius . . . Caelius*: for Octavius and the panthers, see Letter 60.5. Caelius Rufus, successfully defended by Cicero in the extant *Pro Caelio*, was an aedile in 50, and was pestering Cicero for panthers and finances for his games. A letter written to Caelius a few weeks after this in response to the request (*Fam.* II 11) is much more accommodating and jocular.

22 *Lepta*: Paconius Lepta was Cicero's Prefect of Engineers in the province, and was thereafter a firm friend.

that most celebrated oath: on the closing day of his consulship, when he was prevented by the tribune Nepos from making a valedictory speech to the Assembly, Cicero took the oath in ringing tones to declare that he had fulfilled the office according to the laws. See Letter 4.7.

I was magnus: a veritable Pompey in civilian dress!

or pour bronze: Homer, *Iliad* 6.236.

23 *unencumbered*: that is, free of debts, which they are discharging by sales of property. The quotation that follows is from Homer, *Iliad* 7.93, probably with reference to confession of debts.

25 *fifty talents out of Caesar*: text and sense are uncertain, but Caesar has doubtless donated money for public works. He owed Pompey money, which would explain Pompey's displeasure. For Caesar's mansion by Lake Nemi, see Suetonius, *Julius* 46.

Vedius: Augustus has a friend of that name who was said to feed slaves to his eels (Pliny, *Natural History* 9.77).

Curio: Scribonius Curio, earlier a supporter of Clodius, was at this time allied with the optimates. In 50 as tribune he sought to have both Caesar and Pompey disarmed, but the consul Marcellus refused to accept the proposal. In 49 he joined Caesar, and tried to win over Cicero, who wrote seven extant letters to him. There is no record of the passage of this bill.

Pompeius Vindillus' . . . Vennonius: Vindillus was probably a freedman of Pompey. Cicero may have got this anecdote from his friend Vennonius.

'brutish' enough to be associated with Vedius: 'brutish' because the lady was the half-sister of Brutus, and *lepidus* because her husband was Aemilius Lepidus.

26 *the Roman mysteries*: see Letter 60.14.

the 765th day after . . . Leuctra: a joking reference to the street-battle between Clodius and Milo, in which Clodius was killed on 18 January 52. The famous battle of Leuctra, in which Thebes defeated Sparta, took place in 371.

Letter 62 (*Att.* VI 4)

1 *Mescinius . . . Coelius*: Coelius Caldus came out from Rome to succeed Mescinius Rufus as quaestor, but he had not yet arrived.

3 *My wife's freedman*: Philotimus; see Letter 61.19 n.

the Crotonian tyrannicide's property: Milo is jocosely so cited as the assassin of Clodius, and as homonymous with Milo the famous athlete from Croton. When Cicero's friend was condemned and exiled, his property was sold, and Cicero was negotiating for its purchase.

Letter 63 (*Fam.* XV 6)

This letter is in reply to the extant epistle from Cato (*Fam.* XV 5) which reveals that in a speech in the Senate Cato had praised Cicero's performance as governor, but had opposed his application for a triumph. The high-flown compliments in this reply mask Cicero's disappointment, not to say resentment.

1 *Hector in Naevius*: see Letter 40.7 n.

your school: Cato was famed as an adherent of the Stoics.

2 *the drafting of the supplication*: this was the formal application for a triumph, customarily framed by the applicant's supporters.

Letter 64 (*Att.* VI 6)

1 *his accuser*: P. Cornelius Dolabella, a dissolute patrician, had divorced his wife in 50 prior to marrying Tullia. In 46 he divorced her in turn, defaulting in the repayment of her dowry. His indictment of Appius was predictably unsuccessful.

Tiberius Nero: Ti. Claudius Nero was quaestor in 48.

Notes to Pages *145–149* 317

2 *not largesse . . . but generosity*: in a section of his *De republica* now lost, Cicero condemned ambitious politicians who sought to win votes by such free distribution of corn.

Hortensius: Cicero had heard from Caelius Rufus (*Fam.* VIII 13.2) that the optimate leader was close to death. Later at Rhodes he heard that he had died (*Brutus* 1).

3 *Coelius*: see Letter 62.1 n. A letter to Caelius Rufus (*Fam.* II 15) also discusses the appointment of the young Coelius as temporary governor.

this fellow was a governor for three years: Quintus was governor of Asia 61–58.

4 *Pompey . . . Caesar*: Pompey's nominee, Q. Cassius Longinus, governed Further Spain in Pompey's absence in 52. Mark Antony as quaestor commanded the army in winter quarters in 51 (Caesar, *Gallic War* 8.2).

Letter 65 (*Fam.* XIV 5)

1 *Do travel as far as you possibly can*: Terentia went to Brundisium to meet them (*Fam.* XVI 9.2).

2 *The bequest of Precius*: after a brief expression of regret at the death of Precius (otherwise unknown), Cicero shows more concern that Philotimus, Terentia's grasping freedman, should not handle the bequest. See Letter 61.19 n.; also *Att.* VI 9.2.

Letter 66 (*Att.* VII 1)

1 *Saufeius*: see Letter 61.10. Like his friend Atticus, Saufeius was an Epicurean; hence the joking comment on 'the slow progress of philosophers'.

you know whom: Pompey. This letter documents Cicero's anxiety to maintain good relations with both dynasts.

2 *But never . . . within my breast*: cf Homer, *Odyssey* 9.33, where both Calypso and Circe fail to prevail on Odysseus.

4 *the acceptance of Caesar as candidate in his absence*: that is, for the consulship of 48. The college of tribunes had unanimously sponsored a law allowing Caesar to stand *in absentia*.

at Ravenna: we are to assume that Cicero met Caesar at Ravenna, and that he agreed to urge Caelius Rufus as tribune not to veto the proposal.

that third consulship: that of 52, following those of 70 and 55; 'bestowed by heaven' is heavily ironical.

'the Trojans . . . with his reproaches': Homer, *Iliad* 22.105, 100. Polydamas was noteworthy for his sage advice to Hector, as Atticus was to Cicero.

5 *the two previous consulships*: those of 51 and 50.

'to allow the idiot . . . first': the source of this ancient equivalent of 'fools rush in' is unknown.

6 *Thucydides' phrase*: see Thucydides 1.97.2.

7 *The person who opposed it*: Marcus Cato; cf. Letter 63 n.

7–8 *Favonius . . . Hirrus . . . Scrofa . . . Silius*: Favonius (praetor 49; 'Cato's ape') and Hirrus (on whom, see Letter 46.5 and n.) followed Cato's lead, while Scofa and Silius supported Cicero.

9 *that fellow*: Philotimus. 'Lartidius' must be a stage villain, but the source is unknown.

'But let us . . . forget what is done': Homer, *Iliad* 18.112, 19.65.

Letter 67 (*Att*. VII 4)

2 *Hirtius*: as an influential aide of Caesar, he later obtained the praetorship in 46 and the consulship in 43. After the assassination of Caesar, Cicero persuaded him to oppose Mark Antony. He died at the siege of Mutina in 43.

Balbus had decided to visit Scipio: Cornelius Balbus had earlier transferred his allegiance from Pompey to Caesar, and acted as Caesar's agent in Rome. At this time he plays the role of mediator. Metellus Scipio (consul 52) was a supporter of Pompey. This projected meeting was to further negotiations between the dynasts.

3 *awarded a second consulship*: this offer of the consulship for 48 depended on Caesar's disbanding his troops.

Letter 68 (*Fam*. XVI 11)

Twenty-seven letters (*Fam*. XVI 1–27) are addressed to Cicero's secretary Tiro. They date from April 53 to December 44.

1 *quartan fever*: breaking out every third day, it had earlier been tertian (every other day).

the inconvenience of sea-sickness: Tiro was recuperating at Patrae on the west coast of the Peloponnese.

2 *into the blaze of civil discord*: Caesar had crossed the Rubicon on the day before this letter was written; news of it had not yet reached Cicero.

a threatening and bitter letter: Appian (*Civil Wars* 2.32) reports the gist of the letter delivered by Curio to the new consuls on 1 January. After listing his achievements, Caesar offered to resign his command if Pompey did likewise, and a threat that if Pompey did not comply, he would avenge the wrongs suffered by the country and by himself.

Antony, and Quintus Cassius: they were both tribunes. Appian (*Civil Wars* 2.33) reports that the consuls ordered the tribunes out of the Senate. Caelius Rufus, hitherto a supporter of Cicero, accompanied them to join Caesar at Ravenna.

3 *I have taken on Capua*: the purpose of this allocation of regions was to levy troops. Cicero, however, swiftly retired to his residences.

Letter 69 (*Att.* VII 10)

1 *the laurelled lictors*: Cicero as *imperator* was entitled to these attendants, but they would have made his movements conspicuous.

stands paralysed in the Italian townships: Pompey had quitted the capital on news of Caesar's impending arrival.

Letter 70 (*Fam.* XIV 18)

1 *Dolabella*: see Letter 64.1 n.

2 *Philotimus*: for Terentia's freedman, see Letter 61.19 n.

Letter 71 (*Att.* VII 17)

1 *heading for Spain*: this was Pompey's province, which he was governing *in absentia* by virtue of his five-year command.

you and Sextus can . . . remain in Rome: in public, Atticus always played the benevolent neutral. Sextus Peducaeus was likewise uncommitted.

property values so low at Rome: Atticus owned several properties in the capital (so Nepos, *Atticus* 14.3), the value of which will have tumbled in the present crisis.

2 *Lucius Caesar*: this son of the consul of 64 was serving with Pompey, and was attempting to mediate with Caesar.

our friend Sestius: with Milo in the 50s he promoted Cicero's return from exile, and fought against Clodius in street-battles. Twice indicted, in 56 and 54, he was defended by Cicero and acquitted. He succeeded Cicero as governor of Cilicia, but subsequently joined Caesar.

3 *Trebatius*: see Letter 45.1 n.

Dolabella or Caelius: see Letters 64.1 n., 68.2 n.

Letter 72 (*Att.* VIII 8)

2 *a letter from Domitius*: Domitius Ahenobarbus (consul 54 and now governor of Cisalpine Gaul) was in command of a large garrison at Corfinium. Pompey was at Luceria, 150 miles away. He urged Domitius to hasten to join him. But Domitius pigheadedly opted to stay. His resistance to Caesar was short-lived. The extant letters of Pompey to Domitius and to the consuls (*Fam.* VIII 12A–D) present a contrasting picture to Cicero's condemnation of Pompey.

Therefore . . . right is on my side: these lines are in origin a passage of Euripides, adapted by Aristophanes, *Acharnians* 650 ff.

Letter 73 (*Att.* VIII 13)

1 *If Caesar has met our Pompey there*: in fact, Pompey refused to meet Caesar. He set sail for Greece on 17 March (26 January by the Julian calendar).

2 *favour the man they feared*: the support for Caesar throughout Italy was a vital factor in his success.

Letter 74 (*Att.* VIII 16)

1 *on this side*: on the western coast, from Formiae.

Philotimus' letters inform me: in spite of Cicero's distrust of the financial dealings of Terentia's freedman, he was clearly his regular informant.

vows on behalf of Pompey: he had been seriously ill in the summer of 50.

2 *this Pisistratus*: Caesar is compared with the tyrant who ruled Athens benevolently for more than thirty years till his death in 527.

Caesar's crafty clemency: the *clementia Caesaris*, a central feature of his policy towards political opponents, ultimately resulted in his murder.

the Body of 360: the panel of jurymen chosen by Pompey for the trial of Milo and others in 52.

'I fear the Trojans': see Homer, *Iliad* 22.105, where Hector refuses to withdraw from the challenge of Achilles out of fear for the criticism of fellow-Trojans.

on the Appian Way . . . to Arpinum: Cicero proposes to avoid an encounter with Caesar by heading eastward away from the road from Capua to Rome.

Letter 75 (*Att.* IX 6)

1 *the consul Lentulus*: this inveterate foe of Caesar had been appointed governor of Asia by the Senate. He brought over two legions from his province to Dyrrhachium, and resisted blandishments to join Caesar.

the younger Balbus: this nephew of Caesar's agent in Rome was, like his uncle, active in diplomacy on behalf of Caesar.

the six cohorts . . . at Alba: see Caesar, *Civil War* 1.24. Vibius Curius was an officer in Caesar's army whom Cicero had earlier defended in court (see § 2). The Minucian Way (*via Minucia*) joined Brundisium to Beneventum.

the white toga: the toga of manhood.

2 *Domitius is in his residence at Cosa*: Caesar had released him after the fall of Corfinium.

3 *Pompey has sailed*: the information is incorrect. Pompey did not sail until 17 March, but an advance party under the consuls sailed a fortnight earlier. See Caesar, *Civil War* 1.25. For the exaggeration of the number of troops, see Letter 76.2. Clodia, mother-in-law of the tribune Lucius Metellus and wife of the consul of 68, was one of Clodius' three sisters.

4 *My heart . . . I am tortured*: Homer, *Iliad* 10.93 f.

6 *Furnius*: as tribune in 51 he had been a reliable supporter of Cicero; see Letters 58.3, 61.11.

the son of Quintus Titinius: the father was a senator and influential friend of Cicero; see Letter 60.5 and n.

his letter: Caesar's brief note is extant (*Att.* IX 6A). Letter 76 reviews the content.

'Two heads together . . .': Homer, *Iliad* 10.234: 'Two heads together grasp advantages which one would miss.'

7 *the popular path*: appeasement of Caesar.

Letter 76 (*Att.* IX 9)

1 *our friend*: Pompey.

the role of sophiste: the Greek sophists examined the different sides of an argument. Cicero contemplates the choices lying before him. In particular he reviews his attitude towards the optimates. The saying 'Dionysius in Corinth' recalls that the Syracusan tyrant when expelled became a schoolmaster in Corinth ('To such a degree was he unable to forgo the right to rule', *Tusculans* 3.27). The younger Titinius (see Letter 75.6) likewise seeks power with Caesar.

2 *Clodia has exaggerated*: see Letter 75.3.

Demetrius' work On Concord: The reference is not to Demetrius of Phalerum, but to a contemporary of Cicero's, Demetrius of Magnesia (see *Att.* IV 11.2, VIII 11.7). Cicero returns this book as being no longer appropriate to his role.

not on conjecture, but on conversations: the Pompeian strategy is revealed here.

the north wind: Atticus feared that it would carry Pompey's ships to Epirus, resulting in plundering by the troops.

Bibulus came: from Syria, where he was governor 51–49. He came to join Pompey, who appointed him to command a fleet which tried unsuccessfully to prevent Caesar's crossing.

3 *Domitius*: see Letter 75.2.

that most despicable . . . individual: not identified.

our augural books: Gellius (13.5.4) cites Messalla, *De auspiciis*, to confirm that the augural books are the authoritative source for this procedure.

Galba . . . Antony: though these four are augurs, Caesar prefers to have Cicero as spokesman for the college.

'Then may the broad earth swallow me': Homer, *Iliad* 4.182.

4 *Trebatius*: see Letter 45.1 n.

5 *Phamea's death*: he had lent his services to Cicero's campaign for the consulship.

Precius: for his legacy, see Letter 65.2.

Letter 77 (*Att.* IX 11A)

This letter to Caesar is included in the Atticus-correspondence because Cicero forwarded a copy of it to his friend.

1 *Furnius*: see Letter 75.6 n.

2 *the distinction*: the consulship.

3 *Lentulus' saviour*: Lentulus Spinther as consul in 57 had been active in the restoration of Cicero. He was released by Caesar at Corfinium, together with Domitius and other senators.

Letter 78 (*Att.* IX 18)

my discussion with him: this is the celebrated account of the meeting with Caesar in March 49.

2 *among them the héros Celer*: Pilius Celer was a relative of Atticus' wife Pilia. In an earlier letter (*Att.* IX 10.7), Atticus is said to have described Caesar's entourage as 'this underworld'. The Underworld is the name used by Homer, *Odyssey* 11, for the place where ghostly heroes rise from Hades to converse with Odysseus. Cicero here sardonically includes Celer among them.

the son of Servius and the son of Titinius: both fathers, Servius Sulpicius Rufus (consul 51) and Q. Titinius, were staunch senatorials.

3 *I await that swallow's gazouillement*: Atticus had optimistically envisaged the impending meeting with Caesar as the swallow's twittering, heralding the spring of a sunnier future.

Letter 79 (*Fam.* IV 1)

Servius Sulpicius Rufus (consul 51) was, after Scaevola, the most eminent lawyer of the late republic. In politics he was a cautious Pompeian. Eighteen letters to him and two from him (one of them the famous consolation on the death of Tullia, *Fam.* IV 5) have survived.

1 *in the neighbourhood of Rome*: Cicero was awaiting his triumph, and could not enter the city.

or rather, the gathering of senators: since the consuls and many senators had departed with Pompey, Cicero was unwilling to regard the rump as representative of the true Senate.

the man who was begging me: Caesar.

Letter 80 (*Att.* X 10)

1 *keeping my son-in-law in mind*: Cicero refers to the fact that Dolabella was working for Caesar.

2 *Your plan*: perhaps the text should be emended to 'Your friends' plan' (so Beaujeu).

3 *Voilà une dépêche laconienne!*: by a 'Laconian dispatch', Cicero indicates its Spartan brevity and bluntness.

Curio: see Letter 61.25 n. Scribonius Curio, soon to govern Sicily for Caesar, was encouraging Cicero to retire to Greece, and expressed confidence that Caesar would approve. He offered to facilitate the journey; see *Att.* X 4.9 ff.

Your dysurie: Atticus was having trouble passing urine.

4 *the news . . . about the Massilians*: that free city had closed its gates against Caesar, who had arrived before it in mid-April (Caesar, *Civil War* 1.14).

Ocella: but this friend of Cicero never appeared (*Att.* X 17.3).

5 *This fellow*: Antony, though married at this time to Antonia, was cavorting everywhere with the freedwoman Cytheris (Plutarch, *Antony* 9).

6 *our young man*: the letters of this time mark the beginning of young Quintus' estrangement from his uncle.

Letter 81 (*Att.* X 14)

1 *Servius*: for Servius Sulpicius, see Letter 79 n.

2 *the report of the two legions*: at *Att.* X 12A, written a couple of days before this letter, Cicero reports that the legions recruited by Caesar in Italy have become disaffected.

3 *I am taking thought about Caelius*: for this mysterious reference to Caelius, see Shackleton Bailey's appendix VI to volume IV of his *Cicero's Letters to Atticus*, where he argues that Caelius is a code word for a project to establish in Africa a force to further the prospect of peace.

Letter 82 (*Fam.* XIV 7)

Caieta: this harbour, from which Cicero now decided to sail to Greece, lay on the coast of Latium, and was the scene of his later murder on the orders of Mark Antony.

1 *dear Tullia*: a letter to Atticus in mid-May (*Att.* X 18) reported that Tullia had given birth to a boy. He was a weakly baby, and did not survive for long.

Letter 83 (*Att.* XI 1)

1 *my private affairs*: the letters surviving from this period in late 49 and early 48 do not discuss political matters. Cicero is preoccupied with his debts. The person criticized here, as often elsewhere, is Terentia's freedman Philotimus.

2 *cistophori*: the Asian currency referred to here probably dates from the time of Quintus' governorship of Asia.

Letter 84 (*Att.* XI 2)

2 *the dowry*: following Tullia's marriage to Dolabella, the second instalment of the dowry to be paid over to him was due on 1 July.

the 60,000 sesterces: it has been suggested that Terentia was implicated in this transaction.

3 *more secure where it is*: it had been loaned to Pompey.

Chrysippus: Vettius Chrysippus was a freedman of Cicero's friend, the architect Vettius Cyrus (on whom see Letter 18.2 and n.). Cicero may have feared that his house would be confiscated by the Caesarians.

Letter 85 (*Att.* XI 3)

1 *my wishes concerning 1 July*: see Letter 84.2 n. Cicero feared that if he paid over the money, he might not get it back in the likely event of a divorce. But he was anxious to avoid a break with Dolabella, now on Caesar's staff.

2 *particular misfortunes*: marital problems are beginning to loom large.

3 *Egnatius*: Cicero regarded this Roman knight as trustworthy in business relations; see *Fam.* XIII 43.1.

the person I accompany here: Pompey. Cicero is chary of naming him in case the letter is intercepted.

Letter 86 (*Att.* XI 4A)

1 *my particular wish*: probably the payment of the second instalment of Tullia's marriage-dowry.

the person who is directing operations: Pompey.

Brutus: the future tyrannicide, after earlier attacking Pompey for aspiring to dictatorship, was formally reconciled to him in 49 and espoused the republican cause.

Letter 87 (*Att.* XI 4)

1 *I have . . . avoided every commission*: Cicero refused to take any part in the raising of the blockade of Dyrrhachium, which was successfully achieved a few days later than this letter.

Letter 88 (*Fam.* XIV 12)

1 *my safe arrival in Italy*: following Pompey's defeat at Pharsalus in August 48, Cicero, who had remained at Dyrrhachium with Cato pleading sickness, refused Cato's invitation to take over the command and opted to return to Italy (Plutarch, *Cicero* 39). He came close to assassination at the hands of the young Pompey.

Letter 89 (*Att.* XI 5)

2 *by travelling at night*: Atticus had made this suggestion so that Cicero might evade the attentions of the Caesarians, who were in control of Italy.

3 *Basilus . . . Servilius*: Minucius Basilus was a legate of Caesar in both the Gallic and the Civil Wars. Servilius Isauricus shared the consulship with Caesar in 48.

4 *Vatinius*: a faithful supporter of Caesar since his tribunate in 59, he was rewarded for his services in Gaul and in the Civil War with the consulship of 47.

Letter 90 (*Att.* XI 6)

2 *the association with barbaric nations*: Caesar (*Civil War* 3.3 ff.) makes great play with the army of foreigners serving with Pompey.

until I was summoned: that is, back to Italy by Caesar. In Letter 91.2 he claims that Caesar had already instructed Dolabella to welcome him back, but the Caesarians proclaimed ignorance of this.

without the lictors: Atticus had recommended an unobtrusive journey, but Cicero was reluctant to dispense with the symbols of his status.

3 *Balbus and Oppius*: Caesarians sympathetic towards Cicero.

Trebonius, Pansa: Trebonius as tribune in 55 proposed the five-year commands for the dynasts, and subsequently fought as legate of Caesar in Gaul and in the Civil War. Pansa likewise served with Caesar in Gaul. He held the consulship in 43.

5 *Pompey would meet his end*: he was murdered on disembarking in Egypt in September 48.

6 *Fannius*: as tribune in 59 he had opposed the dynasts. After his praetorship he was appointed governor of Asia in 49. This report of his death was ill-founded.

Lucius Lentulus: appointed as governor of Asia for 48 after his consulship of 49, Lentulus Crus brought two legions from his province to join Pompey at Dyrrhachium.

Letter 91 (*Att.* XI 7)

1 *your comrades' wishes*: those of Balbus and Oppius.

Sestius: see Letter 71.2 n. Appointed governor of Cilicia in 49, he may never have set foot there. After Pharsalus he crossed over from the republicans to join Caesar.

2 *Antony*: Caesar left him as Master of Horse to control Italy.

Lucius Metellus: as tribune in 49, Metellus Creticus sought to veto all proposals favouring Caesar, including that allocating the money left in the Treasury after Pompey's precipitate departure.

Laelius: the tribune of 54 had like Cicero made his way back to Italy after Pharsalus. See Letters 94.1, 95.2.

3 *the recent occurrence*: Pompey's death.

a most treacherous race: the Numidians.

4 *Sulpicius' decision . . . that of Cato*: after Pharsalus, Servius Sulpicius retired to Samos (see *Brutus* 156). Cato continued the fight in Africa.

6 *you are being harried*: by the creditors of Tullia, who was in dire financial straits.

7 *they will see Caesar*: Cicero expected Caesar to tour the eastern provinces after the Alexandrian War, so a meeting with Quintus was feasible.

Letter 92 (*Fam.* XIV 16)

This is one of fifteen surviving letters to Terentia from Brundisium. They are all curt and loveless, but offer no hint of the impending divorce.

1 *Volumnia*: perhaps Volumnia Cytheris, mistress of Antony (see Letter 80.5).

Letter 93 (*Att.* XI 12)

1 *bitter words and gestures*: this was at Patrae; cf. Letter 89.4.

3 *Spain is now combining with Africa*: in spite of Caesar's earlier successes in Spain, when his legate Trebonius arrived there to take over the province, he was forced out by the mutineers.

4 *do what you have often done*: in other words, send letters on Cicero's behalf and in his name.

the splendid exploits of my son-in-law: an ironical observation on Dolabella's undistinguished operations in Caesar's interests.

Letter 94 (*Att.* XI 14)

2 *in view of the son-in-law I have*: Dolabella's activities on Caesar's behalf will not have endeared him to republican senators. Moreover, as tribune for 47, Dolabella caused mayhem by proposing cancellation of debts.

3 *Pansa and Hirtius*: for Pansa, see Letter 90.3 n. Hirtius, another Caesarian on friendly terms with Cicero, was at Antioch in early 47, and must have met Quintus then.

Minucius: Atticus was negotiating a loan from him on Cicero's behalf.

Letter 95 (*Att.* XI 15)

1 *Caesar . . . held up at Alexandria*: after pursuing Pompey to Egypt, Caesar became embroiled in the family dispute between Cleopatra and Ptolemy, children of Auletes. The Alexandrian War delayed him there from September 48 to March 47, and (more dubiously) a trip up the Nile with Cleopatra may have delayed him for a further three months.

apart from one other: Laelius; see Letter 91.2 n.

2 *Minucius*: see Letter 94.3 n.

made overtures to Fufius: the Pompeians in Achaia surrendered to Fufius Calenus (consul 47), whom Caesar deputed to take over there.

Gaius Cassius: for the earlier career of the tyrannicide, see Letter 58.1 n. His decision to throw in his lot with Caesar at this time was probably taken at Tarsus.

3 *Aesopus' son*: Aesopus was a celebrated tragic actor who had taught Cicero elocution, and who had worked for his restoration from exile. His son Clodius Aesopus, a profligate spendthrift, had a sexual relationship with Caecilia Metella, a notorious adulteress (see Horace, *Satires* 2.3.239).

Letter 96 (*Fam.* XIV 11)

1 *sending our Cicero to Caesar*: Cicero was proposing to send his son to Alexandria to seek an amnesty from Caesar. The visit did not materialize, since young Marcus, who had served as a cavalry-officer at Pharsalus, was still abroad (see *Fam.* XIV 15).

Gnaeus Sallustius: in Letter 98.2 Cicero mentions that he has been pardoned by Caesar.

Letter 97 (*Att.* XI 18)

2 *these associates of yours*: the leading Caesarians.

Letter 98 (*Att.* XI 20)

1 *a freedman of Gaius Trebonius . . . from Pierian Seleucia*: Trebonius (Letter 90.3 n.), the trusty Caesarian, was in Spain at this time. Pierian Seleucia lay on the coast of Syria at the mouth of the Orontes.

Hirtius: see Letter 94.3 n.

2 *If he does so*: Cicero had hoped to meet Caesar when he disembarked at Brundisium. But the reassuring letter from him (see Letter 99) persuaded him that it was safe to proceed to Rome.

Letter 100 (*Fam.* XV 15)

1 *we each sought to withdraw*: for Cassius Longinus' decision to join Caesar, see Letter 95.2 n.

the outcome of a single battle: Pharsalus.

2 *the little-known Pharnaces*: Pharnaces II, son of Mithradates VI Eupator, had been placed on the throne of Bosporus by Pompey. But when Rome was distracted by civil war, he overran several countries in Asia Minor while Caesar was occupied with Alexandria, and defeated a Roman army under Domitius Calvinus. Caesar subsequently routed him at Zela ('Veni, vidi, vici') in Pontus.

3 *our sponsor*: Caesar.

4 *that first letter . . . from Luceria*: Pompey had set up camp there before moving to Brundisium in 49. The letter presumably advised Cicero to stay in Rome rather than to join Pompey.

Letter 101 (*Fam.* IX 1)

2 *I am reconciled . . . with my books*: Varro has earlier in these letters appeared primarily as a supporter of Pompey, though his eminence as a writer is signalled at Letter 46.2. But now that he has been granted clemency by Caesar, Cicero seeks to engage the polymath as scholar to scholar.

Letter 102 (*Fam.* XIII 29)

1 *I am especially close to you*: Plancus (consul 42), the recipient of fifteen surviving letters from this time on, was serving with Caesar in Africa at

this time. Later, as city-prefect in 45, he supervised the confiscation of properties, and may already have had influence with Caesar in cases such as this.

2 *Capito*: tribune in 55. Two later letters to him have survived (*Fam.* XVI 16D and F).

3 *Titus Antistius*: otherwise unknown.

no successor appeared: no successor, that is, to the outgoing governor, who left Antistius in temporary charge.

Pompey entered the province: after crossing from Brundisium in March 49, Pompey spent a year in Macedonia marshalling his forces.

4 *Aulus Plautius*: praetor in 51, he was probably governor of Bithynia at this time.

when Paullus and Marcellus were consuls: in 50 BC.

8 *among your circle*: Cicero's plea appears to have been successful; see *Att.* XVI 16C, 16F.

Letter 103 (*Att.* XII 2)

1 *Murcus*: the rumour was false, for he became praetor in 45. He was a legate of Caesar.

Asinius: the celebrated littérateur Asinius Pollio served with Caesar's forces throughout the Civil War. The reference here is cryptic.

no sign of Pompeius: Pompey's elder son, Gnaeus, after Pharsalus toured Africa, the Balearics (modern Majorca and Minorca), and Spain. Paciaecus was a Caesarian supporter from Further Spain.

2 *games at Praeneste*: the date of this letter is uncertain. If it was written in early April, the games may have been held away from Rome to avoid a clash with the Ludi Cereales (12–19 April). The reference to 'the business' below must refer to the political settlement at Rome.

Balbus . . . il s'en fiche de tout cela: this Caesarian 'couldn't care less'. As an Epicurean whose aim in life was pleasure rather than virtue, he is little concerned with public rather than private concerns.

Le problème: the problem is uncertain. Cicero may be referring to a projected literary work in honour of Caesar.

Letter 104 (*Fam.* V 21)

Mescinius Rufus had served as quaestor under Cicero in Cilicia (*Fam.* XIII 26). He had now arrived back in Italy after fighting under Pompey in Greece.

2 *that person of whom you were never fond*: Pompey.

3 *awaiting events in Africa*: news of the battle at Thapsus and the subsequent suicide of Cato in April 46 had not yet reached Rome.

your injustice: Mescinius had suffered confiscation of his properties.

4 *we are to despise it*: the theme of despising death is to dominate Book 1 of Cicero's *Tusculans*, which Cicero wrote in June–August 45.

5 *other than guilt or sin*: in early spring of 46 Cicero composed the *Stoic Paradoxes*, the third of which discusses sin and virtue.

Letter 105 (*Fam.* IX 7)

1 *at Seius' house*: Seius was an equestrian friend of Cicero and Atticus.

the time now seems ripe to go: news of the events in Africa had now reached Rome.

'When two men march in step . . .': Homer, *Iliad* 10.224.

Lucius Caesar junior: Cato had appointed him commander at Utica. After Cato's suicide, he opened the gates to Caesar and was murdered by Caesarian troops.

What then has he in store for me . . .?: with this quotation from Terence, *Andria* 112, Cicero appears (unjustly) to assume that Caesar had ordered the murder, and wonders what lies in store for himself.

2 *The bristling Afric land's . . . tumult*: Ennius, *Annals*, frag. 306 Warmington.

no chose indifférente: in Stoic philosophy, virtue is the only good and vice the only evil; all else are 'things indifferent'.

Baiae . . . via Sardinia . . . via Sicily: Caesar in fact came via Sardinia to Ostia, leaving Africa on 13 June, and delaying his arrival in Rome until 25 July (*African War* 98).

Dolabella: Cicero's son-in-law (the divorce was to be finalized in November 46) arrived in Rome in mid-June. The source of the ironical Greek quotation which follows is unknown.

Letter 106 (*Fam.* IX 18)

Paetus, a Neapolitan friend of Cicero, is the recipient of a dozen extant letters.

1 *my pupils to meet their friend*: the joking comment describes the departure of Hirtius and Dolabella from Tusculum to meet Caesar on his return from Africa to Rome.

like the tyrant Dionysius: see Letter 76.1 n.

2 *Lentulus, Scipio, Afranius*: Lentulus Crus (consul 49) was murdered in Egypt following Pompey's assassination. Metellus Scipio (consul 52) and Afranius (consul 60) both died in Africa, the former by suicide and the latter at the hands of the Caesarians.

Cato's: after the defeat at Thapsus, he committed suicide rather than accept clemency from Caesar.

3 *my exercises*: his voice-production.

more peacocks than you have pigeons: Hortensius had set the fashion for serving this exotic fare at an augural dinner (Varro, *De re rustica* 3.6).

legal spices . . . gravy: Cicero puns on the two words, *ius* = law and *ius* = sauce or gravy. Haterius was a lawyer, living near Paetus. Hirtius, a leading Caesarian, was one of Cicero's new-found dinner-partners.

les principes . . . the pig teaching Minerva: the sense of the first expression appears to be 'first principles', here of law or oratory. The well-known proverb that follows suggests that Paetus was a competent rhetorician (see § 5).

Letter 107 (*Fam.* VII 28)

Manius Curius was a non-political friend of Cicero and Atticus. He was in business at Patrae. A letter from him to Cicero, and two to him from Cicero (*Fam.* VII 29–31) survive (see Letter 134 below).

1 *'where no mention of the sons of Pelops . . .'*: the quotation is from an unknown Latin drama. 'The sons of Pelops' are the Caesarians, and there is an element of joking, since Pelops is the eponym of the Peloponnese, where Curius resides.

I go to ground in my library: Cicero had already this year published his *Brutus* and *The Stoic Paradoxes*, and was working on his *Orator*. He was also embarking on his ambitious review of the history of philosophy, beginning with the *Hortensius*.

2 *consoled . . . by reflection*: that is, on his past achievements.

on whom rest all our destinies: the reference is to Caesar.

Letter 108 (*Fam.* IV 8)

Claudius Marcellus (consul 51) supported Pompey in the fighting in Greece. After the battle of Pharsalus he retired to Mytilene. Cicero was anxious to welcome back to Rome as many republican sympathizers as possible. See also Letters 111, 114.

Letter 109 (*Fam.* IV 13)

Nigidius Figulus (praetor 58) was regarded as the most learned man of his time after Varro (so Gellius). He had supported Pompey in the Civil War, and was now living in exile.

2 *my private life*: Cicero makes no specific mention of his divorce from Terentia, which must have occurred in 46. We are dependent on the account of Plutarch, *Cicero* 41, for the details.

those notorious fires: the Catilinarian conspiracy of 63.

3 *I could lend assistance*: as an advocate in the courts.

4 *based on specialized argumentation*: the consolation was a staple exercise in the schools of rhetoric.

plagued by those hardships: the loss of citizen-rights, including ownership of property.

5 *the person with boundless power*: Caesar.

Letter 110 (*Fam.* IX 17)

1 *What a joker you are . . . our friend Balbus*: on Papirius Paetus, see Letter 106 n. At this time he feared that lands belonging to townships and estates near his residence at Naples might be confiscated to provide Caesar's veterans with settlements. Balbus as a leading Caesarian would be aware of such plans.

for almost the past four years: reckoning the period from the outbreak of civil war in January 49.

2 *the lands of Veii and Capena*: these cities in southern Etruria were 20 and 27 miles respectively from Tusculum.

Letter 111 (*Fam.* IV 7)

For Marcus Marcellus, see Letter 108 n.

2 *the consulship*: he was consul with Sulpicius Rufus in 51.

4 *at Mytilene or Rhodes*: Marcellus was in retirement at Mytilene, and Cassius Longinus at Rhodes.

5 *assaults of brigands*: this paragraph indicates that Marcellus' properties had not as yet been confiscated. Cicero's mention of brigands may allude to Antony, for he had seized Varro's estate near Casilinum; see *Philippics* 2.103.

6 *Gaius Marcellus*: Marcus' cousin was consul in 50.

Letter 112 (*Fam.* VI 12)

1 *dear Balbus*: T. Ampius Balbus (unconnected with Caesar's supporter in § 2) was tribune in 63 in Cicero's consulship, praetor in 59 and then governor of Asia. He zealously raised troops for Pompey in 49 (*Att.* VIII 11B.2), and accompanied him to Greece with his wife and daughter. He was now in exile.

2 *Pansa . . . Postumus*: of this list of Caesarian trusties who remained friendly to Cicero, the first four are prominent figures; C. Curius Postumus and C. Matius were less known.

my own efforts . . . no time-serving: Cicero indicates that he has not approached Caesar directly on Ampius' behalf.

Tillius Cimber: this close friend of Ampius became praetor in 45, but later turned against Caesar in support of the tyrannicides.

3 *'the trumpet of civil war'*: the label is here attached to the pardon, but it more appropriately stigmatizes Ampius himself, perhaps recalling his zealous recruiting on Pompey's behalf (see § 1 n. above).

your Eppuleia and . . . Ampia: the wife and daughter of Ampius have now returned to Rome without him.

5 *recording the deeds of courageous men*: Suetonius, *Julius* 77, mentions another work of Ampius, a collection of Caesar's political comments.

Letter 113 (*Fam.* VI 14)

After being left as legate in charge of the province of Africa in 50, Ligarius sur-rendered it to the Pompeian Attius Varus in 49, and thereafter espoused the Pompeian interest in Africa till 46, when he was captured by Caesar at Hadrumetum. He was indicted before Caesar, and successfully defended by Cicero in the extant *Pro Ligario*. Caesar granted him immunity, but he joined the conspiracy on the Ides of March 44.

Letter 114 (*Fam.* IV 10)

1 *come as soon as possible*: in Letter 111, Cicero expressed confidence that Marcellus would be granted immunity. The confidence is here trans-muted into certainty.

Letter 115 (*Fam.* XIII 16)

1 *the youthful Publius Crassus*: at *Brutus* 281 f., Cicero delivers a qualified eulogy of the son of the former dynast. He served with distinction with Caesar in Gaul, first as cavalry-commander, and thereafter as legate. He perished with his father in 53 at Carrhae.

Apollonius: his career is known only from this letter. He here aspires to become a writer in residence on Caesar's staff during the operations against Pompey's sons Gnaeus and Sextus.

4 *with the Stoic philosopher Diodotus*: for Cicero's connection with Diodotus, see *Academica* 2.113; *Brutus* 309; *Att.* II 20.6.

Letter 116 (*Fam.* IV 14)

For Plancius, see Letter 31.3 n. Cicero defended him in 54 in the extant *Pro Plancio* against the charge of bribery. Having supported Pompey in Greece in the Civil War, he was now in exile.

3 *my 'proceedings'*: Cicero married the young Publilia in December 46, having divorced Terentia a few months earlier. For the circumstantial details of the divorce and the new marriage, see Plutarch, *Cicero* 41.

Letter 117 (*Fam.* IX 13)

As a leading Caesarian, Dolabella had recently (November 46) moved from Africa to Spain. Though Cicero disapproved of his ill-treatment of Tullia, whom Dolabella divorced in late 46 when she was pregnant with his child, for political reasons he remained on civil terms with him.

1 *a close connection of Lepta's*: see Letter 61.22 n.

with Marcus Varro: see Letter 101.2 n.

following Afranius' defeat: the consul of 60 served as Pompey's legate in Spain in 55–49. In his final year he was defeated by Caesar at Ilerda.

Scapula: this equestrian stirred up revolt among Caesarian troops in Baetica, leading to the expulsion of Caesar's legate Trebonius (see Dio 43.29).

intensified thereafter by Pompeius: the younger Gnaeus Pompeius recruited forces from the Spanish townships; see Ps.-Caesar, *Spanish War* 1.

1–2 *Subernius of Cales . . . Planius Heres*: neither is otherwise known. Cales lay about thirty miles north of Naples.

Letter 118 (*Fam.* VI 18)

1 *what the law specified*: the Caesarian Balbus had presumably been consulted in the drafting of Caesar's law, which excluded auctioneers and undertakers from municipal office. Diviners, traditionally Etruscan, would have been despised by the *snobbisme* of senators like Cicero.

2 *Paciaecus . . . seven legions*: Vibius Paciaecus was a Spaniard, working in support of Caesar. *Spanish War* 7 states that Pompeius had 13 legions, but that 9 of them consisted of runaways or auxiliary forces.

Messalla: Valerius Messalla (consul 53) served as Caesar's legate in Italy, Sicily, and Africa. The brothers Quintus and Publius Curtius are otherwise unknown.

3 *guarantor for Pompey . . . Galba*: Lepta and Sulpicius Galba (praetor 54) had stood surety for a debt of Pompey the Great in 52. Following his death and the confiscation of his property, Galba boldly asked Caesar if he was still liable. Caesar then paid off the debt from the Treasury (so Valerius Maximus 6.2.11).

4 *my Orator*: this extant treatise, composed in the form of a letter to Brutus, was the latest of Cicero's rhetorical works, completed in the second half of 46.

5 *Tullia's child-bearing . . . the first payment*: the sickly child, born in January 45, did not long survive. Cicero was vainly trying to recover the dowry from Dolabella.

Hesiod: see *Works and Days* 289: 'The gods put sweat before excellence.'

Letter 119 (*Att.* XII 14)

1 *my excuses to Appuleius*: Cicero was apologizing for his absence from Appuleius' induction as augur. The three persons named were among those who presented his apologies.

2 *asked for payment*: Cicero had stood surety for Cornificius, who was serving Caesar abroad, and who owed money to Junius.

3 *a literary consolation*: Tullia died in February 45. Cicero's *Consolation*, which has not survived, is preserved in essence in his *Tusculans* I-II. He pioneered the *consolatio* in Latin after wide study of the Greek tradition (see *Tusculans* 1.76; Pliny, *Natural History*, Praef. 22).

I am sinning: Cicero repeats this notion, that relaxation or distraction from grief is sinning, at *Tusculans* 3.64.

4 *when Pansa is setting out*: this Caesarian with whom Cicero enjoyed cordial relations (see Letter 90.3) had been appointed governor of Cisalpine

Gaul as successor to Brutus. Cicero was keen to ascertain when Brutus would return.

Attica . . . Craterus: Craterus was a celebrated physician; see Horace, *Satires* 2.3.161; Persius 3.52, He was now attending Atticus' daughter.

Letter 120 (*Att.* XII 19)

1 *consecrated ground . . . the shrine*: Cicero was planning a memorial garden for Tullia. The Chian Apella is otherwise little known.

2 *Cocceius and Libo . . . Cornificius' agents*: Atticus was coping with Cicero's financial affairs; see *Att.* XII 18.2.

about Antony: perhaps his candidature for the consulship of 44 was being mooted; he duly obtained it.

3 *Pansa . . . Brutus' arrival*: see Letter 119.4 n.

4 *the whole business . . . young Cicero's interests*: Cicero was concerned about repayment of Terentia's dowry, following the divorce. Perhaps Terentia was proposing that young Marcus should be allocated part of the money.

Letter 121 (*Fam.* IV 6)

For Servius, see Letter 79 n. This letter is Cicero's reply to Servius' celebrated consolation (*Fam.* IV 5) sent from Athens on news of Tullia's death.

1 *Maximus . . . Paullus . . . Gaius . . . Marcus Cato*: Fabius Maximus Cunctator, one of the heroes of the Hannibalic war, pronounced the panegyric over his son (Plutarch, *Fabius* 24). Aemilius Paullus, conqueror over Perseus of Macedon, lost both sons on either side of his triumph in 168 (Livy 45.40.7). The deaths of the sons of Cato the Censor and of Sulpicius Galus are recorded in Cicero, *On Friendship* 9; see also *Tusculans* 3.70 for Cunctator, Paullus, and Cato.

Letter 122 (*Fam.* IX 11)

At this time Dolabella was in Spain supporting Caesar. The friendly tone (see Letter 117 n.) acknowledges Dolabella's claim that he is fighting Cicero's battles against critics among the Caesarians.

1 *the calamity*: Tullia's death.

Letter 123 (*Att.* XII 40)

1 *Caesar's censure*: after Cato's suicide in Africa, Cicero wrote a eulogy, in response to which Caesar in Spain in early 45 wrote an *Anticato*. It was in the form of a prosecutor's speech (so Tacitus, *Annals* 4.34.4). Only fragments survive.

the pamphlet which Hirtius has sent me: in *Att.* XII 40.1 we read that Hirtius' letter 'reads like a rough draft of Caesar's abuse of Cato'.

2 *Lettre de Conseil*: Cicero wrote a letter of advice to Caesar which he never sent or published. See the next letter.

the letters of Aristotle and of Theopompus to Alexander: they have not survived.

as many pages as I have written: Cicero was now embarked on his philosophical works. He had by now completed his apologia for philosophy, the *Hortensius*, and was at work on the *Academica*, devoted to the topic of the theory of knowledge. For other works recently completed, see Letters 118.4 and 119.3.

3 *the owner of the finest estate in Baiae*: he has not been identified.

4 *Scapula's estate*: this Scapula (perhaps the Quintus Scapula who had led a defection of Caesarian troops in Baetica; see Letter 117.1 n.) had recently died, and his estate was up for auction. Cicero hoped to bid for it to establish a shrine to Tullia, but the plan came to nothing.

Lentulus: other gardens were being investigated for Tullia's memorial, one belonging to one of the Clodias with whom Lentulus Spinther, son of the consul of 51, was associated.

Letter 124 (*Att.* XIII 27)

1 *the letter to Caesar*: see Letter 123.2. Atticus had submitted a draft to Balbus and Oppius for approval, but their negative response dissuaded Cicero from delivering it.

the Parthian War: in his letter, Cicero must have preferred to speculate about Caesar's projected campaign against Parthia (which never materialized) rather than to dwell on his domestic policies.

hostile people, including your relative: the hostile Caesarians in Spain included Quintus, Atticus' (and Cicero's) nephew.

2 *the gardens*: see Letter 123.4. Faberius was an agent of Caesar, who owed Cicero a sizeable sum.

Letter 125 (*Fam.* XIII 15)

1 *Precilius*: not mentioned elsewhere in the letters.

But never did he win the heart within my breast: So Homer, *Odyssey* 7.258, 9.33 (Odysseus does not budge from his intention to make for home).

Be brave . . . encompassed him: the first line is from *Odyssey* 1.302 (Athena to Telemachus), and the second from *Odyssey* 24.315 (Laertes' response when Odysseus disguised his identity).

2 *May I not die . . . may learn*: Homer, *Iliad* 22.304 f. (Hector despairingly facing Achilles).

I hate the wisdom-teacher . . . not wise: a fragment of Euripides (905 Nauck).

can look both forward and backward: Homer, *Iliad* 1.343.

strive to be best . . . the rest: Homer, *Iliad* 6.208 (Glaucus echoing his father's exhortation). Cicero deploys these citations as a learned apology designed to mollify Caesar for having opted to follow Pompey.

Letter 126 (*Att.* XIII 7)

Sestius: see Letter 71.2 n.

Theopompus: this mythographer was a follower of Caesar, who is said to have awarded his city of Cnidus its freedom to please him (so Plutarch, *Caesar* 48.1).

my letter: the letter of advice to Caesar (see Letter 123.2 and n. Cicero here has second thoughts about withholding it.

Lentulus . . . divorced Metella: see Letter 123.4. Spinther junior's liaison with one of the Clodias may have led to the marital break-up.

Mustela . . . Silius: both were relevant to Cicero's plans for Tullia's memorial garden. Mustela was Scapula's heir, and Silius' gardens were an alternative possibility. See Letter 123.4.

Letter 127 (*Att.* XIII 19)

2 *my speech the Pro Ligario*: see Letter 113 and n. The speech was delivered before Caesar in 46; for the circumstances, see Plutarch, *Caesar* 32.

3 *the whole topic of the Academy*: this refers to the final version of the *Academica*, dedicated to Varro and completed in four books in June 45. Though nominally an Academic, Varro like Cicero rejected in part the scepticism of the school and adopted the standpoint of Antiochus, the founder of the Fifth Academy, who sought a more ecumenical relationship with Stoicism, especially in ethics.

Cotta: Aurelius Cotta is the Academic spokesman in Cicero's *The Nature of the Gods*, in which he criticizes both Epicurean and Stoic theologies.

4 *Heraclides*: this philosopher from Pontus was a pupil of Plato, and headed the Academy in Plato's absence.

De republica . . . De oratore: the first was composed in 54–51 and set in the year 129. Cicero wrote the second in 55–52 and set it in the year 91, when the orators listed dominated the courts.

the Aristotelian mode: Cicero describes here the early treatment of Aristotle in works now lost.

On Ends: the *De finibus*, devoted to the question of the chief aim in life as envisaged by Epicureans, Stoics, Peripatetics, and Academics, was composed earlier in 45.

5 *I entrusted to Catulus, Lucullus, and Hortensius*: Cicero refers to the first edition. He revised it in 45, making Varro, Cicero, and Atticus the spokesmen.

I envisage certain objections: perhaps from Varro; cf. *Att.* XIII 25.3.

Letter 128 (*Fam.* IX 8)

1 *your promise*: two years earlier Varro had promised to dedicate his *De lingua Latina* to Cicero (cf. *Att.* XIII 12.3). That work, which appeared

probably in 43, contained 22 books, of which 5–22 were indeed dedicated to Cicero.

four reminders: the four books of the revised *Academica*.

the younger Academy: the New Academy, with its central doctrine of scepticism, is thus contrasted with the Old Academy of Plato.

the literary genre which lay within my competence: philosophy.

Letter 129 (*Att.* XIII 47A)

1 *Lepidus*: Aemilius Lepidus (consul 46, the future triumvir) was ruling Italy as Caesar's Master of Horse.

to attend the Senate: doubtless preliminary discussions were to be held about Caesar's plans on his return.

2 *the business with Publilius*: after divorcing Terentia, Cicero married his young ward Publilia towards the close of 46, but the marriage lasted only a few weeks. Publilius, brother(?) of the bride, was handling the financial complications.

Letter 130 (*Att.* XIII 46)

1 *a Tom Thumb, and not an index finger*: Cicero plays on the name Pollex (a thumb) to indicate that the slave had brought no information from Puteoli about Cluvius (see § 3 below).

Lepta . . . in his supervision of the entertainments: at *Fam.* VI 19 Cicero urges his friend Lepta not to concern himself too eagerly with preparations for the 'royal show', the gladiatorial contests which Caesar was to mount.

'*. . . before the Roman Games*': they began on 5 September; Caesar intended to make his triumphal entrance then.

my Cato . . . Brutus' Cato: neither has survived. For Cicero's pamphlet, see Letter 123.1 n.

3 *Cluvius' will . . . Vestorius*: these friends of Cicero were bankers at Puteoli. Hordeonius, another legatee, was a local merchant.

4 *Cossinius*: for this friend of Atticus, see Letter 15.11.

Letter 131 (*Att.* XIII 50)

1 *his books against Cato*: see Letter 123.1. Cicero doubtless praised the literary qualities, not the content, of the *Anticato*, which was divided into two books. Dolabella was the recipient of Cicero's letter because he was close to Caesar and was fighting Cicero's corner (see Letter 122).

2 *Vestorius . . . Brinnius' farm*: this Brinnius had made Cicero one of his heirs; see *Att.* XIII 13.4. For Vestorius, see Letter 130.3.

3 *Caesar's arrival*: Atticus' and Cicero's expectations were premature. Caesar did not arrive from northern Italy until early October. Alsium, where Cicero planned to meet him, lay on the Etruscan coast just

north of Latium. Murena, who had a house there, was not the consul of
62 defended by Cicero on a charge of bribery.

Letter 132 (*Fam.* IX 12)

1 *that dear Baiae*: the harsh criticism of this favourite watering-place of
Romans is hard to parallel elsewhere.

the Pro Deiotaro: see Letter 58.2 n. After supporting his patron Pompey
in the Civil War, Deiotarus was pardoned after Pharsalus by Caesar,
whom he thereafter supported. But his grandson Castor accused him of
plotting to murder the dictator. The indictment was heard before Caesar
in late 45. Cicero's speech of defence (the king had supported
him during his governorship of Cilicia) has survived. Caesar deferred
judgement on the case.

Letter 133 (*Att.* XIII 52)

1 *What a guest*: Caesar may have been touring the veteran colonies in
Campania when he accepted Cicero's invitation to dinner on 18 December.
This sardonic description of the event indicates increasing disillusion-
ment with the dictator's political intentions; see the next letter.

Philippus' residence: Marcius Philippus (consul 56 and stepfather of
Octavian) had played no part in the Civil War.

Cassius Barba: a Caesarian officer; see Cicero, *Philippics* 13.3.

Mamurra: Caesar's Prefect of Engineers, who may have died suddenly.

On food well cooked . . . a pleasant meal: Lucilius, frag. 1122 Marx.

2 *cantonnement*: 'billeting'.

the residence of Dolabella . . . Nicias: Nicias, the Greek friend of Cicero and
Atticus, in reporting this gesture may have regarded it as a compliment to
Dolabella.

Letter 134 (*Fam.* VII 30)

For Curius, see Letter 107 and n. This note is a reply to the extant letter (*Fam.*
VII 29), requesting a letter of recommendation to Acilius. That letter has survived (*Fam.* XIII 50).

1 *For my part*: Curius was under the impression that Cicero was keen for
him to return to Rome. The quotation that follows, a favourite of Cicero's
(see e.g. Letter 107.1), is from an unknown source.

Quintus Maximus: Fabius Maximus Sanga had served as Caesar's legate
in the Spanish operations, and became suffect consul for October–
November 45. Cicero's sardonic comment ('called "the consul"') recalls the
cry raised when Maximus entered the theatre: 'He is no consul!' (Suetonius,
Julius 80.3).

the consulship of Caninius: Caninius Rebilus had served as legate of Caesar
in Gaul, and in the Civil War in Africa and Spain. His one-day tenure of
the consulship became proverbial.

2 *into the haven of philosophy*: a summary of his writings, complete and projected, is listed in *On Divination* at the start of Book II.

3 *Acilius*: this Caesarian gets mention four times in caesar, *Civil War* 3. He was probably following Servius Sulpicius Rufus as governor of Achaia. Cicero's speeches defending him have not survived.

Letter 135 (*Att.* XIV 1)

1 *the person whom we were discussing*: Gaius Matius, a close confidant of Caesar.

Lepidus: Aemilius Lepidus, the future triumvir.

2 *to inform me*: Cicero was en route to Campania, away from disorders at Rome following the assassination of Caesar.

the report about Sextus . . . any word of Brutus: Sextus Pompeius was planning to resume operations in Spain. For Brutus, see Letter 119.4.

'What he wants . . . wants a lot': Plutarch's version (*Brutus* 6) is: 'I do not know what the young man wants, but whatever he wants, he wants it badly.'

on behalf of Deiotarus: Brutus had earlier financial dealings with Deiotarus; see Letter 61.4.

at Sestius' request: this long-standing ally of Cicero had joined Caesar after Pharsalus.

Letter 136 (*Att.* XIV 10)

1 *to skulk at Lanuvium*: the conspirators had laid no detailed plans for action after the murder of Caesar, and Brutus had quitted Rome to escape the riots following Caesar's burial.

Trebonius: Caesar had appointed him governor of Asia after his suffect consulship in 45. The disorders hindered a more formal departure.

that first day: the conspirators occupied the Capitol following the murder.

the Liberalia: on that day, 17 March, the Senate ratified Caesar's *acta*, and agreed that the conspirators should be pardoned but not lauded. Cicero concurred. The Senate further approved a public funeral for Caesar, at which Antony delivered the panegyric.

terre au delà de terre: the Greek quotation ('to go to land beyond land') is from Aeschylus, *Prometheus Bound* 682, where Io complains of being hounded by Hera.

2 *men like Tebassus . . . Fango*: these are Caesarians who have profited from the confiscations.

Curtilius . . . all that type: at *Att.* XIV 6.1 (sent a week before this letter), Cicero complains of 'the rascal Curtilius possessing Sestullius' farm', Sestullius being a Pompeian. The names that follow are likewise those of Caesarians who have profited from the confiscations.

3 *Octavian*: the future Augustus, son of M. Octavius (praetor 51) and great-nephew of Caesar, had served with him in Spain in 45, and was named as his heir in the will drawn up by the dictator in September 45.

your Buthrotum problem: see *Att.* XVI 16A for the threatened appropriation of land there. Caesar had intimated that this threat would be lifted.

the Cluvian property: see Letter 130.3. The sums mentioned refer to the value of the bequest to Cicero.

4 *Quintus senior*: Cicero's brother had now divorced Pomponia (see *Att.* XIV 13.5), and his son was taking his mother's part.

Letter 137 (*Att.* XIV 12)

1 *'Oh, what a splendid deed . . . half-done!'*: the source of the quotation is unknown. The comments that follow indicate that 'left half-done' expresses regret that Antony was not murdered as well.

my position as their patron: his relationship with the Sicilians had been forged by his successful indictment of Verres in 70.

the Latin franchise: this was probably awarded to only a few communities, for Pliny (*Natural History* 3.91) indicates that many did not possess it even by his time. The franchise allowed intermarriage and trade-rights with Roman citizens, and full citizenship could be obtained by migration to Rome.

Deiotarus . . . Fulvia: for Deiotarus, see Letters 58.2 n., 61 4. According to Cicero, *Philippics* 2.94 f., Antony received ten million sesterces for the award of the kingdom. Fulvia was Antony's wife.

Buthrotum: see Letter 136.3 n.

2 *Octavian . . . Philippus*: for Octavian, see Letter 136.3 n.; for Philippus, Letter 133.1 n.

'Where neither names . . . son': see Letter 134.1 and n.

the consuls-designate: Hirtius and Pansa, who were staying with Cicero, and being coached in rhetorical skills.

3 *Vestorius' house*: see Letter 130.2 and n. As a banker, he was more at home with numbers than with philosophy!

Letter 138 (*Att.* XIV 13B)

1 *your communication to me*: that letter is extant (*Att.* XIV 13A). It asks Cicero to approve Antony's request to recall Cloelius from exile. He had been condemned for complicity in the riots following Clodius' murder on the Appian Way in January 52.

4 *young Clodius*: the son of Cicero's bitter enemy may have preferred to spell his name 'Claudius'.

5 *One final word*: Cicero's hypocritical pose of respect and friendship, so alien to his true feelings, was exploited by Antony, who read the letter out in the Senate (*Philippics* 2.7).

Letter 139 (*Fam.* XII 1)

1 *Cassius*: for his heroism after Carrhae, see Letter 58.1 n. In the Civil War he fought under Pompey. He was pardoned by Caesar after Pharsalus, but played a leading part in his assassination. At this time he was at Lanuvium with Brutus.

Decimus Brutus: though favoured by Caesar, he had participated in the assassination. He later left for his province in Cisalpine Gaul.

Dolabella's . . . coup: when appointed consul for this year (44), he quashed the pro-Caesarian riots (see *Att.* XIV 15) during Antony's absence from Rome.

Letter 140 (*Fam.* IX 14)

This letter is duplicated at *Att.* XIV 17A.

1 *the glory you have gained*: see Letter 139.1 n.

2 *a Nestor . . . for Agamemnon*: for examples of Nestor's salutary advice, see *Iliad* 1.254 ff., 9.96 ff., 10.204 ff.

a young consul: according to Appian (*Civil Wars* 2.129), Dolabella was only 25, but he may have been a few years older.

3 *Lucius Caesar*: the consul of 64 served with Caesar in Gaul, but after Caesar's death he opposed his own nephew Antony.

5 *Marcus Brutus . . . his outstanding intellect*: Cicero dedicated to him not merely his oratorical works *Brutus* and *Orator*, but also the philosophical treatises *On Ends*, *Tusculans*, and *The Nature of the Gods*.

What person could possibly believe . . . feel for you?: by thus linking his regard for Dolabella with that for Brutus, Cicero hoped that his former son-in-law would emerge as a champion of the republic. He was to be disappointed.

Letter 141 (*Att.* XV 11)

1 *including Servilia, Tertulla, and Porcia*: that is, Brutus' mother, half-sister, and wife.

Favonius: this vehement Pompeian (praetor 49) had been pardoned by Caesar after Pharsalus, and had taken no part in the conspiracy.

Brutus . . . Sicily: the Senate proposed that Brutus should be appointed to purchase corn in Asia, and that Cassius should act likewise in Sicily (*Att.* XV 9).

2 *charges against Decimus*: presumably he had failed to deploy his troops in his province of Cisalpine Gaul in support of Brutus and Cassius.

another person ought to have been dealt with: Antony.

your lady friend: for Atticus' friendship with Servilia, see Nepos, *Atticus* 11.4.

Servilia promised: Brutus' formidable mother had many influential contacts in the Senate. Cassius, having rejected Sicily, was appointed to govern Cyrene, but in September–October travelled to Asia, and from there to Syria.

the games . . . in his name: the Ludi Apollinares, held 6–11 July, were to be mounted by Brutus as *praetor urbanus* (these games and the *Ludi Victoriae Sullae* were the responsibility of that office, while the rest were administered by aediles).

3 *'Prophet . . . journeying now?'*: the quotation is from an unknown Greek drama.

Neither names . . . sons I hear: see Letter 134.1 and n.

4 *a votive commission*: magistrates who had made a vow when in office could be granted a commission to discharge it subsequently. This privilege was offered to Cicero as a softener.

Letter 142 (*Fam*. XI 29)

1 *my entire plan of departure*: convinced that he had no role to play in politics, Cicero had for some months contemplated a visit to Athens to supervise the education of his son.

your closest friend: Caesar.

2 *when I was away from Rome*: Cicero refers to his period as governor of Cilicia.

after the death of Caesar: Cicero's letters between April and July 44 reflect Oppius' greater intimacy with Cicero.

Letter 143 (*Att*. XVI 7)

1 *I set out from Leucopetra*: having decided to retire to Athens, Cicero crossed to Sicily, and put out from Syracuse on 2 August. But he was forced back by contrary winds to Leucopetra on the south-west tip of Italy. Rhegium lies immediately to the north.

the edict: mention of this at *Fam*. XI 3 suggests that Brutus and Cassius were offering to resign their praetorships, but were rebuffed by Antony.

scheduled for the 1st: that is, 1 August See § 5 below.

2 *at the beginning of January . . . into the firing line*: the new magistrates entered office on 1 January.

4 *our Phaedrus' school*: Phaedrus (*c.*140–70 BC) was the celebrated president of the Epicureans, who advocated retirement from the active life of politics to achieve tranquillity of mind. Atticus claimed adhesion to the school.

justify it to Cato: Cato the Younger was the leading Stoic of the age. Participation in public life was for Stoics a primary duty.

5 *at Velia*: this Lucanian coastal town was famous as the centre of the Eleatic school of philosophy.

Piso: Calpurnius Piso Caesoninus (consul 58 and father-in-law of Caesar) had been a Caesarian, but remained neutral during the Civil War. His advocacy on behalf of Brutus and Cassius won little support in the senate; see *Philippics* 1.10.

to watch the Olympic Games: they were held every four years at Olympia. But Cicero's tepid interest in such activities made it improbable that many contemporaries would harbour such suspicions.

7 *Antony's edict . . . and their admirable reply*: see *Fam.* XI 3.

Letter 144 (*Fam.* X 1)

1 *I have never been left in peace*: Cicero reached Rome at the end of August, and delivered the First Philippic to the Senate on 2 September, a measured criticism of Antony's activities since Caesar's death. In retaliation, on 19 September Antony launched an attack on Cicero's entire career; see Letter 146.1.

the prospect of your consulships . . . so distant: Munatius Plancus, a former Caesarian officer and consul designate for 42, had retired to his province of Gallia Comata after the murder of Caesar.

4 *our friend Furnius*: as tribune in 51 he was a supporter of Cicero, and thereafter became a go-between between Caesar and Cicero.

Letter 145 (*Fam.* X 2)

1 *The distinction*: this was the formal thanksgiving for Plancus' victory over the Raeti, for which he later obtained a triumph.

Letter 146 (*Fam.* XII 2)

1 *my motion and my speech*: a reference to the First Philippic. See Letter 144.1 and n.

much more wicked than . . . 'the most wicked man ever killed': Cicero was much more hostile to Antony than to Caesar, whose despotism he loathed while regarding him personally with affection.

Piso: see Letter 143.5 and n., and *Philippics* 1.14 for Piso's speech on 2 August.

I followed suit thirty days later: with the First Philippic on 2 September.

Publius Servilius: Servilius Isauricus (consul 48) was earlier a supporter of Cato, but joined Caesar in the Civil War. After initially opposing Antony, they were later reconciled. He became consul again in 41.

on 19 September: see Letter 144.1 n.

in Metellus' house: this was at Tibur. Caecilius Metellus was a fervent Pompeian who committed suicide after Thapsus. Antony acquired his house when it was confiscated (see *Philippics* 5.19).

vomiting as usual: cf. *Philippics* 2.50; Plutarch, *Antony* 9.

2 *your kinsman*: L. Aemilius Paullus (consul 50). His nephew had recently married Antony's daughter.

your brother: Cassius' brother Lucius was tribune this year. The applause which greeted him in the theatre (*Att.* XIV 2) may have been a tribute to Cassius himself.

That other family connection: Claudius Marcellus (consul 50) was the cousin of Cassius' wife. He presumably benefited from favourable mention in Caesar's newly discovered diaries.

a certain individual: Marcius Philippus (consul 56), cousin of Cassius' wife. His son, praetor in 44, was eligible for the consulship of 41, as were his fellow-praetors Brutus and Cassius.

that brigand: Antony.

3 *Lucius Cotta*: consul in 65 and a supporter of Cicero against Clodius, he offers an excuse with a Stoic ring for non-attendance.

Lucius Caesar: see Letter 140.3 and n.

Servius Sulpicius: the consul of 51, a pro-Pompeian and a lawyer of distinction, had left Rome hoping to broker a peace-agreement; see *Att.* XIV 18.3, XV 7.

the consuls-designate: Hirtius and Pansa, Caesarian friends of Cicero.

Letter 147 (*Fam.* XII 3)

1 *Your friend's madness*: an ironical reference to Antony's behaviour.

2 *Cannutius*: though as tribune he was responsible for introducing the consul to the Assembly, he was an intransigent foe of Antony; see *Philippics* 3.23, Velleius 2.64.3. Hence the implicit suggestion of Antony's hostility towards him in this section.

your legate: Cassius had been appointed governor of Cyrene. The identity of his legate is unknown.

Letter 148 (*Fam.* XII 23)

1 *your command*: Q. Cornificius, literary friend of Catullus and Cicero, had been appointed governor of Africa Vetus, but found two legates of his predecessor, Calvisius Sabinus, still active in the province, in the expectation that Antony would reappoint him.

2 *the plot of Caesar Octavian*: Antony arrested members of his bodyguard (including Myrtilus) on suspicion that they were complicit with Octavian in planning his assassination. See *Att.* XV 13A.2. Octavian denied the charge.

the four Macedonian legions: they had been sent to Macedonia for Caesar's projected expedition against the Parthians, which never materialized.

3 *Cannutius*: see Letter 147.2 n. This outburst of Antony implied that the conspirators no longer belonged to the Roman community.

the great blessing of philosophy: in his review of the history of philosophy, Cicero constantly adopts a Stoic attitude.

Letter 149 (*Att.* XVI 8)

1 *the veterans at Casilinum and Calatia*: Caesar had established colonies for his veterans in these Campanian towns.

2 *the legion of the Larks*: Suetonius (*Julius* 24.2) states that Caesar raised the famous Fifth Legion at his own expense in Cisalpine Gaul, and gave it the Celtic name of Alaudae, which means 'Crested Larks' (so Pliny, *Natural History* 11.37). They marched 'under the standards' as though in hostile territory.

the three Macedonian legions: these were three of the four mentioned at Letter 148.1, the fourth being that of the Larks. Of the three, two joined Octavian.

Brutus, where are you?: Cicero would have preferred to see Brutus in command in Italy, rather than in the East, when Octavian marched on Rome.

Letter 150 (*Att.* XVI 9)

the Senate cannot meet: with Dolabella the suffect consul away in the East, and Antony hostile, there was no prospect of a meeting of the Senate until the new consuls entered office.

without your friend Pansa: he was consul-designate for 43, and his future colleague Hirtius was ill at this time (*Fam.* XII 22.2).

Varro: pardoned by Caesar after Pharsalus, he was so hostile to Antony that he was later proscribed.

Letter 151 (*Att.* XVI 15)

1 *Dolabella*: Cicero has now abandoned hope of securing him as political ally, and is pressing for recovery of Tullia's dowry.

3 *the boy*: Octavian. For the statue of Caesar, see Letter 147.1. This speech of Octavian causes Cicero anxiety for the safety of the tyrannicides.

our friend Casca: Servilius Casca, one of the conspirators, was due to assume office as tribune on 10 December. Octavian did not oppose this.

a letter from Lepta . . . our famous Stratyllax: for Paconius Lepta, close associate of Cicero, see Letter 61.22 n. Stratyllax, presumably the name of a braggart soldier in a lost comedy, sardonically designates Antony.

4 *Sextus*: Sextus Peducaeus, one of the praetors of 47, was a favoured protégé of Cicero; see *Att.* XIII 1.3.

5 *on behalf of Montanus*: Publius Montanus had escorted young Marcus to Athens. For Cicero's involvement in his finances, see *Att.* XII 32, XIV 16; *Fam.* XVI 24.

Cocceius' response: he appears to have been standing surety for Dolabella; see *Att.* XII 13.2.

Letter 152 (*Fam.* XI 5)

The formal address in this letter is to 'Decimus Brutus, Imperator and consul-designate'. He had served Caesar with distinction in the Gallic and Civil wars, and was rewarded with the governorship of Cisalpine Gaul, and designated as consul for 42.

1 *to meet Pansa at once*: see Letter 150.1 n.

2 *if a province is obtained*: Antony had awarded himself the province of Cisalpine Gaul by a law passed in June 44. When Decimus refused to surrender the province, civil war ensued.

Letter 153 (*Fam.* X 5)

For Munatius Plancus, see Letters 144.1 n., 145.1 n. This letter replies to *Fam.* X 4, itself a response to *Fam.* X 3.

2 *your loyalty to the state*: after serving with distinction as a follower of Caesar, Plancus at this time proclaims adhesion to the republic. But the letters from him also counsel peace with Antony, whom he subsequently supported, becoming consul with Lepidus in 42.

3 *rest on you and your army*: as governor of Gallia Comata, he commanded armed forces with which he had subdued the Raeti.

Letter 154 (*Fam.* XII 4)

1 *there would have been nothing left over!*: Cicero sounds his now ritual lament that Antony had been allowed to escape death.

Our present consuls: Hirtius and Pansa, former Caesarians, but now supporters of the Senate and Cicero.

Philippus and Piso: on 4 January the Senate voted to send an embassy to Antony, who was now besieging Decimus Brutus at Mutina. They were to instruct Antony to raise the siege and to evacuate the province. The three ambassadors were Marcius Philippus (consul 56 and stepfather of Octavian), Calpurnius Piso (consul 58), and Servius Sulpicius Rufus, who died en route.

they brought back . . . intolerable demands: see *Philippics* 8.25 ff. for Antony's response. He offered to resign his claim to Cisalpine Gaul in exchange for a five-year tenure of Gallia Comata with six legions.

2 *Rumour has it that you are in Syria*: he was in fact in Syria, where the governors of both Syria and Bithynia turned their armies over to him. He later intercepted a force dispatched to reinforce Dolabella and enlisted the men in his army.

Brutus is closer to us: he was in Macedonia, having secured the eastern province for troops and finances.

Dolabella: a five-year command in Syria had been assigned to him, but he did not leave Rome until November. In early 43 he entered Asia, where he treacherously assassinated the governor Trebonius at Smyrna.

He moved into Syria in May, but by then Cassius (and Brutus) had been given authority over the eastern provinces; Dolabella was besieged by Cassius in Laodicea, and committed suicide.

Letter 155 (*Fam.* X 28)

The Caesarian Trebonius was rewarded for his participation in the Civil War with the consulship of 45, but he subsequently joined the conspirators. At this time he had been appointed governor of Asia. But this letter never reached him, for he was imprisoned and murdered by Dolabella; see Letter 154.2 n.

1 *no left-overs*: see Letter 154.1 n.

took that plague-ridden man aside: Trebonius was credited with saving Antony's life by diverting him when the conspirators encircled Caesar. See *Philippics* 2.34, 3.22; Plutarch, *Brutus* 17.

a meeting of the Senate: Antony rushed to Cisalpine Gaul because the Martians and the Fourth Legion had defected to Octavian. When the Senate met on 20 December, Cicero delivered the Third Philippic.

3 *the death of Servius*: see Letter 154.1 n.

Lucius Caesar: see Letter 140.3 and n.

two legions of Antony's: see n. to § 1 above, and *Philippics* 3.6 ff.

Letter 156 (*Fam.* XII 5)

1 *your location*: see Letter 154.2 n., and *Fam.* XII 11.

the most reliable citizens: primarily Brutus and Cassius, but also Trebonius in Asia (his death not yet reported) and Tillius Cimber in Bithynia.

2 *to hinge on Decimus Brutus*: besieged by Antony in Mutina, he was unable to emerge until Hirtius and Octavian defeated Antony in April.

Mutina . . . Claterna . . . Forum Cornelium: these towns all lay on the Via Aemilia, the first north of Bononia (modern Bologna) and the other two south. The capture of Claterna by Hirtius was announced in the Senate on 3 February (*Philippics* 8.6).

your dependants beyond the Po: nothing is known of these.

the death of Servius Sulpicius: see Letter 154.1 n.

Letter 157 (*Fam.* XII 25)

For Cornificius, see Letter 148.1 n. His opposition to Antony, and later to the triumvirs, led to his being proscribed and later killed in Africa.

1 *Liberalia . . . Quinquatrus*: 17 and 19 March respectively. The second initiated the festival of Minerva (19–24 March).

my statue of Minerva: Cicero had dedicated this in the temple of Capitoline Jupiter before retiring into exile in 58. Her role as city-guardian was adapted from that of Athena Polias at Athens.

affronted the Minotaur: Cicero jokes at the expense of Calvisius Sabinus, who hoped for a renewal of his appointment as governor of Africa, and his henchman Statilius Taurus.

2 *On 20 December*: see Letter 155.1 n. for the occasion of Cicero's Third Philippic. His proposal on the tenure of the provinces amended Antony's appointments made on 28 November.

the man who sought to govern your province in his absence: this was Calvisius Sabinus; see Letter 148.1 n.

3 *the matter of Sempronius*: this cryptic reference may have concerned Sempronius Rufus. Cornificius' misdemeanour is uncertain.

I made headlong for Greece: see Letter 143 and nn.

next day: in fact Cicero reached Rome on 31 August, and delivered the First Philippic on 2 September.

4–5 *from Brundisium . . . what ensued*: Antony returned from Brundisium to Rome in mid-November, but left for Cisalpine Gaul on learning that two legions had defected to Octavian. The siege of Mutina then ensued.

5 *the day now brings fresh life . . . ways*: Terence, *Andria* 189.

Letter 158 (*Fam.* X 27)

Lepidus had been appointed by Caesar as governor of Narbonese Gaul and Nearer Spain, controlling seven legions. This letter reflects his cool relations with Cicero and the Senate. He was to join Antony in May 43.

1 *the highest honours*: in early January Cicero proposed formal thanks to Lepidus for inducing Sextus Pompeius to lay down his arms. An equestrian statue was to be erected in his honour (so *Philippics* 5.41).

Letter 159 (*Fam.* X 12)

For Plancus, see Letter 153.3 and n.

1 *our friend Furnius*: see Letter 144.4 n. In several subsequent letters Cicero praises him as a valued friend.

2 *Munatius*: this is Munatius Plancus Bursa (tribune 51 and brother(?) of the addressee. He was a partisan of Antony, frequently vilified in the *Philippics* but lauded here (§ 5) out of courtesy to Plancus.

3 *Cornutus*: Caecilius Cornutus, urban praetor in this year, shared Cicero's political ideals. He committed suicide when Octavian marched on Rome in August 43 (so Appian, *Civil Wars* 3.92).

Servilius: earlier an adherent of Cato, Servilius Isauricus had joined Caesar and shared the consulship with him in 48. Bitterly hostile to Antony, he was later reconciled to him. The reason for hostility to Plancus is uncertain.

Letter 160 (*Brut.* I 3)

1 *a turn for the better*: in addition to the promising signs listed here, news of the defeat of Antony at Forum Gallorum reached Rome on 20 April, the day before this letter was written.

2 *Three or four days before this most happy development*: rumours of defeat circulated before the good news came; see *Philippics* 14.15.

to have you come to Rome: Brutus was in Macedonia.

3 *the three brothers*: the Antonii. Lucius was serving with Antony (*Fam.* X 14.1). For Gaius' capture by Brutus at Apollonia, see Letter 161.

Letter 161 (*Brut.* II 5)

2 *the memorable almost divine dead . . . repels all words of blame*: blame for failing to dispose of Antony as well as Caesar.

the dispatch which you sent: Cicero refers to the first of three, which was received about 12 February; see *Philippics* 10.

your dispatch: the second dispatch, which was received on 19 March, announcing the capture of Gaius Antonius; see *Philippics* 13.30.

among them my son Cicero: at *Philippics* 10.13 the proud father reports that a legion commanded by Lucius Piso surrendered to his son. For young Marcus' further successes, see Plutarch, *Brutus* 26.

following the consul Pansa's departure: to Cisalpine Gaul, to confront the forces of Antony.

3 *Pilius Celer*: this kinsman of Atticus' wife Pilia was, according to *Att.* X 1A, 'a man of greater eloquence than wisdom'.

Servilius . . . Cornutus: see Letter 159.3 nn.

'Antonius Proconsul': eyebrows were raised because though Antony had appointed his brother Gaius as governor of Macedonia, the appointment had been rescinded by the Senate. Brutus allowed his captive to use the title so that he would be treated more leniently by the Senate.

'Dolabella Imperator': see Letter 154.2 n. His claim to the title *Imperator* (confirmed by Josephus, *Jewish Antiquities* 8.2.5) may have been based on this 'victory' over Trebonius.

4 *Sestius followed me*: after his earlier stormy career in support of Cicero against Clodius, he joined Caesar after Pharsalus, and after the dictator's death remained inconspicuous.

our friend Labeo: denounced as a gossip and mischief-maker by Cicero; see *Fam.* XI 21.1 f.

5 *whom do we spare*: Cicero here advocates the execution of C. Antonius.

Letter 162 (*Brut.* I 3A)

1 *We have lost our two consuls*: on 21 April 43, in the battle outside Mutina, the senatorial forces won a second victory; six days earlier the consuls

and Octavian had triumphed at Forum Gallorum, eight miles north of Mutina. Decimus Brutus was now free to emerge.

when I myself cited . . . Gaius Antonius: Cicero here withdraws his advice to execute him, advocated in Letter 161.5.

Letter 163 (*Fam.* XII 8)

the heinous activitity of your kinsman Lepidus: the wives of Cassius and Lepidus were sisters, daughters of Servilia. On 29 May 43, Lepidus, governor of Narbonese Gaul and Nearer Spain, defected to Antony with his six legions. Cicero's condemnation of his duplicity echoes that of Brutus: 'That most volatile man . . . will never behave in a principled way' (*Fam.* XI 9).

Decimus Brutus and Plancus: Decimus Brutus pursued Antony into Gallia Comata, but Munatius Plancus, the governor there, deserted him and defected to Antony. Decimus Brutus was later killed on Antony's orders by a Gallic noble.

2 *Dolabella*: a public enemy after his murder of Trebonius, he was now reported to have taken his own life at Laodicea.

Letter 164 (*Brut.* I 10)

1 *against his father-in-law*: this was Q. Fufius Calenus (consul 47), one of Antony's most prominent supporters.

2 *Hirtius merited some censure*: no evidence of his failings survives.

Unstable . . . friendly in adversity: the quotation is from a lost drama.

Decimus Brutus was guilty: at *Fam.* XI 13 he explains why he did not pursue Antony at once. This was the substance of the criticism (*Fam.* X 17).

Lepidus . . . the fickleness: see Letter 158 n.

3 *letters from certain individuals*: 'presumably Philippus and Marcellus' (so Syme, *The Roman Revolution* (Oxford, 1939), 182). Despite Cicero's optimism, Octavian was to march on Rome on 19 August and claim the consulship.

the self-indulgence of the troops: so in the next month (July) a deputation of 400 centurions demanded the consulship for Octavian. Their leader brandished his sword before the Senate, saying: This will make him consul if you do not (Suetonius, *Augustus* 26).

4 *a fate which had . . . befallen me*: with reference to his exile in 58.

Letter 165 (*Brut.* I 15)

1 *Messalla*: Messalla Corvinus, soldier, statesman, and littérateur, fought at Philippi under Cassius, briefly joined Antony, but then defected to Octavian. At this time in 43, prior to his fame as statesman and literary patron (of Tibullus amongst others) he was a promising young rhetorician of 21.

3 *Solon . . . one of the Seven Sages*: the list including Solon is found first in Plato, *Protagoras* 343A.

His dictum: the source of this attribution is unknown.

4 *the action which you . . . failed to take*: Cicero again harps on the obsessive theme of the failure to remove Antony with Caesar.

5 *I thought that I too should depart*: for what follows, see Letter 143 and nn.

6 *I call this policy 'Brutine'*: Cicero forms the adjective from the name of L. Iunius Brutus (consul 509), who was traditionally credited with the inauguration of Roman liberty and the end of the kingship. See Livy 2.1 ff.

7 *The sole distinctions*: Cicero now delivers a detailed riposte to Brutus' criticism in § 2.

his age as a candidate . . . be advanced: by a law passed during Sulla's dictatorship, the minimum age for a consul was 42. Though the regulation was increasingly honoured in the breach rather than in the observance, Octavian at 19 was by far the youngest to stand.

8 *Larentia . . . on the Velabrum*: Acca Larentia was according to the tradition the wet-nurse for Romulus and Remus (see Livy 1.4.6 ff.). The Velabrum lay between the Capitol and the Palatine at Rome, and was hallowed as the alleged site of the feeding of the twins.

a most welcome victory: at Mutina (Letter 162.1 and n.).

on Aquila as well: Pontius Aquila (tribune 45) was killed at Mutina (*Fam.* XI 18.1).

9 *to enter the city in ovation*: at *Brut.* I 17.2 (Brutus to Atticus, sharply critical of Cicero's enthusiastic support of Octavian) this is termed a triumph. It was probably never celebrated. See the summary of Livy, book 119.

we also demolished it: this will have been the consequence of the declaration of Lepidus as public enemy by the Senate on 30 June.

11 *the children of Themistocles*: at *Themistocles* 32, Plutarch reports that there were five children by his first wife, and several daughters by his second. Though his property was confiscated when he was banished, his friends were able to retrieve some of it on his behalf.

Letter 166 (*Brut.* I 18)

1 *your mother*: the dominant role of Servilia is reflected in this and an earlier meeting described in Letter 141, at which Brutus and Cassius were also present.

Casca, Labeo, and Scaptius: for Servilius Casca, see Letter 151.3 and n.; for Segulius Labeo, Letter 161.4 n.; for Scaptius, agent of Brutus and friend of Servilia, *Fam.* XV 13.4.

2 *our army commander*: Antony.

your brother-in-law: Cassius Longinus.

3 *the person for whom you have stood surety*: Octavian.

5 *the 1 per cent tax*: direct taxation on Roman citizens had been abolished in 167 BC, and revenues from overseas had dried up with the levies imposed for raising military forces. This passage provides evidence of direct taxation, and the resentment it aroused.

No letters survive to document the months after July.

GLOSSARY OF TERMS

aedile the third of the annual magistrates, below consul and praetor. There were four aediles, two curule and two plebeian; they were responsible for city administration, the corn supply, and for putting on public games. Cicero was plebeian aedile in 69 BC, and gave three sets of games.

allies the *socii* or 'federate states', native communities, in Italy or overseas (e.g. in Sicily), linked to Rome by treaties of alliance; they provided Rome with troops and received certain benefits in return. In 91–87 BC the Italian allies rebelled against Rome in the Social War (the war against the *socii*) and won their goal of Roman citizenship and incorporation within the Roman state.

assembly (1) centuriate: the *comitia centuriata*, an assembly consisting of all Roman citizens divided into 193 'centuries' (military units), grouped into five census classes based on wealth; it elected the consuls, praetors, and censors, and occasionally passed legislation (it passed the law recalling Cicero from exile in 57 BC). The centuries were unequally composed so as to give greater voting power to the rich, and the voting system also favoured the rich. A result was usually declared before the poorest citizens had had the opportunity to vote. (2) Tribal: the *comitia tributa*, consisting of four urban and thirty-one rural tribes, elected the lower magistrates (tribunes, plebeian and curule aediles, quaestors). Seventeen of the tribes, chosen by lot, nominated members of the priestly colleges, including the *pontifex maximus*. (3) Curiate: the *comitia curiata* conferred the *imperium* on magistrates elected by the centuriate assembly and appointed by the consuls.

augur a member of the college of augurs, the official interpreters of religious auspices (sacred signs or omens revealing the gods' approval or disapproval of an action contemplated or in progress). When an augur announced that an omen was unfavourable, the action that was in progress (e.g. the passage of a law, or an election) would be suspended. As with the college of pontiffs, there were fifteen members, all high-ranking aristocrats. Cicero was elected to membership in 53 (or 52) BC.

Campus Martius the 'Plain of Mars', a flood plain to the north-west of the city, between the Capitol and the Tiber. It was used for military training, for elections, and as the place where the census was taken. In Cicero's time it was already starting to be built over.

censor one of two magistrates elected every five years for a maximum period of eighteen months. They conducted the census (register of names, ages, and property of all adult male citizens), and revised the list of senators and *equites* by excluding the unworthy; they also leased out the right to collect taxes and acted as guardians of public morals. The office was of great importance and prestige, and was normally held by ex-consuls.

colony a town founded by official authority and settled by Roman citizens.

conscript fathers the ancient term for senators, which senators used formally in the Senate.

consul the most senior of the annual magistrates. The two consuls held office for the calendar year, which (in the absence of any numerical system) was named after them. Ex-consuls were called 'consulars' and were influential in the Senate.

curule magistrates consuls, praetors, censors, and curule aediles were known as curule magistrates and enjoyed special privileges, including the right to sit on an ivory 'curule' chair (*sella curulis*). (Plebeian aediles, such as Cicero, also enjoyed these privileges by 70 BC.)

dictator in the early republic, an extraordinary magistrate with supreme powers appointed in an emergency for a maximum of six months. He appointed a deputy who was called Master of the Horse. In the later republic, Sulla and Caesar revived the office for their own ends, Caesar taking it for life. In some other communities, the dictator was simply the chief magistrate.

equestrians, *see equites*

equites the members of the Roman middle class who were not senators (originally, the *equites* were the cavalry); there was a property qualification of 400,000 sesterces. Unlike senators, *equites* were permitted to engage in trade, and some were involved in tax-farming in the provinces. Cicero came from an equestrian, not senatorial, family, and viewed himself as a representative of the *equites* and defender of their interests; but, as a senator, he wished to minimize conflict between the two groups and promote 'harmony between the orders' (*concordia ordinum*). Atticus, Oppius, and Balbus were prominent *equites*.

federate states, *see* **allies**

freedman an ex-slave. A freedman/freedwoman would normally remain a dependant of his/her former master.

legate a senator serving as an assistant to a general or provincial governor.

lictors attendants of senior magistrates. A consul had twelve, a praetor six. Each lictor carried *fasces*, a bundle consisting of an axe and some long rods tied together with red straps; the axe and the rods symbolized the right to inflict capital and corporal punishment respectively (though the axe was omitted within Rome, in recognition of Roman citizens' right of appeal).

Master of the Horse, *see* **dictator**

military tribune a senior officer in the legions. The tribunes of the first four legions recruited each year were elected by the tribal assembly and enjoyed considerable prestige; those in the other legions were appointed by their commander, and were not necessarily military men.

new man a *novus homo*, the first man of a family to reach the Senate. Cicero was therefore a new man, but Lucius Licinius Murena being descended from praetors, was not. The Senate contained many new men, but few rose high (in the first half of the first century BC, only four besides Cicero reached the consulship).

noble a direct descendant of a curule magistrate through the male line. Plebeians as well as patricians might be noble. Cicero was not a noble; his son was.

optimate an aristocrat of conservative opinions, at the opposite end of the political spectrum from 'popular' politicians, Sulla was an optimate, but Marius and Caesar were popular politicians. In the 50s, Cicero wished to broaden the term 'optimate' to include all citizens who were concerned for the welfare of their country.

patricians members of a select group of Roman clans (*gentes*). The distinction dated back to the regal period: it was believed that the patricians were descended from the 100 fathers (*patres*) chosen by Romulus to form the original senate. In early Rome, the patricians monopolized the priesthoods and the political offices, but by the late republic the offices had long been opened up to the plebeians (i.e. non-patricians) and, from a practical point of view, patrician birth brought more disadvantages than advantages (patricians were ineligible for the offices of tribune of the plebs and plebeian aedile: Clodius had to be adopted into a plebeian family to become tribune). At the end of the republic, only fourteen patrician clans were still in existence. Cicero was not a patrician.

people-pleasers, *see* **popular politicians** (*populares*)

plebeian assembly the *concilium plebis* (council of the plebs), an assembly consisting of plebeians only and organized on tribal lines (*see* **tribal assembly**). It elected tribunes of the plebs and plebeian aediles, and passed plebiscites (which had the force of law from 287 BC).

plebeians, *see* **patricians**

pomerium the religious boundary of the ancient city, into which generals with *imperium* and their troops were forbidden to enter.

pontifex a member of the college of pontiffs in charge of Rome's religious affairs. There were fifteen members, holding office for life, and their head was called *the pontifex maximus* ('chief pontiff'). Caesar was *pontifex maximus* from 63 BC until his death. The office of *pontifex maximus* still exists: it is held by the Pope.

popular politicians (*populares*) politicans who set out to win the favour of the people in ways that more conservative politicians (optimates) would consider controversial or objectionable, for example by proposing land redistribution or cheaper grain. The tribunate, with its powers to initiate and veto legislation, was a natural ambition for aspiring popular politicians (e.g. Tiberius Gracchus in 133, Gaius Gracchus in 123 and 122, Saturninus in 103 and 100, and Clodius in 58). The civil conflict which resulted from the growth of popular politics was a major cause of the fall of the republic. Before he reached the consulship Cicero sometimes backed popular causes, for example the appointment of Pompey to the Mithradatic command in 66, but he was always opposed to the more extreme manifestations of popular politics.

praetor the second most senior of the annual magistrates. In the late republic there were eight praetors each year. The city praetor (*praetor urbanus*) handled civil suits between citizens and the foreign praetor (*praetor peregrinus*) civil suits between citizens and non-citizens; the remaining six praetors presided over the permanent criminal courts (not all the criminal courts were presided over by a praetor). Cicero was praetor in 66 BC, and presided over the extortion court. After their year of office, praetors regularly went out to govern a province as propraetors (consuls did the same as proconsuls).

prefecture a district of Italy governed by a magistrate sent out annually from Rome to administer justice.

proconsul a magistrate who was not a consul but was given a consul's authority in order to command an army or govern a province. Similarly, a propraetor was a magistrate who was not a praetor but was given a praetor's authority, for the same reasons. A proquaestor was an acting quaestor, appointed by a provincial governor to fill a vacancy in the quaestorship.

propraetor, *see* **proconsul**

proquaestor, *see* **proconsul**

publicani, *see* **tax-farmers**

quaestor the most junior of the annual magistrates and the first stage in the 'sequence of offices' (*cursus honorum*); quaestors automatically became members of the Senate. Twenty quaestors were elected annually (their year of office began on 5 December, not 1 January); the two city quaestors were in charge of the treasury, while the rest were officials, mainly dealing with financial matters, in Italy and the provinces. Cicero was quaestor in 75 BC, in western Sicily.

rostra the speaker's platform in front of the Senate House in the Forum. It was named after the *rostra*, the bronze prows which adorned it, taken from warships of Antium (in Latium) captured in 338 BC.

Senate the supreme council of the Roman state, consisting of all ex-magistrates (except those expelled as unworthy by the censors). The Senate passed decrees, advised the magistrates, assigned provinces, negotiated with foreign embassies, and voted funds, but could not legislate. Its most famous (and controversial) decree was the emergency decree (*senatus consultum ultimum*, 'ultimate decree of the senate' or 'SCU'), passed at moments of civil crisis. The 600 or so senators enjoyed a very high social status (and were forbidden to engage in trade), but only a minority were influential in politics: a small number of families predominated. The Senate House was at the north-east corner of the Forum, but the Senate sometimes met elsewhere.

sesterce a silver coin, the equivalent of four *asses*.

tax-farmers *publicani*, private businessmen of equestrian rank whose companies leased from the state the right to collect taxes in the provinces. The system varied from province to province. For the most lucrative one, Asia, the state auctioned the right to collect taxes for a period of five years. The company which submitted the highest bid would be awarded the contract: it would pay the agreed amount up-front, and then set about recouping its outlay, plus an element of profit, from the province; the companies had no power, however, to alter the rates of tax, which were set by the state. If a company overestimated the likely revenue and bid too high, as happened towards the end of the Third Mithradatic War (perhaps in 65 BC), its members could end up heavily out of pocket; in that particular case, the company was, exceptionally, refunded one-third of what it had paid, in 59. Cicero supported their applications in the Senate, and maintained harmonious relations with them in his province, in his central policy of *concordia ordinum*. *See equites*.

tribal assembly *see* **assembly**

tribune (of the plebs) one of ten annual officers (their year of office began on 10 December, not 1 January) elected to protect the interests of plebeians (the office was closed to patricians). A tribune could initiate legislation, exercise some jurisdiction, and veto any law, senatorial decree, election, or other act of a magistrate—powers which gave the office great political importance. In 81 Sulla removed or curtailed all these powers, and in addition disqualified tribunes from further public office; but the disqualification was removed in 75, and the other powers restored in 70. Tribunes of the plebs are not to be confused with military tribunes or with *tribuni aerarii*.

tribuni aerarii 'treasury tribunes', originally treasury officials, but from 70 to 46 BC one of the three classes of jurors, after senators and *equites*.

They may be considered as *equites*; there may have been a lower property qualification or merely of lower social status.

triumvirs boards of three established for varying roles and elected by the citizen-body in the tribal assembly. Boards were regularly appointed to ensure Rome's safety by night (*tresviri nocturni*), to investigate criminal charges (*tresviri capitales*), and to superintend the coinage (*tresviri monetales*). The first triumvirate, between Caesar, Pompey, and Crassus in 60, was not a triumvirate in the normal sense, whereas that between Mark Antony, Octavian, and Lepidus in 43 was duly elected.

INDEX

References are to letters and sections; aed cur = curule aedile, cos = consul, cos suff = suffect consul, pr = praetor, tr pl = tribune

Bhagavad Gita

The Bible Authorized King James Version
  With Apocrypha

Dhammapada

Dharmasūtras

The Koran

The Pañcatantra

The Sauptikaparvan (from the
  Mahabharata)

The Tale of Sinuhe and Other Ancient
  Egyptian Poems

The Qur'an

Upaniṣads

ANSELM OF CANTERBURY   The Major Works

THOMAS AQUINAS   Selected Philosophical Writings

AUGUSTINE   The Confessions
                        On Christian Teaching

BEDE   The Ecclesiastical History

HEMACANDRA   The Lives of the Jain Elders

KĀLIDĀSA   The Recognition of Śakuntalā

MANJHAN   Madhumalati

ŚĀNTIDEVA   The Bodhicaryàvatàra

Travel Writing 1700–1830

Women's Writing 1778–1838

WILLIAM BECKFORD   **Vathek**

JAMES BOSWELL   **Life of Johnson**

FRANCES BURNEY   **Camilla**
Cecilia
Evelina
The Wanderer

LORD CHESTERFIELD   **Lord Chesterfield's Letters**

JOHN CLELAND   **Memoirs of a Woman of Pleasure**

DANIEL DEFOE   **A Journal of the Plague Year**
Moll Flanders
Robinson Crusoe
Roxana

HENRY FIELDING   **Jonathan Wild**
Joseph Andrews and Shamela
Tom Jones

WILLIAM GODWIN   **Caleb Williams**

OLIVER GOLDSMITH   **The Vicar of Wakefield**

MARY HAYS   **Memoirs of Emma Courtney**

ELIZABETH INCHBALD   **A Simple Story**

SAMUEL JOHNSON   **The History of Rasselas**
The Major Works

CHARLOTTE LENNOX   **The Female Quixote**

MATTHEW LEWIS   **Journal of a West India Proprietor**
The Monk

HENRY MACKENZIE   **The Man of Feeling**